AI, Economic Perspectives, and Firm Business Management

Abdelkader Mohamed Sghaier Derbali
Taibah University, Saudi Arabia

IGI Global
Scientific Publishing
Publishing Tomorrow's Research Today

Vice President of Editorial	Melissa Wagner
Managing Editor of Acquisitions	Mikaela Felty
Managing Editor of Book Development	Jocelynn Hessler
Production Manager	Mike Brehm
Cover Design	Phillip Shickler

Published in the United States of America by
IGI Global Scientific Publishing
701 East Chocolate Avenue
Hershey, PA, 17033, USA
Tel: 717-533-8845
Fax: 717-533-8661
Website: https://www.igi-global.com E-mail: cust@igi-global.com

Copyright © 2025 by IGI Global Scientific Publishing. All rights reserved. No part of this publication may be reproduced, stored or distributed in any form or by any means, electronic or mechanical, including photocopying, without written permission from the publisher.
Product or company names used in this set are for identification purposes only. Inclusion of the names of the products or companies does not indicate a claim of ownership by IGI Global Scientific Publishing of the trademark or registered trademark.

Library of Congress Cataloging-in-Publication Data

Names: Derbali, Abdelkader Mohamed Sghaier, 1985- editor.
Title: AI, economic perspectives, and firm business management / edited by Abdelkader Mohamed Sghaier Derbali.
Description: Hershey, PA : IGI Global Scientific Publishing, [2025] | Includes bibliographical references and index. | Summary: "This book provides a study agenda on the elements of AI, Economic Perspectives, and Firm Business Management"-- Provided by publisher.
Identifiers: LCCN 2024042839 (print) | LCCN 2024042840 (ebook) | ISBN 9798369373576 (hardcover) | ISBN 9798369373583 (paperback) | ISBN 9798369373590 (ebook)
Subjects: LCSH: Artificial intelligence--Economic aspects. | Information technology--Economic aspects. | Management--Technological innovations.
Classification: LCC HC79.I55 A427 2025 (print) | LCC HC79.I55 (ebook) | DDC 658/.0563--dc23/eng/20241107
LC record available at https://lccn.loc.gov/2024042839
LC ebook record available at https://lccn.loc.gov/2024042840

British Cataloguing in Publication Data
A Cataloguing in Publication record for this book is available from the British Library.

All work contributed to this book is new, previously-unpublished material.
The views expressed in this book are those of the authors, but not necessarily of the publisher.
This book contains information sourced from authentic and highly regarded references, with reasonable efforts made to ensure the reliability of the data and information presented. The authors, editors, and publisher believe the information in this book to be accurate and true as of the date of publication. Every effort has been made to trace and credit the copyright holders of all materials included. However, the authors, editors, and publisher cannot assume responsibility for the validity of all materials or the consequences of their use. Should any copyright material be found unacknowledged, please inform the publisher so that corrections may be made in future reprints.

Table of Contents

Detailed Table of Contents

Due to the increasing digitization of several sectors, businesses are utilizing robotic process automation (RPA) to digitize different aspects of their operations. RPA uses computer codes and rules-based software robots to automate repetitive tasks. It has completely changed the manner in which we approach work. Financial forecasting is not exempt from this evolution, since digital technology present enormous opportunities. By digitally managing and tracking financial transactions, robotic financial forecasting technologies are essential to preserving the financial stability of organizations. This research, is an attempt to deepen understanding of the quickly developing subject of artificial intelligence in finance. In addition to fostering innovation, the use of AI in financial services has the potential to boost economic expansion and establish countries as leaders in the financial technology industry. Fundamentally, this study highlights the various ways that technology—especially artificial intelligence and robotic process automation—affects the finance industry.

The real time price optimization is the need of the hour for attaining the competitive edge in the industry and act as a catalyst for the strategic evolution of corporate practices in this cut throat world of competition Pillai (2023). This research is a step towards understanding as to how the future sustainable business operations of the company can be built in the advent of the technology; AI to optimize the business operations; qualitative and quantitative models to transform business operations; future of business in technological era. Also, the various diagrams through pictorial representation will enlighten as to how the AI will improve the operations of the organization.

In the pursuit of the optimal level of debt that maximizes the firm's value, the predecessors to Modigliani and Miller (MM, 1958) acknowledged the existence of an optimum point, but they failed to calculate it. This failure primarily stems from their inability to find the mathematical expression linking the required rate of return by shareholders to the risk associated with their assets. The purpose of this paper is to demonstrate that even though the two mathematical expressions differ due to the introduction of corporate taxes, the result remains the same. Moreover, even in an imperfect market, no theory suggests that the required rate of return depends on the presence or absence of taxes. We believe that this demonstration does not exist elsewhere and we consider it valuable from a theoretical standpoint.

This chapter looks at how artificial intelligence (AI) has changed the FinTech business by demonstrating its evolution and pointing out key applications, problems, and future trends. From the early days of electronic fund transfers to today's advanced financial services driven by AI, FinTech has always been trying to make things faster, easier to use, and more personalized. Using big data and sentiment analysis to make intelligent choices, AI has transformed how fraud detection, risk management, credit scoring, algorithmic trading, and customer service. Even with these advancements, challenges like data accuracy, bias, cybersecurity, and following regulations exist. Some real-life examples such as JPMorgan Chase's COIN AI system, and more. These examples show how leading companies in the financial sector are using AI to improve customer service, streamline processes, and lower risks. This chapter talks about emerging trends in AI, such as explainable AI(XAI), quantum computing, decentralized AI, and edge computing. It emphasizes the importance of using AI ethically.

The aim of this study is to examine the systemic risk in the Europe region in 2023. In this analysis, we employ SRISK as a metric for systemic risk, with the goal of capturing the strain and potential for systemic impact within financial institutions across countries. These metrics not only evaluate the vulnerability of individual financial institutions, but also consider the interdependencies between them, as well as the connections between systemic risk and factors such as GDP, market capitalization, and total assets of each country. The empirical results indicate that the level of systemic risk reaches its peak between 2020 and 2023. The countries most affected by systemic risk are United Kingdom and France with varying degrees.

The purpose of this paper is to study the implications of the main macroeconomic components on the financial markets of OECD countries under asymmetric uncertainty shocks. By uncertainty shocks, this paper refers to uncertainty shocks emanating from economic policies or geopolitical risks. Using monthly data over the January 2009-May 2022 period, a non-linear panel ARDL-PMG model (Shin et al., 2014) is applied to estimate the relationship between inflation, industrial production, long-term interest rates, uncertainty (economic policy uncertainty, geopolitical risks) and stock prices. In the long term, the results indicate a stable relationship between the selected variables and the different stock prices. However, the asymmetric results show that uncertainty has a negative impact on stock prices in both the short and long term. The results suggest important implications for political and economic decision-makers, especially after the succession of endogenous and exogenous financial crises in recent years.

The purpose of studying the nexus between Artificial Intelligence and Business management through a bibliometric perspective is to systematically analyze and understand the existing body of scholarly literature on this topic.This paper aims to review articles related to Artificial Intelligence and Business management with the help of bibliometric analysis. A total number of 699 documents were drawn from the Scopus database out of which 593 articles were selected. To accomplish the overview of Artificial Intelligence and Business management Research, bibliometric techniques such as performance analysis and scientific mapping were applied. The data was also organized, analyzed, and presented using the Bibliometrix package. The study found that research on Artificial Intelligence and Business management has a significant growth rate of 7.05 percent. It was also discovered that Chen Y and Zhang Y has produced the most influential articles in this field and Industrial Marketing Management was the top-ranked journal.

This chapter examines how automating business processes and changing management practices can be achieved through the use of artificial intelligence (AI). It draws attention to the increasing use of AI across a range of industries and emphasizes how it can improve productivity judgment and overall business performance. The chapter looks at the major managerial tasks that AI supports like employee engagement and performance management and offers case studies and real-world application insights. Businesses can use AI without sacrificing data security or fairness by taking ethical issues privacy concerns and the significance of responsible AI deployment into account. The potential for ongoing innovation and the difficulties businesses may encounter in putting these technologies into practice are highlighted in this exploration of future trends in AI-powered automation. Businesses looking to implement AI in their processes can use the best practices and practical lessons gleaned from industry case studies as a guide.

Preface

Artificial Intelligence (AI) has become a transformative influence in the domains of economics and business administration, fundamentally altering the operational strategies and decision-making processes of organizations. As we navigate an era defined by rapid technological advancements, the intersection of AI with economic perspectives and firm business management presents an unprecedented opportunity to innovate, optimize, and excel in diverse domains. This volume explores these synergies, providing insights into how AI reshapes economic research and business practices while addressing the attendant challenges.

In the realm of economics, AI has unveiled novel pathways for research and examination. The utilization of machine learning algorithms possesses the capacity to scrutinize intricate economic data and detect patterns, resulting in more precise forecasts and prognostications. AI models can be harnessed to scrutinize market trends, consumer behavior, and macroeconomic indicators, thereby assisting policy-makers, investors, and corporations in making well-informed decisions. Additionally, AI-powered algorithms play a pivotal role in the advancement of automated trading systems and tools for managing financial risks, redefining the contours of economic decision-making and strategy formulation.

Within business administration, AI assumes a critical function in the optimization of operations and the enhancement of productivity. AI algorithms can streamline the management of supply chains, regulate inventory, and predict demand, culminating in cost reductions and heightened customer contentment. Natural language processing (NLP) facilitates AI-driven chatbots and virtual assistants in handling customer queries and offering tailored recommendations, thereby enriching customer service experiences. Furthermore, AI methodologies are leveraged for the analysis of sentiments in social media data, enabling enterprises to comprehend public sentiment and customize their marketing strategies accordingly. These advancements underscore AI's transformative potential in creating efficient, agile, and customer-centric organizations.

Despite its transformative capabilities, the escalating integration of AI in economics and business management also gives rise to challenges. Ethical dilemmas, privacy issues, and potential biases ingrained in AI algorithms necessitate resolution to ensure equitable and responsible application. Moreover, the fluid nature of AI demands a continuous enhancement of competencies and expertise for professionals in these domains, alongside a conscientious and persistent endeavor towards modernizing the educational curriculum in institutions of higher learning. Addressing these challenges is essential to unlocking AI's full potential while fostering trust and accountability.

This book is designed for a diverse audience, including leaders seeking organizational enhancement, mid-level managers focused on team innovation, and human resources professionals fostering a learning culture. It provides valuable insights for learning and development practitioners, individual contributors at all levels, and consultants offering organizational guidance. Additionally, educators, researchers, students, and professionals in dynamic sectors will find practical strategies for continuous learning and achieving organizational excellence. Through comprehensive exploration and practical guidance, this volume aims to serve as an invaluable resource for fostering a culture of continuous learning and innovation across various roles and contexts.

Chapter 1 delves into the transformative power of robotic process automation (RPA) in the financial sector. As businesses increasingly adopt RPA to streamline operations, this chapter highlights its pivotal role in revolutionizing financial forecasting. By digitizing transaction management, RPA and artificial intelligence (AI) are not only fostering innovation but also solidifying economic stability and advancing financial technology on a global scale.

Chapter 2 emphasizes the critical importance of real-time price optimization in securing a competitive edge in today's marketplace. This chapter offers insights into leveraging AI to enhance sustainable business operations, showcasing qualitative and quantitative models that redefine corporate strategies. Through illustrative diagrams, it demonstrates how AI fundamentally transforms organizational efficiency.

Chapter 3 revisits the seminal theories of Modigliani and Miller on corporate finance, offering a fresh perspective on optimal debt levels in maximizing firm value. Through rigorous mathematical analysis, it reconciles the theoretical impacts of corporate taxes on shareholder returns, providing valuable insights into financial theory's evolution.

Chapter 4 examines the profound influence of AI on the FinTech industry, tracing its journey from electronic fund transfers to contemporary AI-driven services. Highlighting innovations like fraud detection and algorithmic trading, this chapter addresses ethical challenges while exploring future trends such as explainable AI (XAI) and quantum computing.

Chapter 5 investigates systemic risk in Europe, particularly from 2020 to 2023. By employing SRISK metrics, this chapter identifies the vulnerabilities within financial institutions and their interdependencies. The analysis underscores the link between systemic risks and macroeconomic factors, offering critical insights for policymakers and economic strategists.

Chapter 6 explores the impact of macroeconomic variables on OECD financial markets under asymmetric uncertainty shocks. By employing a non-linear panel ARDL-PMG model, the chapter demonstrates the negative effects of geopolitical and economic policy uncertainties on stock prices, providing essential considerations for economic decision-making in turbulent times.

Chapter 7 addresses strategic security management in the hospitality industry, emphasizing the importance of proactive measures against macro-level challenges. By identifying risks and integrating tools like Key Risk Indicators (KRIs) and foresight skills, this chapter offers a comprehensive framework for enhancing organizational resilience in an increasingly uncertain environment.

Chapter 8 investigates the transformative potential of AI in B2B sales. Focusing on international trade, it highlights AI's role in automating tasks, improving personalization, and fostering trust in customer interactions. By presenting best practices and case studies, this chapter illustrates the shift from traditional sales models to data-driven strategies.

Chapter 9 presents a bibliometric analysis of the intersection between AI and business management. By synthesizing findings from 593 scholarly articles, it identifies key research trends, influential authors, and prominent journals. This chapter underscores the growth trajectory of AI in management, offering a roadmap for future exploration.

Chapter 10 explores the integration of AI in automating business processes and evolving management practices. Through real-world case studies, it highlights AI's role in enhancing productivity, performance management, and ethical considerations. The chapter also addresses the challenges and opportunities associated with AI-powered innovations in business.

Chapter 11 focuses on the sensitivity analysis of public companies' market activity metrics in relation to dividend policy and AI integration. By constructing elasticity models, the chapter provides a framework for forecasting and assessing market behavior under neutral dividend policies, offering valuable tools for financial strategists.

Chapter 12 concludes with an examination of AI maturity models as critical tools for guiding organizations through AI integration. It identifies strategic dimensions—strategy, data, technology, people, and governance—and analyzes empirical case studies to illuminate the pathways for achieving AI maturity and leveraging advancements like Large Language Models (LLMs) in business contexts.

As the editor of this volume, I extend my heartfelt gratitude to the contributing authors, whose expertise and dedication have enriched the discourse on AI's integration into economics and business management. I also express my appreciation to the reviewers and collaborators whose insights and feedback have shaped this work. Together, we present this book as a step forward in understanding and harnessing the transformative power of AI for economic and business advancement. It is my hope that this volume will inspire readers to embrace AI as a tool for innovation, collaboration, and sustainable progress in the modern era.

Abdelkader Mohamed Sghaier Derbali
Taibah University, Saudi Arabia

Chapter 1

Impact of Artificial Intelligence on Investment Decision-Making

Babalpreet Kaur
Chandigarh University, India

Manjit Kour
https://orcid.org/0000-0003-1043-3187
Chandigarh University, India & North-West University, South Africa

ABSTRACT

Due to the increasing digitization of several sectors, businesses are utilizing robotic process automation (RPA) to digitize different aspects of their operations. RPA uses computer codes and rules-based software robots to automate repetitive tasks. It has completely changed the manner in which we approach work. Financial forecasting is not exempt from this evolution, since digital technology present enormous opportunities. By digitally managing and tracking financial transactions, robotic financial forecasting technologies are essential to preserving the financial stability of organizations. This research, is an attempt to deepen understanding of the quickly developing subject of artificial intelligence in finance. In addition to fostering innovation, the use of AI in financial services has the potential to boost economic expansion and establish countries as leaders in the financial technology industry. Fundamentally, this study highlights the various ways that technology—especially artificial intelligence and robotic process automation—affects the finance industry.

DOI: 10.4018/979-8-3693-7357-6.ch001

Copyright © 2025, IGI Global Scientific Publishing. Copying or distributing in print or electronic forms without written permission of IGI Global Scientific Publishing is prohibited.

INTRODUCTION

The world has altered due to technology. It is evolving quickly and making it possible for us to accomplish more tasks at a lower cost than ever before. Our relationship with work is changing as a result of its application. In recent years, digitization has gained relevance in all fields. Robotic process automation, machine learning, and process redesign are all combined in intelligent process automation to improve customer satisfaction, productivity, and efficiency (Federico et al., 2019). Robotic process automation is enabling businesses all over the world to quickly digitize portions of their operations. This procedure automates some manual processes using computer algorithms and robots that follow regulations. Previous studies have already shown the enormous potential that digitalization offers in the field of financial forecasting. It is also difficult to introduce digital technologies, particularly when it comes to the financial consequences. As a digital financial advisory solution, businesses all over the world are expanding their use of robot advisors (robos), which upend conventional financial forecasts and investment services (Tretyak et al., 2021). Through digitally regulating and tracking financial activities, robotic financial forecasting solutions for businesses assist in keeping the organization financially sound (Lee, 2020). The goal of this study is to investigate how artificial intelligence (AI) functions in robo-advising services, how it affects investment decision-making, and how to apply machine learning and algorithmic techniques used in financial forecasting on this platform. These include statistical techniques, business analytics, and similar approaches, whereas software handles all aspects of digitalized processes, including full automation. By enhancing productivity, the study will support the usage of robotics, and by raising awareness, it may draw in more investors. According to the report, interest in sustainable and socially conscious investing is rising, which is consistent with societal values and concerns. By offering insights on the use of AI in finance, the study advances academic research by encouraging more investigation and learning in this quickly developing field.

THE ROLE OF ARTIFICIAL INTELLIGENCE (AI) IN ROBO-ADVISORY SERVICES

Since artificial intelligence (AI) is the foundation of these automated investing platforms, artificial intelligence (AI) plays a critical role in Robo-Advisory services. This study should take into account a number of important factors, including the possibility that AI may affect investor behavior and the growing importance of robot advisers and AI-powered analytics in helping investors make financial decisions.

When AI is used to process large volumes of data fast and precisely, it becomes possible to identify trends, risks, and investment possibilities more effectively than with traditional approaches by using algorithms to build investment portfolios. Artificial intelligence (AI) methods outperform traditional models in a variety of financial activities, including stock price prediction, bankruptcy prediction, portfolio optimization, and genetic algorithms and Robo-advisors (Kour, 2024a). Applications of AI in finance are expanding, particularly in banking (Zekan et al., 2022). The accounting and financial process greatly benefits from AI applications, particularly in domains like expert systems, intelligent agents, machine learning, and decision making (Berdiyeva, 2021). AI-powered solutions have the potential to improve investment choices and increase profits. The growing incorporation of artificial intelligence (AI) into commercial operations gives rise to ethical and legal issues that influence public opinion and the regulatory environment, ultimately influencing investment values. Through the mediation of firm creativity, AI innovation management, and AI-driven decision making, AI innovation management has a favorable impact on business performance (Kasztelnik, 2024).

Artificial intelligence (AI) is a technology that managers can utilize to improve their performance in a number of areas, including risk assessment and management, portfolio rebalancing to preserve the appropriate risk-return profile, and user communication through natural language processing. This makes the interface more user-friendly (Eriksson & Djoweini, 2020). Artificial intelligence can help financial services by compiling facts and data from the public domain. Because public data encompasses a wide range of services, companies are generally obliged to protect its secrecy. Artificial intelligence (AI) technologies are used for security and fraud detection. Robo-advisors offer highly customized investment plans based on the preferences of specific investors (Kaur & Kour, 2024; Rani, 2022). Along with these risks and obstacles, AI also presents issues like bias, explainability, regulation, and trust, all of which need for cautious handling and teamwork. AI was crucial in generating a timely, pertinent financial statement that is comparative, verifiable, and clear, and machine learning was effectively vital in data collecting, recording, categorization, and identification of abnormalities in accounting activities (Osamor & Adeniran, 2023). AI may improve efficiency, accuracy, and creativity, which has broad and revolutionary effects on society, the economy, and finance (Jel et al., 2022).

Thus, artificial intelligence (AI) improves efficiency, customization, and flexibility in robo-advising services, increasing the responsiveness of automated investment platforms to the demands of specific investors and market fluctuations. Artificial Intelligence is a word that has been developed by socio-behavioral rationales of human capacities. It has worldwide, far-reaching ramifications for economic sectors, societies, and the workplace.

Figure 1. Role of AI in Robo advisory services

IMPACT OF ROBO ADVISORS ON INVESTMENT DECISION-MAKING

Indeed, the field of investment decision-making has seen tremendous transformation as a result of the integration of artificial intelligence (AI) in robo-advising services. Financial institutions and businesses have been able to increase financial forecasts, streamline processes, and increase efficiency through the incorporation of cutting-edge technologies like automation and algorithms (Kour, 2024b). The way that people make investing decisions and how individuals and institutions manage their portfolios has been greatly impacted by robo-advisors. Because they are automated, they usually have reduced costs and enable participation in the financial markets by people with different degrees of capital and financial expertise.

The outcomes of foreign direct investment projection that are the most accurate are those produced by learning machine models. New competencies, such as creativity, intelligence, agility, networking, sustainability, social responsibility, innovativeness, digital learning, curiosity, and knowledge-drivenness, are needed for researchers and decision-makers when using artificial intelligence in economic analysis. These competencies are necessary for wise decision-making that takes into account the welfare of the whole and the economy's long-term viability (Bruneckiene et al., 2019). In addition to developing a decision framework that emphasizes resilience to unforeseen scenarios, machine learning techniques and models can facilitate multidisciplinary research by allowing it to forecast and monitor the complicated evolution of work in tandem with technology advancements (Frank et al., 2019).

Customer happiness and better customer experience results have been demonstrated to positively connect with the use of AI in government service delivery. These have the power to remove emotional biases from decision-making and have an impact on judgment that promotes a more methodical approach to risk management. Artificial intelligence adoption has enhanced financial performance, operational efficiency, decision-making, and service delivery quality (Abdulla & Darwish, 2022).

Robo-advisors help investors who might otherwise find it difficult to decide when and how to rebalance their investments. It frequently makes goal-based investing easier, enabling investors to make choices that are more in line with their long-term goals. These are employed in predictive analytics to find possible trends in the market and profitable ventures. In order to ensure openness and accountability, investors have the option to modify their strategy in response to market fluctuations and produce reports that are mandated by regulatory bodies. Robo-advisors possess the capability to cater to the intricate investing requirements of investors, particularly those in the millennial generation, and provide impartial, transparent, and affordable advising services (Mathew, 2023).

Robo-Advisors rely on sophisticated algorithms combined with vast volumes of digital data to work. They make it possible for the system to automatically learn by reading and interpreting patterns and data. Its main benefit is that it can complete jobs hundreds of times more accurately than a human can, and it can do them considerably faster. Without it, some actions would not even be feasible. This can help with decision-making by providing intricate financial data in a way that is easy to comprehend (Barros & Popplewell, 2021).

In the financial services industry, it is extensively used, particularly in credit research, investment management, and customer experience (Jel et al., 2022).

Robo-Advisors use machine learning and algorithms, which are essential for portfolio optimization. These technologies build diverse and well-balanced investment portfolios by analyzing market patterns, historical data, and other pertinent information. Robo-Advisors can continuously enhance their effectiveness using machine learning, which learns from fresh data and modifies methods accordingly. Investors may keep an eye on their portfolios and make decisions at any moment thanks to this real-time accessibility. Financial institutions are currently using robo-advisors to improve customer experience, streamline back-office procedures, improve revenue models, develop new business models, change the workforce, and alter the competitive environment.

As online platforms that provide automated financial guidance, robo-advisors employ artificial intelligence (AI) to analyze a range of variables, such as a user's risk tolerance, financial objectives, and market circumstances, to create a personalized investment portfolio for them. In order to facilitate successful communication between users and the Robo-Advisor and make the interaction more intuitive and user-friendly, natural language processing (NLP) is also used. These platforms' instantaneous nature can influence decision-making by enabling quick reactions to shifts in the market. This influence on decision-making is a reflection of the public's increased interest in sustainable and socially conscious investing. Robo-Advisors have had a significant impact on democratizing access to financial markets. These platforms facilitate investing participation for people with different levels of financial literacy. Furthermore, Robo-Advisory services are sometimes more affordable for investors than traditional financial advisors due to their lower fees. The capacity of robot advisors to remove emotional biases from investing decision-making is another important benefit. Human emotions can frequently impair judgment and cause impulsive behavior, particularly when markets are fluctuating. Because they are algorithm-driven, robo-advisors provide systematic risk management by basing judgments on data and pre-established rules.

Figure 2. Impact of AI on financial services

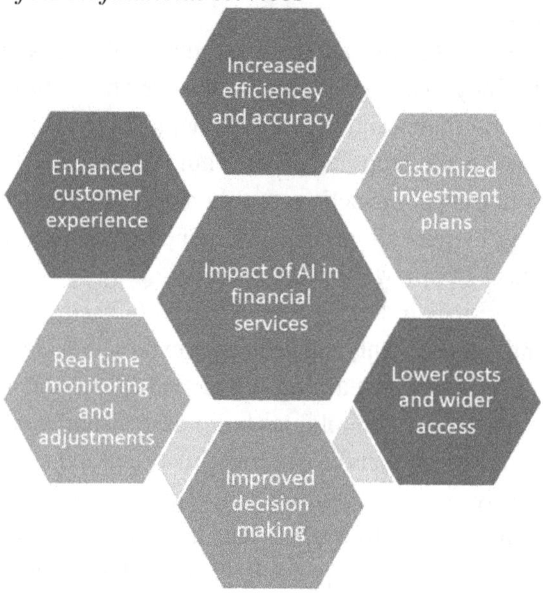

THE ALGORITHMS AND MACHINE LEARNING TECHNIQUES EMPLOYED AT ROBO ADVISORS PLATFORM

Robo-advisors offer automated and data-driven investing advice through a variety of machine learning and algorithms. Robo-Advisors can now evaluate enormous volumes of financial data, spot trends, and make well-informed investing decisions thanks to this technology. Several important machine learning methods and algorithms used by robo-advisor companies include

For portfolio optimization, the Mean-Variance Optimization (MVO) model is a useful tool. Robo-advisors use MVO to build portfolios that minimize risk for a desired level of return or maximize predicted returns for a given level of risk. The goal of the model is to maximize portfolio risk by taking asset class covariance and predicted returns into account. MVO looks for the best asset weights in a portfolio to reduce risk for a given level of expected return or maximize expected returns for a given level of risk (Guliashki & Stoyanova, 2023).

Robo-advisors evaluate the possible future performance of investment portfolios using Monte Carlo simulations. Financial analysts use Monte Carlo simulations extensively when managing their portfolios. They reduce ambiguity by creating a range of potential outcomes, which helps in evaluating the risks and rewards of different investment approaches. Simulations are a potent tool for well-informed portfolio decisions since they analyze the effects of risks, aid in the construction of the best possible strategy, and consider the tax ramifications.

In the machine learning paradigm known as reinforcement learning, algorithms pick up knowledge through interacting with their surroundings. The trial-and-error approach used by machine learning systems is how the data is gathered. Without a training dataset, the agent learns optimal behavior by trial and error. This decision-making science uses algorithms that are able to learn on their own by receiving feedback after every move. It works best for automated systems that make decisions on a regular basis without human assistance, putting an emphasis on learning by doing in order to maximize incentives and produce the best results.

Predictive analytics is a tool used by robo-advisors to predict future asset values and market movements. Big data, data mining, statistical modeling, and machine learning are all used in predictive analytics to examine both recent and old data. Organizations can recognize patterns, evaluate risks, and uncover possibilities by identifying trends and forecasting occurrences based on particular factors. Models are designed to assess situations, facilitating well-informed decision-making in domains such as procurement and supply chain management, and augmenting strategic planning to achieve superior business results.

NLP is used by certain Robo-Advisors to evaluate and interpret textual data, including sentiment from social media, analyst reports, and financial news. A component of artificial intelligence called natural language processing, or NLP, enables machines to understand and interpret human language. Finance uses natural language processing (NLP) to simulate human interpretation by drawing conclusions from a variety of data sources. To help computers comprehend and react to natural language input, it combines computational linguistics, machine learning, and statistical modeling.

Robo-advisors choose assets that are not significantly correlated in order to efficiently diversify portfolios using the clustering technique. By using a cluster trading strategy, investors can create a diversified portfolio with the use of cluster analysis, a useful tool. This entails combining assets from various market segments that have comparable returns. Investors can carefully purchase and group these linked assets together by using cluster analysis, which will increase diversification. The potential of cluster analysis to protect an investor's portfolio from systemic hazards is one of its main benefits in the financial industry. Through the identification and pooling of assets with associated returns, possible losses are lessened. By strengthening the portfolio's resilience, this risk management component helps create a more stable and well-rounded investing strategy.

In a study of (Korzeniewski, 2018) Building diverse stock portfolios from 85 Warsaw Stock Exchange businesses is made easier with the use of cluster analysis. Cluster analysis is helpful in building portfolios; K-means outperforms PAM algorithm; Because short-term investments have higher profitability and lower risk than long-term investments, the Sharpe ratio is crucial for representative selection.

Bagging and Boosting: Both techniques seek to improve model performance by merging several models; however, they use different approaches to addressing misclassifications and creating variety. To generate various models and aggregate their predictions, an ensemble learning technique is used to combine multiple models and improve overall predictive performance. To combat overfitting and lower variance, bagged predictions combine identical predictions. Weights for independently constructed models are equalized. Boosting uses a variety of forecasts combined with performance-based model weights to reduce bias. It emphasizes misclassifications in sequential model training to mitigate significant bias in stable, basic classifiers.

Financial data can be analyzed using deep learning, and neural networks in particular, to find complicated and nonlinear patterns (Mathew & Arul, 2021). When evaluating complicated financial data that is reflecting changes over time, deep learning has shown to be a very effective technique. Deep learning models can help discover trends, correlations, and anomalies in financial markets, where patterns can be altered by a variety of circumstances. This can help with portfolio optimization. Future market movements, stock prices, and other financial indicators can be predicted using models such as recurrent neural networks (RNNs) and long short-term memory networks (LSTMs), which can be trained on past data. These work well at identifying fraudulent activity by looking for trends and irregularities in financial transactions. Large volumes of data can be processed and utilized using neural networks.

CONCLUSION

The use of artificial intelligence (AI) in Robo-Advisory services has brought about a revolution in the process of making financial decisions. Advanced algorithms and robotic process automation (RPA) have made it possible for businesses to digitize financial procedures, which have improved financial forecasts and streamlined operations. As digital financial advisory solutions, robo-advisors utilize artificial intelligence (AI) to manage risks, build customized investment portfolios, and converse with users using natural language processing. Robo-advisors have a significant influence on investing decision-making since they democratize access to financial markets and offer affordable options. These automated tools help investors with different degrees of financial understanding and long-term goals make decisions easier by removing emotional biases and promoting disciplined risk management. Robo-Advisors use algorithms and machine learning approaches that are essential for portfolio optimization, predicting future returns, and spotting market patterns.

REFERENCES

Abdulla, M., & Darwish, A. (2022). The Effect Of Artificial Intelligence In Smart Decision-Making In The UAE Government. *International Business Research.*

Berdiyeva, O. (2021). Artificial Intelligence in Accounting and Finance. *Meta-Analysis.*, (August). Advance online publication. DOI: 10.37435/NBR21032502

Bruneckiene, J., Jucevicius, R., Zykiene, I., & Rapsikevicius, J. (2019). *Assessment of Investment Attractiveness in European Countries by Artificial Neural Networks : What Competences are Needed to Make a Decision on Collective Well-Being ?*

Eriksson, M., & Djoweini, C. (2020). Artificial Intelligence's Impact on Management. *The Innovation Journal.*

Federico, B., Graeme, N., Giambattista, T., & Rob, W. (2019). Intelligent process automation: The engine at the core of the next-generation operating model | McKinsey. *The McKinsey Quarterly, 45*(October), •••. https://www.mckinsey.com/business-functions/mckinsey-digital/our-insights/intelligent-process-automation-the-engine-at-the-core-of-the-next-generation-operating-model

Frank, M. R., Autor, D., Bessen, J. E., Brynjolfsson, E., Cebrian, M., Deming, D. J., Feldman, M., Groh, M., Lobo, J., Moro, E., Wang, D., Youn, H., & Rahwan, I. (2019). Toward understanding the impact of artificial intelligence on labor. *Proceedings of the National Academy of Sciences of the United States of America, 116*(14), 6531–6539. DOI: 10.1073/pnas.1900949116 PMID: 30910965

Guliashki, V., & Stoyanova, K. (2023). Portfolio Risk Optimization Based on MVO Model. *Rcvt.Tu-Sofia.Bg, February.* http://rcvt.tu-sofia.bg/ICEST2018_14.pdf

Jel, O., Pandey, M. K., Sergeeva, I., Пандей, М. К., & Сергеева, И. (2022). *Менеджмент Научная статья Artificial Intelligence Impact Evaluation : Transforming Paradigms in Financial Institutions Оценка воздействия искусственного интеллекта : трансформация парадигм в финансовых учреждениях. 22*(1), 147–164. DOI: 10.25205/2542-0429-2022-22-1-147-164

Kasztelnik, K. (2024). *The Study on the Impact of Business Artificial Intelligence Innovation on Fair Value Investments in the United States The Study on the Impact of Business Artificial Intelligence Innovation on Fair Value Investments in the US. January.*

Kaur, B., & Kour, M. (2024, September). Exploring the Growth and Future research directions on Robo advisors: A Bibliometric Study. In *2024 International Conference on Advances in Computing Research on Science Engineering and Technology (ACROSET)* (pp. 1-6).

Korzeniewski, J. (2018). Efficient Stock Portfolio Construction by Means of Clustering. *Acta Universitatis Lodziensis.Folia Oecologica, 1*(333), 85–92. DOI: 10.18778/0208-6018.333.06

Kour, M. (2024a, September). Revolutionizing Finance: Unleashing Machine Learning's Potential for a New Financial Era. In *2024 International Conference on Advances in Computing Research on Science Engineering and Technology (ACROSET)* (pp. 1-5). IEEE.

Kour, M. (2024b), Dynamics of Big Data Analytics in the Banking Sector. *2024 IEEE International Conference on Interdisciplinary Approaches in Technology and Management for Social Innovation (IATMSI)*, (Vol. 2, pp. 1-6). IEEE. DOI: 10.1109/IATMSI60426.2024.10502648

Kumar, B., Kumar, B., Nagesh, Y., Singh, S., & Rani, J. (2022). The continuous investment in artificial intelligence and its impact on ensuring customer satisfaction. Korea review of international studies, 15(03).

Lee, J. (2020). Access to Finance for Artificial Intelligence Regulation in the Financial Services Industry. *European Business Organization Law Review, 21*(4), 731–757. DOI: 10.1007/s40804-020-00200-0

Mathew, A., & Arul, A. (2021). *Deep Learning Techniques : An Overview Deep Learning Techniques : An Overview. August 2020.* DOI: 10.1007/978-981-15-3383-9

Mathew, N. (2023). *Artificial Intelligence an enabler in Robo-Advisory services to enhance Investment returns – Empirical. 10*, 4008–4016.

Osamor, I. P., & Adeniran, O. S. (2023). *Effects of Artificial Intelligence on Financial Reporting : Evidence from KPMG and PwC Effects of Artificial Intelligence on Financial Reporting : Evidence from KPMG and PwC. April.*

Tretyak, V., Lyakina, M., & Volkova, E. (2021). The ways of business digitalization in global corporations. *SHS Web of Conferences, 92*, 05027. DOI: 10.1051/shsconf/20219205027

Zekan, Y., Sekt, F., & Co, E. A. L. P. (2022).. . *The Role of Artificial Intelligence in Investment Decisions and Applications in The Turkish Finance Industry., 21*(4), 2208–2222.

Chapter 2
Role of Artificial Intelligence in Pricing:
An Industry Orientation

Ashwani Panesar
https://orcid.org/0000-0003-0605-8951
Lovely Professional University, India

Rohit Sood
https://orcid.org/0000-0002-4127-7781
Lovely Professional University, India

ABSTRACT

The real time price optimization is the need of the hour for attaining the competitive edge in the industry and act as a catalyst for the strategic evolution of corporate practices in this cut throat world of competition Pillai (2023). This research is a step towards understanding as to how the future sustainable business operations of the company can be built in the advent of the technology; AI to optimize the business operations; qualitative and quantitative models to transform business operations; future of business in technological era. Also, the various diagrams through pictorial representation will enlighten as to how the AI will improve the operations of the organization.

DOI: 10.4018/979-8-3693-7357-6.ch002

Copyright © 2025, IGI Global Scientific Publishing. Copying or distributing in print or electronic forms without written permission of IGI Global Scientific Publishing is prohibited.

MINI CASE

Figure 1. Case-let: Artificial Intelligence and Pricing Strategy Evaluation

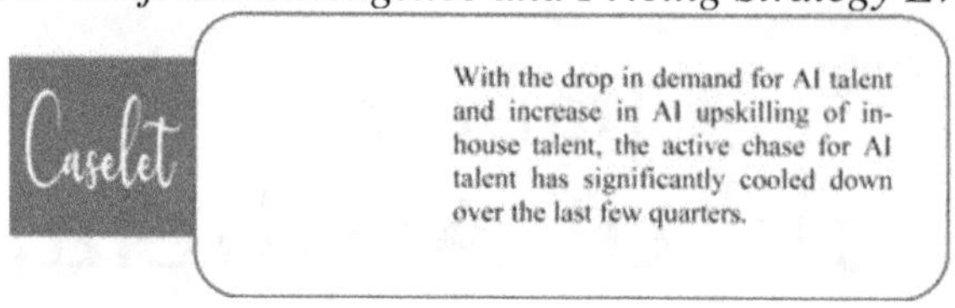

In the dynamic environment of retail sector, pricing strategies play a crucial role in determining a company's sustainability. Traditional methods fall short as they are not able to gauge the changing market scenario. Artificial Intelligence (AI), has truly become a game-changer in the context of pricing strategies. Previously, retailers had relied on static pricing models, often set based on fixed factors such as production costs, demand forecasts, and competitor pricing to arrive at products pricing. But these approaches became redundant in the light of dynamic business environment. Lately, dynamic pricing has helped the corporations to adjust their prices in real-time based on various aspects, such as demand fluctuations and competitor activities. AI, with its computational expertise, brought an innovative dimension to dynamic pricing. Machine learning (ML) algorithms process huge amounts of data, analyzing customer behavior, market trends, and external influences. This empowers retailers to make more informed decisions on pricing strategies, optimizing for competitiveness and profit margins.

The case of "Retail Innovations Inc.," a mid-sized retailer that decided to embrace AI for its dynamic pricing strategy. Initially employing traditional methods, the company faced challenges in staying competitive and adapting swiftly to market shifts. Upon integrating AI algorithms, Retail Innovations Inc. witnessed a remarkable transformation. However, challenges abound. Ethical considerations surrounding personalized pricing, customer perception of AI-driven pricing changes, and the need for skilled personnel to manage and interpret AI algorithms are aspects that warrant careful consideration. Based on the above information, few questions came to the mind like:

- Should the company always follow demand-based pricing?
- Can the dynamic pricing be applied to Festival /Occasions only?
- Can AI be used effectively to ensure more realized profits?

The answers to the foresaid questions will be continued in the forthcoming sections of the chapter for better application-oriented learning.

INTRODUCTION

The business operations of the corporations are passing through a very tough time in the dynamic business environment. The geo-political and economic crises coupled with the liquidity crunch have taken the entire business operations by surprise but only few of them were able to salvage their position as true global business corporations. Globally, gone are the days that business will be build and sustain on single products and be the brand leaders without any competition. Last 20 years have witnessed some corporations like Kodak, Xerox etc. being vanished from the market as they were not able to stand to the need of the market or they were late in adapting the technology. These situations create questions like:

- Did the business got changed or products became obsolete?
- Did AI or technology impact their pricing strategy?
- Did competitors expand business in unrelated area due to intense competition?

The answers to the questions have very complex answer in the light of environment but the steps need to be taken by them so that they don't become obsolete. This chapter is a step towards understanding as to how the future sustainable business operations of the company can be built in the advent of the technology; AI to optimize the business operations; qualitative and quantitative models to transform business operations; future of business in technological era. Also, the various diagrams through pictorial representation will enlighten as to how the AI will improve the operations of the organization.

Figure 2. DID YOU KNOW 1

Technology and Talent has been classified as the most important disruption in the business.

Source: Accenture Pulse of Change, 2024 Index.

Artificial Intelligence (AI) is revolutionizing pricing and business operations by offering unparalleled insights and automation capabilities. In pricing, AI algorithms analyze vast amounts of data in real-time, including customer behavior, market trends, and competitor actions, enabling businesses to optimize pricing strategies dynamically. This data-driven approach enhances competitiveness, maximizes profitability, and allows for personalized pricing tailored to individual customer preferences. Moreover, AI extends beyond pricing to streamline various aspects of business operations. From supply chain management to inventory optimization and predictive maintenance, AI-driven solutions optimize efficiency, reduce costs, and improve decision-making across the entire value chain. As AI continues to evolve, its integration into pricing and business operations promises to reshape industries, unlocking new opportunities for growth and innovation.

FACTORS AFFECTING THE FUTURE GLOBAL BUSINESSES OF CORPORATIONS:

The future global businesses of corporations will be influenced by a variety of factors. While it's challenging to predict the future with certainty, several key trends and influences are likely to play a significant role. Here are some factors that can affect the future global businesses of corporations:

1. Technological Advancements: The digital t analytics and transformation has empowered the business of today in the light of intervention of digital technologies, including artificial intelligence, automation, blockchain, and the Internet of Things (IoT) to give better informed decisions to enhance the customer experience to optimize the operations.

Figure 3. DID YOU KNOW 2

The franchise of global pizza brand was able to use technologies like AI to infuse better customer experiences and productivity to help them sustain in the competitive world.

Source: Springer

2. Globalization and Trade Policies: With entire world being seen as one market, the national, regional of global integration of businesses are required to ensure that the scalability of the business can be improved with the insight of entering

into developing nations. Also, the geo-political dynamics have further put a point of concern for these conglomerates.

3. Environmental, Social, and Governance (ESG) factors: corporation have started to expand their businesses by influencing the customer preferences by concerning for the ESG and adopt them to give absolute advantage.
4. Demographic Shifts: Changes in global demographics, including population growth, aging populations, and urbanization, will impact consumer markets and labor forces. Embracing diversity and inclusion will be crucial for corporations to attract and retain talent and appeal to diverse consumer bases.

Figure 4. Factors affecting the Future Global Businesses of Corporations

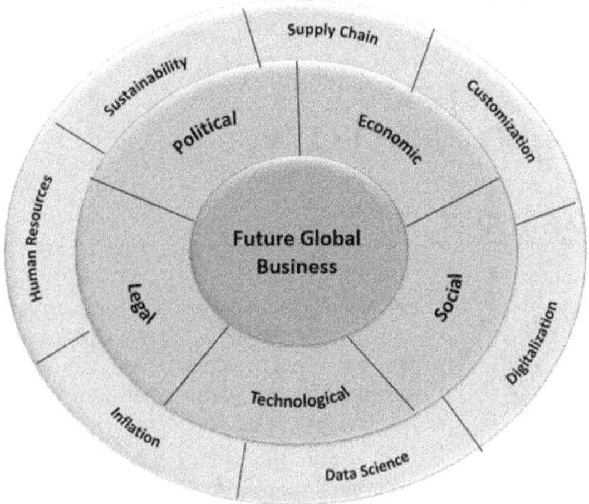

5. Regulatory Environment: Alterations in local, national and international regulations can affect corporations differently, as to influence their strategic decision making and compliance requirements. With consumers going for more privacy, corporations need to invest more on adapting technologies for better compliance.
6. Consumer Behavior and Expectations: With better digitalization and digitization, consumers have shifted to online shopping paving the way for the companies to incorporate more of the technology element in their services to provide them better personalized services. Changing consumer preferences, influenced by factors such as cultural shifts and lifestyle changes, will impact product and service demands.

7. Talent and Workforce Trends: The acceptance and prevalence of remote work may alter traditional workforce models and influence office space requirements. Corporations need to consistently invest in the training and development to upskill their workforce to adapt them to the evolving skills landscape.
8. Financial Market Dynamics: Fiscal & Monetary policies, balance of trade, foreign exchange rates and accessibility to capital will influence corporations' decision for growth and innovation. Stock market fluctuations will further impact their valuations and confidence of investor.

Corporations need to be agile, innovative, and responsive to this dynamic environment to ensure their business scale it through. It's also crucial for them to stay informed, engage with stakeholders, and adopt a forward-looking mindset to thrive in an ever-evolving business environment.

INTEGRATION OF ARTIFICIAL INTELLIGENCE AND CASH FLOWS:

Figure 5. DID YOU KNOW 3

AI seamlessly integrates with existing systems and platforms, providing real-time updates and alerts. This automation streamlines the data-intensive aspects of cash flow management, reducing human error and improving efficiency

Source: Springer

The use of Artificial Intelligence in marketing has revolutionized the entire businesses, the way they communicate and interact with their customers. AI-powered customer service systems have transformed the customer experience by providing innovative solutions and efficient support. This transformation has not come without its challenges.

The top layer of the pyramid shown below brings us that as to how AI has helped the companies to to make their customers realize the experience, journey and supremacy. Customer service leaders face the challenge of selecting the most valuable use cases for AI, integrating AI technology with legacy systems, and finding the right talent and organizational structure to effectively implement and manage AI solutions (Kraus et al., 2023). However, when successfully implemented, AI-enabled customer service can unlock significant value for businesses. AI-enabled customer service can enhance efficiency and accuracy in resolving customer inquiries and issues, leading to improved satisfaction and engagement. With AI-powered customer service, businesses can also analyze customer data and behavior patterns in real-time, allowing them to personalize their interactions and increase customer loyalty(Rust & Huang, 2014). Additionally, AI-powered customer service systems based on big data and machine learning are capable of analyzing large amounts of customer data to provide personalized recommendations and solutions (Kong & Yao-ping, 2021). This transformation in customer service has the potential to greatly improve the overall customer experience and increase business growth. However, implementing such a holistic customer service system will not, and cannot, be achieved using any single AI technology or branch (Kraus et al., 2023).

Figure 6. 4P's Integration with Quantitative and Qualitative Variable

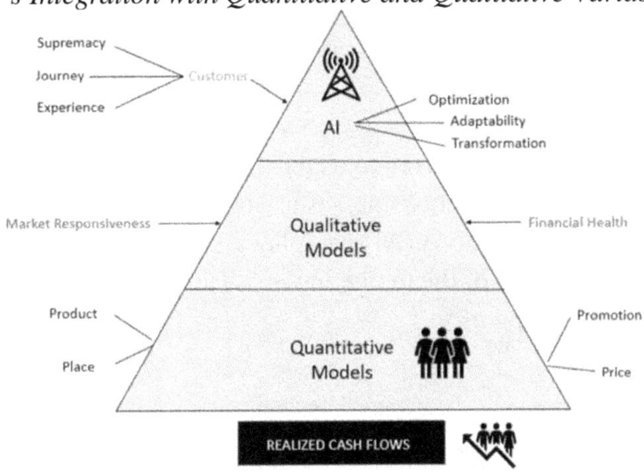

The image above brings us a better insight as to how the various qualitative, quantitative models integrate with the 4P's to have better cash flows. The relationship between market responsiveness and artificial intelligence (AI) is a dynamic and multifaceted one. AI has the potential to significantly impact market responsiveness in various ways. Here are some key aspects of this relationship in the table below:

Table 1. Market responsiveness indicators and support provided

Indicators	Support Provided
Real-time Decision Making	Process data, Quick decision making, Timely decisions, Response to dynamic Environment
Predictive Analytics	Predict trends, anticipate shifts in demand, customer preferences.
Customer Personalization	Tailor products & services, Customization, marketing messages to individual customer preferences, build loyalty.
Supply Chain Optimization	Predict demand fluctuations, identifying potential bottlenecks, and suggesting efficient routes for transportation.
Chatbots and Customer Service	Improve market perception, Instant customer support, addressing inquiries and resolving issues 24/7.
Market Research and Insights	Social media trends, consumer behavior, providing valuable insights.
Competitive Advantage	Build competitive edge, cost optimization, product innovation, create agile business model.
Risk Management	identifying potential risks & threats, proactive risk management strategies, responsive approach to mitigating risks.

The marketing mix, often referred to as the 4Ps (Product, Price, Place, Promotion), is a set of tactical tools that businesses use to promote and sell their products or services. Artificial Intelligence (AI) can play a significant role in shaping and optimizing various elements of the marketing mix. Here's how AI is related to each component of the marketing mix:

Figure 7. DID YOU KNOW 4

Airlines Industry globally rely on dynamic pricing to make up for the losses in the lean season. Augment human intelligence rather than replace human workers, aiming toward increased innovation, creativity, and productivity.

Augment human intelligence rather than replace human workers, aiming toward increased innovation, creativity, and productivity.

Table 2. AI augmentation through 4P's of Marketing

Element	Outcome
Product	Product Customization
	Innovation
Price	Dynamic Pricing
	Personalized Pricing
Place	Supply Chain Optimization
	Retail Automation
Promotion	Targeted Advertising
	Content Personalization
	Social Media Management

From the table, it is pivotal that AI helps the corporations to provide augmented customer relationships by adding new customers through improved customization; personalization; dynamic pricing for seasonal sales; optimize the supply chain for better penetration of the promotional material.

RELATIONSHIP OF ARTIFICIAL INTELLIGENCE (AI) AND PRICING

AI has become increasingly significant in the retail industry, mainly in pricing strategies of consumer goods. By analyzing vast amounts of data, AI algorithms can classify patterns and trends in the consumer behavior, allowing vendors to optimize their pricing strategies (Mazilescu, 2020). This includes implementing dynamic pricing, where in prices can be adjusted in real-time basis in context of factors like demand, competition, and market conditions (Chung et al., 2012). This use of AI in pricing can lead to several advantages for both retailers and consumers.

1) It allows retailers to maximize their profits by setting prices that are tailored to several business conditions and customer preferences.
2) It also supports retailers to successfully manage inventory and prevent stockouts or overstocking by predicting real demand.

Additionally, AI-powered pricing can also augment consumers shopping experience. By analyzing data on factors like consumer behavior, competitor prices, and market conditions, AI can ensure that consumers are offered viable prices that too align with their preferences and purchasing power (Mazilescu, 2020). Almost all companies struggle to determine the fair price for a product or service, how customers will react to different prices and how to extract the maximum value for each customer segment in a market. This is where ML comes into play. It gives companies the opportunity to optimize prices, their pricing strategy and managers' effectiveness.

Setting prices accurately is difficult mainly because of the complexity and proliferation of the available internal and external data that needs to be analyzed. ML can accurately analyze large amounts of data in a short timeframe and derive business-guiding insights from it. It can help companies maximize profits via value-based pricing and optimal price tiering. It also allows decision makers to understand customers' willingness to pay for a product and their reactions to different pricing strategies.

Figure 8: DID YOU KNOW 5

Generative artificial intelligence (AI) will reshape job dynamics, skills, tasks, and occupations, fostering upward social mobility.

Source: The Economic Times

Apple has opened negotiations in recent weeks with major news and publishing organizations, seeking permission to use their material in the company's development of generative artificial intelligence systems, according to four people familiar with the discussions. The technology giant has floated multiyear deals worth at least $50 million to license the archives of news articles

ML helps firms build a more rational global pricing strategy by gathering data from multiple sources: historical transactions, win/loss analysis, the competitions' price levels and contextual data (e.g., what does the customer say about our product on social media, overall market trends, etc.). By looking at such prescriptive and predictive data, leaders can take better and faster decisions. It's important to note that the impact of AI on the pricing of companies can vary based on industry, specific use cases, and how organizations leverage AI technologies. Here's a general overview of how AI can affect pricing in a tabular form.

Table 3.

Aspect	Impact of AI on Pricing
Competitive Advantage	Companies using AI for pricing strategies may gain a competitive edge by optimizing prices based on real-time market conditions, demand fluctuations, and competitor pricing.
Dynamic Pricing	AI enables dynamic pricing, allowing companies to adjust prices dynamically based on various factors such as demand, inventory levels, and customer behavior, leading to improved revenue and profitability.
Personalization	AI-driven personalization can enhance pricing strategies by tailoring prices to individual customer preferences, buying history, and behavior, potentially increasing customer satisfaction and loyalty.
Market Analysis	AI helps in analyzing vast amounts of market data, identifying trends, and predicting market changes. This information can inform pricing decisions, helping companies stay responsive to market dynamics.
Cost Optimization	AI can optimize cost structures by automating processes, reducing operational inefficiencies, and identifying cost-saving opportunities, which can influence overall pricing strategies.
Fraud Detection	AI-powered fraud detection systems can prevent revenue loss due to fraudulent activities, contributing to more accurate pricing and protecting companies from financial losses.
Supply Chain Management	AI in supply chain management can improve inventory management, reduce stockouts, and minimize excess inventory, impacting pricing through better control of supply and demand dynamics.
Customer Segmentation	AI helps in more precise customer segmentation, allowing companies to target specific customer groups with tailored pricing strategies based on their unique characteristics and purchasing behaviors.
Predictive Analytics	Predictive analytics powered by AI can forecast future market conditions, enabling companies to adjust pricing strategies proactively and anticipate changes in consumer behavior.
Operational Efficiency	Improved operational efficiency through AI automation can contribute to overall cost reduction, potentially influencing pricing decisions to maintain competitiveness.
Regulatory Compliance	AI can assist in ensuring pricing strategies comply with regulations and industry standards, helping companies avoid legal issues and potential fines.

APPLICATION OF AI IN THE CURRENT BUSINESS

The application of AI in current business has to be inculcated for the future sustainable business for the current organizations as well as for the new business firms. The current business operations need to be aligned with the external environment forces and the future objectives have to be fulfilled through aligning the current future goals of the organization with the business strategy to strive through the existing competition.

AI or artificial intelligence has to be considered by the organizations to imbibe the technological advancements in pricing strategies in an increasingly competitive market landscape to enhance customer loyalty and purchase intentions. The dynamic price strategies attained through AI can help the organization to increase the revenue growth margin and it will in turn leads to higher operational efficiency with effective risk management. Revenue growth will provide the enhanced realized margin as AI can help the organization to achieve price optimization and the combination of task automation along with human cognitive intelligence can transform the organization traditional thinking and pave the way for modern technological approach, with price optimization playing a pivotal role.

Figure 9. DID YOU KNOW 6

In a Global CEO Survey found 85% of CEOs agreeing that AI will significantly change the way they do business in the next five years, even if AI's penetration in companies is not yet impressive

Source: AIMS International

The intensity of competition, customer experience and ESG factors impact the organization future cash flows and in turn having an impact on the revenues as well as operational profits of the organization. The current sales have to be analyzed and the automation should be taken into consideration through tools like Artificial intelligence, Machine learning, Block-chain and Internet of things (IOT) for overall enhanced financial performance.

Artificial Narrow Intelligence (ANI) is working on specific input-based model through generative AI and analyzing the respective data related to input. The analytics tools like historical data of sales can be analyzed through data analytics tools like Chat GPT, Bard, Dall-E, Mid Journey and Dup Mind should be used to analyze the historical data of sales with logical assumptions to predict the future cash flows and in turn unleashing the operational feasibility and in turn leading to incremental EPS (Earning per share) and higher free cash flows for the organization. The ANI along with reactive artificial intelligence model can pave the way for enriching cognitive experiences for the user and in turn force the organization to adopt the adaptable marketing strategy with dynamic pricing or pricing the product on the basis of customized specifications to gain the competitive advantage and attaining operational excellence. The specificity of the ANI has led to the evolution of another tool to predict, analyze and present the data in accurate and precise manner to the known input variables.

Artificial general intelligence (AGI) is working on the general input and provides the response on the basis of infused input along with identification and analysis of different permutations and combinations for the user to attain the different solutions to infused output and makes a rational decision as per one's experience. The AGI is also known as a response-based model, as it has been able to use its cognitive expertise through the analysis of the data and use that experience in output generation as per the infused commands by the user. AGI uses the data available in public domain to generate the different inputs by using the cognitive experiences and provide the same outputs for the same type of data infusion by the user on the interface. The cognitive experiences being bestowed by the AGI can pave the way for the companies to work as per the generated output and adapting the marketing strategy for a specific product to adhere to the market environment and attain the competitive advantage. The companies can use response base models through AGI model and adapt the marketing strategies as per the generated output to achieve operational excellence.

Figure 10. DID YOU KNOW 7

Samsung Semiconductor India Research has inaugurated its 'Samsung Innovation Campus' Programme at the Visvesvaraya Technological University to upskill 1000youth in future tech domains such as Artificial Intelligence (AI) and Internet of Things (IoT) and make them job-ready. engineering students across Karnataka.

The repetitive nature and same type of analysis for the same infused input has led to the evolution of ultimate integration of human based intelligence and artificial intelligence, known as Super AI for attaining operational feasibility and ultimately enjoying the higher market share through stakeholders' wealth maximization.

Figure 11. Unleashing Operational Excellence Through the Power of AI

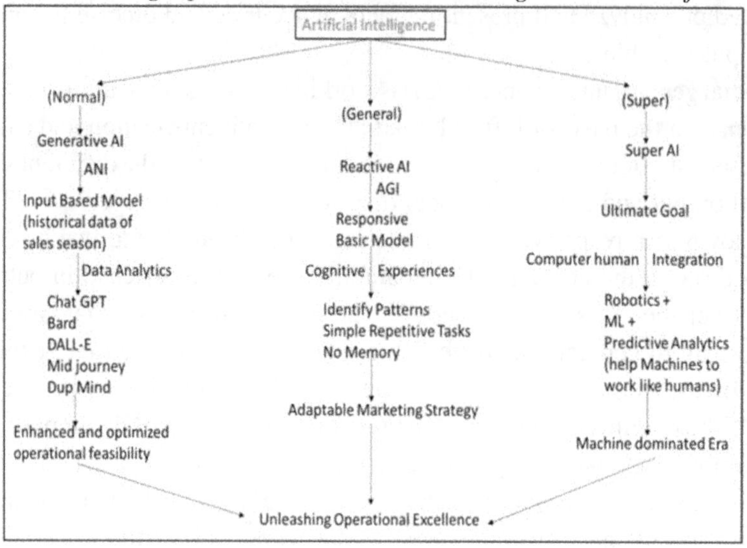

Super AI works on integration of computer and human intelligence to adapt to the current environment to achieve the ubiquitous goal of unleashing operational excellence. The Super AI works through robotics, machine learning, block-chain and assist the human brain to work like the machine and attain the desired results as required. The Super AI era is termed as the machine dominated era to get the requisite outputs with predictive analysis and projecting the enhanced future cash flows with precision and accuracy to the logical assumption being infused by the human in the machine. The machine then analyzes and generate the outputs through predictive analysis to help machines to work like humans for enhanced operational excellence.

AI PRICING MODEL

Figure 12. Dynamic Pricing Model Through Artificial Intelligence

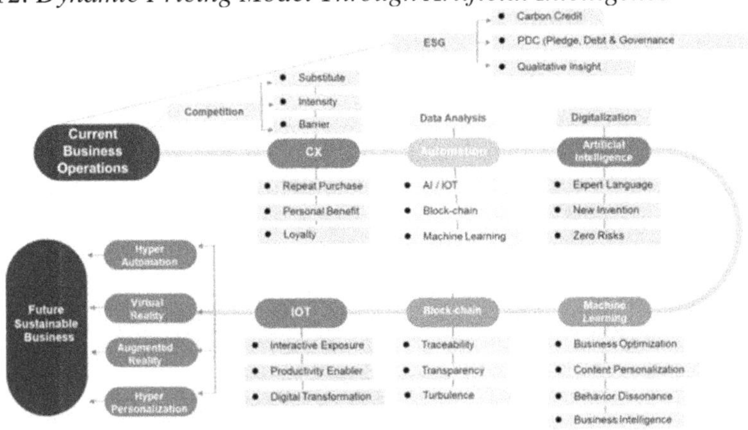

In today's highly competitive business landscape, customer experience has emerged as a crucial factor in determining the success or failure of a company. Organizations that prioritize and invest in delivering exceptional customer experiences consistently outperform their competitors. Customer experience plays a vital role in shaping a company's reputation and fostering customer loyalty (Foroudi et al., 2016). By understanding and responding to customer needs, preferences, and pain points, businesses can gain a competitive advantage. They can distinguish themselves from their peers by delivering adapted, notable experiences that could meet or exceed customer expectations. This will actually help the corporations for better customer satisfaction, increased customer retention, and constructive word-of-mouth referrals.

Automation and the use of Internet of Things (IoT), Machine Learning (ML), and Blockchain technologies have further revolutionized the future existence of various industries. These technologies bring enhanced efficiency, better decision-making capabilities, higher security, and new business prospects (Sethi & Sarangi, 2017). By automating processes and connecting physical devices to the internet, the IoT enables real-time monitoring, data collection, and control of assets, leading to upgraded supply chain management. ML and AI algorithms further analyze the collected data to identify patterns, make estimates, and optimize operations (Reyes et al., 2020). On the contrary, Blockchain provides a secure and decentralized platform for data storage and transactions.

Digitalization comprises the transformation of analog or physical assets, processes, and information into digital formats using advanced technologies like cloud computing, AI, automation, and IoT. On the other hand, AI includes components such as learning, reasoning, problem-solving, perception, and language understanding, allowing AI systems to replicate human intelligence and effectively process the information. The integration of AI with digitalization plays a crucial role in driving digital transformation initiatives across various industries.

Figure 13. DID YOU KNOW 8

India's digital footprint has tripled in less than a decade. 60 percent of Indians now have access to the internet. This digital expansion has changed the lives of millions of people across the country.

Source: DW News

This integration to result into intelligent automation, efficient data analysis for personalized customer experiences, and, enabling organizations to optimize operations through better decisions.

Advances in ML have the potential to revolutionize various industries and occupations. These advances offer opportunities to streamline processes, improve efficiency, and enhance decision-making. By leveraging machine learning algorithms, businesses can analyze large volumes of data to uncover valuable insights and patterns that can drive strategic decision-making(Attaran & Deb, 2018). Utilizing machine learning in business can lead to improved forecasting, optimization of operations, personalized customer experiences, and enhanced risk management(Attaran & Deb, 2018). Machine learning can also help businesses automate repetitive tasks, freeing up employees to focus on more strategic and creative aspects of their work (Brynjolfsson & Mitchell, 2017).

As we move towards a more sustainable future, businesses need to adopt innovative strategies that align with environmental and social goals. These businesses should focus on developing green technologies, implementing sustainable supply chain practices, and promoting green innovation and marketing. By doing so, they can not only contribute to the preservation of our planet but also gain a competitive advantage in the market (Sharma et al., 2010). Integrating sustainability into supply chain operations allows firms to build a competitive advantage in the market (Khan et al., 2021).

Figure 14. DID YOU KNOW 9

6% of US employees fear that many people will lose their jobs to AI and automation and almost a third (31%) believe that trend will manifest during the next two to five years.

Source: Forrester's research

In the realm of business, pricing strategies play a critical role in the overall sustainability and success of a company. Price is not just a financial figure; it serves as a key tool for balancing supply and demand, setting profitability levels, and influencing consumer behavior. Therefore, it is essential for businesses to carefully consider the impact of their pricing decisions on the environment, society, and long-term financial performance. By adopting sustainable pricing practices, corporations can align their financial goals in line with the ESG (Environmental, Social and Governance) responsibilities. Businesses can also contribute SDG goals through protection and preservation of natural resources; reduced waste and emissions; promote fair labor practices, and adapt long-term sustainability.

CONCLUSION

Industry 4.0 has helped companies incorporate AI at various levels to bring more efficiency in their business operations. E- commerce companies, supply chain, mobility solution providers being biggest beneficiaries of these AI intervened pricing decisions. AI's unique promise of combined cost reduction and increased variation makes it generally attractive across the board. However, the benefits of AI in pricing depends on as to what scale the company has implemented taking into cognizance the potential risks. The use of AI in pricing has the potential to impact the businesses by reducing costs and providing a competitive advantage. Also, AI's ability to analyze data and make predictions can help businesses optimize their pricing strategies. Furthermore, AI can provide deeper insights into customer behavior and preferences, allowing businesses to adapt their pricing strategies for homogenous or heterogenous markets to be competitive and sustainable. Additionally, AI can help businesses identify sales opportunities and improve inventory management, leading to better overall performance.

Figure 15. Case Analysis

Case for discussion

Read the case below and answer the questions after the case.

A Company XYZ being the established player in the Petro-chemical Industry wants to diversify in the apparels market. On doing the SWOT analysis, it was found that the market is highly cluttered with majority of the sales going to the unorganized sector largely due to the price point. On discussion with the stakeholders, it was decided to ensure that 4P's of the marketing mix play a pivotal for companies to sustain their businesses. Among them Price being the most important of them as money helps the corporations to help make break even. In one of the reports by PwC found that majority of the marketers feel their decisions of keeping the price as they feel "price is right". The challenge to set the right price may be complex in nature but cannot be left at the mercy of the salesman or customer. Moreover, with the e-commerce companies going for the killing to get more traffic to their websites by announcing heavy discounts has made the entire apparel market more disruptive. The use of AI by the corporations has lately helped them for better realizations per customer. The company XYZ is lately struggling as the foot fall to the Mall and the store has declined rapidly. The company is making all out efforts to reach to various consultants to revive their business.

The consultant proposed that with the better technology penetration, today's customer is the informed consumer, thanks to online catalogues, search tools and collaborative platforms, and is further compounded by the increasing amount of variables to consider in pricing decisions lime optimal pricing, surge pricing, dynamic pricing etc. with the advent of AI. Moreover , the recent report from the PwC's has added that around 2/3rd of the retailers are planning to use intelligent automation to enhance their pricing and promotion.

- *How do you think that AI has practical implications on the future sustainability of the business?*

REFERENCES

Adu-Gyamfi, M., (2016), 'The bankruptcy of Lehman Brothers: Causes, effects and lessons learnt', Journal of Insurance and Financial Management, Vol. 1(4).

Ahmad, H., Yaqub, M., & Lee, S. H. (2023). Environmental-, social-, and governance-related factors for business investment and sustainability: A scientometric review of global trends. *Environment, Development and Sustainability*, *26*(2), 2965–2987. Advance online publication. DOI: 10.1007/s10668-023-02921-x PMID: 36714213

Aims History – Aims international. (n.d.). http://www.aimsinternational.org/aims

Bhat, A. (2023). Employee morale: definition, affecting factors, and how to boost morale. QuestionPro. https://www.questionpro.com/blog/employee-morale/

BrandEquity. E. (2021, July 23). Theatres to OTT: A shift in the wake of pandemic. ETBrandEquity.com. https://brandequity.economictimes.indiatimes.com/news/digital/theatres-to-ott-a-shift-in-the-wake-of-pandemic/84666148

Bureau of Competition. (2021, October 27). Federal Trade Commission. https://www.ftc.gov/about-ftc/bureaus-offices/bureau-competition

Competition Commission of India, Government of India. (n.d.). https://www.cci.gov.in/about-us

Contractor, F. J. (2021). The world economy will need even more globalization in the post-pandemic 2021 decade. *Journal of International Business Studies*, •••, 1–16. PMID: 33551513

Gomory, R., & Sylla, R. (2013). The American Corporation. Daedalus, 142(2), 102-118. Freeman, R. E. (2010). Strategic management: A stakeholder approach. Cambridge university press.

Koenig, M. (2023a, March 13). CFO at Lehman Brothers worked at SVB - while risk manager worked at Deutsche Bank. Mail Online. https://www.dailymail.co.uk/news/article-11855245/CFO-Lehman-Brothers-worked-SVB-risk-manager-worked-Deutsche-Bank.html

Koenig, M. (2023b, March 13). CFO at Lehman Brothers worked at SVB - while risk manager worked at Deutsche Bank. Mail Online. https://www.dailymail.co.uk/news/article-11855245/CFO-Lehman-Brothers-worked-SVB-risk-manager-worked-Deutsche-Bank.html

Magness, V. (2008). Who are the stakeholders now? An empirical examination of the Mitchell, Agle, and Wood theory of stakeholder salience. *Journal of Business Ethics, 83*(2), 177–192. https://economictimes.indiatimes.com/news/economy/policy/govt-amends-rules-governing-corporate-social-responsibility/articleshow/94381725.cms?from=mdr. DOI: 10.1007/s10551-007-9610-2

Morgan, B. (2019, September 16). 10 Examples Of Customer Experience Turnarounds. Forbes. https://www.forbes.com/sites/blakemorgan/2019/09/16/10-examples-of-customer-experience-turnarounds/?sh=1f7c3deb4415

Nova, M. (2020). Globalization-its influences & impacts on specific regions of Africa. In *SHS Web of Conferences* (Vol. 74, p. 06020). EDP Sciences., https://www.indiatimes.com/worth/news/svb-employee-joseph-gentile-worked-at-lehman-brothers-and-arthur-anderson-595887.html DOI: 10.1051/shsconf/20207406020

Pillai, K. A. (2023). AI-DRIVEN DYNAMIC PRICING STRATEGIES FOR SUBSCRIPTION FEATURES: LEVERAGING ARTIFICIAL INTELLIGENCE FOR REAL-TIME PRICING OPTIMIZATION. *Cem Dilmegani (2023). Dynamic Pricing Algorithms in.*

Shah, S. (2014). Corporate social responsibility: A way of life at the Tata Group. *Journal of Human Values, 20*(1), 59–74. DOI: 10.1177/0971685813515591

Chapter 3
Some New Slights About Capital Cost:
Modigliani et Miller (1958) versus MM (1963)

Nizar Elouni
University of Sfax, Tunisia

Abdelfettah Bouri
University of Sfax, Tunisia

ABSTRACT

In the pursuit of the optimal level of debt that maximizes the firm's value, the predecessors to Modigliani and Miller (MM, 1958) acknowledged the existence of an optimum point, but they failed to calculate it. This failure primarily stems from their inability to find the mathematical expression linking the required rate of return by shareholders to the risk associated with their assets. The purpose of this paper is to demonstrate that even though the two mathematical expressions differ due to the introduction of corporate taxes, the result remains the same. Moreover, even in an imperfect market, no theory suggests that the required rate of return depends on the presence or absence of taxes. We believe that this demonstration does not exist elsewhere and we consider it valuable from a theoretical standpoint.

1. INTRODUCTION

In order to accept or reject a new project, the firm has to verify if the net present value (NPV) is positive or negative. A positive NPV is a synonym of a project that increasing investors' wealth. The NPV of a project is "the sum of the present

DOI: 10.4018/979-8-3693-7357-6.ch003

Copyright © 2025, IGI Global Scientific Publishing. Copying or distributing in print or electronic forms without written permission of IGI Global Scientific Publishing is prohibited.

values of all the cash flows – positive or negative – that are expected to occur over the life of the project". (Chandra, 2005, p. 293). So we have to calculate adequately the rate used to discount cash flows; any mistake can leads to accept a project that well be rejected or to reject a project that will be accepted. This rate is the weighted average cost of various sources of finance noted by WACC (Weighted Average Cost of Capital).

In order to finance a project that has implicitly positive NPV, firms can use a variety of financing instruments such as debts, equity, preferred stocks, leasing, hybrid securities, etc. In this paper we suppose, according to Modigliani & Miller (1958, 1963) contributions, that firms will use only the broad categories of debt and equity, so the formula of WACC is: $\rho= w_d k_d + w_e k_e$.

While the cost of debt can be determined fairly easily, the cost of equity is rather difficult to estimate. Two famous 'approaches are considered to calculate the cost of equity, Modigliani & Miller (1958, 1963) approach [R....] and the Security Market Line (SML) one. The two expressions of MM (1958) and (1963) defining the equity' cost, noted by k_l, are:

$$MM(1958): k_l = k_u + (k_u - r)\frac{B}{S}; MM(1963): k_l = k_u + (k_u - r)(1 - T)\frac{B}{S}$$

From a mathematical 'point of view, it's clear that the two expressions are different and lead to different results. The two expressions are equivalent only when T (the corporate taxes) is equal to zero. In fact from a financial point of view, this conclusion is completely false. In fact the two expressions are developed in the frame of efficient market hypothesis (EMH) that suppose that the only factor that determine the cost of equity is the risk (operational and financial) attached to the equity, so the corporate tax or any another factor do not have any influence in the cost of equity. So the application of Modigliani & Miller (1958) expression or the Modigliani & Miller (1963) one can lead to the same result. The aim of this paper is to give some slights about this ambiguity.

This article is organized as follows: In the second section, we will present the contribution of Modigliani & Miller (1958). The third section will discuss the contribution of 1963. Finally, the fourth section will present our contribution aimed at clarifying the raised ambiguity.

2. CONTRIBUTION OF THE MODEL (1958)

Starting from a series of rather restrictive assumptions and relying on the mechanism of arbitrage, Modigliani and Miller (1958) proved, on the one hand, that the value of a firm is independent of its capital structure, and on the other hand, that the required rate of return by shareholders increases with the level of leverage (B/S). By relaxing in 1963 the assumption related to corporate taxation, the two authors arrived at new expression, seemingly distinct from the one developed in 1958. This difference has led several finance professionals to believe that the two expressions, which are clearly different, yield different results. The objective of this purely theoretical paper is to contribute to removing such ambiguity and to explain that the required rate of return by a shareholder (cost of equity capital), in the context of a perfect market assumption considered in both the 1958 and 1963 articles, depends solely on the level of risk (operational and financial) the shareholder is willing to bear. In other words, corporate taxation has no effect, meaning that the difference in the expressions is illusory, and the 1958 and 1963 expressions should lead to the same result.

The purpose of this section is to present the assumptions, variables, and two propositions of the Modigliani & Miller (1958) article.

2.1. Assumptions of the Model

Several assumptions are assumed by Modigliani & Miller (1958) in order to develop their two propositions. The fist assuming that the value of levered firm is equal to the value of unlevered firm. The second is about the expression of the cost of equity capital. These hypotheses are:

H_1: The capital markets are perfect, meaning that markets are frictionless and that all investors have the same information, Efficient Market' Hypothesis (EMH);
H_2: Levered firms and unlevered ones are assumed in the same operational risk, that means that they will have the same net operating income$E(NOI)$;
H_3: Firms issue only two types of claims: risk-free debt (B) and Equity (S);
H_4: Firms do not assume income taxes; (this assumption will be relaxed in the article published by the two authors in 1963);
H_5: All cash flows are constant and perpetuities;
H_6: All free cash flows are paid as dividends;
H_7: All investors (individual or carters) can borrow and limit any amount at the same risk – free rate;
H_8: There are no costs to bankruptcy;
H_9: Managers always maximize shareholders' wealth (that means that there are no agency costs);

Copeland and Weston (1992) noted: "Many of these assumptions are unrealistic, but later we can show that relaxing many of them does not really change the major conclusions of the model of firm behavior that Modigliani and Miller provide." (p. 439)

2.2. Definitions and Notations

Let:

- U: Unlevered firm (firm without debt);
- L: Levered firm (firm with debt);
- I: The perpetual stream of risk-free payments to bondholders ;
- r: Risk free rate;
- B: Market value of debt;
- k_u: Required rate of return by shareholders of the unlevered firm;
- k_l: Required rate of return by shareholders of the levered firm;
- S_u: The value of equity of an unlevered firm;
- S_l: The value of equity of a levered firm;
- ρ_u: the weighted average cost of un levered firm ;
- ρ_l: the weighted average cost of levered firm;
- V_u: The value of unlevered firm ;
- V_l: The value of levered firm ;
- FCF: The free cash flow ;
- NOI: Net operating income;
- T: Corporate taxes;
- $WACC$: Weighted Average Cost of Capital;

Before presenting the two propositions of MM (1958), it is appropriate to provide a more explicit definition of certain concepts mentioned above, such as the value of an unlevered firm, the value of a levered one, the value of debt, etc.

Considering that the present value of a financial asset is equal to the sum of after-tax stream of cash flows (FCF) discounted at the appropriate risk-adjusted rate, so the value of equity of an unlevered firm will be $S_u = \sum E(FCF)\,(1 + k_u)^{-t}$.

Taking into consideration H_5 we shall have

$$S_u = \frac{E(FCF)}{k_u}$$

According, respectively to H_6 and H_4 we obtain:

$$S_u = \frac{[E(NOI) - I](1 - T)}{k_u} = S_u = \frac{[E(NOI) - I]}{k_u}$$

Finally, since the unlevered firm U has no debts, we have

$$S_u = V_u = \frac{E(BAII)}{\rho_u}\left(a\right)$$

Similarly, we can write:

$$B = \frac{I}{r}\left(b\right) \text{ and } S_l = \frac{E(BAII) - I}{k_l}\left(c\right)$$

On the side of the levered firm, its value is equal to the sum of the values of all its financial assets, so we will have: $V_l = B + S_l$,

$$WACC = \rho_l = r\frac{B}{V_l} + k_l\frac{S_l}{V_l}$$

$$\Rightarrow \rho_l \times V_l = r \times B + k_l \times S_l = I + k_l\frac{E(BAII) - I}{k_l} \Rightarrow V_l = \frac{E(BAII)}{\rho_l}(d)$$

Taking into consideration (a) and (d) we can note that the value of levered firm or an unlevered one can be calculated by discounting its FCF by its appropriate WACC.

2.3. Propositions of MM (1958)

Based on the assumptions and definitions mentioned earlier, MM (1958) demonstrated, relying on the arbitrage mechanism, two propositions that truly revolutionized financial thinking.

The first proposition suggests that in a world without taxes, the value of a firm is independent of its capital structure; in other words, the value of a levered firm is equal to that of an unlevered firm. Therefore, we have $V_l = V_u$. MM noted that if the above expression is not satisfied, arbitrage operations quickly restore equilibrium.

The second proposition of Modigliani and Miller (1958) states that the required rate of return by shareholders increases as the firm's debt ratio grows, due to the increasing financial risk supported by shareholders.

Considering the equilibrium condition $V_l = V_u$, and based on equations (a) and (d), we shall have $\rho_l = \rho_u$, so we obtain: $k_l = k_u + \left(k_u - r\right)\frac{B}{S}$ (e)

3. THE MM MODEL IN THE PRESENCE OF CORPORATE TAXES

The merit of the 1958 paper was primarily its use as a reference for extending research on capital structure by taking into account market imperfections. Among these extensions is the one carried out by the same authors in 1963, which considers corporate taxes. The two propositions from 1958 will be reformulated to incorporate taxes. Thus, for the first proposition related to the value of a levered firm, we have $V_l=V_u+TB(f)$

According to equation (f), we obtain:

$$k_l = k_u + \left(k_u - r\right)\left(1 - T\right)\tfrac{B}{S}(g)$$

4. OUR CONTRIBUTION: CLARIFICATION OF AMBIGUITY

By comparing equation (2) and equation (4), one might think that the two expressions can only yield the same result in the absence of corporate taxes,, which is not true at all. In fact, the two expressions are always equivalent regardless of the tax rate T. The levered ratio (B/S) in the second expression varies with T (the role of taxes in wealth redistribution among shareholders and bondholders), but the required rate of return by shareholders remains at the same level (as long as the risk has not changed).

4.1. Proof of Equality between the Two Expressions

To simplify, we use the index 1 to refer to the context without taxes (1958) and the index 2 to refer to the context with taxes (1963).

$$V_{l_1} = V_{u_1} + TB = B + S_{l1} \quad (1)$$

$$V_{l_2} = V_{u_2} + TB = B + S_{l2} \quad (2)$$

$$V_{u_1} = \frac{E(NOI)}{\rho_u} \quad (3)$$

$$V_{u_2} = \frac{E(NOI)(1 - T)}{\rho_u} \quad (4)$$

From (3) and (4), we will have:

$$V_{u2} = V_{u1}(1 - T) \ ; V_{u2} = V_{u1}(1 - T) = \left(B + S_l\right)(1 - T) \quad (5)$$

When we combine (2) and (5), we obtain:

$$V_{l_2} = V_{u_2} + TB = (B + S_{l1})(1 - T) + TB = B - TB + S_{l1}(1 - T) + TB = B + S_{l1}(1 - T) \tag{6}$$

From (2) and (6), we shall have:

$$V_{l_2} = B + S_{l2} = B + S_{l1}(1 - T) \Rightarrow S_{l2} = S_{l1}(1 - T) \tag{7}$$

According to the definition of cost of levered equity in the two frames (1958 and 1963), we will have:

$$k_l = k_u + (k_u - r)(1 - T)\frac{B}{S_{l2}} = k_u + (k_u - r)(1 - T)\frac{B}{S_{l1}(1 - T)} = k_u + (k_u - r)\frac{B}{S_{l1}}$$

4.2. Illustration

Consider Firm U as an unlevered firm and firm L as a levered one. The amount of L' Debts is 800. Both firms have exactly the same perpetual net operating income before taxes, (*NOI*=240). The before-tax cost of debt is the same risk-free rate (k_b=r=6%). The expected rate of return on Firm U is k_u=10%. We are concerned by calculating the expected rate of return on firm L when T=0%, T=20% and T=30%.

$$(a) T = 0\% \Rightarrow V_u = \frac{240}{0.10} = 2400 = V_l = B + S_l = 800 + 1600 \Rightarrow$$

$$k_l = 0.1 + (0.1 - 0.06)\frac{800}{1600} = 12\%$$

$$(b) T = 20\% \Rightarrow V_u = \frac{240 \times 0.8}{0.10} = 1920 \Rightarrow V_l = V_u + TB =$$

$$1920 + 0.2 \times 800 = 2080 = B + S_l = 800 + 1280 \Rightarrow$$

$$k_l = 0.1 + (0.1 - 0.06) \times 0.8\frac{800}{1280} = 12\%$$

$$(c) T = 30\% \Rightarrow V_u = \frac{240 \times 0.7}{0.10} = 1680 \Rightarrow V_l = V_u + TB =$$

$$1680 + 0.3 \times 800 = 1920 = B + S_l = 800 + 1120 \Rightarrow$$

$$k_l = 0.1 + (0.1 - 0.06) \times 0.7\frac{800}{1120} = 12\%$$

5. CONCLUSION

In order to evaluate any investment projects, we need to calculate its net present value that requires determining the minimum expected rate of return which is the cost of capital used to finance the project.MM (1963) have proposed a formula to express the cost of capital which appears to be different from a purely mathematical 'point of view to that proposed in 1958. In a fact, at a time when the 1963 formula took corporate tax into account, the 1958 one did not.

We have demonstrated in this paper that the difference is only an illusion and that the two formulae must lead to the same final result.

To conclude, we can advance the following general rule: In an efficient market, company tax rate or any other factor, other than risk, has no effect in the cost of capital.

WACC- Weighted Average Cost of capital
w_d- Proportion of debts
k_d- Cost of debts (After tax)
w_e- Proportion of equity
k_d- Cost of equity

The Security Market Line (SML) or the Capital Assets Pricing Model (CAPM) is "A model that indicates what should be the expected or required rates of return" (Reilly and Brown, 2000, p. 295). The mathematical expression of SML is: $\widehat{R}_i = Rf + \beta_i[E(R_M) - Rf]$. We must draw the reader's attention to the difference between the Capital Market Line (CML) and the SML. On the one hand the first only applies to portfolio' assets and it measures risk by volatility (standard deviation). On the contrary, the second applies either to portfolio' assets, or to securities and it measures risk by the beta (The covariance of an asset with the market portfolio divided by the variance of the market portfolio).

The Efficient Market Hypothesis (EMH) has been used in financial literature under three vocations: allocation' vocation, operational' vocation and informational' one. In the context of MM (1958) and MM (1963) context, it is the informational' vocation that had been taken into consideration.

Many authors have contributed to the development of this theory but the famous are Eugene Fama (1970) and Paul Samuelson (1965). A financial market is informationally efficient when market prices reflect all available information about value (past prices, public information, so and so,..., any kind of information). In the EMH' context no investor can beat the market, so financial transactions using the available information are zero NPV activities.

Stiglitz (1969), Rubinstein (1973) and Hsia (1981) have relaxed the assumption related to risk free-rate. Stiglitz studied the effect of risky debt in the absence of bankruptcy costs using a state-preference framework, and Rubinstein provided a proof using a mean-variance approach. Hsia combines the Option Pricing Model (OPM), the CAPM and the MM theorems. The conclusion is the same: Risky debt without bankruptcy costs does not alter the basic MM results. Copeland and Weston (1992) note: "…Therefore so long as there are no costs of bankruptcy (paid to third parties like trustees and law firms), it should not make any difference whether debt is risk free or risky. The value of the firm should be equal to the value of the discounted cash flows from investment.

In addition to making the model more realistic, Miller (1977) introduces personal as well as corporate taxes. He assumes two types of personal tax rates: the rate on income received from holding shares and the rate on income from bonds.

DeAngelo and Masulis (1980) extend Miller's contribution by analyzing the effect of tax shields other than interest payments on debt.

In foot note number 4, it is noted that in a world without transactions costs, risky debt has no effect on the value of the firm. Baxter (1967), Kim (1978) and others consider that when we consider bankruptcy costs, the value of the firm is reduced by the fact of payments must be made to third parties than bond or shareholders, such as trustee fees, legal fees, so and so.

Jensen and Meckling (1976) use agency costs to argue that the probability distribution of cash flows provided by the firm is not independent of its ownership structure and that this fact may be used to explain optimal leverage. For an interesting exposition of this idea the reader is referred to Watts and Zimmerman (1979).

$$S_l = \frac{E(BAII) - I}{k_l} = \frac{E(BAII) - rB}{k_l} \Rightarrow k_l = \frac{E(BAII) - rB}{S_l}$$

$$V_u = \frac{E(BAII)}{k_u} = V_l = B + S_l \Rightarrow E\left(BAII\right) = k_u\left(B + S_l\right) \Rightarrow$$

$$k_l = \frac{E(BAII) - rB}{S_l} = \frac{k_u(B + S_l) - rB}{S_l} = k_u + \left(k_u - r\right)\frac{B}{S_l}$$

$$V_l = B + S_l$$

- Streams of CF of debts: $I=rB$;
- Streams of CF of equity: $[E(BAII) - rB](1 - T)$;
- Streams of CF of all assets: $[E(BAII) - rB](1 - T)+rB=E(BAII)(1 - T)+TrB$

$$V_l = \frac{[E(BAII)](1 - T)}{k_u} + \frac{TrB}{r} = V_u + TB$$

$$S_l = \frac{[E(BAII) - rB](1 - T)}{k_l} \Rightarrow k_l = \frac{E(BAII)(1 - T)}{S_l} - \frac{rB(1 - T)}{S_l} k_u = \frac{E(BAII)(1 - T)}{S_u}$$

$$\Rightarrow E(BAII)(1 - T) = k_u S_u = k_u V_u = k_u \left(V_l - TB\right) \Rightarrow k_l$$

$$= \frac{k_u\left(V_l - TB\right)}{S_l} - \frac{rB(1 - T)}{S_l} = k_u\left(\frac{B + S_l}{S_l} - T\frac{B}{S_l}\right) - \frac{rB(1 - T)}{S_l}$$

$$= k_u + \left(k_u \frac{B}{S_l}\right)(1 - T) - \frac{rB(1 - T)}{S_l} = k_u + \left(k_u - r\right)(1 - T)\frac{B}{S_l}$$

REFERENCES

Baxter, N. D. (1967). Leverage, Risk of Ruin and the Cost of Capital. *The Journal of Finance*, (September), 395–403.

Chandra, P. (2005). *Financial Management: Theory and Practice* (6th ed.). Tata McGraw-Hill Publishing Company Limited.

Copeland, T. E., & Weston, I. F. (1992). *Financial Theory and Corporate Policy* (3rd ed.). Addison-Wesley Publishing Company.

DeAngelo, H., & Masulis, R. (1980). Optimal capital Structure under Corporate and Personal taxation. *Journal of Financial Economics*, *8*(1), 3–30. DOI: 10.1016/0304-405X(80)90019-7

Fama, E. F. (1970). Efficient Capital Market: A Review Theory and Empirical Work. *The Journal of Finance*, *25*(May), 383–417. DOI: 10.2307/2325486

Hsia, C. C. (1981). Coherence of the Modern Theories of Finance. *Financial Review*, *16*(Winter), 27–42. DOI: 10.1111/j.1540-6288.1981.tb01617.x

Jensen, M., & Meckling, W. (1976). Theory of the Firm: Managerial Behavior, Agency Costs, and Ownership Structure. *Journal of Financial Economics*, *3*(October), 305–360. DOI: 10.1016/0304-405X(76)90026-X

Kim, H. (1978). A mean-Variance Theory of Optimal Capital Structure and Corporate Debt Capacity. *The Journal of Finance*, (March), 45–64.

Miller, M. H. (1977). Debt and Taxes. *The Journal of Finance*, (May), 261–275.

Modigliani, F., & Miller, M. H. (1958). The Cost of Capital, Corporation Finance, and the Theory of Investment. *The American Economic Review*, (June), 261–297.

Modigliani, F., & Miller, M. H. (1963). Corporate Income taxes and the Cost of Capital. *The American Economic Review*, (June), 433–443.

Reilly, F. K., & Brown, K. C. (2000). *Investment Analysis and Portfolio Management* (6th ed.). The Dryden Press.

Rubinstein, M. E. (1973). A Mean-Variance Synthesis of Corporate Financial Theory. *The Journal of Finance*, (March), 167–181.

Samuelson, P. A. (1965). Proof that Properly Anticipated Prices Fluctuate Randomly. *Industrial Management Review*, (Spring), 41–49.

Stiglitz, J. E. (1969). A Re-examination of the Modigliani-Miller Theorem. *The American Economic Review*, (December), 784–793.

Watts, R., & Zimmerman, J. (1979). The Demand for and Supply of Accounting Theories: The market for Excuses. *The Accounting Review*, (April), 273–305.

Chapter 4
Financial Evolution: Tracing the Roots of AI in Finance

P. Surenthran David
https://orcid.org/0009-0001-7665-2406
St. Joseph's College of Engineering, India

D. Joel Jebadurai
https://orcid.org/0000-0002-6947-8497
St. Joseph's College of Engineering, India

D. Chris Sherin
St. Joseph's College of Engineering, India

A. S. Princy
Sathyabama Institute of science and Technology, India

K. Velu
The New College, University of Madras, India

M. Abdul Sibiril
https://orcid.org/0009-0004-0566-8541
The New College, University of Madras, India

L. Rajeshkumar
https://orcid.org/0009-0007-8513-206X
St. Joseph's College of Engineering, India

ABSTRACT

This chapter looks at how artificial intelligence (AI) has changed the FinTech business by demonstrating its evolution and pointing out key applications, problems, and future trends. From the early days of electronic fund transfers to today's advanced financial services driven by AI, FinTech has always been trying to make things faster, easier to use, and more personalized. Using big data and sentiment analysis to make intelligent choices, AI has transformed how fraud detection, risk management, credit scoring, algorithmic trading, and customer service. Even with these advancements, challenges like data accuracy, bias, cybersecurity, and following regulations exist. Some real-life examples such as JPMorgan Chase's COIN AI system, and more. These examples show how leading companies in the financial

DOI: 10.4018/979-8-3693-7357-6.ch004

Copyright © 2025, IGI Global Scientific Publishing. Copying or distributing in print or electronic forms without written permission of IGI Global Scientific Publishing is prohibited.

sector are using AI to improve customer service, streamline processes, and lower risks. This chapter talks about emerging trends in AI, such as explainable AI(XAI), quantum computing, decentralized AI, and edge computing. It emphasizes the importance of using AI ethically.

INTRODUCTION

FinTech is a short way of saying "financial technology". It refers to any business that uses technology to provide financial services. The fusion of finance and technology is causing significant changes in the financial sector which is transforming financial management. It includes a wide range of innovative financial services and solutions based on cutting-edge technology such as mobile platforms, artificial intelligence, blockchains, etc. These innovations aim to make financial services more efficient, convenient, and cost-effective. The financial sector has been completely transformed by digitalization, resulting in streamlined traditional services and the emergence of new business opportunities and innovative models. The current era of technological advancements has brought about a significant shift in the way we conduct financial transactions. This evolution has brought about a shift in focus, moving beyond the improvement of existing tasks to the creation of entirely new possibilities for financial service companies (Gomber et.al., 2017).

Driven by government initiatives that encourage the adoption of digital financial systems and a cashless economy, the Indian FinTech industry has witnessed remarkable growth in recent years. The transaction value of digital payments in India has experienced a significant surge, more than doubling from $107.72 billion in 2020 to $216.18 billion in 2023. This developing sector has attracted considerable interest from investors such as SoftBank, who are actively supporting promising FinTech startups. The outcome is a thriving ecosystem where developing companies such as Paytm, Pine Labs, PayU, and Faircent are revolutionizing the financial landscape in India. Their digital solutions are meeting the changing needs of Indian consumers and promoting financial inclusion throughout the country. FinTech has made financial services smoother by making them simpler to access and affordable. The FinTech industry will certainly be transformed by these innovations, which will bring new possibilities and challenges that must be solved (mordorintelligence.com).

Figure 1. Transaction Value of Digital Payments, In USD Billion, India, 2020 - 2023

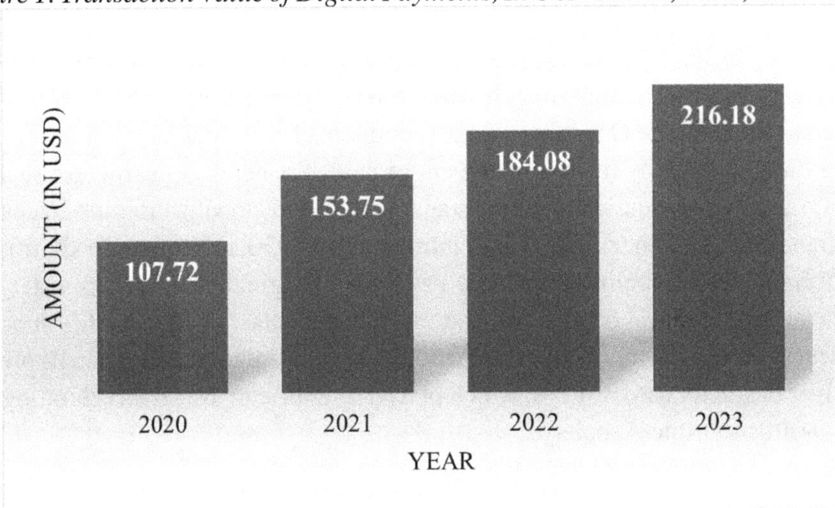

EVOLUTION OF FINTECH

From the first electronic money exchanges to the latest mobile payment apps and blockchain-based payment systems, FinTech has always been pushing the limits of what is possible in finance. Efforts have been continuously made to enhance the efficiency, accessibility, and inclusivity of financial services at every stage. The following table goes into more detail about some major shifts in FinTech that had a big impact on the world of finance.

Table 1. Evolution of FinTech

Era	Period	Key Developments	Technology Focus	Impact on Financial Services
FinTech 1.0	1866-1967	First transatlantic cable, Fedwire (US), credit cards	Telegraph, railroads, steamships	Financial globalization, early electronic fund transfers
FinTech 2.0	1967-2008	ATMs, SWIFT, electronic stock exchanges, online banking	Mainframe computers, internet	Increased automation, faster transactions, rise of online banking
FinTech 3.0	2008-Present	Mobile payments, blockchain, AI, robo-advisors, neobanks	Smartphones, cloud computing, big data	Disruption of traditional banking, personalized financial services, emergence of new players
FinTech 4.0	Emerging	Decentralized finance (DeFi), embedded finance, open banking, hyper-personalization	Web3, AI/ML, APIs	Democratization of finance, integration of financial services into non-financial platforms, increased competition

FinTech 1.0

The start of FinTech 1.0 can be traced back to the late 19th century, with the introduction of transatlantic cables. (Transatlantic cables are underwater cables that run across the Atlantic Ocean to connect continents for communication purposes). The era was marked by the establishment of early financial infrastructure such as Fedwire and credit cards, which set the stage for financial globalization and electronic fund transfers. The Diner's Club Card, introduced in 1950, represented a significant advancement in the realm of cashless payments. Originally limited to restaurant transactions, its modest origins set the foundation for the advancement of modern payment systems. This major development was accompanied by American Express's launch of the credit card in 1958, which played a significant role in accelerating the shift towards a cashless society.

FinTech 2.0

FinTech 2.0 (1967–2008) witnessed the rise of automated teller machines (ATMs), international payment SWIFT networks, electronic stock exchanges, and online banking. The introduction of the ATM by Barclays in 1967 is widely recognized as the start of the FinTech 2.0 era. This advancement was driven by mainframe computers and increased internet use, which changed how we interacted with financial institutions. The rise of online banking enabled individuals to manage their finances from the comfort of their own homes, reducing the need for physical visits to traditional brick-and-mortar banks.

FinTech 3.0

Under FinTech 3.0 (2008–present), mobile payments were introduced, and AI, blockchain technology, robo-advisers, and neobanks (Neobanks are a type of digital bank that operates exclusively online without traditional physical branches) came into operation. All this innovation was facilitated by smartphones, big data analytics, and cloud computing, which have disrupted traditional banks and offered customized financial services to individuals. A statistic released by Statista in 2023 predicted that up to about 1.31 billion people would be global users of mobile payment transactions as of this year or at the latest by the next three years, thus showing a wide adoption rate for mobile-based money solutions.

FinTech 4.0

Emerging FinTech 4.0 promises more developments through decentralized finance (DeFi), embedded finance, open banking, and hyper-personalization. Powered by Web3, AI/ML, and APIs (Application Programming Interfaces), this new phase aims to involve many more people in the industry since it will make finance more accessible and integrated into our everyday lives. While still in its infancy, Global investment in blockchain solutions is experiencing significant growth, with a projected surge from $6.6 billion in 2021 to nearly $19 billion by 2024, according to Statista. This substantial increase in spending underscores the widespread adoption and recognition of blockchain technology's potential across diverse industries.

IMPORTANCE OF TECHNOLOGY IN SHAPING MODERN FINANCIAL SERVICES

From paper-based, manual processes to a digital landscape, technology has not only improved traditional financial systems but has also created new business models and opportunities. Emerging technologies like artificial intelligence, blockchain, and big data are reshaping the industry. These advancements address not only the challenges but also the ethical considerations that coincide with them.

Increased Accessibility

Unlike in the past when one had to visit a physical banking hall, technology has made it possible for people from different walks of life to access financial services. Mobile banking has lowered barriers to entry, hence increasing the accessibility of financial services for previously underserved populations (Maged et.al., 2023). Digital banking improves the availability of financial services in rural areas, giving individuals more control over their finances. This is particularly important in regions where traditional physical bank branches may be limited or non-existent. Financial inclusion and digital finance help governments, consumers of financial services, and the economy as a whole. For instance, it lowers the cost of financial intermediaries for banks and FinTech companies, simplifies loan applications for customers, and boosts overall government spending (Ozili P K 2020).

Hyper-Personalization

FinTech companies are utilizing cutting-edge technologies such as AI, machine learning, and big data analytics to customize their products and services according to the unique needs and preferences of each customer. The transition from one-size-fits-all solutions to tailored experiences is seen in fields such as investment recommendations, loan offerings, and financial planning advice. Customer data can be used by FinTech companies to make sure that financial products and services are tailored to each person's wants and preferences. This could include specific suggestions based on each person's unique financial situation (Lee I et.al., 2020).

Speed and Efficiency

Automation speeds up transactions, simplifies processes and reduces errors. Technology optimizes activities so that they take less time, which enhances productivity. For example, if a customer shops frequently online, they can save time by being able to transfer funds between accounts quickly or pay bills over the internet instead of doing it manually where there's room for error. Although the advantages of this new AI tool for businesses have been extensively covered by multiple sources, it is crucial to acknowledge the potential drawbacks. They pose reputational and legal risks by compromising privacy, enabling fraudulent transactions, etc. (Yogesh K et.al., 2023).

Data-Driven Innovation

The FinTech industry is heavily investing in big data analytics. The banking sector generates a vast amount of data, including customer data, financial product data, and transaction data. The data is used to support decision-making systems by integrating it with external data from social media or marketing websites (Saleem et.al., 2020). In today's competitive landscape, many banks are leveraging the power of big data to gain an edge in their business (Assis et.al., 2019). The data, which includes transactions, market movements, customer interactions, and more, offers a valuable source of information that can be utilized through advanced analytics. The global data landscape is projected to experience significant growth, with an estimated total data generation of 180 zettabytes by 2025, as stated in a 2023 report by Statista. The financial sector will generate a significant portion of this data, which highlights the growing volume and complexity of financial transactions and interactions.

Better Security

Security measures for financial transactions have been improved by new technologies such as biometrics, and encryption. This has greatly reduced cases of fraud as well as other online risks. Biological characteristics such as fingerprints or face recognition offer more robust authentication than traditional methods, particularly when used in combination with multi-factor authentication. While acknowledging the need for privacy, adopting techniques such as data anonymization and encryption can effectively protect biometric information. (Rui et.al., 2019).

Real-Time Insights

Technological advancements allow for keeping track of financial markets and portfolios in real-time. AI-enhanced algorithmic trading has a significant impact on financial markets. It uses advanced technology to analyze important data and provides accessible tools that benefit individuals beyond just companies. Machine learning algorithms are utilized to identify patterns in data and make predictions. (Ta et.al., 2018 & Li et.al., 2020). Real-time insights can enable investors to make more informed decisions on investments by quickly reacting to market changes.

Lower Costs

Technology-based solutions are cheaper than traditional methods therefore operational expense is reduced hence charging lower fees for services rendered which benefits customers. FinTech utilizes technology to automate procedures, optimize operations, and remove intermediaries, leading to reduced operational expenses. In addition, FinTech frequently bypasses traditional banking channels and associated expenses, resulting in additional cost reductions. The inherent attributes of FinTech, along with heightened competition and inventive business models, enable it to provide services at reduced expenses compared to traditional financial institutions (Schueffel P 2021).

APPLICATIONS OF AI IN FINTECH

AI has transformed the FinTech sector, providing exceptional prospects for creativity, productivity, and interaction with customers. FinTech organizations may optimize various services such as fraud detection, credit scoring, customer support, and personalized financial advice by utilizing AI's strengths in data analysis, pattern recognition, and automation. AI plays a crucial role in shaping the future of financial services by redefining traditional approaches and establishing new benchmarks for business excellence.

Table 2. Applications of AI in FinTech

Area	Application	How AI is Applied
Risk Management	Anomaly Detection	Machine learning models identify unusual patterns or outliers
	Credit Scoring	Advanced algorithms assess creditworthiness using various data sources
	Portfolio Optimization	AI algorithms suggest optimal investment allocations based on risk profiles
Investment and Trading	Robo-Advisors	Algorithms create and manage portfolios based on risk tolerance and goals
	Algorithmic Trading	High-frequency algorithms analyze data and execute trades at high speeds
	Market Prediction	Machine learning models analyze historical data to predict market trends
Regulatory Compliance	Know Your Customer (KYC) and Anti-Money Laundering (AML)	Computer vision and NLP automate identity verification and transaction monitoring
	Regulatory Reporting	AI automates data collection, analysis, and report generation
	Compliance Monitoring	AI continuously monitors transactions and activities for potential violations
Operational Efficiency	Process Automation	Robotic Process Automation (RPA) handles repetitive tasks like data entry
	Document Analysis	NLP and machine learning extract and interpret information from documents
	Back-office Operations Optimization	AI streamlines processes like claims processing and reconciliation
Financial Inclusion	Alternative Credit Scoring	Algorithms use non-traditional data (e.g., mobile phone usage) for credit scoring
	Microloans and Microlending	AI streamlines loan origination and risk assessment
	Financial Education	AI-powered tools provide personalized financial advice and education
Insurance	Underwriting	Machine learning assesses risk more accurately for personalized premiums
	Claims Processing	AI automates claim assessment, verification, and settlement
	Fraud Detection	AI identifies fraudulent claims based on patterns and anomalies

continued on following page

Table 2. Continued

Area	Application	How AI is Applied
Financial Product Development	Market Research	NLP and sentiment analysis gauge customer preferences and market trends
	Product Personalization	AI tailors products based on individual financial profiles and behavior
	Product Pricing	AI optimizes pricing based on real-time market conditions and customer data
Customer Service	Chatbots and Virtual Assistants	Natural Language Processing (NLP) to understand and respond to customer inquiries
	Personalized Recommendations	Machine learning algorithms analyze user data to tailor suggestions
	Sentiment Analysis	NLP assesses customer sentiment from social media and reviews to gauge satisfaction

Fraud Detection and Prevention

The role played by AI in fraud detection lies in its ability to analyze massive datasets in real-time. Machine learning algorithms can detect patterns, anomalies, and unusual behaviors that may indicate signs of fraudulent activity (Hilal et.al., 2022). Mastercard, a world leader in payment processing, has successfully put in place an AI-powered fraud detection system to deal with the growing number and complexity of fraudulent transactions. Machine learning algorithms are used by the system to look at huge datasets in real-time and find trends and outliers that could be signs of fraud. Mastercard says that by 2024, its advanced AI model, Decision Intelligence Pro, will be able to get rid of up to 300% more scams. This has not only cut down on false declines by 80%, but it has also led to a significant decrease in fraud-related losses (cnbc.com).

Risk Assessment and Management

AI models can analyze vast amounts of structured and unstructured data, such as financial statements, market data, and news articles, to detect potential risks and evaluate their consequences. Financial institutions can make better decisions regarding lending, investments, and risk mitigation strategies (Khattak et.al., 2023). JPMorgan Chase & Co. has successfully implemented AI in their risk management processes. They have made risk assessment much more accurate and faster by using AI models that look at structured and unstructured data sources, such as news stories and financial statements. These models quickly find possible threats, which lets people make quick decisions and develop good ways to mitigate their risks.

According to the JPMorgan Chase 2022 Annual Report, early warning signs from AI models have helped the company curb credit losses by a large amount. These models' ability to constantly learn and change based on new data has also made risk management more effective. This has helped JPMorgan Chase stay ahead of new risks and improve its overall performance (jpmorganchase.com).

Credit Scoring and Underwriting

AI-powered credit scoring models surpass conventional credit history by integrating additional data sources like social media activity, utility bill payments, and even mobile phone usage habits, to get a better and more accurate picture of an individual's creditworthiness (Addy et.al., 2024). This results in credit decisions that are more equitable and inclusive. This data-driven method not only makes credit decisions more accurate but also helps more people get access to money. LenddoEFL, a leading alternative credit scoring platform, said that their AI-powered models have helped improve approval rates for thin-file borrowers by up to 30%. This shows that they can reach groups of underserved populations by promoting financial inclusivity (lenddoefl.com).

Algorithmic Trading and Portfolio Management

AI algorithms swiftly execute trades based on predetermined criteria. These algorithms utilize advanced analysis techniques to evaluate market trends, news updates, and historical data to make informed investment decisions. Machine learning (ML) looks at a huge amount of financial data, from both traditional market data and data from sources like news and social media opinion. Machine learning methods, like deep learning and natural language processing, can find patterns and signals that help systems make trading choices. This could make trading more efficient, faster, and more profitable. By using sentiment research, investors can learn more about how the market works, which could give them an edge over other investors. However, some risks come with algorithmic trading, like market manipulation and systemic risk. To lower these risks, it's important to have responsible AI development and regulatory systems (Nuti et.al., 2020).

Customer Service and Chatbots

AI-powered robots provide 24/7 customer service, address questions, solve problems, and help with financial tasks. This automation of customer service not only makes the experience better for customers in general but also cuts costs significantly. Juniper Research did a study that says using chatbots in banks will save a staggering

$7.3 billion by 2023. This big reduction in expenses comes from chatbots being able to handle a lot of queries from consumers all at once. This frees up employees to work on more complicated tasks and cuts down on the need for a lot of customer service staff. Also, chatbots can answer questions right away and help customers in a way that is specific to their needs. This makes customers more satisfied and loyal (juniperresearch.com).

Personalized Financial Advice and Recommendation Engines

The AI system carefully examines your personal financial information to offer customized suggestions regarding investments, savings, and budgeting. A recent survey conducted by Accenture revealed that a significant majority of consumers, approximately 95%, are open to sharing their data in exchange for personalized financial advice. As AI technology keeps getting better, we can expect even smarter and more personalized financial assistance in the future. This will make it easier for everyone to get expert financial advice and give people more control over their finances (accenture.com).

AI-POWERED DATA ANALYTICS

AI-driven data analytics is revolutionizing how businesses understand and harness their data. AI leverages advanced algorithms and machine learning approaches to efficiently analyze large volumes of data, reveal underlying patterns, and generate actionable insights with unmatched precision and speed. With the increasing size and complexity of data, AI-driven analytics have become an essential tool for decision-makers. It provides a competitive advantage and facilitates more intelligent, data-driven strategies (Yaiprasert et.al., 2024).

Big Data and its Role in FinTech

The FinTech business has been significantly impacted by the emergence of big data, which is distinguished by its vast volume, diversity, and speed of information. This includes structured data such as financial transactions and consumer demographics, as well as unstructured data like social media posts and news articles. Big data analytics to find trends, patterns, and correlations that would be unattainable through human examination. It results in a deeper understanding of customer behaviour, market dynamics, and risk factors (Mhlanga et.al., 2024). The global big data and business analytics market size was valued at $225.3 billion in 2023 and is projected to reach $665.7 billion by 2033, growing at a CAGR of 11.6% from 2024 to

2033. The rapid growth mentioned here reflects an increasing acceptance of the vital part that big data plays in stimulating innovation while offering a competitive edge in the FinTech industry (alliedmarketresearch.com).

Predictive Analytics for Financial Markets

AI programs can very accurately predict future market trends, asset prices, and possible risks by looking at past data and finding patterns. The ability of AI to adapt and learn from new data enables ongoing enhancement of predictive models, ensuring their accuracy even while changing market conditions. Predictive analytics powered by AI can help algorithmic trading by analysing and makimg decisions on data in real time, making trading methods more efficient and profitable. AI systems can quickly adapt to changes in the market by constantly watching and analysing it. This lowers risks and raises profits (Dakalbab et.al., 2024).

Sentiment Analysis and Social Media Data in Trading

AI-driven sentiment analysis is becoming more prevalent in extracting important insights from social media data and assessing market mood. AI algorithms can forecast market moves by studying the mood and emotions conveyed in tweets, postings, and comments. AI-driven sentiment analysis surpasses just the identification of positive or negative words in the text; it comprehends the underlying emotions and tone of the message. This enables organizations to assess interest in particular subjects, find dominant market attitudes, and acquire essential insights into their competitors' performance. Through the utilization of AI-powered sentiment analysis, businesses may enhance their decision-making process, optimize their strategy, and eventually gain a competitive edge in the market (Taherdoost et.al., 2023)

Customer Behavior Analysis for Targeted Marketing

AI-powered customer behavior analysis has emerged as a game changer in the FinTech business, transforming how financial institutions interact with their clients. Firms can now examine massive volumes of data from a variety of sources, including transaction history, website interactions, mobile app usage, social media activity, and even demographic information which provides useful insights into customer preferences, needs, pain points, and financial objectives. This insight enables them to provide highly tailored experiences, adapting financial goods, services, and marketing efforts to specific needs and preferences. For example, AI can suggest customized investment possibilities depending on a customer's risk profile, budgeting tools to help them better manage their finances, and even bespoke loan conditions based on their credit history and salary (Dwivedi, Y. K., et.al., 2021). Furthermore, AI-powered consumer behaviour research enables financial organizations to predict client wants and address any difficulties before they arise. By spotting early warning indications, such as a sudden surge in expenditure or late payments, these organizations may provide timely assistance and guidance, preventing future difficulties and strengthening client connections. The influence of AI-powered customisation is evident. According to Accenture's poll, 91% of consumers prefer firms that provide tailored offers and recommendations. This demonstrates the increased desire for customized services in the FinTech sector, where customers want their financial providers to understand their specific requirements and give suitable solutions (accenture.com).

REGULATORY CONSIDERATIONS

The rapid integration of AI in FinTech presents regulatory concerns that require attention to guarantee security and safe implementation. With the increasing prevalence of AI-driven solutions in financial services, regulatory frameworks need to adapt and address concerns related to data privacy, algorithmic transparency, and accountability. Ensuring a careful balance between innovation and stringent regulatory supervision is essential for fostering confidence, safeguarding consumers, and upholding the stability and integrity of financial markets. The interaction between innovation in technology and compliance with regulations is crucial for achieving sustainable growth in the AI-powered FinTech industry (Pattnaik et.al., 2024).

Compliance Challenges in Deploying AI in FinTech

AI models usually lack transparency, posing challenges for authorities to evaluate their fairness and readability. The decision-making process of AI models is often compared to a "black box" that lacks transparency (Buckley et.al., 2021; Milana et.al., 2021; Ryll et.al., 2020). Possible remedies for achieving openness in AI decision-making include technical solutions like utilizing simpler models with inherently less complex structures can make their decision-making processes easier to interpret, auditing AI models, encompassing code, data, and outputs, by experts can identify potential biases or flaws, ensuring fair and equitable outcomes. Non-technical solutions also play a crucial role in promoting transparency. Regulations and laws can mandate a certain degree of transparency, compelling companies to prioritize explainability even if it means sacrificing some algorithmic performance.

Public pressure and consumer demand for understandable AI can act as a powerful motivator for companies to adopt more transparent practices. Lastly, educational initiatives focused on improving technical literacy can empower individuals to comprehend the fundamental principles of AI, facilitating informed discussions and decision-making regarding its use (Burrell 2016). In a 2020 survey conducted by the World Economic Forum in collaboration with Deloitte, it was found that 76% of financial services executives view regulatory uncertainty as a major barrier to the implementation of artificial intelligence. It also underscores the demand for clearer norms and frameworks to guarantee the responsible and ethical utilization of AI in the FinTech industry (weforum.org).

Regulatory Frameworks Governing AI Applications in Finance

Multiple regulatory authorities globally are formulating frameworks to regulate the use of artificial intelligence in the FinTech sector. These frameworks have the objective of solving concerns such as algorithmic bias, data privacy, cybersecurity, and consumer protection. The General Data Protection Regulation (GDPR) in the European Union establishes strict standards for the handling of personal data, which include data used in decision-making powered by AI. Moreover, the proposed Artificial Intelligence Act (AIA) seeks to provide a comprehensive regulatory framework for AI, targeting high-risk AI systems, especially those employed in the field of finance. The significance of regulatory frameworks in guaranteeing the responsible and ethical advancement of AI systems is essential for addressing issues such as algorithmic bias, transparency, accountability, and data privacy. Regulatory frameworks can foster public trust in AI technologies and pave the way for wider adoption and innovation while mitigating potential risks and harm to individuals and society (Lepri et al., 2017).

Ethical Considerations and Responsible AI Practices

The use of AI in the field of FinTech gives rise to significant ethical concerns, including the possibility of bias, unintended outcomes, and the decline of human control. AI can acquire and amplify biases present in the data it is trained on, which could result in an unjust denial of loans to eligible borrowers based on their demographic characteristics. Moreover, intricate AI systems have the potential to generate unanticipated outcomes, such as an AI stock platform triggering a market collapse as a result of unexpected interactions with other algorithms. Ultimately, excessive dependence on AI has the potential to reduce human supervision in crucial financial judgments, hence giving rise to concerns over responsibility in the event of malfunctions. (Bathaee 2018). To deal with these concerns, FinTech companies need to implement responsible AI policies, which involve guaranteeing transparency, equity, and liability in their AI systems. This involves carrying out regular audits of AI models to identify and address any biases, providing transparent explanations for decisions made by AI systems, and implementing methods to ensure human supervision and intervention.

CHALLENGES OF AI IN FINANCE

The integration of AI presents immense opportunities for innovation and growth, but it also poses numerous ethical, practical, and regulatory challenges that require careful consideration. It is crucial to find the optimal balance between harnessing the potential of AI and ensuring responsible implementation. The use of AI in the FinTech industry presents significant potential, although it does not lack challenges (Mennella et.al., 2024).

Data Integrity and Availability

The journey to achieving seamless AI integration in finance is full of barriers associated with data integrity and availability. One major challenge is the problem of data silos and fragmentation, which leads to the dispersion of critical financial information across various systems and departments. The fragmentation of data poses a challenge to the consolidation and optimal utilisation of information for AI training. Inconsistencies in data formats from different sources often demand significant standardisation efforts before they can be effectively utilised in AI applications. (Pranckutė R 2021). Another challenge is the scarcity of high-quality, labelled data required for supervised learning. Obtaining such data can be quite expensive and time-consuming, which can hinder the progress of creating accurate and dependable AI models. (Alzubaidi et.al., 2023). To tackle these challenges, it is crucial to implement strong data management strategies and make major investments in data infrastructure.

Interpretability and Explainability

The concepts of interpretability and explainability revolve around the ability to comprehend and express the decisions made by an AI system or model. AI models, particularly deep learning models, often lack transparency, making it challenging to understand the reasoning behind their decision-making processes. The lack of transparency in AI systems can erode trust and acceptance, especially in the FinTech sector, where decisions carry substantial implications. The uncertainty that surrounds the operation of these models often creates doubt and hesitation among users and stakeholders. In addition, there is a growing requirement from regulatory bodies for AI systems to be explainable. This means that FinTech companies must focus on developing strategies to improve the transparency of their AI models.

Talent Acquisition and Skills Gap

The FinTech sector is facing a major challenge in acquiring and developing the necessary skills in AI. FinTech companies are in a fierce battle to attract top professionals, not just from their own industry but also from major tech companies and other sectors that are aggressively seeking AI talent. In addition, the current workforce lacks the necessary skills to effectively work with AI technologies, which requires significant investment in training and development programmes (Zirar et.al.,2023). To address this gap, financial institutions should prioritize the establishment of strong talent development lines, cultivate partnerships with educational institutions, and provide attractive incentives to attract highly skilled AI professionals.

Challenges in AI Model Development

Although AI techniques have made significant advancements in recent years, financial organisations continue to face challenges in developing accurate and high-performing AI models. For example, NLP plays a crucial role in sentiment analysis, enabling the prediction of stock prices and the generation of trading signals through the analysis of extensive financial text data (Osterrieder, 2023). This task presents difficulties when it comes to interpreting language. Although humans have a natural ability to understand the different meanings of words based on context, NLP models face challenges in performing this task. Just like humans, people often use various terms to convey the same concept, which can make it difficult to analyse language and create algorithms. Homonyms pose a significant challenge for question-answering and speech-to-text applications since they lack a written form (Khurana et al., 2023).

CASE STUDIES AND SUCCESS STORIES

The combination of AI and FinTech is revolutionizing the industry, bringing about new opportunities, and producing tangible results. The real-world case studies and success stories provide a clear picture of how AI is revolutionizing the FinTech industry. It demonstrates how AI can optimize operations, improve customer experiences, and foster innovation in various areas of the financial sector (Babina et.al., 2023). These case studies explore the practical applications of AI in various areas such as fraud detection, personalized financial advice, algorithmic trading, and customer service. They showcase how FinTech companies are utilizing AI to stay ahead of the competition and provide value to their customers.

From Manual to Automated: JPMorgan Chase's Success Story with AI-Driven Contract Review

A global financial powerhouse like JPMorgan Chase must deal with the huge job of processing a huge number of complicated legal documents. This is necessary for their business to run smoothly and follow all the rules set by regulators. JPMorgan Chase handles hundreds of thousands of contracts every year. Legal teams used to spend a lot of time going through these papers manually and finding important clauses, terms, and responsibilities. The tedious procedure not only took a long time, but it was also subject to mistakes.

JPMorgan Chase created COIN (Contract Intelligence), an AI-powered tool that speeds up and automates the review of documents, to change the way this process works. Machine learning, natural language processing, and optical character recognition are some of the cutting-edge technologies that COIN uses to look at legal papers at a speed and scale that has never been seen before. COIN gives legal teams a full picture of the information they've extracted and any problems that might arise by turning papers into machine-readable text, extracting relevant data points, finding, and categorizing clauses, evaluating risks, and making insightful reports. COIN reviewed 12,000 credit agreements in seconds in a test program. This is a job that would have taken 360,000 hours of work by lawyers alone (jpmorgan.com).

Putting COIN into use has changed everything for JPMorgan Chase. It has cut down on the time needed to review documents by a huge amount, giving lawyers more time to do more creative work. The AI's ability to gather data with great accuracy has cut down on mistakes, which has led to better decision-making and risk management. COIN's automation features have also streamlined processes, making operations more efficient and boosting efforts to meet regulatory requirements. By automating tasks that used to be done by hand with AI, JPMorgan Chase has cut costs by a large amount. This shows how AI can change the law and financial fields. AI-powered contract review tools like COIN can cut the time it takes to review a contract by up to 90% (LawGeex,2021).

The Future of Fraud Prevention: PayPal's AI Revolutionizes Online Security

PayPal is one of the major players in online payments around the world, and each working day it handles an enormous number of transactions. In 2023 alone, it handled 24.981 billion payments. This scale makes it a great target for fraudsters, who constantly alter their methods to take advantage of vulnerabilities. Rule-based systems and manual review, which are two common ways to find fraud, often struggle to keep up with these complex strategies. Furthermore, Juniper Research did a study in 2022 that showed that global losses from retail online payment fraud amounted to $41 billion in 2022 and are expected to exceed $48 billion in 2023. This shows how essential it is to find more effective approaches(juniperresearch.com).

PayPal has employed the power of artificial intelligence to fight this constant threat. Their AI-powered fraud detection system looks at a huge amount of real-time transactional data and uses machine learning algorithms to find trends and patterns that could be signs of fraud. This system evaluates transactions by looking at numerous variables, such as customer profiles, device information, location, and patterns of behaviour. Fraudsters are altering their methods at an alarming rate, and PayPal wants to stay ahead of them by using such in-depth data analysis. Cybercrime is expected to cost the world $10.5 trillion every year by 2025 (cybersecurityventures.com).

The outcomes of PayPal's adoption of AI have been truly impressive. Fraud losses have gone down significantly because of the method, which protects both the company and its customers from losing money. In 2023, PayPal's fraud rate dropped from 0.37% of revenue the previous year to 0.32% of revenue. PayPal has made all aspects of customer service better by quickly and accurately spotting fraud. This has built trust and faith in their platform. This advanced security measure has also helped PayPal's reputation as a safe and trustworthy payment service, which has brought additional customers and businesses to their site. Machine learning models are flexible, so the system learns and changes all the time to keep up with the evolving landscape of fraud. This makes PayPal even more of an industry leader in safe online payments (newsroom.paypal-corp.com).

Fargo: Addressing the Digital Banking Demand

In response to the growing need for digital banking services and customized customer interactions, Wells Fargo introduced Fargo, its AI-driven virtual assistant, in October 2022 (Wells Fargo Newsroom). Fargo utilizes natural language processing to manage customer requests, provide tailored financial guidance, and execute fundamental banking operations, such as verifying account balances and freezing cards. This not only simplifies everyday interactions but also enables employees to focus their skills on higher-level consumer requirements.

A majority of customers who utilize virtual assistants, such as Fargo, report favourable experiences. Specifically, 70% of customers emphasize that one of the key advantages is the time-saving aspect (Wells Fargo Newsroom). These findings indicate that Fargo is having a beneficial effect on consumer satisfaction, minimizing wait times, and improving agent productivity. In addition, Fargo plays an important part in Wells Fargo's broad strategy to enhance its digital banking services, thereby enhancing the client experience by making it more streamlined and customized to individual needs. With the increasing adoption of AI-powered chatbots in the banking industry, Fargo is positioned to have a significant impact on the development of AI-driven customer care.

Beyond Traditional Metrics: AI's Role in Expanding Credit Opportunities

Ant Financial has introduced Sesame Credit, an AI-powered alternative, to address the exclusion of the 1.7 billion unbanked people globally from existing credit rating systems (World Bank). Sesame Credit evaluates creditworthiness for a majority of Chinese citizens, including those who do not have traditional credit records, by examining various data points such as internet activities, buying patterns, and social networks. This new methodology, utilizing advanced machine learning algorithms, claims greater precision in forecasting the likelihood of loan defaults when compared to traditional approaches.

The impact of Sesame Credit is significant: by 2018, more than 500 million individuals, primarily those who were previously unbanked or underbanked, have obtained credit scores. Moreover, the customized financial services provided by Sesame Credit have achieved a significant level of satisfaction, as more than 80% of users have expressed their acceptance (www.creditsesame.com). Despite ongoing debates about privacy, Sesame Credit demonstrates the transformative power of artificial intelligence in transforming credit assessment and promoting financial inclusivity, especially for marginalized communities.

Square – Democratizing Payment Processing

Square, founded in 2009 by Jack Dorsey, one of the co-founders of Twitter, brought about a major shift in the financial services sector by making payment processing accessible to small businesses. Traditional payment methods were burdened by high expenses, complex setups, and restricted availability, limiting the expansion of small businesses. Square tackled these obstacles by developing a simple card reader that can be connected to smartphones, thus reducing the necessity for costly equipment. In addition, the company implemented a transparent and fixed-rate fee system, ensuring that enterprises of any scale accurately predict their transaction expenses. Square's efforts to enhance payment processing accessibility and affordability have encouraged several small businesses to take card payments, broaden their customer base, and flourish in the digital era.

LESSONS LEARNT AND BEST PRACTICES

Analyzing real-life examples of how artificial intelligence is used in the FinTech industry offers valuable knowledge about real-world challenges encountered by leading businesses. These practical examples highlight the knowledge gained and optimal methods that can assist other firms in effectively integrating AI into their business processes.

Embrace AI for Efficiency and Accuracy

AI technology offers organizations a chance to greatly improve operational efficiency and accuracy. Through the automation of mundane and time-consuming tasks, AI allows human resources to dedicate their efforts to more crucial and strategic activities. This not only saves time and money but also ensures precision by minimizing errors inherent in manual processes. With AI, organizations can enhance efficiency and accuracy, leading to streamlined operations, increased productivity, and a boost in innovation across different business functions.

Utilize Diverse Sources

Having access to a wide range of data sources is essential for improving the efficiency and precision of AI systems. Through the utilization of a diverse array of data sources such as transaction records, customer profiles, and behavioral trends, organizations can acquire profound insights and enhance their decision-making capabilities. The multifaceted approach employed enhances the understanding and predictive capabilities of AI models, allowing them to identify intricate patterns and correlations that may not be immediately evident with limited data. Using a wide range of data sources enables organizations to remain flexible, adjust to evolving market conditions, and achieve long-term growth(Verhoef, P. C. et.al., 2020).

Invest in Data Infrastructure and Talent

Building a strong data infrastructure and having highly skilled talent is crucial for effectively implementing AI. The presence of a reliable data infrastructure is crucial for organizations to effectively handle and analyze large amounts of data, empowering them to make well-informed decisions and gain valuable insights (Mikalef et.al.,2019). It is essential to hire highly skilled data scientists and AI engineers to successfully build, manage, and improve AI systems, guaranteeing their optimal performance and success.

Prioritize Customer Experience and Security

Emphasising the importance of both customer experience and security is crucial in establishing trust and loyalty in AI-driven financial services (Rane et.al.,2024). The use of AI technology can greatly improve the customer experience by offering faster and more personalized services, as well as enhancing security measures to safeguard customers' financial assets (Bhuiyan et.al.,2024). The perfect harmony between experience and security guarantees customer satisfaction, creating lasting loyalty and retention.

TRENDS IN AI

This symbiotic relationship has not only streamlined traditional processes but has also made way for innovative new ideas. Trends in AI in FinTech are changing how we manage, invest, and deal with money.

Generative AI

It possesses the capability to generate material such as text, graphics, or code, and is being utilized in several domains such as personalized financial advice, fraud identification, and risk evaluation(Gupta et.al.,2024). Generative AI can examine vast quantities of data to detect patterns and trends that may go unnoticed by humans. As a result, it enhances the precision and efficiency of these operations.

Quantum Computing

Though it is in its early phase, can transform AI in FinTech by significantly increasing computational capabilities. This has the potential to result in (Kadve et.al., 2024). Additionally, it could create new opportunities in fields like cryptography.

Decentralized AI and Blockchain

The integration of AI and blockchain technology can facilitate the development of decentralized financial systems that offer enhanced security, transparency, and efficiency. (Shamsan Saleh, A. M.,2024). For instance, the utilization of artificial intelligence in smart contracts might automate complex financial operations, while the implementation of blockchain technology could guarantee the confidentiality and immutability of financial data.

Edge Computing

It refers to the practice of performing data processing near where the data is generated, rather than depending on centralized cloud servers. Edge computing in the field of FinTech can facilitate immediate decision-making for tasks such as identifying and preventing fraudulent activities, as well as executing algorithmic trading strategies (Shoetanmet.al., 2024). This is particularly crucial in circumstances where latency, which refers to the time it takes for data to transit, can have a significant impact like online banking.

CONCLUSION

AI in FinTech is not a distant future but an evolving present. To successfully integrate AI, technologists, financial experts, regulators, and customers will need to keep adapting, learning, and collaborating. The use of AI in FinTech aims to enhance human skills rather than replace them. The most effective FinTech solutions leverage the collaboration between human expertise and AI skills, resulting in a strong relationship that stimulates innovation and achieves exceptional results. The partnership between AI and humans, as discussed in the paper Artificial Intelligence in Service in the Journal of Financial Services Research (Huang & Rust, 2018) fosters a mutually beneficial connection where AI enhances human abilities and addresses their limitations. This results in improved productivity, efficiency, and innovation in the FinTech industry.

Humans possess crucial attributes such as creativity, analytical reasoning, and ethical judgment, which are essential for comprehending complex situations and establishing credibility with consumers. AI, in contrast, demonstrates exceptional proficiency in handling extensive quantities of data, recognizing patterns, and automating processes. The synergy between Artificial Intelligence and human agents is evident in customer service, where AI-driven chatbots manage common questions, enabling human agents to concentrate on intricate financial advisory tasks. The most important component of this collaboration lies in achieving the optimal balance and creating a cooperative atmosphere between man and machine.

REFERENCES

Abdelfattah, R. M. M. (2023). The Impact of Fintech on Financial Inclusion in Egypt (Doctoral dissertation, The German University in Cairo).

Addy, W. A., Ajayi-Nifise, A. O., Bello, B. G., Tula, S. T., Odeyemi, O., & Falaiye, T. (2024). AI in credit scoring: A comprehensive review of models and predictive analytics. *Global Journal of Engineering and Technology Advances*, *18*(02), 118–129.

Allied Market Research. (2023). Allied Market Research. Retrieved May 20, 2024 from www.alliedmarketresearch.com

Alzubaidi, L., Bai, J., Al-Sabaawi, A., Santamaría, J., Albahri, A. S., Al-dabbagh, B. S. N., Fadhel, M. A., Manoufali, M., Zhang, J., Al-Timemy, A. H., Duan, Y., Abdullah, A., Farhan, L., Lu, Y., Gupta, A., Albu, F., Abbosh, A., & Gu, Y. (2023). A survey on deep learning tools dealing with data scarcity: Definitions, challenges, solutions, tips, and applications. *Journal of Big Data*, *10*(1), 46. DOI: 10.1186/s40537-023-00727-2

Assis, L. F., Ferreira, K. R., Vinhas, L., Maurano, L., Almeida, C., Carvalho, A., & Camargo, C. (2019). TerraBrasilis: A spatial data analytics infrastructure for large-scale thematic mapping. *International Journal of Geo-Information*, *8*(11).

Babina, T., Fedyk, A., He, A., & Hodson, J. (2023). Artificial intelligence, firm growth, and product innovation. *Journal of Financial Economics*, *151*, 103745. DOI: 10.1016/j.jfineco.2023.103745

Bathaee, Y. (2017). The artificial intelligence black box and the failure of intent and causation. *Harv. JL & Tech.*, *31*, 889.

Bhuiyan, M. (2024). The Role of AI-Enhanced Personalization in Customer Experiences. *Journal of Computer Science and Technology Studies.*, *6*(1), 162–169. DOI: 10.32996/jcsts.2024.6.1.17

Buckley, R. P., Zetzsche, D. A., Arner, D. W., & Tang, B. (2021). Regulating Artificial Intelligence in Finance: Putting the Human in the Loop, 2021. 43 Sydney Law Journal 43 University of Hong Kong Faculty of Law Research Paper 2021/016

Burrell, J. (2016). How the machine 'thinks': Understanding opacity in machine learning algorithms. *Big Data & Society*, *3*(1), 2053951715622512. DOI: 10.1177/2053951715622512

CNBC. (2024). CNBC. Retrieved May 12, 2024 from www.cnbc.com

. Cyber Security Ventures (2020). Cyber Security Ventures. Retrieved May 13, 2024 from cybersecurityventures.com

Dakalbab, F., Talib, M. A., Nasir, Q., & Saroufil, T. (2024). Artificial intelligence techniques in financial trading: A systematic literature review. *Journal of King Saud University. Computer and Information Sciences*, *36*(3), 102015. DOI: 10.1016/j.jksuci.2024.102015

Dwivedi, Y. K., Ismagilova, E., Hughes, D. L., Carlson, J., Filieri, R., Jacobson, J., Jain, V., Karjaluoto, H., Kefi, H., Krishen, A. S., Kumar, V., Rahman, M. M., Raman, R., Rauschnabel, P. A., Rowley, J., Salo, J., Tran, G. A., & Wang, Y. (2021). Setting the future of digital and social media marketing research: Perspectives and research propositions. *International Journal of Information Management*, *59*, 102168. DOI: 10.1016/j.ijinfomgt.2020.102168

Dwivedi, Y. K., Kshetri, N., Hughes, L., Slade, E. L., Jeyaraj, A., Kar, A. K., & Wright, R. (2023). Opinion Paper: "So what if ChatGPT wrote it?" Multidisciplinary perspectives on opportunities, challenges and implications of generative conversational AI for research, practice and policy. *International Journal of Information Management*, *71*, 102642.

Fargo, W. (2022). Wells Fargo Newsroom. Retrieved May 12,2024 from www.newsroom.wf.com

Gomber, P., Koch, J. A., & Siering, M. (2017). Digital Finance and FinTech: Current research and future research directions. *Journal of Business Economics*, *87*(5), 537–580. DOI: 10.1007/s11573-017-0852-x

Gupta, P., Ding, B., Guan, C., & Ding, D. (2024). Generative AI: A systematic review using topic modelling techniques. *Data and Information Management*, *8*(2), 100066. DOI: 10.1016/j.dim.2024.100066

Hilal, W., Gadsden, S. A., & Yawney, J. (2022). Financial Fraud: A Review of Anomaly Detection Techniques and Recent Advances. *Expert Systems with Applications*, *193*, 116429. DOI: 10.1016/j.eswa.2021.116429

Huang, M.-H., & Rust, R. T. (2018). Artificial intelligence in service. *Journal of Service Research*, *21*(2), 155–172. DOI: 10.1177/1094670517752459

Intelligence, M. (2024). Mordor Intelligence. Retrieved May 01,2024 from www.mordorintelligence.com

JPMorgan Chase. (2022). JPMorgan Chase. Retrieved May 15, 2024 from www.jpmorganchase.com

Juniper Research. (2019,2021). Juniper Research. Retrieved May 15, 2024 from www.juniperresearch.com

Kadve, Dipak, Kumar, Binod, Suryawanshi, Vaishali, Gupta, Karan, & Koul, Ritesh & Shreyash, (2024). *Impact of Quantum Computing on Artificial Intelligence.21.* 71-78.

Khattak, B. H. A., Shafi, I., Khan, A. S., Flores, E. S., Lara, R. G., Samad, M. A., & Ashraf, I. (2023). A systematic survey of AI models in financial market forecasting for profitability analysis. *IEEE Access : Practical Innovations, Open Solutions*, *11*, 125359–125380.

LawGeex. (2021). LawGeex. Retrieved May 19, 2024 from www.lawgeex.com

Lee, I., & Shin, Y. J. (2020). Fintech: Ecosystem, business models, investment decisions, and challenges. *Business Horizons*, *63*(3), 357–370.

Lenddo, E. F. L. (2023). LenddoEFL. Retrieved May 16, 2024 from www.lenddoefl .com

Lepri, B., Oliver, N., Letouzé, E., Pentland, A., & Vinck, P. (2018). Fair, transparent, and accountable algorithmic decision-making processes: The premise, the proposed solutions, and the open challenges. *Philosophy & Technology*, *31*(4), 611–627.

Mhlanga, D. (2024). Big Data and Financial Technology (Fintech) Towards Financial Inclusion. SSRN Electronic Journal. 10.2139. DOI: 10.2139/ssrn.4697365

Mikalef, P., Boura, M., Lekakos, G., & Krogstie, J. (2019). Big data analytics and firm performance: Findings from a mixed-method approach. *Journal of Business Research*, *98*, 261–276. DOI: 10.1016/j.jbusres.2019.01.044

Milana, C., & Ashta, A. (2021). Artificial intelligence techniques in finance and financial markets: A survey of the literature. *Strategic Change*, *30*(3), 189–209. DOI: 10.1002/jsc.2403

Newsroom, P. (2024). Paypal Newsroom. Retrieved May 05,2024 from www .newsroom.paypal-corp.com

Nuti, G., Mirghaemi, M., Treleaven, P., & Yingsaeree, C. (2020). Algorithmic trading with machine learning and sentiment analysis: A survey. *The Journal of Financial Data Science*, *6*(4), 148–170.

Ozili, P. K. (2020). Impact of Digital Finance on Financial Inclusion and Stability. *Borsa Istanbul Review*, *20*(4), 329–340. DOI: 10.1016/j.bir.2017.12.003

Pattnaik, D., Ray, S., & Raman, R. (2024). Applications of artificial intelligence and machine learning in the financial services industry: A bibliometric review. *Heliyon, 10*(1), e23492. DOI: 10.1016/j.heliyon.2023.e23492 PMID: 38187262

Pranckutė, R. (2021). Web of Science (WoS) and Scopus: The Titans of Bibliographic Information in Today's Academic World. *Publications / MDPI, 9*(1), 12. DOI: 10.3390/publications9010012

Rane, N., Paramesha, M., Choudhary, S., & Rane, J. (2024). Artificial Intelligence in Sales and Marketing: Enhancing Customer Satisfaction, Experience and Loyalty. SSRN Electronic Journal. DOI: 10.2139/ssrn.4831903

Rui, Z., & Yan, Z. (2019). A Survey on Biometric Authentication: Toward Secure and Privacy-Preserving Identification. *IEEE Access : Practical Innovations, Open Solutions, 7*, 5994–6009. DOI: 10.1109/ACCESS.2018.2889996

. Ryll, L., Barton, M.E., Zhang, B.Z., McWaters, R.J., Schizas, E., Hao, R., Bear, K., Preziuso, M., Seger, E., Wardrop, R., Rau, P.R., Debata, P., Rowan, P., Adams, N., Gray, M., Yerolemou, N., (2020). Transforming Paradigms: A Global AI in Financial Services Survey.

. Saleem, H., Yongjun, L., Ali, Z., Mehreen, A., & Mansoor, M. S. (2020). An empirical investigation on how big data analytics influence China SMEs performance: Do product and process innovation matter? Asian Pacific Business Review, 1-26.

Schueffel, P. (2021). Taming the Beast: A Scientific Definition of Fintech. *Journal of Innovation Management, 9*(4), 32–54. DOI: 10.24840/2183-0606_004.004_0004

Sesame, C. (2018). Credit Sesame. Retrieved May 23, 2024 from www.creditsesame .com

Shamsan Saleh, A. M. (2024). Blockchain for secure and decentralized artificial intelligence in cybersecurity: A comprehensive review. Blockchain: Research and Applications, 100193.

Shneiderman, B. (2020). Human-centered artificial intelligence: Reliable, safe & trustworthy. *International Journal of Human-Computer Interaction, 36*(6), 495–504. DOI: 10.1080/10447318.2020.1741118

Shoetan, P., & Familoni, B. (2024). TRANSFORMING FINTECH FRAUD DETECTION WITH ADVANCED ARTIFICIAL INTELLIGENCE ALGORITHMS. *Finance & Accounting Research Journal., 6*(4), 602–625. DOI: 10.51594/farj.v6i4.1036

Ta, V. D., Liu, C. M., & Addis, D. (2018). Prediction and portfolio optimization in quantitative trading using machine learning techniques. In *Proceedings of the 9th International Symposium on Information and Communication Technology* (pp. 98-105). DOI: 10.1145/3287921.3287963

Taherdoost, H., & Madanchian, M. (2023). Artificial Intelligence and Sentiment Analysis: A Review in Competitive Research. *Computers*, *12*(2), 37. DOI: 10.3390/computers12020037

Verhoef, P. C., Broekhuizen, T., Bart, Y., Bhattacharya, A., Qi Dong, J., Fabian, N., & Haenlein, M. (2020). Digital transformation: A multidisciplinary reflection and research agenda. *Journal of Business Research*, *122*, 889–901. DOI: 10.1016/j.jbusres.2019.09.022

World Economic Forum. (2020). World Economic Forum (2020). Retrieved May 15,2024 from www.weforum.org

Yaiprasert, C., & Hidayanto, A. N. (2024). AI-powered ensemble machine learning to optimize cost strategies in logistics business. *International Journal of Information Management Data Insights*, *4*(1), 100209. DOI: 10.1016/j.jjimei.2023.100209

Zirar, A., Ali, S. I., & Islam, N. (2023). Worker and workplace Artificial Intelligence (AI) coexistence: Emerging themes and research agenda. *Technovation*, *124*, 102747. DOI: 10.1016/j.technovation.2023.102747

Chapter 5
Global Analysis of the Systemic Risk in the Europe Region

Abdelkader Mohamed Sghaier Derbali
https://orcid.org/0000-0003-4098-3120
Applied College, Taibah University, Saudi Arabia

ABSTRACT

The aim of this study is to examine the systemic risk in the Europe region in 2023. In this analysis, we employ SRISK as a metric for systemic risk, with the goal of capturing the strain and potential for systemic impact within financial institutions across countries. These metrics not only evaluate the vulnerability of individual financial institutions, but also consider the interdependencies between them, as well as the connections between systemic risk and factors such as GDP, market capitalization, and total assets of each country. The empirical results indicate that the level of systemic risk reaches its peak between 2020 and 2023. The countries most affected by systemic risk are United Kingdom and France with varying degrees.

1. INTRODUCTION

Systematic risk refers to the risk of failure or failure of a company, firm, financial institution, or the economy as a whole. The risk of a major breakdown in the financial system occurs when providers of capital such as bankers, investors and capital markets lose confidence in users of capital such as banks, creditors and investors. A means of exchange, such as the US dollar, the Japanese yen, or gold. Systemic failure is a feature of the market system and cannot be avoided. An important char-

DOI: 10.4018/979-8-3693-7357-6.ch005

Copyright © 2025, IGI Global Scientific Publishing. Copying or distributing in print or electronic forms without written permission of IGI Global Scientific Publishing is prohibited.

acteristic of systematic risk is its spread through the transfer process from weaker firms to relatively stronger firms.

The ripple effect caused by a systemic crisis can have a devastating effect on the economy. Managing and reducing systemic risk is a major concern for regulators, especially as consolidation in the financial sector has resulted in the largest banks (Derbali, 2017b; Derbali and Sy, 2016). After the 2008 global crisis, financial managers turned their attention to increasing the resilience of the financial system to economic shocks. They implemented firewalls to minimize the damage caused by system failure. In addition, regulators developed macroeconomic and microeconomic policies and paid more attention to supervisory regulations and established procedures to ensure the stability of the financial system. Macroprudential regulation is meant to protect banks or the financial system, while micro-prudential regulation focuses on regulating individual financial institutions such as commercial banks, lenders and insurance companies.

The financial crisis started in 2007 with the mortgage market in the USA. Eventually, the housing bubble burst, causing a major housing and mortgage crisis in America. This situation led to a financial and credit crisis that spread throughout the credit and financial markets. These factors together created the biggest economic shock ever. The financial crisis caused a general depression in the United States, which caused a sharp drop in investment and business worldwide. The impact of the recession also extended to the most advanced economies.

The implementation of the inflationary policy will increase the pressures on the financial system. As a result, the banking crisis turned into a sovereign debt crisis, which culminated in the global financial crisis with the collapse of Lehman Brothers, an investment bank. The high level of risk taking by Lehman Brothers and other financial institutions further influenced global finance. These results worsened the situation of depression.

Later, this crisis was accompanied by a global economic downturn known as the Great Recession of 2008-2009. This crisis later became the European debt crisis, which affected the financial systems of European countries that used the euro. Although the recession ended in late 2009, countries burdened by debt since the financial crisis have continued to grow. The purpose of insurance and investing is to change risks. Therefore, it is necessary to analyze the potential limitations of risk spreading. One of these limitations arises from the presence of systematic risk affecting all policies simultaneously (Figure 1).

The aim of this paper is to analyze the systemic risk in the European region in 2023. In this study, we use SRISK as a measure of systemic risk, aiming to captures the stress and capacity of the system in financial institutions in each country. These measures assess not only the vulnerability of individual financial institutions, but also the interdependence between them and between systemic risk and GDP, market capitalization and total assets of each country. Official findings show that the level of systemic risk will reach its peak in the period 2020 to 2023. The countries most affected by the system crisis are the UK and France to varying degrees.

Our paper is organized as follow: the second part is a literature review. The third describes the methodology and economic model used. The fourth section presents empirical findings based on the proposed model. Finally, the fifth section concludes our study.

Figure 1. Systemic Risk in the 2008 Financial Crisis

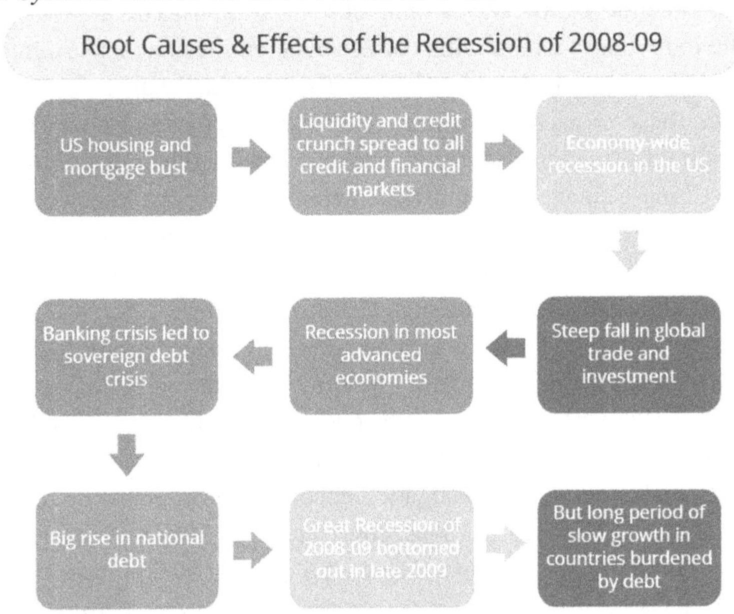

Source: *Corporate Finance Institute (2012)*

2. LITERATURE REVIEW

The existing body of literature reveals a diverse array of findings regarding U.S. banks. Research by De Jonghe (2010), Moore and Zhou (2014), and Bostandzic and Weiss (2018) establishes a positive relationship between noninterest income and systemic risk. Conversely, Engle et al. (2014), Weiss et al. (2014), and Saunders et al. (2020) report an insignificant link between these two variables.

Furthermore, De Jonghe et al. (2015) indicate that noninterest income has a diminishing effect on systemic risk for large banks while increasing it for smaller institutions. Their analysis also suggests that the benefits of reduced systemic risk for larger banks are negated in environments characterized by corruption, concentrated banking sectors, and asymmetric information. When applying these findings to the United States, where such factors are less pronounced, a negative correlation for large banks and a positive correlation for small banks is inferred.

In a separate study, Derbali (2017a) investigates the systemic risk associated with Chinese financial institutions in the wake of the 2007 financial crisis. This research aims to quantify the systemic risk of a sample comprising 70 Chinese financial entities from January 2, 2008, to June 30, 2015. The study utilizes SRISK as a metric for systemic risk, designed to evaluate both the stress levels and the potential for systemic significance within these institutions. This approach not only assesses the individual vulnerabilities of financial entities but also examines their interconnections within the broader Chinese financial landscape.

Moreover, these metrics are instrumental in identifying banks deemed systematically important. The empirical results indicate a markedly high level of systemic risk among Chinese financial institutions, with each entity making a considerable contribution to the overall risk profile of the financial system. The analysis further reveals that institutions with elevated debt levels significantly and positively impact systemic risk, aligning with the findings of Derbali (2016).

To effectively tackle systemic events and their adverse externalities, it is crucial to formulate methodologies that quantify systemic risks and evaluate their individual impacts. The primary aim of the research conducted by Derbali and Hallara (2016) is to assess the systemic risk associated with European banks in the aftermath of the 2007 financial crisis. This investigation encompasses a sample of 281 financial institutions across 16 European nations, covering the period from January 1, 2006, to December 31, 2012. The Marginal Expected Shortfall (MES) serves as the metric for systemic risk assessment.

The empirical findings reveal a notable degree of systemic risk present among European banks. Additionally, the role of financial institutions in contributing to the risk within their respective systems is significant, given the strong correlation observed between institutional returns and market returns. This correlation is analyzed through the DECO-GARCH (1,1) model, which is employed for the first time to assess systemic risk in financial entities. The heightened systemic risk levels have necessitated intervention from international authorities, as evidenced in Eurozone countries, where organizations such as the International Monetary Fund, the European Central Bank, and the World Bank have taken action. Regrettably, these interventions have not resulted in a lasting resolution to the issue of systemic risk accumulation.

In a related study, Derbali et al. (2016) investigate the conditional dependence among Greek banks. This research employs two distinct methodologies: GARCH-DCC, which focuses on the dynamic nature of dependence, and GARCH-DECO, which examines a constant dependence process. These approaches are applied to a dataset comprising 18 Greek banks listed on the Athens Exchange, spanning from January 2, 2006, to December 31, 2012. The results underscore the influence of time-varying variance and dynamic correlations on the returns of all banks within the Greek stock market. It is clear that the returns of these banks exhibit a strong positive correlation, particularly following the onset of the 2007 financial crisis.

3. METHODOLOGY

The Systemic Risk Analysis presents a diverse range of risk measures for prominent Global Financial Firms. These measures are updated on a weekly basis and unveil multiple facets of risk. The historical estimations of each of these risk measures can be graphed to observe the evolving performance of individual firms (Adrian and Boyarchenko, 2012; Adrian and Brunnermeier, 2014; Acharya, 2009; Acharya et al., 2010; Acharya et al., 2012; Brownlees, 2012).

Systemic Risk (SRISK) refers to the expected capital shortfall that a firm would experience in the event of another crisis. The SRISK% is a metric used in the NYU Stern Systemic Risk Ranking, which represents the firm's percentage of financial sector capital shortfall. Firms with a high percentage of capital shortfall during a crisis are not only the most heavily impacted, but also contribute significantly to the overall crisis.

The capital shortfall (SRISK) is computed using the following formula:

$$SRISK = k * DEBT - (1 - k) * EQUITY * (1 - LRMES)$$

In this formula, k represents the capital requirement, LRMES represents the Long-Run Marginal Expected Shortfall, EQUITY represents the current market capitalization of the firm, and DEBT represents the book value of debt, which is calculated as the book value of assets minus the book value of equity.

During calm periods for insurance companies, when 40% of separate accounts are included in the total liabilities, capital ratios typically hover around 8%, which aligns with our default capital requirement. As a result, we adjust the value of DEBT so that only 40% of liabilities attributed to separate accounts are included by default.

In our paper, we use a data composed of 275 financial institutions from Europe region. For the details of the data used in this paper, we present all details of all financial institutions used in the Table 1.

Table 1. List of financial institutions used in this paper

Region		Europe	
Number of countries		34	
Number of financial institutions		275	
List of countries	**List of countries**	**List of countries**	**List of countries**
Austria Belgium Croatia Cyprus Czech Republic Denmark Estonia Finland France	Germany Greece Guernsey Hungary Iceland Ireland Italy Jersey Liechtenstein	Lithuania Luxembourg Malta Netherlands North Macedonia Norway Poland Portugal	Romania Russian Federation Slovenia Spain Sweden Switzerland Turkey United Kingdom

Source: Owen elaboration

4. RESULTS

In this section, we present the empirical results of the estimation with the systemic risk measures as used in this paper. The objective of this study to examine the systemic risk in the global economy in 2023. First, we discuss the global systemic risk by country and the total SRISK in the global world. Second, we examine the proportion of the systemic risk by the principal economic indicators such as GDP, Market Capitalization, and total assets for each country. Third, we present the SRISK estimation for financial institutions in each countries used in this paper.

For the first part, we analyze the global systemic risk by country (US$ billion) which is presented in the Figure 2. From this figure, we can observe that the higher level of global systemic risk is for China (2100 US$ billion) followed respectively by Japan (800 US$ billion), United States (700 US$ billion), United Kingdom (350 US$ billion), France (340 US$ billion), Canada (290 US$ billion), Korea (200 US$ billion), Spain (180 US$ billion), and Germany (150 US$ billion).

Figure 3 presents the evolution of the total of SRISK of all countries in the world during the period from January 2014 to December 2023. Based on this figure, we can show that the total of systemic in the world attains his maximum especially during the period from 2020 to 2023 which 6000 US$ billion.

In the second part, we present the proportion of the systemic risk by the principal economic indicators such as GDP, Market Capitalization, and total assets for each country. For the first indicator GDP, we find that the higher level of the global systemic risk by GDP is for Cayman Islands (175%), followed by, Japan (19%),

Hong Kong (17%), China (14%), Canada (14%), France (13%), United Kingdom (13.5%), and Korea (12%).

For the second indicator market capitalization, we find that the higher level of the global systemic risk by market capitalization is for Nigeria (155%), followed by, France (137%), Japan (136%), Togo (135%), Korea (117%), China (116%), Pakistan (84%), and Spain (61%).

For the third indicator total assets, we find that the higher level of the global systemic risk by total assets is for Japan (5.4%) followed by, Korea (5.1%), China (4.7%), Nigeria (4.5%), Cayman Islands (4.3%), Togo (4.2%), France (3.7%), and Pakistan (3.7%).

Figure 2. Global Systemic Risk by Country (US$ billion)

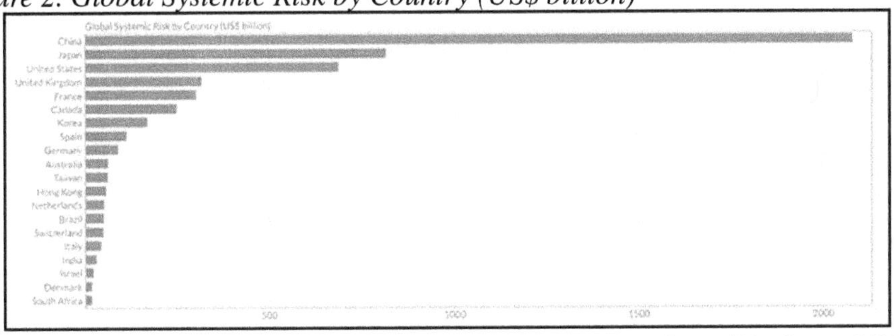

Note: In this figure, we present the SRISK for the most affected countries in the world for the year 2023.

Figure 3. Total SRISK (US$ billion)

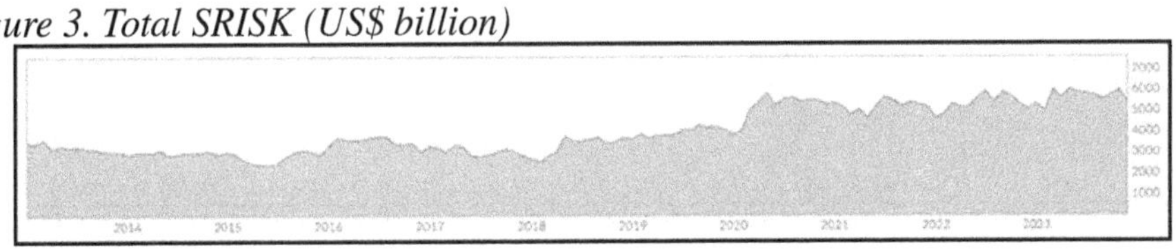

Note: In this figure, we present the evolution of the total of SRISK of all countries in the world during the period from January 2014 to December 2023.

Figure 4. Global Systemic Risk by GDP

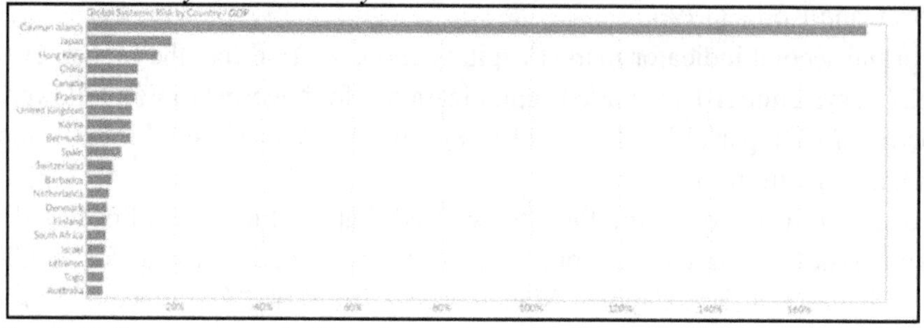

Note: In this figure, we present the Global Systemic Risk by GDP for the most affected countries in the world for the year 2023.

Figure 5. Global Systemic Risk by Market Capitalization

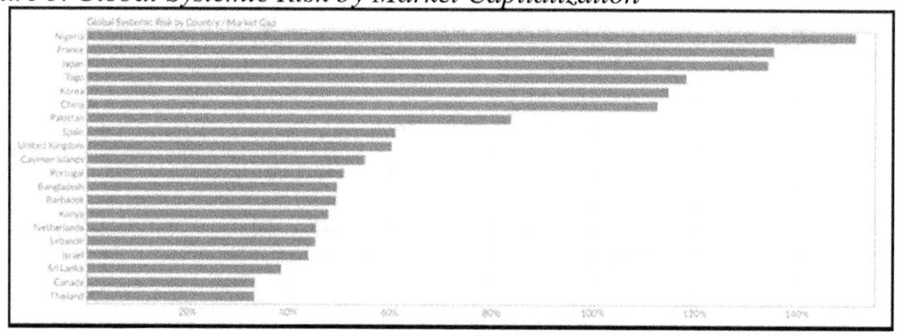

Note: In this figure, we present the Global Systemic Risk by Market Capitalization for the most affected countries in the world for the year 2023.

Figure 6. Global Systemic Risk by Total Assets

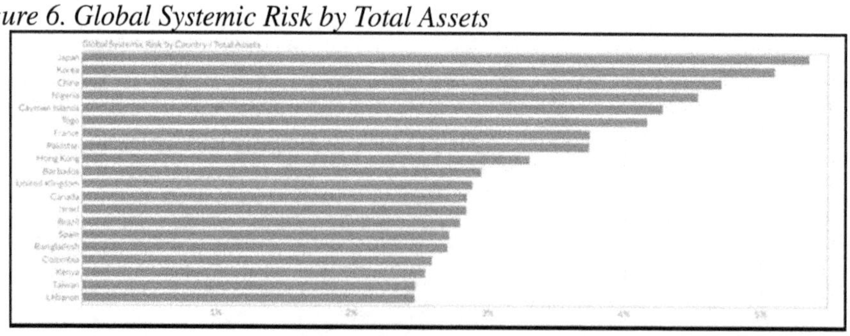

Note: In this figure, we present the Global Systemic Risk by Total Assets for the most affected countries in the world for the year 2023.

For the third part of this section, we present the SRISK estimation for the selected financial institutions in each region used in this paper. Then, we consider for each region the 100 most affect financial institutions. We justify our consideration by the level of SRISK for each financial institution.

For the European region, we use a sample of 275 financial institutions for 34 countries (Table 2). We consider only the results for the 100 most affected financial institutions. The higher level of SRISK is equal to 121248.64 $ million (Credit Agricole SA*). The biggest level of the Long-Run Marginal Expected Shortfall is equal to 59.46 (Raiffeisen Bank International AG). The high level of the market beta which refer to the current market capitalization of the firm is equal to 1.48 (Barclays PLC & UBS Group AG). Finally, the biggest level of the correlation is equal to 0.56 (SpareBank 1 SR-Bank ASA).

After the analyzing of the SRISK estimation for the selected financial institutions in each region used in this paper, we can observe that the Asian region present the biggest level of SRISK, followed by, the American region, European region, and African region.

Table 2. SRISK estimation for financial institutions in the European region

Institution	SRISK %	SRISK ($ m)	LRMES	Market β	Cor
Credit Agricole SA*	11.52	121248.64	46.30	1.16	0.32
BNP Paribas SA	11.48	120751.15	33.57	0.78	0.09
Barclays PLC	9.84	103625.24	55.42	1.48	0.44
Societe Generale SA	8.60	90515.24	43.90	1.08	0.30
Banco Santander SA	7.83	82443.85	54.33	1.44	0.43
Deutsche Bank AG	6.67	70208.31	51.96	1.36	0.33
HSBC Holdings PLC	6.15	64804.11	33.79	0.78	0.43
UBS Group AG	4.66	49068.43	55.51	1.48	0.40
Lloyds Banking Group PLC	4.27	44859.78	43.88	1.08	0.44
Standard Chartered PLC	3.62	38112.73	50.83	1.31	0.41
Natwest Group PLC	3.58	37659.28	48.10	1.22	0.43
ING Groep NV	2.54	26755.21	42.08	1.02	0.20
Commerzbank AG	2.30	24218.20	45.33	1.13	0.32
London Stock Exchange Group PLC	2.30	24202.44	42.11	1.02	0.43
ABN AMRO Group NV	1.79	18862.19	30.03	0.68	0.38
Phoenix Group Holdings	1.75	18442.90	40.22	0.97	0.48
Danske Bank A/S	1.69	17844.55	45.49	1.14	0.31
Intesa Sanpaolo SpA	1.62	17029.43	35.27	0.83	0.31
CaixaBank SA	1.47	15447.03	34.13	0.79	0.15

continued on following page

Table 2. Continued

Institution	SRISK %	SRISK ($ m)	LRMES	Market β	Cor
Nordea Bank Abp	1.33	14093.14	51.76	1.35	0.43
Legal & General Group PLC	1.32	13958.93	54.77	1.46	0.48
Banco Bilbao Vizcaya Argentaria SA	1.21	12730.04	45.11	1.13	0.38
Aegon Ltd	1.07	11246.66	46.53	1.17	0.47
Banco de Sabadell SA	0.90	9432.30	20.36	0.44	0.09
VTB Bank PJSC	0.87	9228.98	0.00	0.00	0.17
Raiffeisen Bank International AG	0.84	8865.93	59.46	1.63	0.41
Banco BPM SpA	0.79	8330.37	51.85	1.35	0.41
St James's Place PLC	0.79	8294.72	50.80	1.31	0.32
Erste Group Bank AG	0.74	7743.07	38.56	0.92	0.39
Aviva PLC	0.69	7320.44	45.33	1.13	0.45
Svenska Handelsbanken AB	0.66	6883.33	50.54	1.30	0.47
Poste Italiane SpA	0.55	5773.00	31.54	0.72	0.35
BPER Banca	0.43	4536.29	20.44	0.44	0.23
Banca Monte dei Paschi di Siena SpA	0.41	4402.66	39.03	0.93	0.23
Unicaja Banco SA	0.41	4335.62	37.13	0.87	0.26
Caisse Regionale de Credit Agricole Mutuel de Paris et d'Ile-de-France*	0.38	4019.48	23.22	0.51	0.28
KBC Groep NV	0.38	3940.02	45.20	1.13	0.29
UniCredit SpA	0.36	3764.99	24.50	0.54	0.22
Skandinaviska Enskilda Banken AB	0.36	3715.88	54.49	1.45	0.52
Basler Kantonalbank	0.32	3404.23	19.30	0.41	0.32
Bank of Ireland Group PLC	0.32	3375.37	41.19	1.00	0.35
Bankinter SA	0.31	3327.99	35.48	0.83	0.26
Jyske Bank A/S	0.31	3235.53	45.89	1.15	0.39
Wuestenrot & Wuerttembergische AG	0.29	3040.03	32.94	0.76	0.40
Swedbank AB	0.29	2970.34	52.47	1.37	0.54
Deutsche Pfandbriefbank AG	0.28	2854.42	48.84	1.24	0.31
DNB ASA	0.26	2726.31	54.21	1.44	0.52
Banco Comercial Portugues, S.A.	0.23	2466.52	35.33	0.83	0.26
Credito Emiliano SpA	0.22	2297.13	42.63	1.05	0.36
Turkiye Halk Bankasi AS	0.22	2289.54	41.62	1.01	0.07
Caisse Regionale de Credit Agricole Mutuel Nord de France*	0.22	2239.51	30.53	0.69	0.25
Turkiye Vakiflar Bankasi TAO	0.21	2203.98	37.75	0.90	0.07
NN Group NV	0.20	2084.03	30.44	0.69	0.32
Credit Agricole Atlantique Vendee*	0.17	1850.24	29.50	0.67	0.21
Credit Agricole Sud Rhone Alpes*	0.16	1710.17	16.47	0.35	0.21
Alpha Services and Holdings SA	0.15	1599.31	43.88	1.08	0.33

continued on following page

Table 2. Continued

Institution	SRISK %	SRISK ($ m)	LRMES	Market β	Cor
Caisse Regionale de Credit Agricole Mutuel Alpes Provence*	0.15	1551.47	22.93	0.51	0.23
Just Group PLC	0.14	1460.50	43.31	1.07	0.29
Metro Bank Holdings PLC	0.14	1447.39	36.77	0.86	0.15
Caisse Regionale de Credit Agricole Mutuel de Normandie-Seine*	0.14	1443.71	26.51	0.59	0.30
Unipol Gruppo Finanziario SpA	0.12	1257.30	24.52	0.54	0.35
Piraeus Financial Holdings SA	0.12	1194.39	42.62	1.05	0.30
Aareal Bank AG	0.12	1172.31	21.14	0.46	0.40
NUERNBERGER Beteiligungs AG	0.12	1169.32	14.64	0.31	0.17
Caisse Regionale de Credit Agricole Mutuel d'Ille-et-Vilaine*	0.10	1105.27	21.19	0.46	0.17
Storebrand ASA	0.10	1035.81	53.90	1.43	0.43
BAWAG Group AG	0.09	980.26	49.88	1.28	0.47
Sparebanken Vest	0.09	943.00	44.29	1.09	0.51
Banca Popolare di Sondrio SCARL	0.09	940.93	25.60	0.56	0.17
Valiant Holding AG	0.09	931.96	23.66	0.52	0.38
Caisse Regionale de Credit Agricole Mutuel de la Touraine et du Poitou*	0.09	920.69	21.34	0.46	0.21
Graubuendner Kantonalbank	0.08	823.86	16.54	0.35	0.21
Credit Agricole Loire Haute-Loire*	0.08	812.59	20.32	0.44	0.23
Assicurazioni Generali SpA	0.07	786.37	27.91	0.62	0.36
Banco di Desio e della Brianza SpA	0.07	781.31	35.57	0.83	0.33
Credit Agricole du Morbihan*	0.07	702.65	21.49	0.47	0.23
Close Brothers Group PLC	0.06	631.47	54.18	1.44	0.17
Luzerner Kantonalbank AG	0.06	628.82	24.24	0.53	0.25
Credit Bank of Moscow PJSC	0.05	540.62	27.31	0.61	0.31
Chesnara plc	0.05	528.66	32.13	0.74	0.25
Julius Baer Group Ltd	0.05	462.88	56.41	1.52	0.51
Berner Kantonalbank AG	0.05	431.71	15.49	0.32	0.28
Haci Omer Sabanci Holding AS	0.03	361.22	50.98	1.32	0.38
Hellenic Bank PLC	0.03	338.79	20.77	0.45	0.18
St Galler Kantonalbank AG	0.02	271.52	33.68	0.78	0.44
Aktia Bank OYJ	0.02	259.90	34.60	0.81	0.39
VP Bank AG	0.02	238.05	21.37	0.46	0.24
Sparebanken More	0.02	230.23	30.43	0.69	0.39
Paragon Banking Group PLC	0.02	195.04	46.72	1.17	0.33
ProCredit Holding AG	0.01	175.38	26.65	0.60	0.21
UmweltBank AG	0.01	168.82	29.64	0.67	0.05
Vienna Insurance Group AG Wiener Versicherung Gruppe	0.01	135.47	37.33	0.89	0.46
Albaraka Turk Katilim Bankasi AS	0.01	125.93	27.60	0.62	0.13

continued on following page

Table 2. Continued

Institution	SRISK %	SRISK ($ m)	LRMES	Market β	Cor
SpareBank 1 SR-Bank ASA	0.01	124.32	52.04	1.36	0.56
illimity Bank S.p.A.	0.01	102.47	42.52	1.04	0.40
Bank of Valletta PLC	0.01	97.87	11.96	0.24	0.14
Van Lanschot Kempen NV	0.00	57.16	38.30	0.91	0.39
SpareBank 1 Nord Norge	0.00	54.51	44.46	1.10	0.47
Paysafe Ltd	0.00	48.99	87.57	3.23	0.48
Bank Millennium SA	0.00	46.81	50.84	1.31	0.39

5. CONCLUSION

The primary aim of this study is to examine systemic risk within the global economy in 2023. Utilizing SRISK as a measure for systemic risk, the objective is to capture the stress and potential systemic impact in financial institutions worldwide. These measures not only assess the susceptibility of individual financial institutions but also consider the interconnectedness among them, along with the associations between systemic risk and variables such as GDP, market capitalization, and total assets of each nation.

The empirical findings suggest that systemic risk peaks between 2020 and 2023. Among the countries impacted most by systemic risk are the United Kingdom and France each to varying extents.

Upon analysing the SRISK estimation for the chosen financial institutions in each region as utilized in this study, it is evident that the Asian region exhibits the highest level of SRISK, followed by the American region, European region, and African region.

REFERENCES

Acharya, V. (2009). A theory of systemic risk and design of prudential bank regulation. *Journal of Financial Stability*, *5*(3), 224–255. DOI: 10.1016/j.jfs.2009.02.001

Acharya, V., Engle, R., & Richardson, M. (2012). Capital shortfall: A new approach to ranking and regulating systemic risks. *The American Economic Review*, *102*(3), 59–64. DOI: 10.1257/aer.102.3.59

Acharya, V., Pedersen, L. H., Philippon, T., & Richardson, M. (2010). Measuring systemic risk, Working Paper, NYU Stern Schook of Business.

Adrian, T., & Boyarchenko, N. (2012). Intermediary leverage cycles and financial stability, Working Paper, Federal Reserve Bank of New York.

Adrian, T., & Brunnermeier, M. (2014). *CoVaR*. Federal Reserve Bank of New York Staff Reports.

Bostandzic, D., & Weiss, G. N. F. (2018). Why do some banks contribute more to global systemic risk? *Journal of Financial Intermediation*, *35*, 17–40. DOI: 10.1016/j.jfi.2018.03.003

Brownlees, C. T., & Robert, E. (2012). Volatility, correlation and tails for systemic risk measurement, Working Paper, NYU Stern School of Business.

De Jonghe, O. (2010). Back to basics in banking? A micro-analysis of banking system stability. *Journal of Financial Intermediation*, *19*(3), 387–417. DOI: 10.1016/j.jfi.2009.04.001

De Jonghe, O., Diepstraten, M., & Schepens, G. (2015). Banks' size, scope and systemic risk: What role for conflicts of interest? *Journal of Banking & Finance*, *61*, S3–S13. DOI: 10.1016/j.jbankfin.2014.12.024

Derbali, A. (2016). Global systemic risk ranking of Chinese financial institutions. *Journal of Chinese Governance*, *1*(2), 340–372. DOI: 10.1080/23812346.2016.1165403

Derbali, A. (2017a). Systemic risk in the Chinese Financial System: Measuring and Ranking. *Chinese Economy*, *50*(1), 34–58. DOI: 10.1080/10971475.2016.1211904

Derbali, A. (2017b). Systemic risk ranking of US financial institutions. *International Journal of Management and Network Economics*, *4*(1), 1–41. DOI: 10.1504/IJMNE.2017.087574

Derbali, A., & Hallara, S. (2016). Systemic risk of European financial institutions: Estimation and ranking by the Marginal Expected Shortfall. *Research in International Business and Finance*, *37*(15), 113–134. DOI: 10.1016/j.ribaf.2015.10.013

Derbali, A., Hallara, S., & Sy, A. (2016). Athen's game of chicken or the conditional dependence between the Greek banks. *International Journal of Economics and Accounting*, *7*(1), 1–26. DOI: 10.1504/IJEA.2016.076747

Derbali, A., & Sy, A. (2016). The volatility of exchange rate between the US dollar and African emerging currencies: Analysing by GAS-GARCH-Student-t model. *International Journal of Critical Accounting*, *8*(2), 132–143. DOI: 10.1504/IJCA.2016.077538

Engle, R., Moshirian, F., Sahgal, S., & Zhang, B. 2014. Banks non-interest income and global financial stability. Working Paper, New York University.

Moore, K., & Zhou, C. 2014. The determinants of systemic importance. Discussion Paper, London School of Economics and Political Science.

Saunders, A., Schmid, M., & Walter, I. (2020). Strategic scope and bank performance. *Journal of Financial Stability*, *46*, 100715. DOI: 10.1016/j.jfs.2019.100715

Weiss, G. N. F., Bostandzic, D., & Neumann, S. (2014). What factors drive systemic risk during international financial crises? *Journal of Banking & Finance*, *41*, 78–96. DOI: 10.1016/j.jbankfin.2014.01.001

Chapter 6
On the Asymmetric Long-Run Nexus Between Uncertainty, the Macroeconomic Sphere, and Stock Markets:
Fresh Evidence From a Nonlinear Panel Cointegrated

Nizar Elouni
University of Sfax, Tunisia

ABSTRACT

The purpose of this paper is to study the implications of the main macroeconomic components on the financial markets of OECD countries under asymmetric uncertainty shocks. By uncertainty shocks, this paper refers to uncertainty shocks emanating from economic policies or geopolitical risks. Using monthly data over the January 2009-May 2022 period, a non-linear panel ARDL-PMG model (Shin et al., 2014) is applied to estimate the relationship between inflation, industrial production, long-term interest rates, uncertainty (economic policy uncertainty, geopolitical risks) and stock prices. In the long term, the results indicate a stable relationship between the selected variables and the different stock prices. However, the asymmetric results show that uncertainty has a negative impact on stock prices in both the short and long term. The results suggest important implications for political and economic decision-makers, especially after the succession of endogenous and exogenous financial crises in recent years.

DOI: 10.4018/979-8-3693-7357-6.ch006

Copyright © 2025, IGI Global Scientific Publishing. Copying or distributing in print or electronic forms without written permission of IGI Global Scientific Publishing is prohibited.

1. INTRODUCTION

Many economic and financial players have shown significant interest in the intricate connection between the stock market and macroeconomic factors. Finance researchers have persistently delved into this relationship to determine and understand financial market behavior. Consequently, an extensive theoretical and empirical literature on economic systems' operations has surfaced, primarily centered on the concept of financial market efficiency.

Examination of stock market dynamics remains intricately intertwined with the study of economic fluctuations, as price expectations inherently mirror anticipations of economic fundamentals. To elucidate the unpredictable swings in financial asset prices, it is imperative to elucidate the underlying factors behind economic fluctuations.

The financial literature has extensively explored the connections between stock markets and several economic indicators, such as interest rates, industrial production, inflation, commodity prices, money supply and consumption. These linkages have undergone scrutiny in both developed markets (Erfan M. Bhuiyan and Murshed Chowdhury, 2020; Taufiq Choudhry et al., 2016; Amado Peir'o, 2016; Gan, Lee et al., 2006; Humpe and Macmillian, 2009) and emerging financial markets (Hosseini and Ahmad, 2011 ; Kandir, 2008). Although this body of theoretical and empirical literature provided comprehensive insights into the diverse interactions between the real economy and stock markets, the applied financial and economic models have yielded varying and occasionally paradoxical conclusions on these economic relationships. In their study, Hacker, Karlsson, and Månsson (2014) did not uncover substantial connections between stock market indices and interest rates, which contradicts conventional long-term financial theories. Likewise, Valcarcel (2012) found potential ambiguity in the relationship between macroeconomic variables and stock prices. Consequently, we propose that the observed evidence may occasionally present contradictions because of the use of different proxies to simulate a particular economic parameter. For this purpose, the results may be contingent on specific countries or periods.

In general, previous studies have faced challenges in clearly and precisely determining the direction and significance of the relationships between macroeconomic variables and stock prices, particularly within an environment marked by uncertainty. Consequently, there is a need for additional empirical and theoretical research in the financial literature to delve deeper into these intricate connections. The primary objective of this paper is to investigate the repercussions of key macroeconomic components on the financial markets of OECD countries under asymmetric uncertainty shocks. These uncertainty shocks, as defined in this paper, arise from factors like economic policy changes or geopolitical risks.

There are two compelling reasons for pursuing this objective. First, an examination of the trend patterns and cyclical behavior of economic and financial components over the past two decades reveals a succession of major events affecting the dynamics of these components. These events typically give rise to uncertainty originating from various sources, including endogenous factors such as the sub-prime crisis, exogenous factors like the COVID-19 health crisis, or geopolitical factors such as the recent Russo-Ukrainian war. To effectively address various forms of uncertainty in situations primarily exposed to it, such as the interplay between the macroeconomic realm and financial market performance, several key considerations come into play.

Firstly, when facing significant events and their ensuing uncertainty, it is imperative to adopt an asymmetric approach that aligns with the inherent consequences of these events. Ideally, each event is expected to induce one or more structural disruptions, resulting in pronounced fluctuations of the macroeconomic components and a heightened, sometimes even excessive, volatility in financial assets. Thus, it is more pragmatic to examine the targeted dynamics through an asymmetric lens.

This paper is structured as follows: The subsequent section provides a review of the relevant literature. Section 3 offers a summary of the adopted methodology, while Section 4 describes the dataset and the sample used. Section 5 presents the empirical findings, and Section 6 concludes the paper, offering policy and economic implications.

2. LITERATURE REVIEW

2.1. Relationship Between Stock Market and Macroeconomic Indicators

The relationship between macroeconomic variables and stock markets has been examined by several authors (Silvio John Camilleria et al., 2019; Valcarcel, 2012; Antonakakis et al., 2017; Erfan M. et al., 2020; Taufiq Choudhry et al., 2016; Trang Nguyen et al., 2020), highlighting the interaction between the financial sphere and the real and monetary sphere which is of capital interest for the different actors on the political and scientific scene. Recently, financial market liberalization and technological advances have dramatically increased interdependence between equity and money markets. At this stage, we focus on the reaction of stock market indices and interest rates following changes in economic fundamentals. In what follows, we summarize the results of previous research, focusing on the macroeconomic parameters that we consider in this study to explain stock prices. These are inflation (CPI), industrial production (IPI) and long-term interest rates (IR).

Beginning with the inflation rate, we distinguish a very rich financial literature that shows that the latter is not simply a monetary instrument, but that it necessarily influences stock market activity and fundamentally determines the relationship between financial policy and monetary policy as Suhaibu et al., (2017) has indicated. This link has its origins in Gordon's (1962) model, which showed that stock prices depend in part on dividend expectations. Therefore, the observed increase in stock prices reflects the stimulation of expectations of economic activity caused by inflation following an increase in money supply. Inflation can exert a detrimental influence on stock prices primarily through an expansive monetary policy, which increases long-term interest rates. This results in a decline in stock prices as the present value of future dividends decreases (Cogley and Sargent, 2001; Sargent, 1999).

Likewise, Chen, Roll, and Ross (1986), Humpe and Macmillian (2009), Naik and Padhi (2012), Akbar, Ali, and Khan (2011), Anderson, Balli, and Godber (2018), as well as Silvio John Camilleria, Nicolanne Sciclunaa, and Ye Baib (2019) collectively reaffirm the notable and negative relationship between inflation and stock market performance.

Contrary to previous research findings, a number of authors, including (Ratanapakorn and Sharma, 2007; Asmy et al., 2010; Alam, 2017; Kolluri and Wahab, 2008; Antonakakis et al., 2017; Al-Shami and Ibrahim, 2013; Balcilar et al., 2017), have advanced an alternative hypothesis suggesting a positive relationship between the two variables. This relationship exhibits a distinct pattern, fluctuating between positive and negative depending on the specific periods and countries under consideration.

For the industrial production index, numerous studies have put forth arguments supporting a positive relationship between stock prices and industrial production, as a gauge of real economic activity. This viewpoint has garnered endorsement from authors such as Mayasami et al. (2004), Humpe and Macmillian (2009), Gurgul and Lach (2010), Ikoku (2010), Naik and Padhi (2012), Hsing and Hsieh (2012), Narayan, Narayan, and Singh (2014), Plíhal (2016), Peiró (2016), and Silvio John Camilleria, Nicolanne Sciclunaa, and Ye Baib (2019) who have provided empirical support for this hypothesis using various analytical techniques.

However, other authors have revealed that the relationship between these factors is far from straightforward and does not consistently align with the anticipated positive trend. In their study, Anderson and Coll (2018) uncovered variations in the impact of industrial production announcements on different sectoral indices in both the EU and the US. Laopodis (2011) documented disparities in the relationship between stock prices and the Industrial Production Index (IPI) across different countries. More recently, Erfan M. et al (2020) highlighted results marked by ambiguity, which contradicted established theoretical assumptions.

As for interest rates, they remain of a paramount importance to decision-makers as they represent a fundamental and indispensable instrument of monetary policy. In addition to the reaction of stock markets to different monetary policy decisions, they also serve as valuable sources of information for central banks regarding sectoral expectations about macroeconomic variables. Drawing from insights put forth by Chen et al (1986), Mok (1993), Alam (2017), Ratanapakorn, and Sharma (2007), we acknowledge a notable negative relationship between stock prices and interest rates.

Consistent with the proposed hypothesis, Humpe and Macmillian (2009), Bernanke and Gertler (2000), Adam and Tweneboah (2008), Bjørnland and Leitemo (2009), Gurgul and Lach (2010), Laopodis (2011), Hussain, Rafique, Khalil, and Nawaz (2013), Andries, Ihnatov, and Tiwari (2014), Peiró (2016), and Alam (2017) have consistently shown that interest rates have a negative effect on stock prices.

Conversely, Ratanapakorn and Sharma (2007), Abugri (2008), Silvio John Camilleri, Nicolanne Scicluna, and Ye Bai (2019), as well as Erfan M. Bhuiyan and Murshed Chowdhury (2020) have reported mixed relationships. Their study of the link between interest rates and stock prices have unveiled both significant positive and negative associations, which vary in line with the period studied and the specific country under consideration.

2.2. Uncertainty Impact on Stock Market

The concept of uncertainty holds considerable significance for both political and economic decision-makers, exerting an effect with both microeconomic and macroeconomic nature (Chiang, 2021; Brogaard and Detzel, 2015; Bartsch, 2019; Duong et al., 2020; Goodell et al., 2020; He et al., 2020; Liang et al., 2020; Ma et al., 2018; Wen et al., 2022). Notably, heightened uncertainty tends to prompt businesses and individual investors to adopt more cautious approaches, resulting in a significant decline in consumption. This, in turn, contributes to increased unemployment rates and reduced levels of investment, ultimately leading to decreased debt issuance (Ashraf and Shen, 2019; Bloom, 2009; Caggiano et al., 2017; Canh et al., 2020; Chu and Fang, 2020; Hsieh and Vu, 2021; Kahle and Stulz, 2013; Wen et al., 2021).

Moreover, numerous studies have produced compelling evidence on the adverse effects of economic policy uncertainty on stock markets (Arouri M et al., 2016; Buchinsky M, 2001; Cheng CHJ, 2017; Liu L and Zhang T, 2015; Ma F et al., 2019; Phan D et al., 2018; Sharif A et al., 2020).

Additionally, Brogaard and Detzel (2015), Phan et al (2018), Istiak and Serletis (2018), Chiang et al. (2019) and Dai, Xiong, Liu et al. (2021) have explored the relationship between uncertainty and stock prices. For this purpose, Kang and Ratti (2013) highlighted the substantial effect of economic policy uncertainty (EPU) on real equity returns. Examining data from 11 different countries, the authors found a negative relationship between domestic uncertainty in policy-related risks (UPR) and domestic stock prices using a wavelet analysis (Ko and Lee, 2015). Bekiros et al., (2016) emphasized the importance of considering the content of UPR when predicting US equity returns. Chiang (2019) found that stock returns in G7 countries were inversely linked to innovation in economic policy uncertainty from both national and international sources.

Similarly, Hong Vo et al. (2021) delved into the impact of economic policy uncertainty on a firm's investment decisions in the US over the 1985 to 2018 period. Their findings contribute to the existing body of literature as they shed light on how firm-level investment behavior corresponds to changes in UPR. Furthermore, Feng Ma et al. (2022) showed that combining the MAI and EPU indices can yield additional insights to predict stock market volatility.

A substantial and current body of literature has also examined the role of geopolitical risks (GPR) in elucidating the dynamics of financial markets, like B.A. Kusi et al. (2020), J.A. Sonnenfeld et al. (2022), R. Rigobon and B. Sack (2005), T. Choudhry (2010), I. Yousaf, R. Patel, and L. Yarovaya (2022), S.K. Agyei (2022), B. Bedowska-Sojka (2022), A. Bossman, M. Gubareva, and T. Teplova (2023), Z. Umar (2022), and Ahmed Bossman and Mariya Gubareva (2023). These authors underscored the significance of geopolitical risks in the decision-making processes of economic stakeholders.

Geopolitical risks often referred to as GPR wield considerable influence on business cycles and financial markets. Caldara and Iacoviello (2016) note that economic decision-makers consider them as pivotal factors in shaping investment choices. These so-called geopolitical risks (GPR) exert a notable impact on economic cycles and financial markets through macroeconomic ramifications of terrorist incidents and national and global conflicts. In their study, Blomberg et al. (2004) documented a significant and economically adverse impact of these events on economic activity. Additionally, terrorism tends to affect economic growth by diverting investment spending towards public expenditure.

Several studies have examined the existing relationship between financial market activity and terrorist attacks. Overall, these studies have revealed that domestic terrorist attacks not only influence stock market performance and economic activity but also they have a notable impact on stock market volatility and returns. One major advantage of Caldara and Iacoviello's GPR indices, as established in their 2016 study, is their broad scope. These indices include not only terrorist attacks but also other geopolitical tensions such as military threats and war risks in addition to tensions in the Middle East. Consequently, they are able of detecting a wider array of external global uncertainties.

Mehmet Balcilar et al. (2016) introduced a fresh perspective to this body of research by examining the movements of major BRICS emerging stock markets using GPRs as a basis. Their results revealed the impact of geopolitical risks, measured via a continuous events-based index, across different financial market situations, including normal, bearish and bullish states.

More recently, Caldara and Iacoviello (2022) pointed to the substantial effect of geopolitical risks on both economic activity and the stock market. Furthermore, they have uncovered an interconnectedness between economic policy uncertainty and the propagation of geopolitical risks-related shocks. Using a geopolitical risk index founded on these shocks allowed for a more accurate estimation of the economic landscape.

3. EMPIRICAL METHODOLOGY

As previously mentioned, our primary objective is to examine stock prices behavior while incorporating macroeconomic variables and uncertainty shocks. The fundamental idea is to initially assess the dynamic consequences of asymmetric shocks stemming from long-term uncertainty on stock prices in a sample of OECD countries. Achieving this goal inherently needs the use of a non-linear empirical model, ensuring the adjustment of variable dynamics from short-term to long-term equilibrium. We draw upon the methodology proposed by Shin et al. (2014), specifically their Nonlinear Panel ARDL approach. We model the dynamic relationship between stock prices, the industrial production index, the consumer price index, and long-term interest rates via an asymmetric panel ARDL model in the presence of two uncertainty metrics. Specifically, we will investigate economic policy uncertainty (EPU) in Model 1 and geopolitical risks (GPR) in Model 2.

3.1. Economic Specification

The connections between stock prices and macroeconomic factors held significant importance and were intricately tied to studies that clarified the criteria used to select macroeconomic variables when investigating their relationship with the overall stock market. As highlighted by Chen et al. (1986), most researchers grounded their choice of variables in financial theory. This theory posits that stock prices are determined by anticipated cash flows and discount rates. Therefore, if a change in a macroeconomic variable leads to changes in expected cash flows or discount rates, it will inevitably result in corresponding changes in stock prices. Consequently, this paves the way to study the links between the said macro-economic variable and stock prices.

Put differently, numerous studies have delved into the different interactions between stock prices and macroeconomic variables. Researchers such as Fischer and Merton (1984), Stock and Watson (1990), Mukherjee and Naka (1995), Cheung and Ng (1998), Maysami and Koh (2000), Nasseh and Strauss (2000), Ratanapakorn and Sharma (2007), Humpe and Macmillan (2009), Silvio John Camilleri, Nicolanne Scicluna, and Ye Bai (2019), as well as Erfan M. Bhuiyan and Murshed Chowdhury (2020), have scrutinized the intricate relationships between various sets of variables. Their aim has been to determine which variables should be included in their respective studies.

Accordingly, we adopt the following model to estimate stock prices for a panel of OECD countries:

$$Stock_{it} = \beta_{0i} + \beta_{1i} IPI_{it} + \beta_{2i} CPI_{it} + \beta_{3i} IR_{it} + \beta_{4i} UNC_{it} + \mu_{it}$$

Where β_0 denotes the fixed country effect and μ_{it} is an error term assumed to be independently and normally distributed. $Stock_{it}$ is the stock price, IPI_{it} is the industrial production index, CPI_{it} represents the consumer price index, IR_{it} is the long-term interest rate and UNC_{it} is the measure of uncertainty (EPU or GPR). Index i and index t represent individual and time dimensions, respectively.

3.2. Econometric Approach

As previously indicated, the econometric methodology used in this study is mainly founded upon the non-linear panel Auto-Regressive Distributed Lag (ARDL) - Pooled Mean Group (PMG) approach. This model is constructed with due consideration to the model of Shin et al. (2014), which adapts the nonlinear panel ARDL model to accommodate dynamic representations of heterogeneous panel data under conditions of asymmetry. The selection of this econometric methodology is substantiated by two main rationales.

First, adoption of this non-linear model is warranted and recommended for its ability to capture the asymmetric effects of uncertainty shocks on stock prices. Second, this panel ARDL approach is deemed appropriate for considering both the short-term dynamics of the variables and their adjustment towards long-term equilibrium. We note that in accordance with the studies of Pedroni (2004) and Kao (2016), this adjustment persists especially when it comes to mutually integrated variables and independently of the presence of cointegration. In this regard, and in order to manipulate non-stationary variables with the same order of integration [I(1)] or with a mixed order of integration ([I(1)] and [I(0)],the heterogeneous dynamic panel approach is considered the most appropriate technique.

We distinguish between the Pooled Mean Group (PMG) estimator and the Mean Group (MG) estimator; based on the maximum likelihood approach (Pesaran and Smith (1995) and Pesaran et al. (1999)), as the two main techniques in order to estimate the non-stationary dynamic heterogeneous panel data model. The major contribution of these two techniques is that they take into account the individual particularities of the chosen sample with a deeper understanding of the long-term equilibrium dynamics.

It follows that the MG approach aims to estimate N regressions of time series and to calculate the average of the coefficients (Blackburne and Frank (2007)), which allows for estimating certain heterogeneity in the short and long-term.

On the other hand, using the PMG method yields heterogeneous estimations in the short term but a homogeneous estimation in the long term. However, one can consider conducting the long-term Hausman test to check if there is a difference between the aforementioned methods.

3.2.1. The Linear Panel ARDL

We recall at this stage that the ARDL (Auto-Regressive Distributed Lag) model is an asymmetric version of the linear panel ARDL model (Pesaran et al.; 1999). Therefore, our analysis will begin by assuming that stock prices react in a symmetrical manner following detected changes in macroeconomic variables. Subsequently, in a second step, we transition to an asymmetry assumption to facilitate identification of both positive and negative changes in variables representing long-term uncertainty.

The relationship between $Stock_{it}$, IPI_{it}, CPI_{it}, IR_{it} and UNC_{it} as delineated in Equation (1), is presumed to follow a temporal trend before reaching long-term equilibrium. Consequently, following the insights of Pesaran et al., Equation (1) can be represented within the linear panel ARDL model as follows:

$$\begin{aligned}\Delta Stock_{it} &= \alpha_i + \gamma_{1i} Stock_{i,t-1} + \gamma_{2i} IPI_{i,t-1} + \gamma_{3i} CPI_{i,t-1} + \gamma_{4i} IR_{i,t-1} + \gamma_{5i} UNC_{i,t-1} \\ &\quad + \sum_{j=1}^{P_1} \delta_{1ij} \Delta Stock_{i,t-j} + \sum_{j=1}^{P_2} \delta_{2ij} \Delta IPI_{i,t-j} + \sum_{j=1}^{P_3} \delta_{3ij} \Delta CPI_{i,t-j} \\ &\quad + \sum_{j=1}^{P_4} \delta_{4ij} \Delta IR_{i,t-j} + \sum_{j=1}^{P_5} \delta_{5ij} \Delta UNC_{i,t-j} + \varepsilon_{it}\end{aligned}$$

Where Δ is the first difference operator, αi is a constant, δ_{sij} (s = 1, 2, 3, 4, 5) are the short-term coefficients, γ_{ki} (k = 1, 2, 3, 4,5) are the long-term coefficients and ε_{it} is an error term. The optimal lag orders (P_1,P_2,P_3,P_4,P_5) on the first differentiated variables are chosen according to the Schwarz Information Criterion (SIC) or the

Akaike Information Criterion (AIC). Equation 2 could be formulated as follows in order to take into consideration the error correction term:

$$\Delta Stock_{it} = \varphi_i + \sum_{j=1}^{P_1} \delta_{1ij} \Delta Stock_{i,t-j} + \sum_{j=1}^{P_2} \delta_{2ij} \Delta IPI_{i,t-j} + \sum_{j=1}^{P_3} \delta_{3ij} \Delta CPI_{i,t-j}$$
$$+ \sum_{j=0}^{P_4} \delta_{4ij} \Delta IR_{i,t-j} + \sum_{j=0}^{P_5} \delta_{5ij} \Delta UNC_{i,t-j} + \lambda_i ect_{i,t-1} + \varepsilon_{it}$$

Here,

$$ect_{i,t-1} = Stock_{i,t-1} - \theta_{1i} IPI_{i,t-1} - \theta_{2i} CPI_{i,t-1} - \theta_{3i} IR_{i,t-1} - \theta_{4i} UNC_{i,t-1}$$

represents the linear error correction component for each unit, derived from the long-term relationship. For the parameter λ_i, it denotes the error correction rate in the equilibrium model fitting each unit, which is also denoted as λ_{1i}. The parameters $\theta_{1i}, \theta_{2i}, \theta_{3i}\, et\, \theta_{4i}$ are computed as $\gamma_{2i}/\gamma_{1i}, \gamma_{3i}/\gamma_{1i}, \gamma_{4i}/\gamma_{1i}\ et\ \gamma_{5i}/\gamma_{1i}$, respectively.

Faced with the asymmetric relationships detected between the different studied variables, we use a nonlinear panel ARDL model using the asymmetric ARDL approach developed by Shin et al. (2014), which remains more adequate because it allows us to detect asymmetric movements in the short and long term as well as the specification of an asymmetric error correction model.

3.2.2. The Nonlinear Panel ARDL

To identify stock price reactions to uncertainty with asymmetry, we use the ARDL asymmetric panel model. This asymmetrical approach involves breaking down the exogenous fluctuating variable, denoted as $UMC_{i,t}$ *in our study, into two distinct partial sums: a positive partial sum denoted as* $\Delta UNC^{+}_{i,t}$ to identify upward movements in $UMC_{i,t}$, and a negative partial sum *denoted as* $\Delta UNC^{-}_{i,t}$, to capture negative changes. In this framework, it is anticipated that positive and negative uncertainty shocks will not produce identical impacts on stock prices. Following the methodology proposed by Shin et al., (2014), the panel decomposition of the uncertainty variable is outlined as follows:

$$UNC^{+}_{i,t} = \sum_{j=1}^{t} \Delta UNC^{+}_{i,j} = \sum_{j=1}^{t} \max\left(\Delta^{+}_{i,j}, 0\right)$$
$$\text{and } UNC^{-}_{i,t} = \sum_{j=1}^{t} \Delta UNC^{-}_{i,j} = \sum_{j=1}^{t} \min\left(\Delta UNC^{-}_{i,j}, 0\right) \quad (4)$$

As shown in Equation 2 (Eq. (2)), we construct our nonlinear panel ARDL model by integrating short-term and long-term asymmetric relationships:

$$\Delta Stock\text{Skipping malformed tag: msub} = \eta_i + \gamma_{1i} Stock_{i,t-1} + \gamma_{2i} IPI_{i,t-1} + \gamma_{3i} CPI_{i,t-1} + \gamma_{4i} IR_{i,t-1} + \gamma_{5i}^{+} UNC_{i,t-1}^{+}$$
$$+\gamma_{5i}^{-} UNC_{i,t-1}^{-} + \sum_{j=1}^{P_1} \delta_{1ij} \Delta Stock_{i,t-j} + \sum_{j=1}^{P_2} \delta_{2ij} \Delta IPI_{i,t-j} + \sum_{j=1}^{P_3} \delta_{3ij} \Delta CPI_{i,t-j}$$
$$+\sum_{j=1}^{P_4} \delta_{4ij} \Delta IR_{i,t-j} + \sum_{j=0}^{P_5} (\delta_{5ij}^{+} \Delta UNC_{i,t-j}^{+} + \delta_{5ij}^{-} \Delta UNC_{i,t-j}^{-}) + \varepsilon_{it}$$

The coefficients γ_{5i}^{+} and γ_{5i}^{-}, estimate the long-term asymmetric response of stock prices following positive or negative uncertainty shocks. Whereas in the short term, the coefficients δ_{5ij}^{+} and δ_{5ij}^{-} estimate the response at this time horizon. The asymmetric error correction version of Eq. (5) indicates:

$$\Delta Stock_{it} = \tau_i + \sum_{j=1}^{P_2} \delta_{2ij} \Delta IPI_{i,t-j} + \sum_{j=1}^{P_3} \delta_{3ij} \Delta CPI_{i,t-j} + \sum_{j=1}^{P_4} \delta_{4ij} \Delta IR_{i,t-j}$$
$$+\sum_{j=0}^{P_5} \left[\delta_{5ij}^{+} \Delta UNC_{i,t-j}^{+} + \delta_{5ij}^{-} \Delta UNC_{i,t-j}^{-}\right] + iect_{i,t-1} + \varepsilon_{it}$$

Where $iect_{i,t}$ represents the asymmetric error correction term. $_i$ represents the system's adjustment speed to its long-term equilibrium following a shock.

4. KEY VARIABLES, SAMPLE AND DATA

In this study, our sample consists of 16 OECD economies, which are Canada (CAN), France (FRA), Germany (GER), Australia (AUS), Japan (JPN), South Korea (KOR), the United Kingdom (GBR), Belgium (BEL), the United States (USA), Colombia (COL), Denmark (DNK), Spain (ESP), the Netherlands (NLD), Sweden (SWE), Chile (CHL), and Italy (ITA). The dataset includes monthly observations spanning from January 2009 to May 2022.

Our primary focus is on stock prices, which serve as the dependent variable. To elucidate the relationship, we have selected a set of macroeconomic variables frequently used in both theoretical and empirical research. These include the industrial production index (IPI), inflation (CPI), the long-term interest rate (IR), and two distinct forms of uncertainty: economic policy uncertainty (EPU) and geopolitical risks (GPR). Data for these variables have been sourced from the OECD's economic and financial indicators and the International Monetary Fund's international financial statistics.

For measures of uncertainty, economic policy uncertainty (EPU) data were obtained from Global (Davis[1], 2016), while those relating to geopolitical risks (GPR), the said data were downloaded from https://www.matteoiacoviello.com/gpr.htm January 04, 2023.

4.1. Descriptive Statistics

Table 1 provides a comprehensive overview of stock prices and the different key macroeconomic variables (IPI, CPI, IR, EPU, and GPR) across 16 OECD countries during the period spanning from January 2009 to May 2022, with data collected on a monthly basis. The table presents essential statistics such as means, standard deviations, maximum, and minimum values.

Stock prices, on average, stood at 0.968394 and reached their highest point at 1.996418. Conversely, the industrial production index exhibited an average value of 1.012612, with its maximum value reaching 1.437000. As for the inflation rate, it maintained an average value of 1.004941, while its peak value reached 1.387389. In contrast, interest rates displayed an average value of 2.392949, with a maximum value reaching 10.78000.

Table 1. Descriptive statistics

	CPI	EPU	GPR	IPI	IR	SM
Mean	1.004941	1.617974	0.345007	1.012612	2.392949	0.968394
Median	1.001719	1.316850	0.120832	1.003916	1.963000	0.978208
Maximum	1.387389	11.41796	7.014576	1.437000	10.78000	1.996418
Minimum	0.754453	0.276324	0.000000	0.551954	-0.649091	0.277822
Std. Dev.	0.076501	0.946264	0.580147	0.081021	2.074474	0.247840
Skewness	0.602569	2.363333	3.306879	0.275571	1.060008	0.401230
Kurtosis	4.778738	12.74722	18.40094	5.835654	3.949300	4.025827
Jarque-Bera	495.4792	12595.53	30153.24	895.6635	579.1321	182.0656
Probability	0.000000	0.000000	0.000000	0.000000	0.000000	0.000000
Sum	2588.728	4167.900	888.7386	2608.487	6164.236	2494.583
Sum Sq. Dev.	15.06997	2305.696	866.6702	16.90341	11081.36	158.1688
Observations	2576	2576	2576	2576	2576	2576

Turning to measures of uncertainty, economic policy uncertainty (EPU) showed an average of 1.617974 and reached a maximum of 11.41796. Meanwhile, geopolitical risk (GPR) had an average around 0.345007, with its maximum at 7.014576.

4.2. Panel Unit Root Tests

In order to assess stationarity of the variables under scrutiny, we consider the newest dynamic heterogeneous panel data model, ARDL - PMG, we conduct a panel unit root test on the different series. Moreover, while application of the ARDL approach allows for different levels of integration (I (1)) between the variables to facilitate their adjustment to long-term scenarios, the use of the panel unit root test is fundamental to ensure that none of the variables exceeds an integration of order one.

For empirical purposes, we consider two types of panel unit root tests. Breitung (2000) and Levin et al. (2002) propose a first type of panel unit root tests where the null hypothesis posits a unit root with a common process. A second type of test proposed by Maddala and Wu (1999) and Im et al. (2003) assumes a unit root with an individual unit root process. Our results are presented in Table 2 and indicate that stock prices, long-term interest rates, the consumer price index, and the industrial production index exhibit non-stationarity at the first-order integration level [I (1)] or both types of panel unit root tests. However, the different tests confirm that the uncertainty variable, including both its UPR and GPR measures, remains stationary at a non-integration level [I (0)].

Having assessed the stationarity attributes of the chosen variables, we postulate a mixed integration order, including both [I (0)] and [I (1)] properties. We establish that not all the studied variables present a second-order integration, while the dependent variable (Stock Price Index) shows first-order integration. By satisfying these conditions, we validate the estimation process for the panel ARDL model, making it applicable.

Furthermore, our results once again underscore the significance of our selection of the panel ARDL model, given its capacity to account for heterogeneity and non-stationarity inherent in panel data series.

As previously mentioned, the empirical approach used in this study involves the implementation of our non-linear econometric models in a two-stage process. Initially, we assess the symmetric response of stock prices to variations in three designated macroeconomic variables, along with uncertainty, using two distinct models. In the first model (referred to as "Model 1"), we estimate uncertainty through the Economic Policy Uncertainty (EPU) variable, whereas the second model (referred to as "Model 2") considers geopolitical risks (GPR) as a representation of uncertainty. Subsequently, we incorporate the asymmetry hypothesis to account for both positive and negative fluctuations in uncertainty.

Table 2. Panel unit root test

Test			CPI	IPI	IR	Stock Market	EPU	GPR
LLC	**Level**	Intercept	10.1836 (1,0000)	-0.76873 (0.2210)	-3.59584 (0.0002)	-0.07542 (0.4699)	-2.28075 (0.0113)	2.97006 (0.9985)
		Inter and trend	15.4221 (1,0000)	-2.05000 (0.0202)	10.0849 (1.0000)	0.81050 (0.7912)	-4.34913 (0.0000)	1.23409 (0.8914)
	First Diff	Intercept	0.35599 (0.6391)	-10.4819 (0.0000)	-8.59422 (0.0000)	-9.30711 (0.0000)	-6.13988 (0.0000)	8.10991 (1.0000)
		Inter and trend	-1.04083 (0.1490)	-10.4097 (0.0000)I1	-11.9637 (0.0000)	-9.66888 (0.0000)	-4.22439 (0.0000)	12.6525 (1.0000)
IPS	**Level**	Intercept	13.2875 (1.0000)	-2.52865 (0.0057)	-1.73519 (0.0414)	-0.13277 (0.4472)	-4.91752 (0.0000)	- 5.60055 (0.0000)
		Inter and trend	11.1137 (1,0000)	-4.14277 (0.0000)	4.74723 (1.0000)	-3.44411 (0.0003)	-4.87500 (0.0000)	- 5.67962 (0.0000)
	First Diff	Intercept	-10.0294 (0.0000)	-25.6996 (0.0000)	-15.6191 (0.0000)	-17.2071 (0.0000)	-27.6565 (0.0000)	- 28.4542 (0.0000)
		Inter and trend	-9.35189 (0.0000)	-25.4856 (0.0000)	-15.2791 (0.0000)	-15.8113 (0.0000)	-27.3990 (0.0000)	- 28.5066 (0.0000)
ADF	**Level**	Intercept	1.82485 (1.0000)	71.2586 (0.0001)	36.1352 (0.2814)	31.2271 (0.5055)	96.5289 (0.0000)	122.233 (0.0000)
		Inter and trend	9.55770 (1,0000)	77.4229 (0.0000)	5.02345 (1.0000)	55.9889 (0.0054)	84.6918 (0.0000)	112.456 (0.0000)
	First Diff	Intercept	189.621 (0.0000)	637.017 (0.0000)	315.257 (0.0000)	361.800 (0.0000)	704.305 (0.0000)	737.307 (0.0000)
		Inter and trend	161.687 (0.0000)	568.072 (0.0000)	279.071 (0.0000)	294.731 (0.0000)	626.809 (0.0000)	667.503 (0.0000)
Breitung	**Level**	Inter and trend	-4.45080 (0.0000)	2.77094 (0.9972)	7.21853 (1.0000)	-1.65594 (0.0489)	-0.51589 (0.3030)	5.86657 (1.0000)
	First Diff	Inter and trend	4.09681 (1.0000)	-4.29385 (0.0000)	-1.11789 (0.1318)	-0.25674 (0.3987)	-9.77812 (0.0000)	2.82211 (0.9976)

Values in () are probabilities

5. EMPIRICAL RESULTS AND DISCUSSION

5.1. Symmetric Impact of Uncertainty on Stock Market: Linear Panel ARDL Results

We first use linear models to estimate Eq. (2) via the two techniques MG and PMG. Subsequently, we admit these estimation outcomes to the long-run Hausman test to determine the most suitable estimation approach. If the null hypothesis is not rejected, it is suggested that the PMG estimator should be adopted. Conversely, if the null hypothesis is rejected, it implies a preference for the MG estimator. Essentially, the long-term Hausman test is grounded on a set of hypotheses, assuming hypothesis (0) that the PMG estimator is more efficient than in hypothesis (1), advocating the efficiency of the MG estimator.

The results in Table 3 of the long-run Hausman tests for each of the independent variables (IPI, CPI, IR, and UNC) provide support for not rejecting the null hypothesis, indicating that to model stock prices, the PMG estimator is the efficient technique. Consequently, for the remainder of our empirical study, we exclusively present and discuss results obtained from the PMG estimator.

Table 3. Linear panel ARDL estimation

Variables	Model 1	Model 2
	With EPU	With GPR
Long-run estimates		
CPI	0.435819 (0,3638)	-0.478204 (0.3789)
IPI	**-0.989388**** (0,013)	-0.521033 (0.1438)
IR	**-0.178881***** (0,0000)	**-0.173485***** (0.0000)
UNC	**-0.091467***** (0.0007)	**-0.183847**** (0.0450)
Hausman test	2.84 (0.5851)	2.14 (0.7097)
Short-run estimates		
ECT	**-0.031610***** (0,0000)	**-0.035065***** (0.0000)
Δ(*CPI*)	**0.566716*****(0,0001)	**0.942360***** (0.0000)
Δ(*IPI*)	**0.200397**** (0,0003)	**0.212575***** (0.0002)
Δ(*IR*)	**0.017983*** (0,0875)	**0.023334*** (0.0699)
Δ(*UNC*)	**-0.031340*****(0,0000)	**-0.021387***(0.1018)
C	**0.066675***** (0,0000)	**0.086505***** (0.0000)

***, ** and * denote 1, 5 and 10% significance levels respectively, while values in () are probabilities

From an economic standpoint, beyond the results of the long-term Hausman test, the PMG estimator is considered as the selected technique when addressing the long-term relationship between macroeconomic variables and stock prices in a uniform manner across the entire set of countries. Simultaneously, it enables the identification of the distinct short-term fluctuations that characterize each economy.

Put differently, it is probable that each country will pursue its unique strategy in the short-term depending on its economic situation as well as the structure of its financial market. However, the economies within our sample are anticipated to share a common objective of fostering their financial markets and combatting inflation at the long-term.

Table 3 reports the results of the estimation of the linear model (Equation (2)) for each of the exogenous variables considered in our model. These findings include the estimated long-run elasticities, the estimated coefficients depicting short-term dynamics, and the estimated adjustment speed toward long-term equilibrium.

The error correction term (ECT) shows strong statistical significance at the 1% level in both models, with coefficients of approximately -0.031610 in model 1 and -0.035065 in model 2. This discovery means that the long-term adjustment of the different variables is established. These values indicate an annual adjustment rate towards long-term equilibrium of 3.16% and 3.5% respectively in models 1 and 2.

Examining the estimated long-run coefficients, we observe expected signs and statistical significance for the IPI, IR, and UNC coefficients in model 1. In model 2, only IR and UNC display significance. Specifically, in model 1, long-run elasticities of stock prices concerning long-term interest rates and uncertainty are significantly negative at the 1% level. Additionally, the industrial production index shows a negative and significant impact at the 5% level.

In model 2, a noteworthy and negative relationship emerges between stock prices, on the one hand, and long-term interest rates and uncertainty, on the other hand, with significance levels of 1% and 5%, respectively.

As for the short-term dynamics, the results point to the significance of stock prices' short-run elasticity vis-a-vis all independent variables in both model 1 and model 2.

Beginning with the short-term dynamics in model 1, we observe positive and statistically significant relationships between stock prices and CPI, IPI, and IR. Conversely, elasticity of stock prices concerning uncertainty is significant and negative, notably at the 1% level. These properties of the relationships are true in model 2, where uncertainty is represented by geopolitical risks.

In this linear model, the relationship between inflation and stock prices in the short run is notably significant and positive (0.566716 for EPU and 0.942360 for GPR), both at the 1% level. This finding aligns with those of several previous studies, including those of Ratanapakorn and Sharma (2007), Asmy, Rohilina, Hassama, and Fouad (2010), Alam (2017), and Antonakakis et al. (2017). These findings lend support to the hypothesis that stock prices in our OECD sample serve as effective hedges against inflation. This alignment can be rationalized by Gordon's (1962) model, which posits that stock prices are influenced, in part, by dividend expectations. In this regard, an expansionary monetary policy, which can lead to inflation, may concurrently raise expectations of economic activity, consequently bolstering stock prices.

Furthermore, alternative explanations can be considered, as several studies have indicated that during the initial stages of an inflationary cycle, equities tend to perform positively. This phenomenon often occurs as the initial signs of inflation follow improvements in economic conditions. There is a temporal gap between the onset of inflation and the initial monetary tightening, which can contribute to this observed trend. This phase can extend for several months, or even up to a year. Throughout this period, equities enjoy a highly favourable environment as real bond yields turn negative, reinforcing the notion that there are limited alternatives to stocks. In the subsequent phase, returns on equities decline as central banks hike interest rates above nominal growth and inflation levels, resulting in positive real interest rates. During this stage, equities lose their competitive edge compared to bond investments. In the long run, impact of inflation on stock prices becomes insignificant, regardless of the adopted model.

For the industrial production index, we observe a substantial and negative relationship (-0.989388) in the long term when economic policy uncertainty represents uncertainty (model 1). However, it is not statistically significant in model 2, where geopolitical risks represent uncertainty. In contrast, this relationship exhibits a reversal between its two parameters in the short term, reaching values of 0.566716 in Model 1 and 0.942360 in Model 2.

Table 3 which indicates the relationship between the industrial production index, serving as an indicator of real economic activity and stock prices, shows a degree of ambiguity when compared to the findings of previous studies. While there is a validated relationship between stock prices and the industrial production index in our panel, this relationship does not consistently align with long-term expectations. Our results remain different from those of several other studies (Chen et al., 1986; Fama, 1990; Abdullah and Hayworth, 1993; Mukherjee and Naka, 1995) and agree with others (Anderson et al. 2018) whose sectoral indices in the United States and the EU react differently to industrial production announcements. Even the expected positive direction of these effects has not been confirmed. It is therefore important to emphasize that the relationship between stock prices and the industrial production index varied according to several parameters. Then, we distinguish the country and the period dimensions (Laopodis, 2011).

In the short term, the relationship between the industrial production index and stock prices, in the presence of either EPU or GPR, confirms the hypothesis that an increase in real production will lead to a development in stock market activity. The positive relationship between stock prices and IPI is consistent with thenfindings of Humpe and Macmillian (2009), Narayan et al. (2014), Silvio John Camilleri (2019), and others. The idea here is that IPI emerges as the most crucial macroeconomic variable positively interacting with the financial sphere.

As for long-term interest rates, the relationship between stock prices and the industrial production index showed variable signs within our panel of countries over time, despite the strong theoretical links between these two parameters. Indeed, the relationship is around -0.178881 in Model 1 and -0.173485 in Model 2 (indicating a significant and negative relationship). However, in the short term, this relationship is significantly positive at 0.017983 in Model 1 and 0.023334 in Model 2. As described in our literature review, these results remain consistent with our mixed expectations in terms of sign and significance.

To elucidate the positive relationship outlined in Table 3, we can consider two plausible explanations. First, it is possible that monetary policymakers are aiming to temper excessive exuberance in the stock market by increasing interest rates. Alternatively, growth in stock market activity can stimulate real activity, which leads to an increase in interest rates following increased financing needs.

Additionally, it is worth noting that during periods of financial and economic instability, investors often shift from equities to high-quality bonds. This transition leads to lower equity prices and reduced bond yields, thereby establishing a positive correlation. In this regard, it is noteworthy that our study period from January 2009 to May 2022 includes the subprime crisis, which had a profound impact on various financial, real, and monetary activities. Furthermore, we should acknowledge the effect of the COVID-19 crisis and the Russian-Ukrainian war during this timeframe.

In essence, the persistent negative long-term relationship between stock prices and long-term interest rates aligns consistently with the theoretical principles and the literature, including studies by Bernanke and Gertler (2000), Bjørnland and Leitemo (2009), Humpe and Macmillian (2009), Adam and Tweneboah (2008), Hussain et al. (2013), and Peiró (2016).

Chen et al., (1986) showed that stock prices are influenced by variations detected in interest rates since the latter influence dividends. Furthermore, Mok, (1993) mentioned another transmission channel of the effect of interest rates on stock prices. The author proposes that interest rates influence cost of financing and, consequently, the opportunity cost of borrowing and the stock price. Another possible explanation postulated by (Alam 2017) for the inverse relationship between stock prices and interest rates is that if interest rates climb, investors tend to substitute bonds for stocks.

For uncertainty, this variable consistently maintains the same direction of significance, irrespective of whether it is considered in terms of time (short term or long term) or within different models (UPR in Model 1 or GPR in Model 2). This parameter consistently shows significant negative values, amounting to approximately -0.091467 in Model 1 and -0.183847 in Model 2 in the long term, while these values decrease to around -0.031340 in Model 1 and -0.021387 in Model 2 in the short term.

These recent findings remain entirely consistent with prior research supporting the hypothesis of a negative effect of uncertainty on financial activity. Notable studies reinforcing this notion include those of Arouri M et al. (2016), Buchinsky M (2001), Cheng CHJ (2017), Liu L and Zhang T (2015), Ma F et al. (2019), Phan D et al. (2018), Sharif A et al. (2020), Liang et al. (2021), Li et al. (2022), Ma et al (2022), Salisu et al. (2022), Lee (2023), and Bakhtiar Javaheri et al (2022).

5.2. Asymmetric Impact of Uncertainty on Stock Market: Nonlinear Panel ARDL Results

Recall that given the importance of the questions addressed in this study and the prior discussions on the intriguing linear findings on the effect of long-term macroeconomic variables on stock prices, it was deemed inappropriate to rely solely on the linear version of the panel ARDL model. Instead, it was more plausible to specify a more complex relationship between the studied parameters, such as the non-linear panel ARDL.

Table 4 reports the results found following the estimation of equation 5 for all the macroeconomic variables of our non-linear model. These findings cover the estimated long-term non-linear elasticities, the estimated short-term non-linear coefficients, and the estimated long-term adjustment speed to equilibrium.

In the long term, the non-linear findings indicate predominantly negative signs or relationships that lack statistical significance. Specifically, the coefficient associated with the consumer price index (CPI) is negative (-1.036566 in Model 2) and significantly so at the 1% level, while it remains insignificant in Model 1. Conversely, the coefficient of the industrial production index (IPI) has no discernible impact on stock prices in either models.

For the asymmetric impact of long-term interest rates on stock prices, the non-linear results from both models consistently reveal negative and statistically significant relationships in the long term. These values amount to -0.078487 and -0.095013, respectively, aligning with established findings in the financial literature.

Similarly, focusing on the asymmetric effect of uncertainty on stock prices in the two aforementioned models, we observe that positive changes in uncertainty (UNC+) yield a negative and significant impact on stock prices (-0.066075 in Model

1 and -0.179326 in Model 2). Furthermore, we found that the impact of negative changes in long-term uncertainty is significant at the 1% level, exerting a negative effect on stock prices (-0.079833 in Model 1 and -0.208596 in Model 2). These findings indicate that a detected 1% increase in uncertainty results in a 6.6% decrease in Model 1 and a 17.93% decrease when geopolitical risks represent uncertainty in Model 2. Similarly, a 1% decrease leads to a 7.98% decrease in Model 1 and a 20.85% decrease in Model 2.

Both positive and negative fluctuations in uncertainty show a detrimental effect on stock prices, aligning with the theoretical and empirical literature, albeit with differing magnitudes. Upon reviewing the results in Table 4, it becomes evident that a negative long-term shock has a more pronounced impact than a positive shock in both models. This implies that policymakers in both the political and financial spheres should take note that adverse shifts in uncertainty will result in a more substantial reduction in stock market activity compared to favourable variations.

Turning to the short-term non-linear dimension, the findings indicate that inflation, represented by the consumer price index, has a significant and positive effect on stock prices in both models. This positive impact implies that a 1% change in inflation (consumer price index) leads to approximately a 58.32% variation in share prices in Model 1 and 94.92% in Model 2. Similarly, the industrial production index also maintains a significantly positive relationship with stock prices in the short term, registering values of 0.177917 in Model 1 and 0.201278 in Model 2.

The relationships between interest rates and stock prices also show significant coefficients, with a positive relationship between the two variables in both models. Specifically, a 1% change in long-term interest rates led to an increase of 01.71% in stock prices in Model 1 and 02.21% in Model 2, respectively.

Furthermore, the results from the short-term non-linear model reveal evidence of short-term asymmetry. They indicate that an increase in uncertainty (Model 1 / UPR) exerts a negative asymmetric influence on stock prices, with stock prices responding to an uncertainty shock (1%) by decreasing by 5.24%. In contrast, an uncertainty shock in Model 2 (Model 2 / GPR) remains statistically insignificant. In simpler terms, a decline in uncertainty has no discernible impact on stock prices, whereas only upward shifts in uncertainty negatively affect stock prices in the short term. It follows that stock prices do not react following negative shocks of uncertainty.

Table 4. NonLinear panel ARDL estimation

Variables	Model 1	Model 2
	With EPU	With GPR
Long-run estimates		
CPI	-0.365536 (0,2291)	**-1.036566***** (0.0030)
IPI	-0.217105 (0,2075)	0.175722 (0.4850)
IR	**-0.078487***** (0.0000)	**-0.095013***** (0.0000)
UNC pos	**-0.066075***** (0,0000)	**-0.179326**** (0.0324)
UNC neg	**-0.079833***** (0,0000)	**-0.208596**** (0.0136)
Short-run estimates		
ECT	**-0.058137***** (0,0000)	**-0.046247***** (0.0000)
Δ(*CPI*)	**0.583219***** (0,0006)	**0.949219***** (0.0000)
Δ(*IPI*)	**0.177917***** (0,0010)	**0.201278***** (0.0002)
Δ(*IR*)	**0.017139*** (0.0974)	**0.022176*** (0.0773)
Δ(*UNC pos*)	**-0.052461***** (0,0000)	0.011124 (0.2009)
Δ(*UNC neg*)	-0.002607 (0,5287)	-0.042904 (0.7445)
C	**0.097388*****(0,0000)	**0.093387***** (0.0000)

***, ** and * denote 1, 5 and 10% significance levels respectively, while values in () are probabilities

In both of the considered models, the non-linear error correction term (ECT) is statistically negative and significant at the 1% level. This implies that there is indeed an adjustment of short-term dynamics towards long-term non-linear equilibrium.

6. CONCLUSION AND POLICY IMPLICATIONS

The main aim of this paper was to elucidate the short- and long-term relationship between stock prices and different macroeconomic factors in a non-linear framework. The objective was to uncover the asymmetric aspects of the relationships under examination. This study has revealed a long-term equilibrium relationship between the macroeconomic variables representing inflation, long-term interest rates, the industrial production index, two different measures of uncertainty (UPR and GPR), and the stock prices in our panel of countries over a period spanning from January 2009 to May 2022.

The findings have unveiled an asymmetric relationship between stock prices and the different independent variables across different time horizons. Notably, inflation has a negative long-term effect on stock market activity within the studied economies. Consequently, to foster the growth of the financial sector and maintain robust stock market activity in OECD financial markets, policymakers should address inflation by implementing inflation-reducing economic policies.

For long-term interest rates, our results align with those of previous research, affirming a negative relationship with stock prices. Therefore, central banks in the studied countries should consider the potential adverse impacts of their long-term monetary policies and explore avenues to stimulate financial activity by lowering long-term interest rates. However, the relationship between stock prices and the industrial production index yields inconclusive results. This study lends support to the notion that industrial production may no longer be the useful indicator for making the right decision in the long term, given the shift in international economies towards services-based economies as opposed to manufacturing-driven ones.

Furthermore, our study has extended the finding of a negative long-term relationship between different measures of uncertainty, whether economic policy uncertainty or geopolitical risks, and stock prices. This aligns with prior theoretical and empirical research, endorsing the hypothesis that uncertainty exerts a long-term dampening effect on stock prices, a notion further substantiated by our own results.

It is worth highlighting that a negative long-term shock has a more substantial impact than a positive one in both of the models we examined. This underscores the importance for political and financial decision-makers to take note that adverse fluctuations in uncertainty will result in a more significant reduction in stock market activity than positive fluctuations.

Nonetheless, the results of this study clearly indicate a short-term asymmetric relationship between macroeconomic variables and stock prices, which differs from the dynamics observed in the long term. It is noteworthy that the behavior of stock prices in OECD countries during the studied period varies depending on time horizon.

We emphasize a positive relationship between long-term interest rates, the industrial production index and inflation, with stock prices in the short term. Notably, only positive shocks stemming from economic policy uncertainty exhibit a negative short-term impact on stock prices, while all other impulses fail to show an effect on stock prices. These findings underscore the significance of a robust financial sector in the presence of uncertainty, as it can contribute to restoring financial market stability as desired. Additionally, with the aim of diversifying specific risks for investors, an open economy can be the basis of such an operation. This issue is of particular importance for policymakers to consider, especially given that financial markets often experience the inflow and outflow of 'speculative capital,' which can be at the origin of economic and financial destabilization caused by geopolitical risks, as has been proven in this study.

In conclusion, there is ample room for expanding this study by integrating supplementary macroeconomic indicators, alternative measures of uncertainty, and country-specific variables to assess their impact on stock market dynamics. Previous research has delved into integrating parameters such as short-term interest rates and exchange rates to shed light on a nation's stock market index. Additionally, variables such as other commodity prices and oil prices could hold substantial explanatory power when it comes to understanding stock market returns.

REFERENCES

Abugri, B. A. (2008). Empirical relationship between macroeconomic volatility and stock returns: Evidence from Latin American markets. *International Review of Financial Analysis*, *17*(2), 396–410. DOI: 10.1016/j.irfa.2006.09.002

Adam, A. M., & Tweneboah, G. (2008). Macroeconomic factors and stock market movement: evidence from Ghana. Unpublished Working Paper. https://mpra.ub .unimuenchen. De/11256/.

Agyei, S. K., Owusu, P.Junior, Bossman, A., Asafo-Adjei, E., Asiamah, O., & Adam, A. M. (2022). Spillovers and contagion between BRIC and G7 markets: New evidence from time-frequency analysis. *PLoS One*, *17*(7), e0271088. DOI: 10.1371/ journal.pone.0271088 PMID: 35895731

Al-Shami, H. A. A., & Ibrahim, Y. (2013). The effects of macro-economic indicators on stock returns: Evidence from Kuwait stock market. *American Journal of Economics*, *3*(5C), 57–66.

Anderson, H. D., Balli, F., & Godber, C. (2018). The effect of macroeconomic announcements at a sectoral level in the US and European Union. *Research in International Business and Finance*, *44*(C), 256–272. DOI: 10.1016/j.ribaf.2017.07.095

Andrie , A. M., Ihnatov, I., & Tiwari, A. (2014). Analyzing time–frequency relationship between interest rate, stock price and exchange rate through continuous wavelet. *Economic Modelling*, *41*(C), 227–238. DOI: 10.1016/j.econmod.2014.05.013

Antonakakis, N., Chatziantoniou, I., & Filis, G. (2017). Oil shocks and stock markets: Dynamic connectedness under the prism of recent geopolitical and economic unrest. *International Review of Financial Analysis*, *50*(C), 1–26. DOI: 10.1016/j. irfa.2017.01.004

Arouri, M., Estay, C., Rault, C., & Roubaud, D. (2016). Economic policy uncertainty and stock markets: Long-run evidence from the US. *Finance Research Letters*, *18*(C), 136–141. DOI: 10.1016/j.frl.2016.04.011

Ashraf, B. N., & Shen, Y. (2019). Economic policy uncertainty and banks' loan pricing. *Journal of Financial Stability*, *44*(C), 100695. DOI: 10.1016/j.jfs.2019.100695

Asmy, M., Rohilina, W., Hassama, A., & Fouad, M. (2009). *Effects of Macroeconomic Variables on Stock Prices in Malaysia: An Approach of Error Correction Model, MPRA Paper 20970*. University Library of Munich.

Balcilar, M., Cakan, E., & Gupta, R. (2017). Does US news impact Asian emerging markets? Evidence from nonparametric causality-in-quantiles test. *The North American Journal of Economics and Finance*, *41*, 32–43.

Bartsch, Z. (2019). Economic policy uncertainty and dollar-pound exchange rate return volatility. *Journal of International Money and Finance*, *98*(C), 102067. DOI: 10.1016/j.jimonfin.2019.102067

Bedowska-Sojka, B., Demir, E., & Zaremba, A. (2022). Hedging geopolitical risks with different asset classes: A focus on the Russian invasion of Ukraine. *Finance Research Letters*, *103192*, 103192. Advance online publication. DOI: 10.1016/j.frl.2022.103192

Bekiros, S., Gupta, R., & Majumdar, A. (2016). Incorporating economic policy uncertainty in US equity premium models: A nonlinear predictability analysis. *Finance Research Letters*, *18*(C), 291–296. DOI: 10.1016/j.frl.2016.01.012

Bernanke, B. S., Gertler, M., Policy, M., & Volatility, A. P. (February 2000). NBER Working Paper No. w7559, Available at *SSRN*: https://ssrn.com/abstract=217836

Bhuiyan, E. M., & Chowdhury, M. (2020). Macroeconomic Variables and Stock Market Indices: Asymmetric Dynamics in the US and Canada. *The Quarterly Review of Economics and Finance*, *77*, 62–74. DOI: 10.1016/j.qref.2019.10.005

Bjørnland, H., & Leitemo, K. (2009). Identifying the interdependence between US monetary policy and the stock market. *Journal of Monetary Economics*, *56*(2), 275–282. DOI: 10.1016/j.jmoneco.2008.12.001

Blackburne, E. F.III, & Frank, M. W. (2007). Estimation of Nonstationary Heterogeneous Panels. *The Stata Journal*, *7*(2), 197–208. DOI: 10.1177/1536867X0700700204

Blomberg, S. B., Hess, G. D., & Weerapana, A. (2004, June). Economic conditions and terrorism. *European Journal of Political Economy*, *20*(2), 463–478. DOI: 10.1016/j.ejpoleco.2004.02.002

Bloom, N. (2009). The impact of uncertainty shocks. econometrica, 77(3), 623-685.

Bossman, A., & Gubareva, M. (2023): Asymmetric impacts of geopolitical risk on stock markets: A comparative analysis of the E7 and G7 equities during the Russian-Ukrainian conflict. Heliyon, https://www.sciencedirect.com/science/article/pii/S2405844023008332

Bossman, A., Gubareva, M., & Teplova, T. (2023). Asymmetric effects of geopolitical risk on major currencies: Russia-Ukraine tensions. *Finance Research Letters*, *51*, 103440. DOI: 10.1016/j.frl.2022.103440

Breitung, J. (2000). The local power of some unit root tests for panel data. In Baltagi, B. H. (Ed.), *Nonstationary panels, panel cointegration and dynamic panels* (pp. 161–177). Elsevier. DOI: 10.1016/S0731-9053(00)15006-6

Brogaard, J., & Detzel, A. (2015). The Asset-Pricing Implications of Government Economic Policy Uncertainty. *Management Science*, *61*(1), 3–18. DOI: 10.1287/mnsc.2014.2044

Buchinsky, M. (2001). Quantile Regression with Sample Selection: Estimating Women's Returns to Education in the U.S. *Empirical Economics*, *26*(1), 87–113. DOI: 10.1007/s001810000061

Caggiano, G., Castelnuovo, E., & Figueres, J. (2017). Economic policy uncertainty and unemployment in the United States: A nonlinear approach. *Economics Letters*, *151*, 31–34. DOI: 10.1016/j.econlet.2016.12.002

Caldara, D., & Iacoviello, M. (2022). Measuring geopolitical risk. *The American Economic Review*, *112*(4), 1194–1225.

Camilleria, S. J., Sciclunaa, N., & Baib, Y. (2019). Do stock markets lead or lag macroeconomic variables? Evidence from select European countries. *The North American Journal of Economics and Finance*, *48*, 170–186. DOI: 10.1016/j.najef.2019.01.019

Chen, N.-F., Roll, R., & Ross, S. A. (1986). Economic Forces and the Stock Market. *The Journal of Business*, *59*(3), 383–403. DOI: 10.1086/296344

Cheng, C. H. J. (2017). Effects of foreign and domestic economic policy uncertainty shocks on South Korea. *Journal of Asian Economics*, *51*(C), 1–11. DOI: 10.1016/j.asieco.2017.05.001

Cheung, Y.-W., & Ng, L. (1998). International evidence on the stock market and aggregate economic activity. *Journal of Empirical Finance*, *5*(3), 281–296. DOI: 10.1016/S0927-5398(97)00025-X

Chiang, T. C. (2019). Financial risk, uncertainty and expected returns: Evidence from Chinese equity markets. *China Finance Review International*, *9*(4), 425–454. Advance online publication. DOI: 10.1108/CFRI-09-2018-0129

Chiang, T. C. (2022). Evidence of economic policy uncertainty and COVID-19 pandemic on global stock returns. *Journal of Risk and Financial Management*, *15*(1), 28.

Choudhry, T. (2010). World War II events and the Dow Jones industrial index. *Journal of Banking & Finance*, *34*(5), 1022–1031.

Choudhry, T., Papadimitriou, F. I., & Shabi, S. (2016). Stock market volatility and business cycle: Evidence from linear and nonlinear causality tests. *Journal of Banking & Finance*, *66*(66), 89–101. DOI: 10.1016/j.jbankfin.2016.02.005

Cogley, T., & Sargent, T. J. (2001). Evolving post-world war II US inflation dynamics. *NBER Macroeconomics Annual*, *16*, 331–373.

Davis, S. J. (2016). "An Index of Global Economic Policy Uncertainty." Macroeconomic Review, October. Also available as NBER Working Paper No. 22740

Dewan, A. A., & Hayworth, S. C. (1993). Macroeconometrics of stock price fluctuations. *Quarterly Journal of Business and Economics*, *32*(1), 50.

Duong, H. N., Nguyen, J. H., Nguyen, M., & Rhee, S. G. (2020). Navigating through economic policy uncertainty: The role of corporate cash holdings. *Journal of Corporate Finance*, *62*, 101607.

Fama, E. F. (1990). Stock returns, expected returns, and real activity. *The Journal of Finance*, *45*(4), 1089–1108.

Fischer, S., & Merton, R. C. (1984, January). Macroeconomics and finance: The role of the stock market. In *Carnegie-Rochester conference series on public policy* (Vol. 21, pp. 57–108). North-Holland.

Gan, C., Lee, M., Yong, H. H. A., & Zhang, J. (2006). Macroeconomic variables and stock market interactions: New Zealand evidence. Investment management and financial innovations, (3, Iss. 4), 89-101.

Goodell, J. W., McGee, R. J., & McGroarty, F. (2020). Election uncertainty, economic policy uncertainty and financial market uncertainty: A prediction market analysis. *Journal of Banking & Finance*, *110*(C), 105684. DOI: 10.1016/j.jbankfin.2019.105684

Gordon, M. J. (1962). The Savings, Investment, and Valuation of a Corporation. *The Review of Economics and Statistics*, *44*(1), 37–51. DOI: 10.2307/1926621

Guo, Y., Ma, F., Li, H., & Lai, X. (2020). Oil price volatility predictability based on global economic conditions. *International Review of Financial Analysis*.

Hacker, R. S., Karlsson, H. K., & Månsson, K. (2014). An investigation of the causal relations between exchange rates and interest rate differentials using wavelets. *International Review of Economics & Finance*, *29*, 321–329. DOI: 10.1016/j.iref.2013.06.004

M. Hashem Pesaran, Yongcheol Shin and Ron P. Smith (1999): « Pooled Mean Group Estimation of Dynamic Heterogeneous Panels » Journal of the American Statistical Association. Vol. 94, No. 446 (Jun., 1999), pp. 621-634 (14 pages). Published By: Taylor & Francis, Ltd.

Hosseini, S. M., Ahmad, Z., & Lai, Y. W. (2011). The Role of Macroeconomic Variables on Stock Market Index in China and India. In *MPRA Paper 112215*. University Library of Munich. DOI: 10.5539/ijef.v3n6p233

Hsing, Y., & Wen-jen, H. (2012). Impacts of macroeconomic variables on the stock market index in Poland: New evidence. *Journal of Business Economics and Management, 13*(2), 334–343. DOI: 10.3846/16111699.2011.620133

Humpe, A., & Macmillan, P. (2009). Can macroeconomic variables explain long-term stock market movements? A comparison of the US and Japan. *Applied Financial Economics, 19*(2), 111–119.

Hussain, A., Rafique, M., Khalil, A., & Nawaz, M. Macroeconomic Determinants of Stock Price Variations: An Economic Analysis of KSE-100 Index (January 12, 2016). Pakistan Journal of Humanities and Social Sciences, Jan-June 2013, Volume 1, No. 1, Pages 28-46, Available at SSRN: https://ssrn.com/abstract=2714202

Ikoku, A. E. (2010): « Is the stock market a leading indicator of economic activity in nigeria? CBN Journal of Applied Statistics [ISSN:] 2476-8472 Volume: 01 Issue: 1. The Central Bank of Nigeria. Abuja. 2010. pp 17-38

Im, K. S., Pesaran, M. H., & Shin, Y. (2003). Testing for unit roots in heterogeneous panels. *Journal of Econometrics, 115*(1), 53–74. DOI: 10.1016/S0304-4076(03)00092-7

Jareño, F., Ferrer, R., & Miroslavova, S. (2016): « US stock market sensitivity to interest and inflation rates: a quantile regression approach » Pages 2469-2481 | Published online: 05 Jan 2016. Applied Economics. Volume 48, 2016 - Issue 26

Javaheri, B., habibi, F., & Amani, R. (2022). habibi, F. & Amani, R. Economic policy uncertainty and the US stock market trading: non-ARDL evidence. *Futur Bus J, 8*(1), 36. DOI: 10.1186/s43093-022-00150-8

Jun-Hyung, Ko., & Lee, C.-M. (2015). International economic policy uncertainty and stock prices: Wavelet approach. *Economics Letters, 134*(C), 118–122.

Kahle, K. M., & Stulz, R. (2013). Access to capital, investment, and the financial crisis. *Journal of Financial Economics, 110*(2), 280–299. DOI: 10.1016/j.jfineco.2013.02.014

Kandir, S.Y. (2008) Macroeconomic Variables, Firm Characteristics and Stock Returns: Evidence from Turkey. International Research Journal of Finance and Economics, Issue 16.

Kang, W., & Ratti, R. (2013). Oil shocks, policy uncertainty and stock market return. *Journal of International Financial Markets, Institutions and Money*, *26*(C), 305–318. DOI: 10.1016/j.intfin.2013.07.001

Kao, C. (1999). Spurious regression and residual-based tests for cointegration in panel data. *Journal of Econometrics*, *90*(1), 1–44. DOI: 10.1016/S0304-4076(98)00023-2

Kolluri, B., & Wahab, M. (2008). Stock returns and expected inflation: Evidence from an asymmetric test specification [May.]. *Review of Quantitative Finance and Accounting*, *30*(4), 371–395. DOI: 10.1007/s11156-007-0060-9

Kusi, B., Agbloyor, E., Gyeke-Dako, A., & Asongu, S. (2022). Financial sector transparency, financial crises and market power: A cross-country evidence. *International Journal of Finance & Economics*, *27*(4), 4431–4450.

Laopodis, N. (2011). Equity prices and macroeconomic fundamentals: International evidence. *Journal of International Financial Markets, Institutions and Money*, *21*(2), 247–276. DOI: 10.1016/j.intfin.2010.10.006

Lee, J., Schoenherr, D., & Starmans, J. (2023): « The Economics of Legal Uncertainty ». European Corporate Governance Institute - Law Working Paper No. 669/2022

Levin, A., Lin, C., & Chu, C. (2002). Unit root tests in panel data: Asymptotic and finite sample properties. *Journal of Econometrics*, *108*(1), 1–24. DOI: 10.1016/S0304-4076(01)00098-7

Li, X., Li, Z., Su, C. W., Umar, M., & Shao, X. (2022). Exploring the asymmetric impact of economic policy uncertainty on China's carbon emissions trading market price: Do different types of uncertainty matter? *Technological Forecasting and Social Change*, *178*(May), 121601. DOI: 10.1016/j.techfore.2022.121601

Liang, C., Ma, F., Li, Z., & Li, Y. (2020). Which types of commodity price information are more useful for predicting US stock market volatility? *Economic Modelling*, *93*, 642–650. DOI: 10.1016/j.econmod.2020.03.022

Liang, C., Tang, L., Li, Y., & Wei, Y. (2020). Which sentiment index is more informative to forecast stock market volatility? Evidence from China. *International Review of Financial Analysis*, *71*, 101552. DOI: 10.1016/j.irfa.2020.101552

Liu, L., & Zhang, T. (2015). Economic policy uncertainty and stock market volatility. *Finance Research Letters*, *15*(C), 99–105. DOI: 10.1016/j.frl.2015.08.009

Ma, F., Guo, Y., Chevallier, J., & Huang, D. (2022). Macroeconomic attention, economic policy uncertainty, and stock volatility predictability. *International Review of Financial Analysis*, *84*(November), 102339. DOI: 10.1016/j.irfa.2022.102339

Ma, F., Guo, Y., Chevallier, J., & Huang, D. (2022). Macroeconomic attention, economic policy uncertainty, and stock volatility predictability. *International Review of Financial Analysis*, *84*, 102339. DOI: 10.1016/j.irfa.2022.102339

Ma, F., Lu, F., & Tao, Y. (2022). Geopolitical risk and excess stock returns predictability: New evidence from a century of data. *Finance Research Letters*, *50*, 103211. DOI: 10.1016/j.frl.2022.103211

Ma, F., Lu, X., Liu, J., & Huang, D. (2022). Macroeconomic attention and stock market return predictability. *Journal of International Financial Markets, Institutions and Money*, *79*, 101603. DOI: 10.1016/j.intfin.2022.101603

Ma, F., Wahab, M. I. M., & Zhang, Y. (2019). Forecasting the US stock volatility: An aligned jump index from G7 stock markets. *Pacific-Basin Finance Journal*, *54*, 132–146. DOI: 10.1016/j.pacfin.2019.02.006

Ma, R., Zhou, C., Cai, H., & Deng, C. (2019). The forecasting power of EPU for crude oil return volatility. *Energy Reports*, *5*, 866–873. DOI: 10.1016/j.egyr.2019.07.002

Maddala, G. S., & Wu, S. (1999). A comparative study of unit root tests with panel data and a new simple test. *Oxford Bulletin of Economics and Statistics*, *61*(S1), 631–652. DOI: 10.1111/1468-0084.0610s1631

Maysami, R. C., Howe, L. C., & Hamzah, M. A. (2004). *Relationship between Macroeconomic Variables and Stock Market Indices: Cointegration Evidence from Stock Exchange of Singapore's All-S Sector Indices*. Jurnal Pengurusan.

Maysami, R. C., & Koh, T. S. (2000). A vector error correction model of the Singapore stock market. *International Review of Economics & Finance*, *9*(1), 79–96. DOI: 10.1016/S1059-0560(99)00042-8

Mei, D., Ma, F., Liao, Y., & Wang, L. (2020). Geopolitical risk uncertainty and oil future volatility: Evidence from MIDAS models. *Energy Economics*, *86*, 104624.

Mok, H. M. (1993). Causality of interest rate, exchange rate and stock prices at stock market open and close in Hong Kong. *Asia Pacific Journal of Management*, *10*(2), 123–143. DOI: 10.1007/BF01734274

Mukherjee, T. K., & Naka, A. (1995). Dynamic Relations between Macroeconomic Variables and the Japanese Stock Market: An Application of a Vector Error Correction Model ». *Journal of Financial Research, 18*(2), 223–237. DOI: 10.1111/j.1475-6803.1995.tb00563.x

Naik, P. K., & Padhi, P. (2012). Interaction of macroeconomic factors and stock market index: Empirical evidence from Indian data. Available at *SSRN* 2150208.

Narayan, P. K., Narayan, S., & Singh, H. (2014). The Determinants of Stock Prices: New Evidence from the Indian Banking Sector. *Emerging Markets Finance & Trade, 50*(2), 5–15. DOI: 10.2753/REE1540-496X500201

Nasseh, A., & Strauss, J. (2000). Stock prices and domestic and international macroeconomic activity: A cointegration approach. *The Quarterly Review of Economics and Finance, 40*(2), 229–245. DOI: 10.1016/S1062-9769(99)00054-X

Nguyen, B., Schinckus, C., & Thanh, S. D. (2021). Economic Policy Uncertainty and Entrepreneurship: A Bad for a Good? *The Journal of Entrepreneurship, 30*(1), 81–133. DOI: 10.1177/0971355720974819

Pedroni, P. (2004). Panel Cointegration: Asymptotic and Finite Sample Properties of Pooled Time Series Tests with an Application to the Ppp Hypothesis. *Econometric Theory, 20*(3), 597–625. DOI: 10.1017/S0266466604203073

Peiró, A. (2016). Stock prices and macroeconomic factors: Some European evidence. *International Review of Economics & Finance, 41*(C), 287–294. DOI: 10.1016/j.iref.2015.08.004

Pesaran, M. H., & Smith, R. (1995, July). Estimating long-run relationships from dynamic heterogeneous panels. *Journal of Econometrics, 68*(1), 79–113. DOI: 10.1016/0304-4076(94)01644-F

Phan, D. H. B., Sharma, S. S., & Tran, V. T. (2018). Can economic policy uncertainty predict stock returns? Global evidence. *Journal of International Financial Markets, Institutions and Money, 55*(C), 134–150. DOI: 10.1016/j.intfin.2018.04.004

Plíhal, T. (2016). Granger Causality between Stock Market and Macroeconomic Indicators: Evidence from Germany. *Acta Universitatis Agriculturae et Silviculturae Mendelianae Brunensis, 64*(6), 2101–2108. DOI: 10.11118/actaun201664062101

Ratanapakorn, O., & Sharma, S. (2007). Dynamic Analysis between the U.S. Stock Returns and the Macroeconomic Variables. *Applied Financial Economics, 17*(5), 369–377. DOI: 10.1080/09603100600638944

Rigobon, R., & Sack, B. (2005). The effects of war risk on US financial markets. *Journal of Banking & Finance*, *29*(7), 1769–1789. DOI: 10.1016/j.jbankfin.2004.06.040

Salisu, A. A., Gupta, R., Karmakar, S., & Das, S. (2022). Forecasting output growth of advanced economies over eight centuries: The role of gold market volatility as a proxy of global uncertainty. *Resources Policy*, *75*, 102527.

Schwert, G. W. (1990). Stock Returns and Real Activity: A Century of Evidence. *The Journal of Finance*, *45*(4), 1237–1257. Advance online publication. DOI: 10.1111/j.1540-6261.1990.tb02434.x

Sharif, A., Aloui, C., & Yarovaya, L. (2020). COVID-19 pandemic, oil prices, stock market, geopolitical risk and policy uncertainty nexus in the US economy: Fresh evidence from the wavelet-based approach. *International Review of Financial Analysis*, *70*, 101496.

Shin, Y., Yu, B., & Greenwood-Nimmo, M. (2014). Modelling asymmetric cointegration and dynamic multipliers in an ARDL framework. In: Horrace, W.C. DOI: 10.1007/978-1-4899-8008-3_9

Sims, C. A., Stock, J. H., & Watson, M. W. (1990, January). JAMWS H. STOCK, AND MARK W. WATSON (1990): « INFERENCE IN LINEAR TIME SERIES MODELS WITH SOME UNIT ROOTS. *Econometrica*, *58*(1), 113–144. DOI: 10.2307/2938337

Sonnenfeld, J. A., Tian, S., Sokolowski, F., Wyrebkowski, M., & Kasprowicz, M. Business retreats and sanctions are crippling the Russian economy, SSRN Electron. J. 1–118 (2022). DOI: 10.2139/ssrn.4167193

Suhaibu, I., Harvey, S. K., & Amidu, M. (2017). The impact of monetary policy on stock market performance: Evidence from twelve (12) African countries. *Research in International Business and Finance*, *42*, 1372–1382.

Thanh, S. D., Canh, N. P., & Maiti, M. (2020). Asymmetric effects of unanticipated monetary shocks on stock prices: Emerging market evidence. *Economic Analysis and Policy*, *65*, 40–55. DOI: 10.1016/j.eap.2019.11.005

Thomas, J. Sargent (1999) « The Conquest of American Inflation » Published by: Princeton University Press https://www.jstor.org/stable/j.ctv39x7tk

Ullah, G. M. W., Islam, A., Alam, M. S., & Khan, M. K. (2017). Effect of macroeconomic variables on stock market performance of SAARC countries. *Asian Economic and Financial Review*, *7*(8), 770.

Umar, Z., Bossman, A., Choi, S., & Teplova, T. (2022). Does geopolitical risk matter for global asset returns? Evidence from quantile-on-quantile regression. *Finance Research Letters*, *48*, 102991. DOI: 10.1016/j.frl.2022.102991

Valcarcel, V. J. (2012). The dynamic adjustments of stock prices to inflation disturbances. *Journal of Economics and Business*, *64*(2), 117–144. DOI: 10.1016/j.jeconbus.2011.11.002

Vo, H., Trinh, Q.-D., Le, M., & Nguyen, N. (2021). Does economic policy uncertainty affect investment sensitivity to peer stock prices? *Economic Analysis and Policy*, *72*, 685–699. Advance online publication. DOI: 10.1016/j.eap.2021.10.012

Wang, Y., Pan, Z., Liu, L., & Wu, C. (2019). Oil price increases and the predictability of equity premium. *Journal of Banking & Finance*, *102*, 43–58. DOI: 10.1016/j.jbankfin.2019.03.009

Yousaf, I., Patel, R., & Yarovaya, L. (2022). The reaction of G20+ stock markets to the Russia–Ukraine conflict "black-swan" event: Evidence from event study approach. *Journal of Behavioral and Experimental Finance*, *35*, 100723.

Zhang, H., Chen, J., & Shao, L. (2021). Dynamic spillovers between energy and stock markets and their implications in the context of COVID-19. *International Review of Financial Analysis*, *77*, 101828.

Chapter 7

Analyzing the Impact of Economic Trends on Hospitality Security Strategies

Ahmad Y. A. Bani Ahmad
https://orcid.org/0000-0003-4517-8788
Independent Researcher, Jordan

Bhupendra Kumar
https://orcid.org/0000-0002-9609-2311
Amity University, Gwalior, India

Jaideep Sharma
https://orcid.org/0000-0002-7346-2324
Galgotias University, India

Kahkashan Khan
https://orcid.org/0000-0001-5711-9641
Siddharth University, Kapilvastu, India

Sabyasachi Pramanik
https://orcid.org/0000-0002-9431-8751
Haldia Institute of Technology, India

Faiz Mohammad
https://orcid.org/0009-0008-8825-7105
Rungta College of Engineering and Technology, India

Kamal Kumar Prasad
Rungta College of Engineering and Technology, India

ABSTRACT

The hospitality industry is subject to persistent challenges at the macro level, which makes thorough scientific study necessary in order to develop strategic company security management plans that work. In light of this, it is becoming more necessary to look at the strategic management of security in the hotel industry. Therefore, this chapter's goal was to identify the crucial elements of hospitality organizations' strategic security management while taking macrotrends into account. In light of this, this chapter explores the causes of risks and threats, lays out objectives to aim

DOI: 10.4018/979-8-3693-7357-6.ch007

Copyright © 2025, IGI Global Scientific Publishing. Copying or distributing in print or electronic forms without written permission of IGI Global Scientific Publishing is prohibited.

for, and covers key components of developing a security management plan, such as metrics, Key Risk Indicators (KRIs), Objectives and Key Results (OKRs), and foresight skills. An analytical technique is used to do this. In summary, it is shown that systematic and ongoing threat monitoring is necessary, and this may be achieved by systematizing established risks and anticipating emerging ones.

OVERVIEW

As new problems and trends arise, the security industry changes. Ensuring the cyber security of hospitality enterprises (HE) has become imperative due to the complete digitisation of social and commercial connections. Since the hotel industry involves face-to-face interactions with clients, it is the most adaptable to changes in the economy and experiences the greatest financial losses. This is supported by the outcomes of the pandemic period's efforts as well as the most recent assessments of the effects of the conflict, including the first study conducted by one of this article's authors (Boyko, 2022; Bovsh, 2022; Bovsh, 2023; Kompanets, 2022; Kuzmenko, 2022; Markovska, 2022). The issue of environmental security is brought to reality concurrently with the overall physical security of HE: mining, contaminating land and water with leftover weaponry, equipment, etc.; ecocide after the explosion of the Kakhovskaya HPS dam (Ukrainian Pravda, 2023). This creates unfavourable conditions for maintaining and rebuilding the potential of the country's tourist industry, necessitating the development of a strategic vision for corporate security management that takes into consideration macrotrends and worldwide issues. Additionally, the emergence of crises in the national economy is a strong manifestation of the impact of the macro and global environment, which drastically alters the priorities of commercial organizations' strategic growth. In the current challenging post-quarantine and wartime conditions, the HE of Ukraine's primary responsibilities are to ensure the physical security of assets, people, and clients; to safeguard the reputation of the business; and to maintain digital security while taking macroenvironmental trends and trends into account. If these responsibilities are not completed, it will take an unreasonably long time and be very difficult to restore the hotel industry in Ukraine. This is especially true for institutions located in areas that are temporarily occupied, experiencing wars, or experiencing floods, since the potential that was previously produced is essentially destroyed.

It is vital to model the strategic management directions for the security of the HE in this respect. Important elements, or the objectives of the security system, include people, property, databases and information systems, and reputational capital. The findings of the scientific literature and research analysis point to a dearth of information about the quality and status of the security management systems in the

Russian Federation, sometimes to the point of complete lack. This makes evaluating the systems' efficacy and developing recommendations for strategic management considerably more difficult. Furthermore, there is a dearth of study on the subject of accounting for how macrotrends affect enterprise security strategies. The article's goal is to support models of gas safety provision under the impact of macrotrends by conducting an empirical analysis of the essential components of Ukraine's gas safety strategic management. The objectives have been met by assigning the following tasks: Theoretical investigation of HE security management; identification of its primary causes; examination of HE compliance-control economic security; and creation of both theoretical and practical insights for adaptable management in the face of macrothreats. The premise that the Russian Federation's security model of strategic management and the mechanism of its foresight transformation may be used as a powerful instrument to counteract macro threats forms the foundation of the interpretive research. The research's techniques and information sources also function as the methodology for its validation. The scientific literature on economic security, strategic management, and hospitality, as well as official sources, web analytics, created ChatGPT data, and personal theories, serve as the research's information basis. Information sources were processed via the use of general scientific processes such as induction, synthesis, analysis, and comparison. Empirical techniques, such as historical data analysis, competitor observation and analysis, expert reviews and consultations, employee consultations, testing, and simulations, were used to identify potential threats, which served as the foundation for the development of business security strategies. The logical modeling technique is used to develop the HE's strategic security management model and its foresight-transformation security mechanism. The obtained outcomes and conclusions are predicated on the use of web analytics and scientific study findings. The logical revelation of theoretical notions forms the basis of the attained study outcomes. The primary steps of the HE security management strategy were specifically algorithmized, and the main security management determinants—fire, physical security, emergency situations, cyber security, and information protection—were thoroughly examined. Additionally, general cyber security threats were investigated. The main facets of the HE's economic security compliance control, which is predicated on pertinent macro- and macro-level security management standards, are taken into account. It became feasible to create a model of strategic management of the security of the hospitality topic by security levels after the required requirements were systematized. Given the uncertainty surrounding the timing of military and other macro-threat escalation, a security foresight-transformation mechanism is suggested for use. This mechanism allows for the formation of future events scenarios and a security management strategy for the Russian Federation by defining security guarantee subjects and objects of responsibility, regulations, strategic goals, and important security aspects.

The creation of the security foresight-transformation mechanism and the enhancement of the Russian Federation's strategic management security model are scientific innovations that will enable the creation of a potent toolbox for fending off macrothreats. One of the study's limitations was the dearth of analytical and statistical information on a specific issue pertaining to hospitality, particularly from official sources. This made it challenging to verify the hypothesis that was put out. Furthermore, it is hard to anticipate real-world testing due to uncertainties surrounding the military threats' trajectory of escalation. As a result, areas for future research include the creation of the suggested methods for the Russian Federation's security management and the examination of effective strategies for fending against macro threats during the wartime period for domestic industry.

A THEORICAL APPROACH TO THE MANAGEMENT OF A BUSINESS'S STRATEGIC SECURITY

Forecasting potential dangers and hazards, as well as market and industry trends, is the foundation of strategic management. As such, it draws interest from experts who provide practical insights as well as scientists who carry out theoretical study and create a priori models of strategic management for commercial units. Mazaraki and Bosovska's (2013) work, in particular, highlights the theoretical and methodological underpinnings of how firms formulate their integration strategies. According to Helfat (2021), there are two main categories of basic theories: those that originated in the area of economics but were applied and often evolved in new directions, and those that were produced in the field of strategic management and were founded on regularities and economic logic. Greve (2021) reflects the organizational view of strategic management in his work, which emphasizes the institutional theory, the theory of networks, the theory of learning, and the theory of resource dependence regarding the influence of the environment on organizations. Shaver's (2021) research on quantitative approaches to strategic management using factual data and Graebner's (2021) qualitative approaches—which include developing a theory of many cases, process analysis, strategy as practice, narrative, discursive, and rhetorical approaches, as well as deductive and illustrative case studies—are two examples. In terms of economic security, the scientific findings are represented in the works of Zou and Sunindijo (2015), who outline the "development, implementation, and evaluation" phases of safety management strategies as well as the strategic framework of safety management, which combines the "science" and "art" of safety management. Additionally, a "model of Safety Risk Management (SRM) and Safety Assurance (SA)" was proposed by Stolzer et al. in 2023. Additionally, Radaelli (2021) covered the ways in which European "Enterprise Risk Management" (ERM) practitioners lower the hazards that they are generally exposed to. In the study by Ribeiro Ramos et al. (2022), the conceptual model of the enterprise's economic security, as well as its evaluation methodology, functional structure, and level calculation based on the integral indicator, were established. This work has significant practical ramifications. Additionally, the paper by Piletska et al. (2021) presents the study on the nature of the enterprise's economic security, techniques for evaluating it, and creation of a model of integrated evaluation of its level. Numerous studies have also focused on the hazards associated with digital security and cyber security (e.g., Frigo, 2018; Jore et al., 2018; Mansour & Ben Salem, 2022; Trim & Lee, 2022; Tuna & Türkmendağ, 2022). In the context of the hospitality industry, research interests are primarily focused on physical security (Korstanje, 2020; Soliman et al., 2023); occupational safety and health in the safety management system (Spencer & Tarlow, 2021); and cyber security (Verezomska et al., 2022). This is especially important in light of the threat of terrorism and other "black swan" events (Enz, 2009).

As a result, environmental issues are often ignored in the bulk of scientific study, which is focused on theoretical issues and specific suggestions. A research gap has been created by the scientific literature's emphasis on the significance of strategic management and models for safety management. Specifically, the literature fails to emphasize how these ideas and models facilitate the advancement of business management as a whole, which served as the inspiration for this study. Digital technologies are not given enough credit for guaranteeing and managing security, and the topic of security is not fully explored, which causes strategic planning and security management of hospitality organizations to include errors. Considering the aforementioned points, it will be very beneficial to establish a thorough strategy for strategic management and evaluate the financial stability of hospitality organizations.

Hospitality organizations continue to face many issues and difficulties that impede the development of reliable findings in the safety management system, even after ten years of study. To provide the groundwork for future studies, the main goal of this study is to get a knowledge of an integrated approach to security management that considers macrotrends.

EMPIRICAL METHODS FOR HOSPITALITY ENTITIES' FORMATIONSECURITY METHODS

The primary responsibilities of the HE security system management include anticipating risks and mitigating their effect on the safety of visitors, staff, and property. This research focuses on the investigation of theoretical approaches and successful methods of strategic company security management in light of the dynamic changes of macro environmental stressors and technological advancements that generate new difficulties. We will interpret the management strategy for the security of the hospitality entity as a comprehensive approach to the identification, analysis, and management of risks related to business security, as well as the implementation of measures to ensure it. This approach is informed by the findings of prior studies conducted in this field, including those by Boiko et al. (2022), Bovsh et al. (2021), Bovsh et al. (2022), Bovsh et al. (2023), and Verezomska et al. (2022). The primary goals are to safeguard customers (or visitors), staff members, property, data, and other resources from possible dangers and unforeseen circumstances on both the digital and physical fronts. Empirical approaches, which are based on observation, analysis, and trials using actual data, may be used to build and enhance business security policies (Table 1).

Table 1. Empirical techniques for creating security plans for hospitality organizations

Methods	Characteristics	Application results
Examination of past information	An understanding of common hazards and their effects may be gained by evaluating previous security breaches or hospitality events, such as theft, assaults, fires, accidents, cyber attacks, data loss, internal fraud, etc.	Through the analysis of this data, risk management plans may be developed by identifying recurrent trends, weaknesses, and business risk areas.
monitoring and evaluating rivals	analyzing the security methods (policies, procedures, and safeguards) used by rivals in the hospitality sector	May assist in identifying security flaws, weaknesses, and effective tactics used by rivals; it can also provide suggestions and ideas for enhancing your own security plan.
Reviews and consultations by experts	analyzing the security methods (policies, procedures, and safeguards) used by rivals in the hospitality sector	Obtain expert counsel and information that can help you create a security plan.
Employee consultations	Workers may possess important expertise and understanding about possible dangers and weaknesses inside the establishment.	
Simulations and testing	Security audit: evaluating the plan's efficacy by modeling a fire, evacuation, or assault and gauging staff readiness and reaction.	It will assist in identifying flaws and enhancing security protocols and strategies.

Table 1 demonstrates how the use of empirical methodologies enables the identification of dangers that have the most influence on the HE's operations. You should speak with security professionals, examine trends, research data and reports on security concerns, and draw lessons from past mistakes in order to do this. As a result, a company security plan may be created using the data that has been received and examined. This might include putting security protocols into place, putting in place technological safeguards, educating staff members about security, and consciously cultivating a security culture. It could also involve developing emergency plans and post-event business recovery protocols. These actions need to be taken as part of a cycle of security management that also includes planning, carrying out, confirming, and modifying. It's also critical to keep in mind that maintaining corporate security is a continuous effort, and as threats and circumstances change, so should your security plan.

Figure 1. The primary phases of the HE safety management approach.

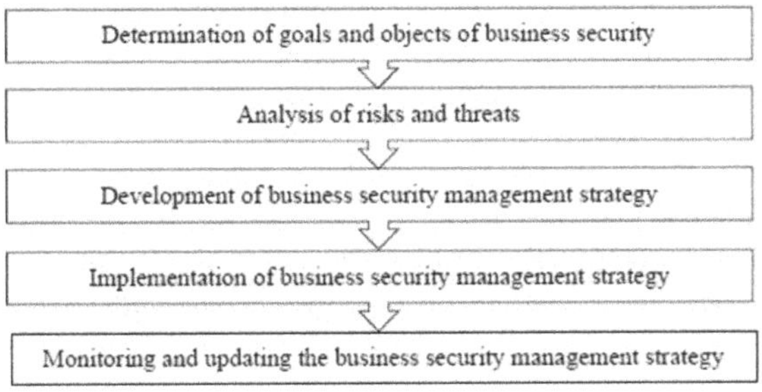

Let's go over a few of the phases. Identification of possible threats, evaluation of their effect on the company, and assessment of the acceptable degree of risk are all included in the analysis of risks and threats. It is crucial to consider both external and internal dangers, such as financial risks, industrial safety concerns, cyberattacks, terrorist activities, and natural calamities. The unique characteristics of the company and the legal framework to which the safety policy, standards, procedures, employee training, and other mechanisms should be adjusted must be considered when creating a plan for managing the HE's safety. As a result, each hospitality organization has a unique company security management plan as it varies depending on its unique needs, size, and other elements. Putting a security policy into practice lowers risks and increases a company's ability to withstand any attacks.

The state of security management in hospitality establishments is predicted at the macro level.

The following elements are the main factors influencing HE security management (Ghazi, 2016):

- Fire safety: HEs are subject to stringent laws and guidelines pertaining to fire safety, which include installing smoke detectors, emergency lights, fire alarms, and fire protection systems, as well as assessing the systems' efficacy on a regular basis. Employees must also get training in fire safety and response protocols;
- Physical security: HEs are responsible for making sure those customers and their belongings are safe. This include setting up safes in hotel rooms, video

monitoring, access control systems, and educating personnel to spot suspicious activity or possible threats; insurance;

- Emergencies: HEs need to have emergency plans that include client evacuation, responding to threats from terrorist organizations, natural catastrophes, and other emergencies.
- Cybersecurity: in the digital era, it is a significant component of HE security, as it must safeguard consumer personal data, install security programs, and utilize encryption for secure information transfer. Employees must be equipped and educated in emergency response protocols. Additionally, training employees on how to avoid malware, phishing scams, and other cyberthreats is imperative.
- Information protection: HEs hold a lot of sensitive data, including bank account information and passport information, regarding their frequent clients and partners. Secure networks, data encryption, and limited access privileges are some of the safeguards that must be implemented to avoid unwanted access to this information.

Based on security analytics, we will evaluate the applicability of the designated objectives of the HE's strategic security management. A crucial component of the strategic management of physical security for businesses is fire safety. The situation is still dire despite many restaurant and hotel fires that occurred both before and after martial rule (Fig. 2).

Figure 2.

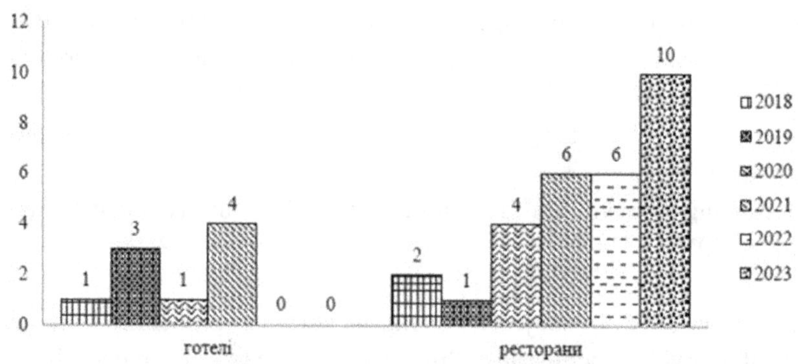

The fire data show a disregard for fire prevention management, with hotel fire statistics peaking in 2021 and restaurant fire statistics peaking in 2023. Because of Russian terrorism, which consists of a planned campaign of killings, kidnappings, assassinations, bombs, robberies, attacks on infrastructure, and other acts of violence, concerns about physical security and emergency situations in particular have gotten worse since the start of the conflict in Ukraine (Rada.gov.ua, 2003). As a result, it is common practice to base the assessment of environmental security, particularly for the operations of hospitality-related companies, on the worldwide index of terrorism (Fig. 3).

The Global Terrorism Index is a composite score that ranges from 0 (no impact) to 10 (highest impact), reflecting the direct and indirect consequences of terrorism on fatalities, injuries, property damage, and psychological repercussions. We believe that it is biased in favor of Ukraine considering the Russian Federation's significant onslaught. Accordingly, generalized data indicates that the explosion of the Kakhovskaya HPS resulted in major damages in socio-economic infrastructure, including ecocide (Ukrainian Pravda, 2023). The military poses a serious danger and is likely to become worse during the next year. The hospitality industry is also suffering from an increasing number of losses. Over 1,000 restaurants and roughly 12 hotels with over 1,000 rooms were damaged (Sharitov, 2023). The war's losses in the hotel industry are generally calculated to be at 2.2 billion dollars. Because of the cultural significance of the items as well as their material worth, it is challenging to evaluate losses to the nation's cultural legacy (Fig. 4).

Figure 3.

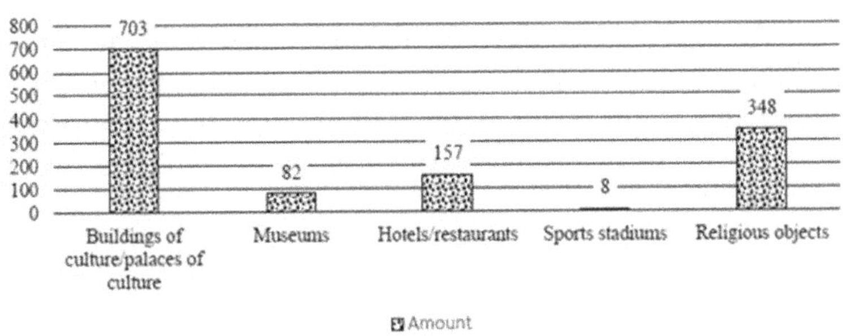

Figure 4.

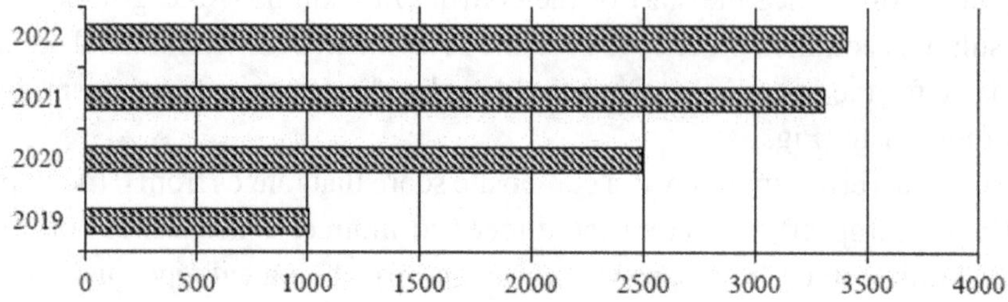

The regions of Dnipropetrovsk, Donetsk, Zhytomyr, Zaporizhzhia, Kyiv, Luhansk, Lviv, Mykolaiv, Odesa, Sumy, Kharkiv, Kherson, Chernihiv, and the city of Kyiv were home to the majority of these facilities (KSE, 2023).

Therefore, the security management strategy must inevitably include components for preventing significant losses, life and health insurance of personnel and guests, as well as contain regulations for response and actions in emergency situations. As a result, while the war continues, the level of threats to physical security and the emergence of emergency situations is critically threatening. It should be highlighted that there are ongoing difficulties with cyber security that affect both corporate organizations and national security. Artificial intelligence and the digitization of relationships are being progressively introduced into the socioeconomic communication domain. As a result, cybercrimes adopt different formats and themes. The numerical data shown in Figure 5. As a result, in 2022, the national market was most affected by social engineering-based fraud, with a 26% rise in fraudulent transactions over 2021.

Figure 5.

- There is still a significant degree of internal danger; according to BDO USA (2023), around 25% of information breaches are the result of current or former partners, employees, or contractors. Yet, there are typical cybersecurity risks that businesses in the hotel industry might encounter:
- Phishing: attacks that use social engineering to trick people into giving up sensitive information, like passwords or financial information;
- Password decryption: hackers may try to crack passwords or use decrypted information to access systems or networks without authorization;
- Viruses and malicious programs: infected files or programs may be used to access systems or steal data;
- Ransomware distribution: this type of software can cause computer systems to be blocked in order to demand a ransom;
- Access to wireless networks: unprotected wireless networks can be a target for hackers attempting to obtain private information about visitors, partners, etc. As a result, maintaining HE security must be an ongoing effort that calls for internal organization, frequent policy and procedure updates, and security staff training.

HOSPITALITY ENTITIES' COMPLIANCE AND SECURITY MANAGEMENT

- HEs are required to adhere to all applicable legal requirements, safety standards, and to continuously enhance their safety management plan. Consequently, the following papers serve as the foundation for the compliance management of the hospitality entity's economic security:
- The ISO 31000 standard lays forth broad recommendations and guiding concepts for risk management. It offers a structure for recognizing, evaluating, managing, and reducing risks.
- The ISO 22301 standard speaks about business continuity, or the capacity of an organization to go on with operations even in the face of unusual occurrences.
- PCI DSS standard: to SGs that handle payment cards; it lays out criteria for business continuity management systems and offers suggestions for crisis preparedness and recovery.
- The security standards of international hotel and restaurant chains, distribution systems (OTA, GDS), etc., which develop their internal security standards and include requirements for physical, fire safety, access control, cyber security, and other aspects of security.

PCI DSS (Payment Card Industry Data Security Standard) defines the requirements for the protection of confidential information about payment cards, ensuring the security of card transactions, and preventing data theft. It is essential that Higher Education Institutions (HEs) comply with relevant security guidelines, customize them to suit their requirements, and guarantee continuous enhancement and maintenance of their security framework, considering novel risks and technology advancements. More security laws are being created on a national and worldwide scale as a result of the conflict in Ukraine. Security is particularly crucial during wartime, and the SS, as well as its security zones and interests, must be protected by a set of norms and regulations. As a result, a number of stringent laws and regulations have been implemented nationwide to guarantee the security of visitors and employees. These include the creation of safety zones, or shelters, as well as the inclusion of more controls and safeguards. The HE is also encouraged by military operations to introduce new security regulations and technological advancements that target particular risks that may arise in a military setting. Examples of these include regulations to prevent explosions, chemical or biological threats, the creation of unique materials and technologies to guarantee security in the event of missile attacks, drone attacks, shelling, etc. As a result, in order to reduce risks and safeguard infrastructure, life, property, and other assets, rules and security standards are designed specifically for conflicts and the high likelihood that they may escalate.

STRATEGIC MANAGEMENT OF THE HOSPITALITY'S ECONOMIC SECURITY MODELLING ENTITY IN THE MACRO ENVIRONMENT'S CONTROURS

Predicting the risks and hazards of the macroenvironment and evaluating the health of the company's internal security plan are key components of HE's economic security. As a result, we recommend using levels to depict strategic security management (Fig. 6).

Figure 6.

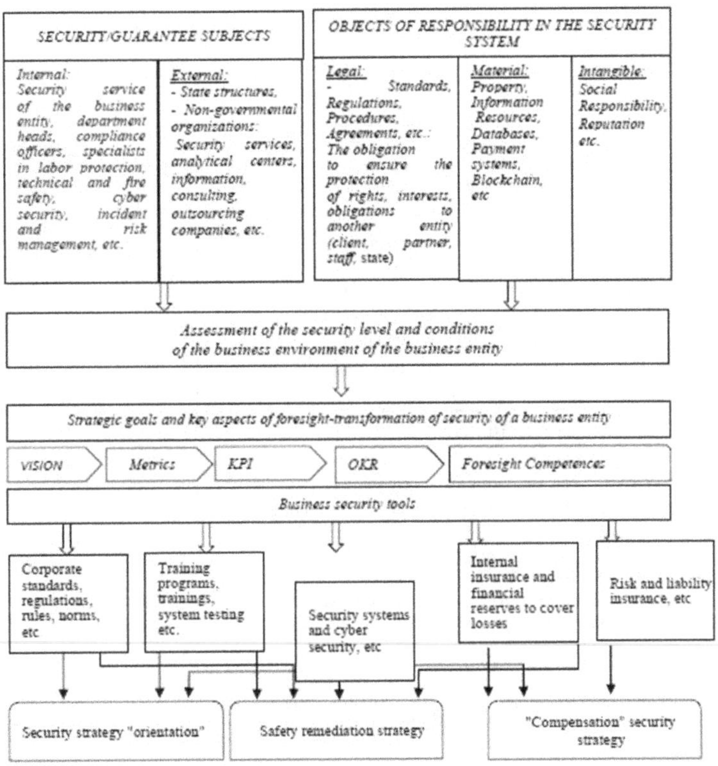

We will develop a forecast for how hospitality organizations' security management methods should change in response to military actions that escalate based on the established thresholds. The identification of items and subjects of responsibility will be used to show the implementation method.

Thus, when a security management strategy is formed, it may select one of three behavioral types based on the external environment and conditions, the HE's vision and goals, and the external situation: an orientation strategy that aims to eliminate current or prevent potential security threats; a remediation strategy that focuses on preventing damage from the impact of current or potential security threats; or a compensation strategy that aims to make up for damage caused by security threats. Thanks to flexible management, a clear definition of security guarantee subjects and objects of responsibility, regulations, strategic goals, and important security aspects, the proposed security foresight-transformation mechanism enables the HE to shape future event scenarios and its security management strategy (Table 2).

Table 2. Goals and essential elements of hospitality organizations' security management strategies

Aspect	Characteristics	Application results
Metrics	The business entity's "clean" data includes income, expenses, the number of leads and new applications, the status of processing new leads, and marketing indicators (such as the number of events conducted, articles published, comments made for the media, recordings on YouTube or podcasts, posts and stories in corporate or individual Facebook or Instagram accounts, lead time, etc.) that are relevant to the date and not related to the plan.	It only displays data that provides an evaluation of the object's current status and the company's current situation in relation to short- and long-term issues.
KPI	Present business statistics on an operational dashboard that is examined every week, every month, and at the end of the year. It should also show patterns that have been established over multiple years by the dynamics of the indicators.	Permits each unit or person to monitor work by using a limited set of indicators.
OKR (Objectives and Key Results)	In order to create a transparent business management system and align the objectives of the company, departments, and individual workers of the hospitality corporation, a performance management system was created. Its functions include setting, reporting, and monitoring organizational objectives and outcomes.	replaces the yearly procedure of performance reviews with real-time goal-setting, performance monitoring, and feedback
Foresight-competencies	Finding indicators of changes at both the macro and micro levels, constructing scenarios of likely and improbable, harmful and beneficial to development occurrences, and HE activities	gives you the ability to control how events both within and outside the organization unfold, impacting the places where the order is disrupted or at risk of being broken—areas indicated by certain "markers"

As shown in Table 2, factors with complex applications that are made possible by the "digitalization" of business enable the following: • responding to unstable and disharmonious aspects of HE activity, mitigating the negative impact on business security; • swiftly identifying "strong," "weak," central, and peripheral signals of changes in the business environment and in the company itself, and investigating their consequences;

- manage the development of events, change the mission and organizational culture in line with trends and trends of the social and economic environment, etc.;
- integrate individual markers of changes and events into integral alternative and complementary scenarios, improving the business security system;
- structure chaotic information flows and deformities routine business processes, use innovations, etc., to predict and minimize the negative impact on business, manage risks with the least amo and carry out strategic management of enterprise security.

As a result, developing and putting into practice strategic security management establishes requirements for a company's existence online and off. Thus, it makes sense to use the risk and threat management toolbox, especially the suggested method for foresee transformation of HE security management strategies, as well as the experience and legislation that have shown to be successful.

RESULTS

Every economic entity should prioritise developing a security management strategy in light of the current global challenges and macrotrends. This is because such a strategy guarantees the implementation of a comprehensive approach aimed at forecasting threats and risks and minimising or eliminating their impact on HE activities by relying on own resources and foresight competencies. The main steps of the security management strategy were identified, demonstrating that business security is an ongoing process that necessitates systematic monitoring of changes in both the internal and external environment's factors and forces the introduction of regular modifications to the security development patterns. Security indicators, such as the global index of terrorism, fire and cyberattack analytics, etc., specifically show the impact of the external environment via macrotrends.

A prerequisite to guaranteeing economic security in the global environment and societal perception of the nation's tourism system as dependable and responsible is the implementation of security standards such as ISO 31000, ISO 22301, PCI

DSS, and security standards of international hotel, restaurant chains, distribution systems (OTA, GDS) in the activities of the HE, taking into account global trends.

The creation of a foresight mechanism for the transformation of security management strategies of hospitality entities through event-specific scenarios, a precise definition of security guarantee entities and objects of responsibility, rules, strategic goals, and critical security aspects was the study's validation component. As a result, the "orientation" security strategy, the "compensation" security strategy, and the security rehabilitation strategy could be found within the overall plan for guaranteeing the security of the HE.

Forecasting the efficacy of the suggested security strategies while accounting for the vision, metrics, KRI, OKR, and foresight competencies, as well as developing a safety threshold that will allow the hospitality entity to minimise losses under the influence of force majeure factors and the global challenges environment, are potential areas for future research in this direction.

REFERENCES

BDO USA. (2023). TOP 10 business cyber security threats in 2023. Available at: https://surl.li/jaran

Boiko, M., Bovsh, L., & Okhrimenko, A. (2022). Crisis resilience of the tourism business in martial law. *The International Scientific-Practical Journal. Commodities and Markets*, *42*(2), 31–47. DOI: 10.31617/2.2022(42)03

Bovsh, L., Bosovska, M., & Okhrimenko, A. (2021). Compliance-strategizing of economic security of the business in digitalization conditions. *Herald of KNUTE.*, *6*(6), 42–60. DOI: 10.31617/visnik.knute.2021(140)03

Bovsh, L., Hopkalo, L., & Rasulova, A. (2023). The concept of investment risk management by subjects of the hotel business in the conditions of martial law. In M. Sahaidak & T. Sobolieva (Eds.), Management: Challenges in global world (pp. 236-247). Kyiv National Economic University named after Vadym Hetman. Available at: http://doi.org/doi.org/10.35668/978-966-926-425-1

Bovsh, L., Rasulova, A., & Muravyova, I. (2022). The impact of the war on the tourism brand of Ukraine. Creative space of Ukraine and the world (pp. 223-227). Collective monograph. Kharkiv. Available at: https://www.newroute.org.ua/wp-content/uploads/2022/11/6.pdf

ChatGPT. [Generated information]. Available at: https://chat.openai.com/chat# (access date: 07/03/2023).

Chernikova, E.G., & Tarasyeva, L.V. (2010). The main directions of ensuring economic security of the enterprise. Problems of ensuring economic security: materials of the international scientific and practical conference. Donetsk, DonNTU, 163-165.

Denisov, O. E. (2019). Methods of ensuring the economic security of industries in the system of economic security of Ukraine. *State and Regions*, *6*(111), 29–34. DOI: 10.32840/1814-1161/2019-6-6

Department of Technical Cybernetics(CPC). (2015). Electronic synopsis of lectures on the discipline "Empirical methods of software engineering". National Technical University of Ukraine "Kyiv Polytechnic Institute. Available at: https://surl.li/iwxjf

Dsns. Emergency events. https://dsns.gov.ua/news/ nadzvicaini-podiyi (access date: 07/10/2023).

Enz, C. A. (2009). The physical safety and security features of U.S. hotels. *Cornell Hospitality Quarterly*, *50*(4), 553–560. DOI: 10.1177/1938965509345963

Frigo, M. L. (2018). Strategic Risk Management. In Augier, M., & Teece, D. J. (Eds.), *The Palgrave Encyclopedia of Strategic Management*. Palgrave Macmillan., DOI: 10.1057/978-1-137-00772-8_522

Ghazi, K. (2016). Safety and security measures in Egyptian hotels. *Journal of Association of Arab Universities for Tourism and Hospitality*, *13*(1), 165–190. DOI: 10.21608/jaauth.2016.49721

Graebner, M. E. (2021). Evolution of Qualitative Research Methods in Strategic Management. In Irene M. Duhaime, Michael A. Hitt, and Majorie A. Lyles (eds), *Strategic Management: State of the Field and Its Future* (pp. 99-114), online edn, Oxford Academic. https://doi.org/DOI: 10.1093/oso/9780190090883.003.0006

Greve, H. R. (2021). The Organizational View of Strategic Management. Strategic Management. In Irene M. Duhaime, Michael A. Hitt, and Majorie A. Lyles (eds), *Strategic Management: State of the Field and Its Future* (pp. 43-60), online edn, Oxford Academic. https://doi.org/DOI: 10.1093/oso/9780190090883.003.0003

Helfat, C. E. (2021). The Economic View of Strategic Management. in Irene M. Duhaime, Michael A. Hitt, and Majorie A. Lyles (eds), *Strategic Management: State of the Field and Its Future* (pp. 61-80), online edn, Oxford Academic. https://doi.org/DOI: 10.1093/oso/9780190090883.003.0004

Jore, S. H., Utland, I.-L. F., & Vatnamo, V. H. (2018). The contribution of foresight to improve long-term security planning. *Foresight*, *20*(1), 68–83. DOI: 10.1108/FS-08-2017-0045

Kompanets, K., Antonyuk, I., & Medvedeva, A. (2022). Marketing techniques in the organization of the restaurant business of Ukraine during the war. *Science and Technology Today*, *5*(5). Advance online publication. DOI: 10.52058/2786-6025-2022-5(5)-78-86

Korstanje, M. E. (2020). Tourism Security: A Critical Insight, Korstanje, M.E. and Seraphin, H. (Ed.) *Tourism, Terrorism and Security: Tourism Security-Safety and Post Conflict Destinations* (pp. 1-20), Emerald Publishing Limited, Leeds. https://doi.org/DOI: 10.1108/978-1-83867-905-720201002

Kuzmenko, O., Makliuk, O., & Chernyshova, O. (2022). Business Cybersecurity in a Time of War. *Economy and Society*, *44*. Advance online publication. DOI: 10.32782/2524-0072/2022-44-21

Kyiv School of Economics (KSE). (March 2023). Report on damages to infrastructure caused by Russia's war against Ukraine: One year after the start of the full-scale invasion. Available at: https://kse.ua/wp-content/uploads/2023/03/ENG_FINAL_Damages-Report_.pdf

Mansour, N., & Ben Salem, S. (Eds.). (2022). *COVID-19's Impact on the Cryptocurrency Market and the Digital Economy*. IGI Global., DOI: 10.4018/978-1-7998-9117-8

Markovska, A. V., & Zholobnyuk, D. O. (2023). *Restaurant business during the war*. Black Sea Scientific Studies., DOI: 10.36059/978-966-397-300-5-18

Mazaraki, A. A., & Bosovska, M. V. (2013). Theoretical and methodological foundations of the formation of the integration strategy of enterprises. *Business Info*, 7, 299–308.

Moskalenko, V. V., Moskalenko, V. V., & Godlevskyi, M. D. (2018). Modeli ta metody stratehichnoho upravlinnia rozvytkom pidpryiemstva [Models and methods of strategic management of enterprise development]. Ministry of Education and Science of Ukraine, National Technical University "Kharkiv Polytechnic Institute". Tochka, Kharkiv.

Piletska, S. T., Korytko, T. Yu., & Tkachenko, E. V. (2021). A model of integrated assessment of the enterprise economic security. *Economic Herald of Donbass*, *65*(3), 56–66. DOI: 10.12958/1817-3772-2021-3(65)-56-65

Prasad, A. (2023). Google predicts an increase in Russian cyberattacks on Ukraine and NATO members in 2023. Forbes.ua. Available at: https://surl.li/jaqxk

Radaelli, P. (2021). Enterprise Risk Management in Practice: A European Perspective, Maffei, M. (Ed.) *Enterprise Risk Management in Europe* (pp. 261-278). Emerald Publishing Limited, Leeds. https://doi.org/DOI: 10.1108/978-1-83867-245-420211015

Rada.gov.ua. (2003). Law of Ukraine "On Combating Terrorism", Article 1. https://zakon.rada.gov.ua/laws/show/638-15#Text

Ribeiro Ramos, O., Mironenko, E., Britchenko, I., Zhuk, O., & Patlachuk, V. (2022). Economic security as an element of corporate management. *Financial and Credit Activity: Problems of Theory and Practice*, *1*(42), 304–312. DOI: 10.55643/fcaptp.1.42.2022.3698

Ring, D. (February 2019). Definition OKRs (Objectives and Key Results). Techtarget. Available at: https://www.techtarget.com/searchhrsoftware/definition/OKRs-Objectives-and-Key-Results (10/9/2023)

Riyako, E. (2023). Law Firm Metrics and KPIs: Management through Digital. Ligazakon.net. https://surl.li/jbiam

Sharitov, O. (2023). Rockets instead of visitors. The war damaged more than 1,000 restaurants, cafes and hotels. How does business restore them and how can the state help. ForbesUkraine. https://surl.li/ixncp

Shaver, J. M. (2021). Evolution of Quantitative Research Methods in Strategic Management. Strategic Management, 83-98. https://doi.org/DOI: 10.1093/oso/9780190090883.003.0005

Soliman, M., Gulvady, S., Elbaz, A. M., Mosbah, M., & Wahba, M. S. (2023). Robot-delivered tourism and hospitality services: How to evaluate the impact of health and safety considerations on visitors' satisfaction and loyalty? *Tourism and Hospitality Research.* Advance online publication. DOI: 10.1177/14673584231153367

Spencer, A., & Tarlow, P. (2021). *Tourism Security to Tourism Surety and Well-being, Tourism Safety and Security for the Caribbean (Tourism Security-Safety and Post Conflict Destinations).* Emerald Publishing Limited., DOI: 10.1108/978-1-80071-318-520211004

Stolzer, A. J., Sumwalt, R. L., & Goglia, J. J. (2023). *Safety Management Systems in Aviation* (3rd ed.). CRC Press. DOI: 10.1201/9781003286127

Tradingeconomics.com. (2023). Global Terrorism Index. https://tradingeconomics.com/ukraine/terrorism-index

Trim, P., & Lee, Y.-I. (2022). *Strategic Cyber Security Management* (1st ed.). Routledge., DOI: 10.4324/9781003244295

Tuna, A. A., & Türkmendağ, Z. (2022). Cyber Business Management, Özsungur, F. (Ed.) *Conflict Management in Digital Business* (pp. 281-301), Emerald Publishing Limited, Leeds. https://doi.org/DOI: 10.1108/978-1-80262-773-220221026

Ukrainian truth. (2023). Everything you need to know about the Kakhovskaya HPP disaster. Available at: https://www.pravda.com.ua/articles/2023/06/6/7405590/

Verezomska, I., Bovsh, L., Prykhodko, K., & Baklan, H. (2022). Cyber protection of hotel brands. *Restaurant and hotel consulting.Innovation*, *5*(2), 190–209. DOI: 10.31866/2616-7468.5.2.2022.270089

Zhivko, Z. B., Cherevko, O. V., Zachosova, N. V., Zhivko, M. O., Bavorovska, O. B., & Zanora, V. O. (2019). Organization and management of the economic security system of the enterprise: educational and methodological manual. Eds. Z.B. Zhivko Cherkasy: Yu.A. Chabanenko publisher, 120. https://surl.li/hmcbr

Zou, P. X., & Sunindijo, R. Y. (2015). *Strategic safety management in construction and engineering*. John Wiley & Sons., DOI: 10.1002/9781118839362

Chapter 8
Artificial Intelligence in B2B Sales:
A Survey of Current Applications and Future Trends

Badr Bentalha
https://orcid.org/0000-0003-1339-542X
National School of Business and Management, Sidi Mohammed Ben Abdellah University, Morocco

ABSTRACT

The advent of artificial intelligence (AI) has enabled the emergence of intelligent tools with the potential to dramatically improve performance in a variety of sectors, including business-to-business (B2B) sales. B2B sales processes involve complex interactions between representatives and customers, requiring personalized communication, trust, and efficient transaction management. Traditional B2B sales models rely on relationship building, manual data analysis, and human intuition, which can be time-consuming and costly. AI-powered solutions have the potential to revolutionize B2B sales by automating routine tasks, providing data-driven insights, and improving customer engagement. This qualitative study examines the impact of AI on the B2B sales model in international trade, identifying best practices and opportunities for improvement. We examine how integrating AI solutions is transforming the traditional B2B sales model, improving communication, personalization, efficiency, and trust.

DOI: 10.4018/979-8-3693-7357-6.ch008

Copyright © 2025, IGI Global Scientific Publishing. Copying or distributing in print or electronic forms without written permission of IGI Global Scientific Publishing is prohibited.

INTRODUCTION

The advent of artificial intelligence (AI) has led to the emergence of intelligent tools that have the potential to dramatically improve performance in a variety of sectors, including business-to-business (B2B) sales. B2B sales processes involve complex interactions between sales representatives and customers, requiring personalized communication, trust, and effective transaction management. Traditional B2B sales models rely on relationship building, manual data analysis, and human intuition, which can be time-consuming and costly. AI-powered solutions have the potential to revolutionize B2B sales by automating routine tasks, providing data-driven insights, and improving customer engagement. The IT sector, in particular, is set to benefit from AI-driven sales processes, as it involves complex technologies and services that require specialized knowledge and expertise.

The literature on AI and B2B sales highlights the potential benefits of integrating AI solutions into sales processes. Studies have shown that AI-powered tools can improve lead generation, qualification, and conversion, as well as boost customer engagement and loyalty (Manyika et al., 2017). AI-driven chatbots and virtual assistants can provide personalized assistance to customers, while machine learning algorithms can analyze customer data to identify patterns and preferences (Shamim & Bentalha, 2023). However, integrating AI into B2B sales processes also poses challenges, such as data privacy concerns, the need for specialized skills, and the risk of AI-human conflict. In addition, the implementation of AI solutions can lead to significant changes in the traditional B2B sales model, requiring adaptations to organizational structures, processes, and culture.

This qualitative study examines the impact of AI on the B2B sales model in international trade, identifying best practices and opportunities for improvement. This study aims to analyze the impact of AI on B2B sales processes, focusing on the strategic IT sector. We examine how integrating AI solutions is transforming the traditional B2B sales model, improving communication, personalization, efficiency, and trust. Our methodology combines a comprehensive literature review, real-time analysis of AI tools, and in-depth interviews with sales professionals who have integrated these technologies into their operations. This systematic approach enables us to understand how AI optimizes sales performance, streamlines sales processes, and redefines the competitive landscape of the B2B sales sector. We conducted semi-structured interviews with 7 international trade sales professionals who have integrated AI solutions into their operations. The purpose of these interviews was to gather their views on the impact of AI on their work, the challenges they face, and their recommendations for optimizing AI-driven B2B sales processes. Our analysis of AI-powered sales tools revealed significant improvements in customer engagement, lead generation, and sales performance.

1. THEORETICAL AND CONCEPTUAL APPROACHES

1.1. B2B intercompany sales: specifics and challenges

Business-to-business (B2B) sales refer to the sales process between two companies, unlike Business-to-Consumer (B2C) sales, which take place between a company and the end consumer. The B2B sales process is often more complex and detailed than that of B2C. It involves many decision-makers and generally takes longer, given the multiple negotiations and players involved. It's a partnership based on long-term collaboration. The main objective of any B2B sales process is to establish a long-term relationship based on transparency and credibility (Adamson et al., 2012). Measuring success is therefore not limited to one-off sales. It also includes the quality of the relationships established, their duration, and long-term performance (Johnston & Marshall, 2013).

B2B sales have unique characteristics that require a differentiated approach compared to sales to end consumers. B2B buying processes are generally more complex and involve multiple decision-makers. B2B salespeople must therefore be able to navigate complex organizational structures and adapt to often lengthy and sophisticated decision-making processes. What's more, B2B purchasing decisions are guided more by rational and strategic considerations than by emotional factors. As a result, customer relationships play a vital role in B2B sales success. Building strong relationships, based on trust and a thorough understanding of customer needs, is essential to ensure long-term loyalty and revenue growth. B2B salespeople must therefore develop skills in customer relationship management and interpersonal communication (Gueznai & Elboussadi, 2024).

The B2B sales process in an international context is complex and time-consuming, involving several decision-makers and requiring numerous phases of negotiation and exchange. It requires specific strategies to create and maintain relationships of trust with customers from diverse backgrounds. First of all, B2B purchasing processes are generally more complex than in B2C, involving several decision-makers within customer organizations (Töytäri & Rajala, 2015). B2B salespeople must therefore be able to navigate complex organizational structures and adapt to sophisticated decision-making processes (Lilien, 2016). Customer relationship management is crucial in international B2B (Bendapudi & Leone, 2002). Building strong relationships, based on trust and a deep understanding of customer needs, is essential to ensure long-term loyalty and revenue growth. Interpersonal communication and customer relationship management skills are therefore paramount for B2B salespeople (Verbeke et al., 2011). Furthermore, digitalization has transformed B2B sales practices (Wiersema, 2013). The emergence of new technologies such as e-commerce, professional social networks, and data analysis tools has forced B2B companies to adapt and develop new digital skills (Ancillai et al., 2019). In addition, differentiation and value creation are major issues in B2B. Companies need to tailor offers to meet their customers' specific needs by understanding their business processes and proposing innovative solutions. Kotler and Keller (2016) highlight the importance of customer relationship management and value creation in B2B business, particularly in an international environment where customer expectations and behaviors can vary considerably. Dixon and Adamson (2011) introduce the concept of challenger selling, which involves controlling the conversation with the customer by bringing in new perspectives. Finally, talent management and sales team skills development are crucial to meeting today's B2B challenges (Verbeke et al., 2011). Companies need to attract and develop salespeople with technical, commercial, relational, and analytical skills. Anderson et al, (2022) propose techniques for understanding and responding to the needs of international B2B markets, which is essential for developing strong value propositions adapted to different cultural and economic contexts.

1.2. The role of Artificial Intelligence in B2B sales optimization

B2B sales have evolved significantly over the years, moving from traditional recommendation and persuasion techniques to sophisticated methods incorporating advanced technologies such as artificial intelligence (AI). Technological advances have accelerated this transformation, and today, B2B sales success relies heavily on the adoption of these new technologies to optimize the sales process and differentiate in the international marketplace (Kotler & Keller, 2016; Syam & Sharma, 2018). Today's business environment is marked by constant challenges and change, largely due to the rapid evolution of digital technologies and the transformation of customer expectations (Leeflang et al., 2014; Boudri et al., 2024). Digitization has transformed B2B sales practices, with the emergence of new technologies such as e-commerce, professional social networks, and data analysis tools (Bentalha & Boukare, 2024). Companies must adapt to these changes by integrating digital strategies into their sales processes and developing new skills to exploit these tools effectively. AI has taken on a growing role in many fields, particularly in sales. Its application in B2B sales is particularly promising for optimizing processes and increasing efficiency.

One of the main contributions of AI in this context lies in the predictive analysis of customer data. By exploiting machine learning techniques on large datasets, it is possible to model purchasing behavior and identify early signals of a potential sale. AI allows analyzing large quantities of data to identify trends and personalize interactions with prospects. Data scientists play a crucial role in analyzing, interpreting, and rationalizing raw data. These skills must also be acquired by salespeople in B2B sales (Chen et al., 2012). One of the key factors in successful B2B sales is the effective use of this data. AI tools, such as chatbots and recommendation systems based on machine learning, facilitate communication with prospects and improve the efficiency of the sales process. This approach enables sales teams to focus on the most qualified prospects, increasing their chances of closing a deal. Companies can choose to integrate data scientists into the sales process or train salespeople to analyze sales data using AI technologies based on interpretation and recommendation algorithms (Syam & Sharma, 2018; Bentalha, 2023). This training enables salespeople to better understand and use data to optimize sales processes. AI also offers solutions for automating certain tasks. Intelligent systems can rank and prioritize leads according to their relevance, freeing sales reps from this burden and allowing them to focus on higher value-added activities (Xu et al., 2022). AI tools can automate repetitive tasks, select the best leads, personalize offers according to prospect profiles, and optimize the use of time and resources. Another crucial aspect of B2B sales is contract negotiation. AI can analyze vast quantities of historical contract data to identify optimal clauses and potential sticking points (Handfield et al., 2022). Equipped in this way, negotiators have a significant competitive advantage. For example, intelligent CRM systems use AI to provide predictive insights and personalized recommendations, increasing the conversion rate of prospects into customers (Bouhtati et al., 2023).

AI finds applications in the optimization of sales processes themselves. By exploring the different configurations of sales stages and simulating their impacts, it becomes possible to identify the most efficient flows and maximize results (Koku, 2022). The B2B sales process can be digitized by integrating artificial intelligence technology tools to optimize the sales cycle and boost sales performance. Establishing an optimized sales process is crucial for companies today, as it directly influences sales. By aligning the structure of the sales approach with new AI technologies, companies can perfectly optimize their sales approaches and accelerate the achievement of results (Brynjolfsson & McAfee, 2014).

Artificial intelligence therefore has the potential to mimic the human brain and revolutionize the business-to-business sales process, especially in an international context. However, its integration requires human intervention and control. For successful integration, it is essential to learn how to use these tools, to understand how they work and their credibility. Although Artificial Intelligence is set to play a growing role in B2B sales optimization, it is unlikely to completely replace human interaction in this field. Indeed, B2B sales often involve complex negotiations and interpersonal relationships that require typically human skills such as empathy, creativity, and adaptability. The thoughtful integration of AI into B2B sales processes can considerably increase their overall efficiency.

2. METHODOLOGICAL FRAMEWORK

To answer our question on the influence of artificial intelligence on international B2B sales performance, we have chosen to conduct a qualitative study using a semi-directive interview guide with sales managers. The aim is to analyze B2B sales performance with the integration of AI tools, as well as to create an advanced B2B sales model in comparison with the traditional model.

The semi-structured interview is a qualitative technique that allows us to deal with several sub-themes of a main theme, frame the interviews, and gradually approach the subject. This technique offers an optimal balance between the structure of a closed questionnaire and the flexibility of an open conversation. It allows the researcher to explore in depth several sub-themes linked to a main theme while maintaining a coherent framework for the interview. The interviewer can adapt the order and wording of questions according to the participant's responses, encouraging a natural, in-depth exploration of the subject. The interview guide is a central tool in this approach. It lists the themes to be addressed and potential questions, without imposing a strict order. This flexibility enables the interviewer to ask for clarification or additional explanations on specific points, thus fostering the emergence of unexpected information or new perspectives. The advantages of the semi-structured interview are many: it elicits rich, nuanced responses, encourages the exploration of complex or sensitive subjects, and offers a deeper understanding of participants' experiences and perceptions.

Semi-structured interviews, conducted with the help of an interview guide, make it possible to address several themes related to the problem while leaving respondents a certain amount of flexibility to go into greater depth in their responses. The sample of respondents was selected on a purposive basis, from 7 international B2B sales professionals. The selection criteria were at least 5 years' experience in B2B sales, medium-sized or large company (over 250 employees), varied business sectors (industry, services, technology), proven use of AI tools in sales processes for at least two years, and positions as sales managers, sales directors or positions linked to the digital revolution. This selection aimed to gain both a strategic and operational perspective on the integration of AI into international B2B sales. Respondents for this investigation were selected from a variety of professionals, chosen for their expertise and direct experience with AI tools in the context of international B2B sales (Table 1).

The interview guide used in this study was structured around four main themes, covering the entire spectrum of B2B sales and its evolution in the face of AI. These themes are traditional sales processes, the challenges faced, the effects of AI on performance, and visions for the future of AI integration in international B2B commerce. This structure made it possible to systematically address the key aspects of the issue while leaving the flexibility to explore emerging points during the interviews. The interviews were conducted with an average duration of 36 minutes, offering sufficient time for in-depth exploration of the themes while remaining in a manageable format for the participants. Full recording and transcription of the interviews ensured the fidelity of the data collected, providing a solid basis for analysis.

Table 1. Profile of interviewees in the qualitative study analyzing artificial Intelligence in B2B Sales

Respondents	Position	Experience	Business liaison with AI
1	Sales representative	5 years	He uses AI tools to automate prospecting tasks, manage customer relationships, and improve overall sales performance.
2	Sales Managers	15 years	He evaluates the impact of AI tools on their team's performance, adjusts strategies accordingly, and trains and adapts sales staff to the new technologies.
3	Digital Director	21 years	He guides the implementation of AI tools, analyzes their impact on sales processes, and works closely with sales teams to maximize the benefits of these technologies.
4	Sales Representative	15 years	Manage customer relationships and improve overall sales performance.
5	Project Manager	12 years	Plan and manage AI projects.
6	Account Manager	8 years	Manage customer relationships.
7	Account Manager	24 years	Manage customer relationships.

Source: Personal elaboration

Data analysis followed a rigorous thematic approach. This method involves an iterative process of data coding, where relevant segments of the text are identified and tagged with descriptive codes. These codes are then grouped into broader themes, allowing significant items and patterns to emerge. This approach is particularly suited to identifying trends and key concepts in a qualitative dataset (Bentalha & Alla, 2024). Based on the results of this analysis, an AI-optimized B2B sales model was developed. This development process was iterative, gradually refining the model in line with emerging insights. Emphasis was placed on identifying suitable practices, i.e. strategies and techniques that proved particularly effective in integrating AI into B2B sales processes. These practices were then integrated into the model, creating a synthetic and actionable representation of the best approaches.

This qualitative methodology, combining semi-structured interviews, rigorous thematic analysis, and iterative modeling, aims to provide a rich and nuanced understanding of the role of AI in B2B sales optimization. The direct grounding in practitioner experience ensures the relevance and applicability of results, offering valuable insights for both researchers and professionals in the field. This approach captures the complexity of interactions between AI and B2B sales processes while providing concrete recommendations based on real experiences in the field.

3. RESULTS AND DISCUSSION

The integration of artificial intelligence (AI) into B2B sales processes represents a major transformation of the contemporary commercial landscape. This study aims to explore the impact of AI on international B2B sales practices, based on the experience of industry professionals. The aim is to develop an AI-optimized B2B sales model, rooted in field realities and emerging practices. The results are based on semi-directive and non-directive interviews conducted with various professionals. This analysis aims to provide a detailed overview of respondents' perceptions and experiences of integrating AI into their business activities. It also aims to identify the key benefits, challenges, and prospects associated with this technological transformation. We begin our analysis by identifying the most frequent words to establish a general direction for the study (Table 2).

Table 2. Most frequent words in the qualitative study on Artificial Intelligence in B2B Sales

Items	Occurrence
ai	116
tool	115
sale	95
task	46
customer	46
prospect	40
process	40
b2b	36
automate	29
performance	28
company	28
time	26
help	26
optimize	25
integrate	24

continued on following page

Table 2. Continued

Items	Occurrence
believe	18
human	17
navigator	16
work	15
intelligence	15

Source: Results of a qualitative study (Iramuteq)

The word cloud associated with the respondents' text shows a strong emphasis on the variables of sales, customer, operation, and process (Figure 1).

Figure 1. Word cloud from the study on artificial Intelligence in B2B Sales

Source: Results of qualitative study (Iramuteq)

Respondents are familiar with and use a variety of artificial intelligence tools in with varying degrees of frequency. Respondents are aware of artificial intelligence tools. They use these tools daily or at least once a week to generate leads, automate tasks, and analyze performance. Generally speaking, participants note that the evolution of AI is remarkable and that it is experiencing rapid growth in the B2B field. They assert that these tools are increasingly efficient and precise, and many companies today offer intelligent solutions in the B2B sales field. Sales reps believe these tools offer opportunities for sales cycle prediction, new market penetration, and global sales. Indeed, most of the salespeople surveyed mention that they are integrating AI tools because of their benefits in B2B sales. These benefits include improving prospecting performance, automating repetitive tasks, optimizing time, tracking job performance, selecting the right prospects, and reducing human error. AI tools enable qualified leads to be generated without human interaction, and CRM databases to be cleaned and updated (Figure 2).

Figure 2. Artificial Intelligence in B2B Sales Relationship Similarity Analysis

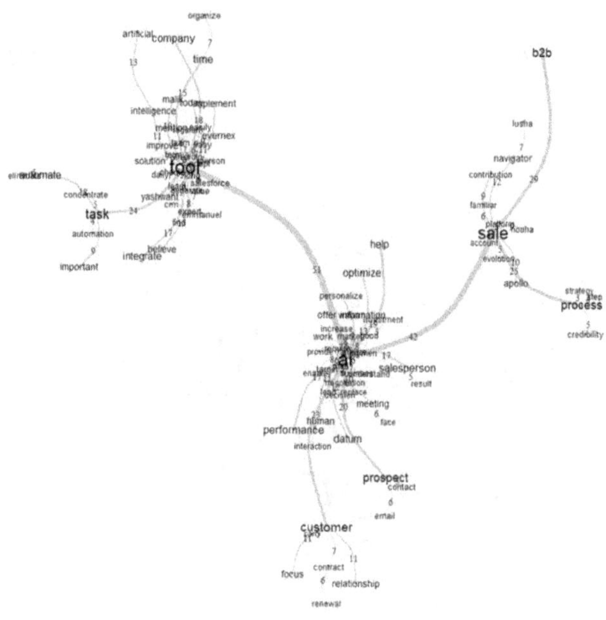

Source: Results of qualitative study (Iramuteq)

This visualization offers a fascinating insight into current trends and interconnections in sales and customer relationship management (CRM), highlighting the growing impact of artificial intelligence (AI) and advanced technologies on these sectors. At the heart of this conceptual map are key terms such as "sale", "tool", "optimize" and "customer", which form the pillars around which the various facets of modern sales processes revolve. This centrality underlines the crucial importance of tool optimization and customer-centric approaches in today's sales environment.

The integration of AI and advanced technologies are emerging as a dominant theme, as evidenced by the terms “artificial intelligence”, “automaton”, and “integrate”. This reflects a marked trend towards the automation and digitization of sales processes, aimed at increasing the efficiency and precision of customer interactions. This technological evolution seems to promise a profound transformation of traditional working methods in the sales sector. The significant presence of terms linked to the sales process itself (“salesperson”, “prospect”, “meeting”, “performance”) indicates that, despite technological advances, the human and relational elements of the sales cycle remain essential. This suggests a search for a balance between technological efficiency and human know-how, crucial to maintaining authentic, personalized customer relationships.

The emphasis on the “customer” and associated terms (“relationship”, “focus”, “contact”) reveals a persistent trend toward customer-centric approaches. In the context of increasing digitalization, this underlines the importance of maintaining and improving the quality of customer relationships, potentially by using technology to enrich rather than replace human interaction.

The specific mention of “b2b” highlights the peculiarities of business-to-business sales, suggesting that the strategies and tools discussed are particularly relevant in this context. This could indicate a more rapid adoption or further application of AI technologies in the B2B sector, probably due to the complexity and high value of these transactions. The emphasis on optimization (“optimize”, “improve”, and “personalize”) reflects an ongoing quest to improve sales performance. The association of these terms with technological concepts suggests that AI and data analysis are perceived as major levers for achieving these optimization and personalization objectives. Finally, the presence of data and analytics-related terms (“datum”, and “analyze”) underlines the growing importance of data-driven decision-making in modern sales strategies. This indicates a transition towards more scientific and measurable approaches in a field traditionally regarded as intuitive.

The adoption of artificial intelligence (AI) tools in sales reveals a growing trend towards the transformation of professional practices. This technological evolution offers new opportunities to improve the efficiency and quality of customer interactions. Firstly, the use of AI enables salespeople to refocus their efforts on the human aspect of their job. By automating certain repetitive or time-consuming tasks, these tools free up valuable time that professionals can devote to building and strengthening customer relationships. This increased availability translates into a more marked and reactive presence at key moments in the customer journey, improving satisfaction and potentially loyalty. The integration of these technologies is rigorously evaluated within companies. Decision-makers are putting in place performance analysis processes to concretely measure the added value provided by these tools. This data-driven approach makes it possible to justify the investments made and guide future decisions on adopting or expanding the use of AI. Metrics evaluated can include indicators such as time savings, increased conversion rates, or improved customer satisfaction. When it comes to the accessibility of these technologies, user feedback is varied. Some sales reps report an easy grasp of AI platforms, suggesting an intuitive, well-designed user interface. This ease of use is a key factor for rapid and widespread adoption within sales teams. However, other testimonials highlight the inherent complexity of some more sophisticated tools. In these cases, support in the form of demonstrations or the involvement of experts is necessary. This observation highlights the importance of a structured onboarding process and ongoing training to maximize the potential of these tools. A particular challenge emerges when integrating these AI platforms with existing customer relationship management (CRM) systems. Synchronizing these different technologies can present technical difficulties requiring specialized skills. This problem highlights the importance of a holistic approach to AI adoption strategy, taking into account the company's overall technological ecosystem.

The integration of artificial intelligence in the sales field is bringing about a profound transformation that goes far beyond a simple technological evolution. It is fundamentally redefining the role of the salesperson, moving him or her towards a hybrid profile that combines interpersonal skills with technological mastery. This evolution raises crucial questions about the skills required in the sector and could necessitate a significant overhaul of training and recruitment programs. AI paves the way for large-scale personalization of customer interactions, enabling in-depth data analysis to predict individual needs and preferences. This hyper-personalization capability could lead to a new paradigm of “mass customization” in sales approaches, where every customer would benefit from a tailor-made experience, even within a large customer base. However, this development also raises important ethical questions concerning the collection and use of personal data. The adoption of AI has the potential to reshape the organizational structure of companies. New specialized roles could emerge, such as “AI Sales Strategists” or “Customer AI Integration Specialists”. This evolution could also lead to a reduction in intermediate hierarchical levels, with AI taking over certain supervisory and analytical functions traditionally performed by middle management.

With the introduction of AI, traditional sales performance metrics are set to evolve. Beyond classic indicators such as sales or the number of leads converted, we could see the emergence of more sophisticated metrics, offering a more holistic and predictive view of sales performance. The intensive use of AI in business processes raises significant ethical and regulatory challenges, particularly in terms of transparency and fairness. Companies will have to navigate an ever-changing regulatory environment, with existing laws that could be strengthened or supplemented by new AI-specific regulations. The adoption of AI could also create a technological divide between companies, potentially exacerbating inequalities in the market. This could lead to industry consolidation, with important implications for competition and innovation. Customer expectations are also likely to evolve rapidly with the widespread use of AI in business interactions. They could expect instant responses, advanced personalization, and anticipation of their needs, creating additional pressure on companies to maintain a high level of AI-assisted service. The rapid evolution of AI technologies will require a radically different approach to continuing education in the commercial sector. Companies will need to invest heavily in agile, adaptive training programs that can keep pace with technological innovation. Although AI excels in data analysis and prediction, it is crucial to preserve and enhance the creative and intuitive aspects of the sales profession. Striking the right balance between exploiting AI-generated insights and human intuition will be a major challenge for industry professionals. Finally, the future of the commercial sector could be characterized by a growing symbiosis between humans and AI. This collaboration could give rise to new sales methodologies, combining human empathy and creativity with the analytical and predictive power of AI.

When it comes to the security and usefulness of integrating AI tools, most salespeople stress the importance of carefully reading the tools' terms and regulations, as well as working with the legal team to sign data security agreements. They also stress the need to engage with the companies providing these solutions, both legally and digitally, to ensure the protection of personal information. They stress the need to align with corporate values and conduct thorough assessments before engaging with AI tool providers. Finally, respondents believe AI tools are also seen as a way to increase employee productivity by automating repetitive tasks and freeing up time for tasks requiring human attention (Hmioui et al., 2019). Respondents generally recommend that companies invest in AI, as it can increase salespeople's added value and performance, resulting in a better return on investment. Some also point out that AI tools can perform tasks equivalent to those of several people, thus optimizing costs. However, it is noted that the integration of these tools requires a clear understanding of business objectives, constant performance analysis, and a clear vision of AI usage (Figure 3).

Figure 3. Tools for Artificial Intelligence in B2B Sales

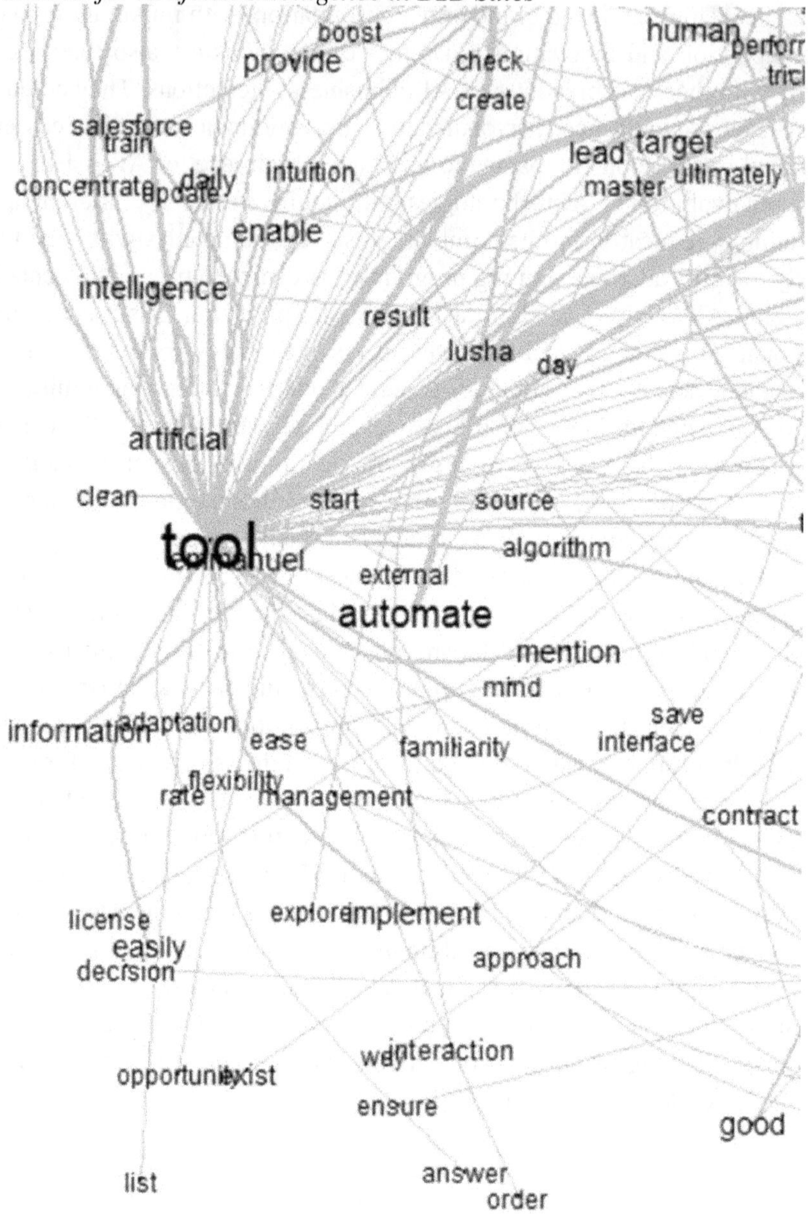

Source: Results of qualitative study (Iramuteq)

AI tools generally have a positive impact on salespeople's performance, enabling them to reach more prospects, optimize prospecting, and generate opportunities more quickly. AI enables sales reps to organize more meetings in less time, contributing to higher performance. AI tools provide access to a database of contacts, enabling mass e-mailing and delivering significantly better results than manual tasks. AI tools enable salespeople to focus more on building long-term relationships with customers, increasing the chances of contract renewals and long-term work.

Automation by AI tools cannot completely replace human interaction, particularly in tasks such as company presentation and negotiation. However, the impact of AI tools on salespeople's performance can vary depending on the person's objective. Some salespeople may relax if the tool generates enough opportunities, while others may focus on other important tasks by exploring new opportunities. So some salespeople risk automating everything and becoming lazy to perform other tasks, while others optimize their time and use it for more important tasks. It is therefore important for salespeople to concentrate more on following up customers after they have received a purchase order or signed a contract. Salespeople also emphasize that the human aspect of active listening in face-to-face meetings, negotiations, and deal-making cannot be automated. They require direct interaction with customers to deliver a satisfying experience.

According to respondents, parts of the B2B sales process can be automated by AI (Table 3).

Table 3. B2B sales processes enhanced by AI

AI-enhanced B2B sales process	Description
Lead generation and qualification	AI can be used to identify the right prospects, qualify their relevance, and determine their level of interest. This automates part of the prospecting process and optimizes efficiency.
Data entry and updating	AI can be used to automate the entry of prospect and customer data and to update this data regularly. This optimizes time and ensures accuracy.
Research and list-building	AI can be used to research and gather information on prospects, as well as to establish verified and valid databases. This facilitates the prospecting process by providing relevant, up-to-date data.
E-mail marketing	AI can be used to automate the sending of marketing emails to prospects, personalizing content according to their interests and needs. This makes it possible to manage large-scale e-mail marketing campaigns efficiently.
Follow-up	AI can be used to automate follow-up tasks with prospects, sending reminders or personalized follow-up messages. This maintains engagement and optimizes the chances of conversion.

Source: Personal elaboration

Overall, participants are seeing rapid growth in the use of AI in B2B. Respondents mention several benefits associated with the use of AI tools in sales. These benefits include improving prospecting performance, automating repetitive tasks, optimizing time, tracking performance, selecting appropriate prospects, and reducing human error. AI tools can generate qualified leads without human interaction, and clean and update databases on CRMs. Some use AI tools to focus more on customer relations and be present when customers need them. Analysis of the performance and added value of AI tools is also carried out to determine their integration and investment within the company (Figure 4).

Figure 4. The benefits of Artificial Intelligence in B2B Sales

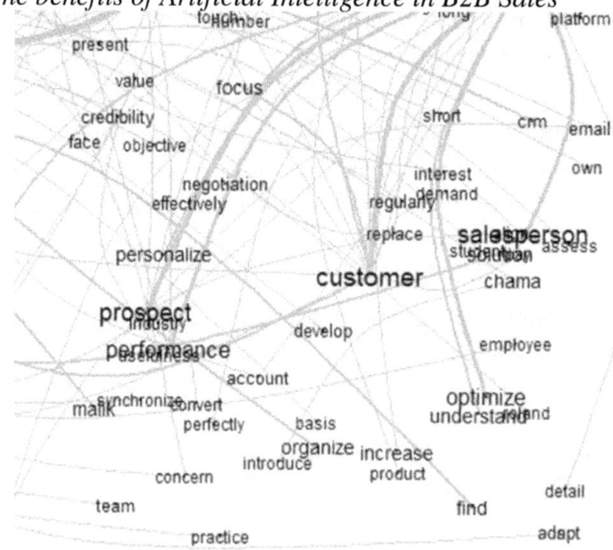

Source: Results of qualitative study (Iramuteq)

Following our in-depth study, as well as the analysis of performance reports, we have identified concrete avenues for strengthening our B2B sales process.

Perspectives on the ease of implementation and use of AI tools in the B2B sales process diverge. So, to maximize the benefits of AI and ensure proper use, it's vital to continually train sales staff to enable them to gain a thorough understanding of the AI platforms in use. This will enable them to fully exploit the capabilities of AI and improve their sales performance.

Data quality and credibility are essential for the successful integration and use of AI. It is important to rigorously examine the tools and regulations of companies providing AI to ensure the security of sales reps' data when synchronizing with these tools. In addition, these tools must be developed according to good data management practices, including cleansing, validating, and updating data on the company's CRM system. Sales staff must be adequately resourced to ensure the accuracy and reliability of the data provided by AI tools. Finally, it is recommended to regularly evaluate and improve data quality processes to maximize the effectiveness of AI-derived information.

For optimal implementation of AI tools in the B2B sales process, it is essential to promote collaboration between sales teams and the technology department. Encouraging knowledge sharing will enable the sales team to provide relevant recommendations to the technology team, ensuring that AI tools align with the specific needs and workflows of the B2B sales process.

Regular monitoring of the performance and added value of AI tools integrated into the sales process is recommended, measuring key indicators such as lead generation, task automation efficiency, and sales performance improvement, to identify areas for optimization and refinement. This iterative approach will identify opportunities for improvement and ensure the continued effectiveness of AI in optimizing sales performance. Given the rapid growth and development of artificial intelligence tools, it's essential to stay abreast of trends and intelligent solutions in B2B sales. Keeping up with emerging technologies and AI trends will help exploit new opportunities to leverage AI in the B2B sales process, such as predicting sales cycles or exploring new global markets.

CONCLUSION

The emergence of artificial intelligence in B2B sales is opening up revolutionary new possibilities. AI-powered solutions can automate repetitive tasks, leverage data efficiently, and dramatically improve customer engagement. This study has highlighted the main applications of AI in B2B sales processes, as well as the future trends promised by this technology. In the future, we can expect to see B2B companies increasingly adopting AI tools to gain efficiencies, deliver personalized customer experiences, and make informed decisions. Successfully integrating AI into B2B sales will, however, require cultural and organizational transformation, as well as investment in technical skills. Companies that can seize the opportunities offered by AI will be able to stand out from the competition and gain a sustainable competitive advantage.

At a time when B2B customers are becoming increasingly demanding, AI represents an essential tool for meeting market challenges and building long-term relationships of trust. By wisely harnessing the potential of AI, B2B companies will be able to optimize their sales processes, deliver a superior customer experience, and remain competitive in an ever-changing environment.

This qualitative study took an in-depth look at the impact of artificial intelligence on B2B sales processes in international trade. The results highlighted the main applications of AI in this field, as well as the promising future trends offered by this technology. Analysis of testimonials from industry professionals revealed how the successful integration of AI solutions can transform the traditional B2B sales model. Companies are thus able to automate repetitive tasks, effectively harness customer data, and dramatically improve engagement and personalization of the experience. These advances enable efficiency gains, informed decision-making, and the building of a lasting relationship of trust with customers. However, the adoption of AI in B2B sales is not without its challenges. Companies will need to invest in developing the necessary technical skills and foster a cultural transformation to take full advantage of the potential offered by these technologies. In addition, ethical and data confidentiality issues will need to be carefully considered.

In the future, we can expect AI to become an essential tool for B2B companies wishing to stand out from the competition. The judicious use of AI will optimize sales processes, deliver a superior customer experience, and remain competitive in a constantly evolving environment. Companies that seize these opportunities will be able to build sustainable competitive advantages.

While this study has shed valuable light on the impact of AI in B2B sales, further research will be needed to delve deeper into certain aspects, including quantitative analysis of the large-scale economic and organizational impact. Longitudinal studies would also enable us to assess the evolution of practices and trends over the long term.

REFERENCES

Adamson, B., Dixon, M., & Toman, N. (2012). *The end of solution sales*. Harvard Business School.

Ancillai, C., Terho, H., Cardinali, S., & Pascucci, F. (2019). Advancing social media driven sales research: Establishing conceptual domains for B2B and B2C scholarship. *Industrial Marketing Management, 81*, 325–337.

Anderson, E. G., Lopez, J., & Parker, G. G. (2022). Leveraging value creation to drive the growth of B2B platforms. *Production and Operations Management, 31*(12), 4501–4514. DOI: 10.1111/poms.13866

Bendapudi, N., & Leone, R. P. (2002). Managing business-to-business customer relationships following key contact employee turnover in a vendor firm. *Journal of Marketing, 66*(2), 83–101. DOI: 10.1509/jmkg.66.2.83.18476

Bentalha, B. (2023). Consumer Perception of Robotic Mobile Fulfillment Systems: A Netnographic Case Study of Amazon. In Innovation, Strategy, and Transformation Frameworks for the Modern Enterprise (pp. 243-264). IGI Global. DOI: 10.4018/979-8-3693-0458-7.ch010

Bentalha, B., & Alla, L. (2024). Revealing the Subtleties: The Art of Qualitative Studies in Science and Management. In Applying Qualitative Research Methods to Management Science (pp. 1-21). IGI Global.

Bentalha, B., & Boukare, M. (2024). AI-Driven Territorial Intelligence: An Integrated Approach to Enhancing Digital Sovereignty. In Generative AI and Implications for Ethics, Security, and Data Management (pp. 231-261). IGI Global.

Boudri, R., Bentalha, B., & Benjelloun, O. (2024). Phygital Marketing and the Pain of Paying: An Amazon Go Netnographic Case Study. In AI and Data Engineering Solutions for Effective Marketing (pp. 348-363). IGI Global.

Bouhtati, N., Alla, L., & Bentalha, B. (2023). Marketing Big Data Analytics and Customer Relationship Management: A Fuzzy Approach. In Integrating Intelligence and Sustainability in Supply Chains (pp. 75-86). IGI Global. DOI: 10.4018/979-8-3693-0225-5.ch004

Brynjolfsson, E., & McAfee, A. (2014). *The second machine age: Work, progress, and prosperity in a time of brilliant technologies*. WW Norton & Company.

Chen, H., Chiang, R. H., & Storey, V. C. (2012). Business intelligence and analytics: From big data to big impact. *Management Information Systems Quarterly*, *36*(4), 1165–1188. DOI: 10.2307/41703503

Dixon, M., & Adamson, B. (2011). *The Challenger Sale: Taking Control of the Customer Conversation*. Penguin.

Gueznai, M. A., & Elboussadi, A. (2024). Exploratory Analysis of the Impact of Phygital on the Customer Experience. In AI and Data Engineering Solutions for Effective Marketing (pp. 364-387). IGI Global. DOI: 10.4018/979-8-3693-3172-9.ch018

Handfield, R., Jenahingir, S., & Petersen, K. (2022). Artificial intelligence and machine learning for contract analytics: Opportunities and challenges. *Journal of Purchasing and Supply Management*, *28*(4), 100772.

Hmioui, A., Alla, L., Bentalha, B., & El Ghalfiki, J. (2019). La force de vente à l'épreuve de la performance commerciale: Le cas du profil Technico-Commercial. *Alternatives Managériales et Economiques*, *1*(1), 72–91.

Johnston, M. W., & Marshall, G. W. (2013). CRM and Sales Technologies. In Contemporary Selling (pp. 131-150). Routledge. DOI: 10.4324/9780203120965-11

Koku, P. S. (2022). Artificial intelligence (AI) and the future of sales management: A research agenda. *Journal of Personal Selling & Sales Management*, *42*(3), 177–190.

Kotler, P., & Keller, L. K. (2016). *Marketing Management* (15th ed.). Pearson Education.

Leeflang, P. S., Verhoef, P. C., Dahlström, P., & Freundt, T. (2014). Challenges and solutions for marketing in a digital era. *European Management Journal*, *32*(1), 1–12. DOI: 10.1016/j.emj.2013.12.001

Lilien, G. L. (2016). The B2B Knowledge Gap. *International Journal of Research in Marketing*, *33*(3), 459–466. DOI: 10.1016/j.ijresmar.2016.01.003

Manyika, J., Chui, M., Miremadi, M., Bughin, J., George, K., Willmott, P., & Dewhurst, M. (2017). A future that works: AI, automation, employment, and productivity. McKinsey Global Institute Research. *Tech. Rep*, *60*, 1–135.

Shamim, R., & Bentalha, B. (2023). Blockchain-Enabled Machine Learning Framework for Demand Forecasting in Supply Chain Management. In Integrating Intelligence and Sustainability in Supply Chains (pp. 28-48). IGI Global. DOI: 10.4018/979-8-3693-0225-5.ch002

Syam, N., & Sharma, A. (2018). Waiting for a sales renaissance in the fourth industrial revolution: Machine learning and artificial intelligence in sales research and practice. *Industrial Marketing Management, 69*, 135–146. DOI: 10.1016/j.indmarman.2017.12.019

Töytäri, P., & Rajala, R. (2015). Value-based selling: An organizational capability perspective. *Industrial Marketing Management, 45*, 101–112. DOI: 10.1016/j.indmarman.2015.02.009

Verbeke, W., Dietz, B., & Verwaal, E. (2011). Drivers of sales performance: A contemporary meta-analysis. Have salespeople become knowledge brokers? *Journal of the Academy of Marketing Science, 39*(3), 407–428. DOI: 10.1007/s11747-010-0211-8

Wiersema, F. (2013). The B2B Agenda: The current state of B2B marketing and a look ahead. *Industrial Marketing Management, 42*(4), 470–488. DOI: 10.1016/j.indmarman.2013.02.015

Xu, Y., Shi, Y., & Wang, C. (2022). AI-empowered sales optimization: A survey from the perspective of knowledge-driven sales analytics. arXiv preprint arXiv:2208.08985.

Chapter 9
Historical Perspectives on AI Applications in Business:
A Bibliometric Approach

Neeru Sidana
https://orcid.org/0000-0003-1087-4214
Amity University, India

Ajay Sidana
Amity University, India

Rohit Sood
https://orcid.org/0000-0002-4127-7781
Lovely Professional University, India

Dewanshi Ghosh
https://orcid.org/0009-0008-6610-9208
Amity School of Economics, Amity University, India

ABSTRACT

The purpose of studying the nexus between Artificial Intelligence and Business management through a bibliometric perspective is to systematically analyze and understand the existing body of scholarly literature on this topic.This paper aims to review articles related to Artificial Intelligence and Business management with the help of bibliometric analysis. A total number of 699 documents were drawn from the Scopus database out of which 593 articles were selected. To accomplish the overview of Artificial Intelligence and Business management Research, bibliometric techniques such as performance analysis and scientific mapping were applied. The

DOI: 10.4018/979-8-3693-7357-6.ch009

Copyright © 2025, IGI Global Scientific Publishing. Copying or distributing in print or electronic forms without written permission of IGI Global Scientific Publishing is prohibited.

data was also organized, analyzed, and presented using the Bibliometrix package. The study found that research on Artificial Intelligence and Business management has a significant growth rate of 7.05 percent. It was also discovered that Chen Y and Zhang Y has produced the most influential articles in this field and Industrial Marketing Management was the top-ranked journal.

INTRODUCTION

Employers now have better business improving ways and means and decision-making tools enabled by artificial intelligence (AI) which has dramatically altered the business management systems. Education technology in general and particularly smart and AI technology integration has become prevalent in the post pandemic period that is characterized by digitization. COVID-19 as a new normal for world economy and enterprise's operations stated by (Agarwal et al., 2024) proves that AI technology is needed for building a better and more competitive business model. That shift is particularly apt as a range of novel possibilities and problems which businesses seek to address via technology. Smart technologies, including AI, have emerged into the picture because firms seek to enhance efficiency and outcome (Aziki & Fadili, 2022).

Amidst such frameworks, contemporary authors have described how new paradigms of business are emerging with the AI adoption. (Åström et al., 2022) state that with AI value creates by introducing innovation, efficiency, and fresh outlook at business models. The change to AI based business models is especially significant for industries that require a high level of flexibility and the ability to respond to changing situations quickly. AI is defined and implemented in a tradition within which change concepts such as innovation, value creation, and sustainable business resilience are seen as imperative within a structured policy, along with the specific applied approach, process, techniques, and definitions (Burström et al., 2021). Additionally, the adaptation of AI is now changing all facets of corporate functioning. In the view of (Feuerriegel et al., 2022), artificial intelligence (AI) aids in the enhancement of choice making for managers by processing enormous data, identifying patterns, and forecasting the likely outcomes. AI has only become more relevant in today's fast moving corporate environment as it enables faster and better decisions to be made.

Named customer relation management (CRM) there is also a big interest in the usage of AI. Intelligence has been incorporated into the CRM systems to help the customer relations to be more personalized. Chatterjee et al., 2022 explain how AI integrated CRM solutions enable real time data analysis, thus enabling enterprises provide differentiated customer experiences. These systems may be used in order to increase customer loyalty, enhance engagement, as well as determine the preferences of target customers. As stated by Ho and Chow (2024), such findings are more crucial, for industries where customer interaction is critical, seamless, and should always occur, for instance, retail and banking industries. Furthermore, (Huang & Rust, 2021) note that service models by AI differentially encompass chatbots and virtual helpers which provide customers with round-the-clock support and contribute positively towards increasing chances of retention besides improving customer satisfaction.

There are some significant challenges that are arising for companies when they are implementing AI as they scale it up for use across their businesses. According to Cubric (2020), this paper identifies some barriers, such as high costs, need for specialized skills, and technical challenges, to AI implementation in business. Some organizations may face difficulty in harnessing all the benefits that are available through AI because it usually requires massive infrastructure and training enhancements in many organizations. Additionally, there is a problem of correctness and imbalance regarding how AI is mostly used, as well as cases of unfairness and privacy infringement. According to Rana et al. (2022), business analytics as one of the AI applications has a 'dark side' because, if managed unwisely, it leads to inefficiency and organizational competitive disadvantage if managed incorrectly.

Furthermore, it has been evidenced that applying AI to marketing strategies has led to bettering the client relations and get the maximum outcomes from the campaign. As cited in (Basri, 2020) the integration of artificial intelligence (AI) to the marketing of SMEs can be helpful to the KSA economy. Thus, analysing customer behaviour and choice, artificial intelligence solutions provide greater personal approach and effectiveness to organization's marketing campaigns and customer targeting. This goes in sync with the arguments made by Borges et al., (2021) who establish that AI utility in managing large datasets and analytical capabilities have made it crucial in digital marketing strategies to enable organizations to reach the right consumers with solutions.

The management of knowledge and decision making of organizations has also been revolutionized fully by the new technology of AI. The integration of AI into human knowledge management is described by (Jarrahi et al., 2023). Because of their capacity to reduce repetitious and monotonous tasks, analyse huge information, and provide recommendations that assist companies with reducing corporative workflow inconsistently and enhancing efficiency in their operations, it optimizes communication and decision-making. AI can bring effectiveness and compliance in diverse fields ranging from the drugs search in pharmaceutical companies and supply chain management (Kulkov, 2021). AI has also been proved that integrating it for the business simulation games will improve the entrepreneurial aptitude and choice making as well (Chen et al., 2022).

Environmental issues are also critical areas that must be resolved together with the help of AI along with the optimization of the business processes. Kong & Yuen, 2024, focus on sustainability risk management through AI adoption in which the authors examine the risks that concern ESG. Business organizations might adopt AI technologies to analyze extensive and complicated information, to predict risk factors, and to optimise the employment of resources all of which helped make business corporations to be more environmentally sustainable. It can be noted that the integration of AI technologies into sustainable activities is relevant primarily for industries with long-term targets, resources for which must be managed, such as manufacturing and energy industries.

The growing number of investigations also reveals the role of AI in stimulating business models based on advanced technologies. As stated by Lee et al., (2019), organisations can harness the power of innovation enabled by artificial intelligence to review the existing strategies and explore new product and services, and new markets. Using the potential of applying AI that encompasses data analysis and decision-making to innovate faster, businesses can target their competition. Similarly, (Di Vaio et al., 2020) argued that AI is strategically relevant in the global market since it is critical in helping organisations to integrate the UN Sustainable Development Goals [SDGs].

Supply chain management, together with enhancement of corporative flexibility is mentioned in the literature as AI's primary use. Chatbots and machine learning facilitate an opportunity for companies to improve how their supply chain operates, changing easily to market conditions, and increasing the effectiveness of organisations according to Wang et al., (2022). In the modern world full of competitions in business one ability that is needed is the ability to adapt quickly to changes in the environment, customers' needs, or laws and regulations.

AI analysis indicates that this approach offers valuable contributions to raised engagement & productivity for employees in personnel management. Opportunities, risks, and benefits of applying artificial intelligence (AI) into people management models is discussed in (Rožman et al., 2022). On that account, this approach enhances the organizational performance as it provides the customized training, anticipate the employee turnover, and simplifies the procedure of hiring. All organisations may need to use AI driven workforce analytics to inform businesses' decisions on improving worker contentment, reducing turnover rates and allocating appropriate labour skills for organisational needs. This is a good example showing how applicable AI is to be applying to issues both tactical and strategic in human resources.

For corporate management using AI, ethical issues are also introduced. Leveraging the previous problems with bias, openness, and data privacy, Dwivedi et al. (2021) call for the development of robust ethical frameworks. This is particularly important because, as the incorporation of AI systems into the procedures of organizations continues to progress, they become more entrenched in the processes of decision making. One of them is applying protection from biased algorithms and focusing on making AI systems safe and accountable for their actions is one manifestation of this.

Nevertheless, some key themes remain still unexplored even though the amount of study regarding the application of artificial intelligence in business management is still growing. There are very few studies on the use of AI in SMEs. Although (Basri, 2020) highlight the impacts of AI to marketing communication on Saudi Arabian SMEs, scanty research has been conducted on how these relatively unsophisticated organizations with limited capital may apply AI in other domains such as operations, financial or human resource management. Moreover, (Cubric, 2020) and (Dwivedi et al., 2021) have provided comprehensive literature on reviewing the ethical dimensions of AI uptake, such as bias, transparency, and privacy; however, a significant part of this accumulated knowledge has been concentrated on the western nations. Further work needs to be done to see how similar ethical problems are managed in other non-Western and emerging countries, as cultural attitudes and legal frameworks may not necessarily reflect those of the developed world.

Secondly, although numerous studies focus on AI applications that support sustainability, including risk management and optimizing resource use, there are no research papers that address the environmental impact of AI technologies on their own (Kong & Yuen, 2024) & (Di Vaio et al., 2020).). Further studies are required to know the real applicability of AI over the long term particularly in fields that require intense power consumption. People cannot know all there is to know about this cooperation of human and artificial intelligence. Though (Jarrahi et al., 2023) have documented how AI supports and enriches human decision-making in the field of knowledge management, little has been done in understanding how this partnership can be taken forward to other organizational activities for bettering organizational performance and innovation.

However, much of the literature (Feuerriegel et al., 2022) & (Åström et al., 2022) focuses on utilization and impact of AI in the developed economies including US and the Europe respectively, resulting in a literature gap regarding the issue of adoption of AI in the emerging economies. While these nations face challenges of infrastructure and human capital development, opportunity and risks in regions such as the South East Asia, Africa, and Latin America are uncharted. In addition, the literature review found little primary longitudinal research on AI's long-term consequences for business performance, competitive advantage, and strategic development despite the emphasis of numerous studies on I's immediate advantages across various industries, including marketing and customer relation management & (Chatterjee et al., 2022) & (Enholm et al., 2022). Another issue that should be discussed is the lack of studies that constitute special industry. Most of the current research studies are addressing the application of AI in banking, marketing, and healthcare industries while the opportunities for utilising AI in education, agriculture, real estate, and others are are still relatively untouched (Aziki & Fadili, 2022). Eliminating these gaps in our research will aid in clarifying exactly what AI can do and what it cannot, in the polycephalic scope of its applications and in a broader spectrum of industries and global markets.

This Chapter will specifically address the following queries:

Q1: How much research on Artificial intelligence and Business management has been developed in the last years using the Scopus database?
Q2: How is the performance evaluation of various scientific entities in the fields of Artificial intelligence and Business management conducted, including sources, keywords, countries, affiliations, documents, and authors?
Q3: What possible avenues for Artificial intelligence and Business management might there be in the future?

The conceptual use of Artificial intelligence in the field of Business management is suggested in this article. Research will give a thorough overview of the field by evaluating the body of existing literature and applying bibliometric analysis. This will aid in developing future research agendas and policy initiatives that centre on Artificial intelligence and Methodology Business . The study's conclusions may serve as a source of motivation and direction for people, groups, and decision-makers as they adopt.

This study employs bibliometric tools to analyse research on Artificial intelligence in the field of Business. The articles are selected based on keywords relevant to the research topic. The Biblioshiny app and VOS viewer programme are used to analyse the filtering results after they are stored in CSV, RIS, and Bib Tex file formats.

To filter search results more carefully, advanced search strategies are used. This approach exclusively considers English-language materials and concentrates on keywords, article titles, and abstracts. The analysis just looks at journals and papers. A crucial component of any bibliometric analysis is data sources. The six steps of the literature review process are as follows. The procedures for carrying out a literature review are as follows.

LITERATURE REVIEW

Artificial Intelligence (AI) is emerging to play an integral role in managing organizations and businesses while transforming multiple sectors in terms of helping to make decisions more effectively, providing ways to attract consumers, increase efficiency, and give businesses tools they need to be creative. As in the past, AI was previously considered as virtually a tool for automation, it is gradually being felt as an influence or a tool for strategic business change across the globe touching many sectors as identified by Agarwal et al. 2024. This paper focuses on the following topics relating to how AI affects company management as discussed in the literature: sustainability, customer relation management, operations efficiency, business model innovativeness, knowledge management and adoption issues.

Artificial Intelligence and Innovative Business Models

AI is recognised as a driver of the invention of business models. From (Åström et al., 2022) A useful and linear three phase framework that can or may be applied to cause and capture value with the help of AI might be structured with: AI is being as applied in businesses for resource management, flexibility, and plasticity, and revised operating models. AI allows for timely decision-making and contributes to sustainable competitiveness; this has been illustrated in numerous innovations in, for example, manufacturing and industrial systems realms (Burström et al., 2021).

AI and its application in recommending business paths for organizations who wish to renew themselves and sustain growth is discussed by (Reim et al., 2020). Organizations may key their processes with state-of-art hardware and respond to changing market requirements and stay relevant by integrating the AI into their models. With the ability to sort through large quantities of data, AI makes it possible for firms to locate trends and acquire the novelty to stay relevant in volatile markets. Similarly, Han et al.'s (2021) bibliometric analysis focuses on how AI is applied to B2B marketing by showing how analytics derived from AI enhance decision processes, enhance customer understanding and increase marketing effectiveness.

AI in Operations

AI has received substantial definition in terms of what it brings to the operational efficiency. The ways that AI approach big data and can generate prediction results may strengthen the human decision as pointed out by (Feuerriegel et al., 2022). Improved organizational performance and reduced cost is realized since human error coupled with efficient manual processes are avoided. RPA, NLP, and ML are three technological solutions that increase the efficiency of decision processes and enhance operations.

In their review of the literature, Enholm et al., (2022) point out that there seems to be further commercial value in the use of AI-driven automation. AI improves using processes in industries such as healthcare, manufacturing, and finance since it does not require human interaction in most tasks done in organizations. The report also grosses up how the use of real time data analysis by AI assist the firms in responding to market changes which indeed enhance their operational flexibility.

About the study: The study, (Basri, 2020) examines the effects of artificial intelligence (AI) on social media marketing for small and medium enterprises (SMEs) in Saudi Arabia. The study further finds that through data-driven insights about consumer behaviour and segmentation, the AI marketing improvement of techniques increases consumer engagement and the success of various marketing campaigns. As stated by (Borges et al., 2021), the adoption of artificial intelligence (AI) has emerged as a necessity for every organization that seeks to process significant amounts of data to drive business performance and chart better promotional strategies.

Application of AI to CRM (Customer Relationship Management)

CRM has thus undergone a tremendous shift due to the integration of artificial intelligence. By implementing AI, businesses have the possibility to improve customer satisfaction and decrease customer churn (Chatterjee et al., 2022). The AI applications analyze the client information within a short duration, thereby helping firms predict preferences, optimize marketing strategies and deliver personalised insights.

Describing how the AI-based CRM systems enhance customer interaction in real-time by responding to questions and personalising the interaction, (Chatterjee et al., 2022). By applying these technologies some companies might adapt unique products and services while nurturing long-term client relationships, which the AI systems are able to predict. Thus, following the words of Huang & Rust (2021), chatbots and virtual assistants bring even more customer satisfaction if they are available without breaks 24/7.

In the field of the financial industry focusing on the retail banking sector, Ho & Chow, (2024) explore the impact of AI for consumer purchase decision. In the report, AI stabilises the relationships between clients by ensuring they receive quality choice of banks, therefore improving market loyalty. These findings agree with the notion that AI is indispensable in improving customer bonding and service provision particularly in industries where customer relations impact organizational performance.

Obstacles to the Adoption of AI

The application of AI in company management is actually beneficial, but facing some issues in practice. Cubric (2020) provides the account of the enablers and barriers to AI and discusses concerning ethical, societal and technological conditions. These challenges consists of the high costs of deployment, the complexity of the

AI systems, and shortage of skilled employees who possess the expertise to manage the use of AI technology.

Thus, (Rana et al., 2022) highlight that there are ethical issues with the help of AI, like algorithmic unfairness, data privacy, and explainability. The study also warns that in case AI is utilized inappropriately, it leads to inefficiency, and a disadvantage when facing competitors. Due to these difficulties, businesses should consider the following aspects that could be negatively affected: The quality and imbalance of the decisions made could therefore lead to dire consequences, and override the morale of workers in an organization.

In more detail, (Gligor et al., 2021) further continue the discussion about the 'dark side' of AI and wonder what threats AI can pose for business-to-business contexts. The mentioned risks are the fear of data misuse, the increased reliance on AI applications, and distrust in AI outcomes. In order not to compromise morality as corporations tap into AI's full potential, these needs to be solved.

AI for Knowledge Management

AI is also being used increasingly for enhancing KM as it provides organisations the tool to address the big information quicker and more efficiently. They suggest that knowledge management may be done by artificial intelligence alongside human intelligence according to the view provided by (Jarrahi et al., 2023). The priceless contribution of ''AI' driven solutions include: Redundant functions can be handled by ''AI'' resulting in generation of likely results and ease in flow of information between business entities. These technologies enable organisations to work more closely together and make enhanced decisions thereby supporting innovation to the improvement of organisational outcomes.

In sectors such as the pharmaceutical, knowledge management using AI should be deployed so as to foster innovation and comply with the legal requirements. The advantage of AI to the pharmaceutical industry According to Kulkov (2021), one way through which AI can help in management of complicated regulatory regulations and ease procedures involved in drug discovery, is AI. It may help to minimize expert involvement to the extent that, by managing knowledge with the help of AI tools, companies can sustain their efficiency in highly controlled industries.

Moreover, (Chen et al., 2022) explores the potential pathways for applying aspects of business simulation games to improve entrepreneurial attitudes with reference to AI. This is highlights the relevance of AI as reinforcing innovation and strategic thinking in the corporate management function Furthering the idea in the study show how such insights from the simulation that has been enhanced by the use of AI may enhance decision making.

Artificial Intelligence and Sustainability

It is possible to note that more and more companies start applying AI technologies to sustainability. According to Kong & Yuen (2024) examine how AI sustains risk by identifying volume of data concerning environmental dangers to make an efficient forecast and utilization of resources. They pointed out that AI is capable of evaluating large information which may help businesses enhance the management of sustainability risks, and activities aligned to ESG goals.

In their study, Burström et al., (2021) argue that AI business model advancements enhance the efficient use of resources hence improved sustainability because they limit operational gaps. This contributes to the importance of AI integration into sustainability projects because knowledge of these sectors compensates for material resource scarcity in the reach of sustainable development goals.

At the same time, (Di Vaio et al., 2020) describe how AI can help companies align their activities with the UN's Sustainable Development Goals. International minded companies might be able to carry out environmentally friendly business promotions while continuing to make good profits due to corporate use of AI that enhances resource utilization. It is in line with the findings of Palanivelu and Vasanthi (2020) who learn that through AI, business functionalities across numerous industries change and develop sustainable business models.

Artificial Intelligence and Business Fluidity

One of the more popular topics explored in recent research is automated intelligence for enhancing business adaptiveness. Due to the infected flexibility with which they adapt to changes in the market, Wang et al., (2022) affirm that agreement is steeped in the application of artificial intelligence (AI) technologies such as chatbots and machine learning algorithms. This is particularly important in areas of the economy that maintaining market advantage and.rf competitiveness depends on timely decision-making.

While relying on AI makes a supply chain more agile, it brings benefits of improved demand forecasting, inventory management, and logistics. Based on (Lee et al., 2019), AI in the supply chain is helpful due to its ability to predict events and allow the organizations to be responsive to disruptions that may occur in the chain and which they never expected. This is particularly so in the volatile environment that most businesses are facing today, where the winner is the most adaptable.

Using AI in HRM

AI has a very large impact on HRM as it can be implemented to improve the interaction with the employees, recruitment and performance appraisal systems. As declared by Rožman et al., (2022), AI-based personnel management models enhance organizational performance through individual training; employee turnover expectation, and fast-tracking the recruitment process. With the help of AI, companies may achieve improved pairing of employee skills with their objectives and potentially enhance the satisfaction of their workers.

Rahman et al., (2023) also examine the integration of AI policy in HRM and the role of technology in enhancing the management of labor and the development of friendly environment, which are socially sustainable aspects. AI helps organizations save precious time to focus on and invest in the most relevant activities, such as staffing the company with great and diverse professionals.

Prospects for the Future and Unfilled Research Needs

However, Platanakis & Zopounidis (2018) have identified that there are at least four main research gaps, given the focus of the literature on the transformative effects of AI in many aspects of corporate functioning. Thus, according to (Aziki & Fadili, 2022), most of the research identified provides information on developed countries, thus lacking information on the application of AI in emerging markets. Further research should seek to unravel how AI might be made unique to enable it overcome challenges that enterprises experience in regions like Southeast Asia, Africa, and Latin America.

Moreover, there is little research on what impact this new trend will have on strategic innovation and long-term corporate performance. While a great deal of literature focuses on the immediate benefits of AI, much more detailed long-term analyses are needed for understanding the impact of AI on competitive advantage and company growth (Enholm et al., 2022) & (Chatterjee et al., 2022).

In conclusion, AI has become an indispensable instrument for managing a corporation focusing on sustainability, efficient operations, and innovation. However, firms must work on adoption related challenges such as ethical issues and technology challenges to realize this potential fully. Therefore, to make sure that these benefits are evident in all organizations, the next research studies should focus on the following suggestions: Acknowledging AI's impact on future organization performance should be explored Further research should take on a look at the function of AI in emerging markets.

RESULTS AND DISCUSSION

Citations Per Year

An effective method for evaluating the caliber and impact of a scientific paper is citation analysis. From 1971 until 2023, trends in citations are shown in Figure 1. These charts demonstrate the variations in citations that occur inside that place. Assessing the impact and influence of published scientific articles in the area may be possible with the use of the data in this graphic. This graphic may also be used to identify notable years or events that have an impact on the domain's citation count.

Figure 1 illustrates how the number of citations rose gradually beginning in 1992 and peaking in 2001, with an average of 55.9 citations per document. Since public data is readily available, this expansion may be linked to significant developments and acknowledgment around artificial intelligence's role in business management during the past several years.

Figure 1. Average citations per year.

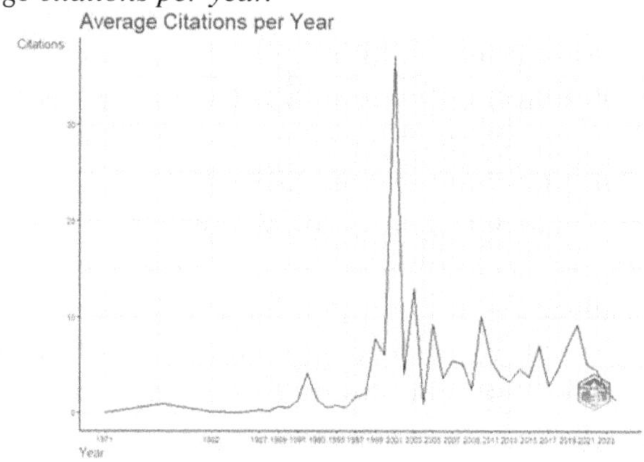

Publications Per Year

Any research topic's foundational, developing, and mature stages may be evaluated by looking at the annual publication activity pattern. Figure 2 and the study analysing the relationship between the function of AI in business management provide the research publications released year between 1971 and 2023. Elsevier B.V.'s Scopus scientific database is the main source of the graph data. The graph pattern demonstrates that after 1986, the number of papers released didn't remain steady; rather, it continued to rise, reaching a high in 2022 and a pick-up in 1989.

The yearly production of scientific publications published in a variety of topics throughout that period may be determined analytically using these graphs.

The graph shows the notable trend in the creation of articles on artificial intelligence about the application of AI in business management over the last several years.

The constant growth seen in Figure 2 peaked in 1986 and increased gradually until 2022. The fact that the number of publications did not decrease despite the COVID-19 pandemic between 1989 and 2023 is noteworthy since it demonstrates the study's endurance and continuing popularity. As per the annual scientific output study, the growth rate of research articles in the subject matter is 7.05 percent every year.

Figure 2. Number of Paper Published on role of AI in business management.

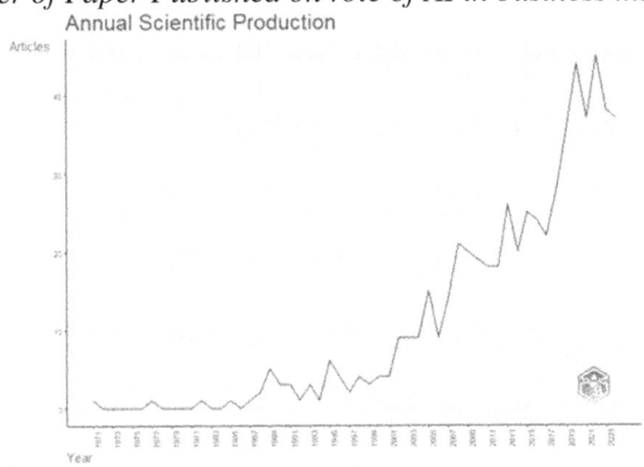

Documents Per Year by Source

A comparison of the quantity of documents from five distinct sources is shown in a line graph in Figure 3. The years 1971 through 2022 and the amount of paper are represented by the X and Y axes, respectively, while each source is represented by several lines. The sources, which include IEEE, Access, Sensors, etc., are identified by different colours. The overall growth in documents for all resources throughout time is depicted in these graphs. An analytical tool for comprehending head publishing partners' perspectives on the application of AI in company management is Figure 3.

This graphic's data may be used to determine which sources are the most active and fruitful for the subject of the study.

> Q1. How is the efficacy of various scientific groups examining the function of AI in company management evaluated? The review considers papers, writers, associations, countries, references, and search terms.

Q2. What are the potential future resource orientations in relation to the function of AI in company management?

Figure 3. Number of sources

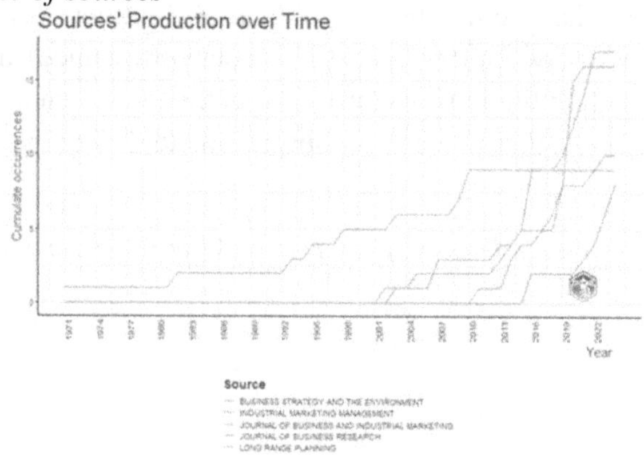

Most Relevant Affiliations

Affiliates for an extended time. Information on each affiliate's pertinent contribution to the rise of document output is included in this table. This table is important as it illustrates the ways in which each colleague influenced the creation of a certain document or work of literature. Using this type of research, the most significant or ongoing relationships related to the topic under investigation may be found.

The graph shows that the Central University of Finance and Economics and the Copenhagen Business School have the most relevant affiliations, with nine for each article. The City University of Hong Kong and Uppsala University have the second-highest number of affiliations, each with eight. Additionally, the number of papers at Arizona State University, Politecnico Di Milano, Renmin University of China, University of Padua, University of Pennsylvania, and Washington State University is the same—7.

Figure 4. Top 10 Research Publication Sources

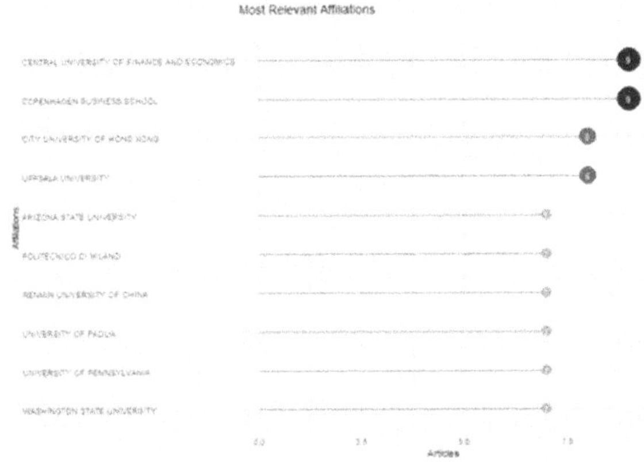

Table 1. Number of articles

Affiliation	Articles
Central Unversity of Finance and Economics	9
Copenhagen Business School	9
City University of Hong Kong	8
Uppsala University	8
Arizona State University	7
Politecnico Di Milano	7
Renmin University of China	7
University of Padua	7
University of Pennsylvania	7
Washington State University	7

Figure 5. Affiliation production over the time.

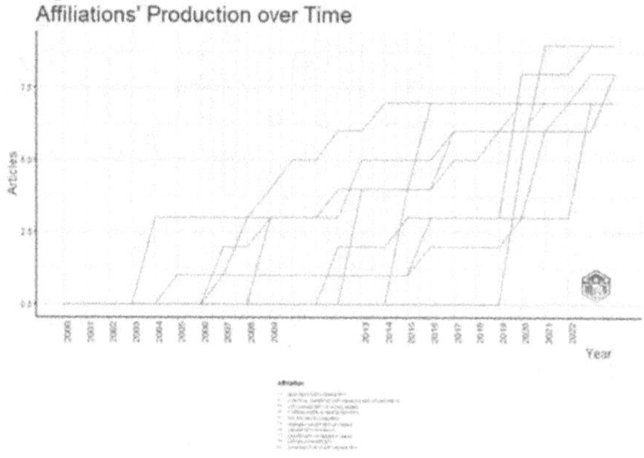

The affiliate's significant contributions to the field's investigation of artificial intelligence's use in business management at that period are what led to this.

Three-Field Plot

"Bibliometrics" is a study methodology that use quantitative approaches and statistical analysis to identify recurring themes within a body of literature. This is an amazing tool, particularly for mapping study where the lights might be useful. In reference to the many, diverse, complex, and occasionally disputed fields of research. Based on Lotka's Law, three-dimensional illustrations of writers' productivity are created using Biblioshiny, an online Bibliometrix interface. Moreover, a word cloud powered by the most frequently used word keys is created using Biblioshiny.

An example of a Biblioshiny three-field plot technique would be the information flow between the sources (left field), publishers, authors, and keywords (right field). To provide a more useful representation, just a small number of objects from each field are examined in this study. This approach offers a comprehensive synopsis of the relationships and structures present in the scientific literature pertaining to a certain topic.

As Figure 6 makes evident, the study's focus on the "Role of AI in Business Management" is evident in most of the publications. Journals such as "Business Strategy and the Environment, Industrial Marketing Management, Journal of Business and Industrial Marketing, Journal of Business Research, & Long-Range Planning," among others, have published these works. The authors with the greatest publications on the use of AI in business management are Chen Y, Zhang Y, and Crick D.

Figure 6. Author Productivity Through Lutka's Law.

Top Author Production Over the Time

The "Authors' Production Over Time" graphic plots the contributions made by leading researchers in the field of business management-related artificial intelligence. Author productivity from 2002 to 2024 is shown in the chart, which includes writers Chen Y, Zhang Y, Crick D, and others. Bigger circles indicate authors Chen Y and Zhang Y, whose article publications have been steadily increasing in the past few years and peaked between 2020 and 2022, when they published numerous papers annually. In addition, a few writers—like Morgan NA and Crick D.—have contributed significantly in the past but less frequently now.

The deeper hue denotes the overall number of citations received annually, with well-known writers receiving more citations in recent years. The size of the circles indicates the number of papers produced. Based on the data, it appears that certain writers have maintained or expanded their influence as AI in business management has developed, which has helped to expand and enhance the field of study.

Figure 7. Author's Production Over Time

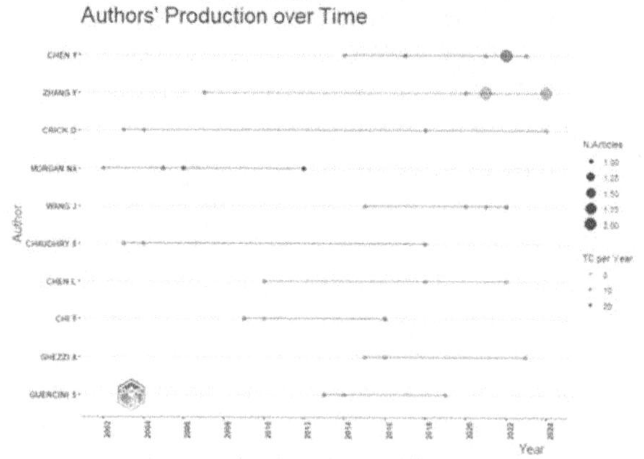

Most Relevant Authors

A line graph illustrating the number of documents authored by the writers who have produced the most pertinent articles is presented in Figure 8. To show the relationship between two variables, a particular kind of graph known as a point graph employs points. On the Y-axis are the authors, and on the X-axis is the total number of papers. Data scales and classifications are shown using axes, which are lines. Vertical or horizontal ones are both possible. Data point locations are shown by the blue dots. Data points include values that indicate the outcomes of measurements or observations of variables. The quantity of references the author included from each source is shown in Figure 8. The dark blue circles represent the most relevant citations, and the light blue circles represent the least relevant citations.

Crick D, Morgan NA, and Wang J come in second with four citations, while Chen Y and Zhang Y are the most prolific writers in the field of the function of AI in corporate management, with six citations. In the domains of artificial intelligence and business management, these writers have authored the most significant studies. They appear to have made significant contributions to the discipline, as evidenced by the widespread recognition of their work among scholars. Additionally displayed in the graph is the current surge in research on AI and the Business Management of continuous learning. Citations for publications published in the last year have increased, indicating this.

Figure 8. Most Relevant Authors

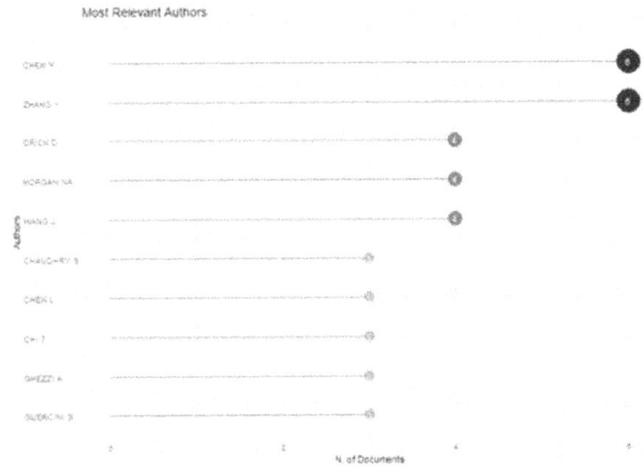

Most Relevant Sources

With reference to Figure 9, For each source, the total number of documents is shown in this line graph. Regarding the overall count of articles with sources, every element in the picture has a distinct function. There are more papers using the source when the X value is higher. Additionally, the names of various sources are represented via the Y-axis. Among these sources are academic periodicals that discuss technology, leadership, HRM, and ongoing education. ten labels make up the Y axis. AI and business management departments can be found at the Central University of Finance and Economics, Copenhagen Business School, City University of Hong Kong, Uppsala University, Arizona State University, Politecnico Di Milano, Renmin University of China, University of Padua, University of Pennsylvania, and Washington State University.

The quantity of articles originating from East sources is shown by the data on the blue dart. Both the source name and the number of documents correspond to each point's X and Y coordinates.

The sources that are most relevant are “Industrial Marketing Management”, “Journal of Business Research”, “Journal of Business and Industrial Marketing”, “Organization Science”, “Strategic Management Journal”, “Business Strategic and the Environment”, “Long Range Planning”, “IEEE Transaction on Engineering Management”, “International Journal of Operation and Production Management”, and “MIS Quarterly: Management Information System” the sources listed in Figure 9. Different numbers of papers are available on each of these sites. “Industrial Marketing Management” is the most often accessed source out of the records that total fourteen.

Out of the 343 sources utilized, the least common categories are "MIS Quarterly: Management Information System," "International Journal of Operation and Production Management," and "IEEE Transaction on Engineering Management," each with just two sources available.

Figure 9. Most relevant sources

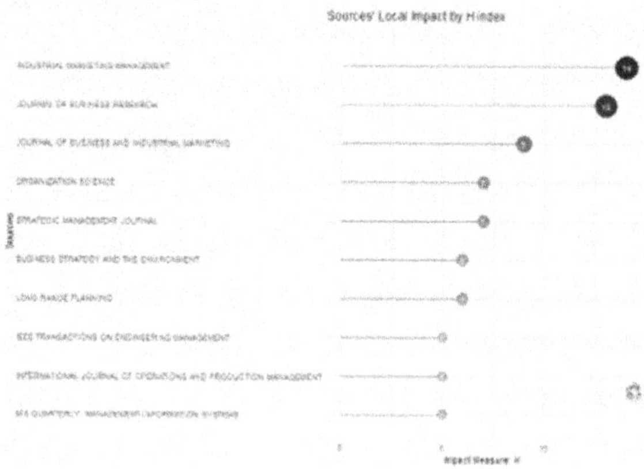

Word Cloud of Titles using Biblioshiny App.

This image is a word cloud that illustrates ideas about role of AI in Business Management. A word cloud is a graphic representation that indicates how frequently or how important a word occurs in a text. In comparison to comparable words, larger words imply a stronger pressure or importance, and their magnitude reflects how frequently or how important they occur.

Figure 10. Word Cloud

A continuous weekly trend in the keywords for AI and business management is predicted by the Biblioshiny Bibliometrix display in the Figure 10 package, which spans the years 1984 through 2024. When used graphically, terms or phrases with more volume and density are shown in a stronger, bigger font. As a result, we may see additional information about the pattern or emphasis of keywords by using these terms in research publications.

Co-occurrence of Keyword

Relationship analysis inside a document is facilitated by Vosviewer's co-occurrence of words feature. The relationships between the themes the text discusses may be understood and keywords that commonly appear together can be found with the help of this tool. A network of relationships exists between subjects and individuals in the fields of artificial intelligence (AI) and business management, as per Vosviewer's interpretation of the image. The network is depicted in the form of a map, with nodes standing in for subjects and relationships between them.

Figure 11. Co-occurrence of keywords

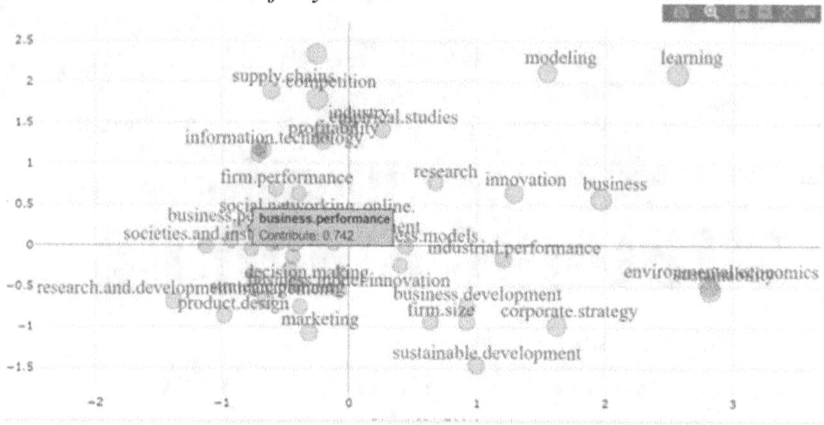

The map illustrates the range of subjects on which AI and business management research is now concentrated. Currently, among the most in-demand competencies in the management sector are artificial intelligence and business management. Artificial intelligence (AI) and business management have several uses, including enhanced decision-making, higher performance, and work automation. Smart systems have the capacity to learn and change. Increasing employee happiness, productivity, and efficiency are just a few of the many AI and business management objectives that smart technologies may be utilized to. The digital transformation of the industry known as Industry 4.0 has a significant impact on AI and business management. It calls for changes to the way employees manage and perform their duties.

Overlay Visualization

The three main types of visualization that Vosviewer offers are overlays, network visualization, and density visualization. Overlays show traces of previous research in a particular area or subject. These overlays are created using a technique called "co-citation analysis". Co-closely related documents are those in which two topics are frequently referenced jointly in another text. A closer look at Figure 12 & 13 reveals a notable increase in research over the past several years on the application of AI in business management.

Figure 12. Co-occurrence of keywords

Several experiments using various keywords have shown this. Here are a few recent advancements in AI. The many studies that employ terminology like data analytics and digital transformation industry 4.0 demonstrate this.

The field of AI is seeing an increase in research on the application of role of AI in business management to global concerns, such as social, economic, and technology-related problems. This is shown by several studies that use terms like environmental management, sustainability, and the ramifications for the economy and society.

Figure 13. Co-occurrence of keywords

Corresponding Author's Countries

The claim made in figures 14 and 15 that the United States has the biggest number of SCP and MCP is supported by the fact that many of the relevant writers are from industrialized countries. China, United Kingdom, Italy, India, Germany, Australia, Canada, Finland, Korea, Spain, Sweden, Denmark, Malaysia, Netherlands, Norway, France, Hong Kong, & Switzerland are among the other countries that collaborate. This trend highlights the significance of academic and research institutions in these fields, which are usually at the forefront of AI and business management research. Nonetheless, emerging economies have made a notable contribution, particularly those in Asia, where countries like USA and China are doing important research at a quick pace. The fact that different geographic regions are represented emphasizes how important transformative AI and business management are in a range of cultural and economic contexts.

Figure 14. Corresponding Author's Countries

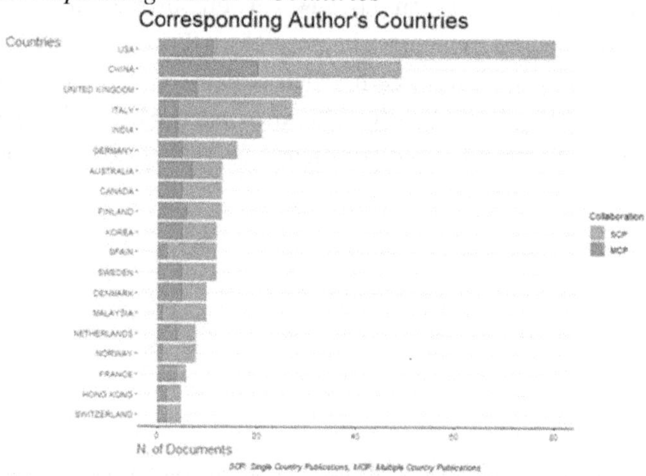

Figure 15. Most Cited Countries

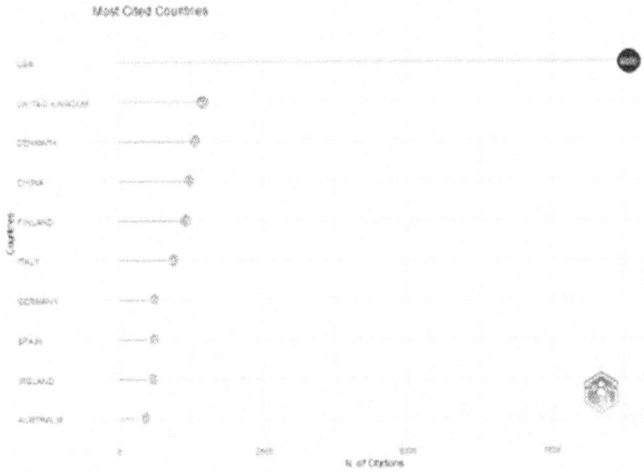

Author's Local Impact by H Index

Because of the constant rise in citations and publications over the years, the article "Role of AI in Business Management" has shown substantial local effect, as evidenced by its H-index. A consistent increase in citations was seen for the article between 1992 and 2023, reaching a peak with an average of 55.9 citations per document, indicating the growing acceptance of AI's position in corporate management. With renowned sources like "Industrial Marketing Management" and "Journal of Business Research" contributing to the topic, its significance is further reinforced by the yearly publishing growth rate of 7.05%. Prominent writers with a high citation count and regular publications, such Chen Y, Zhang Y, and Crick D, have substantially improved their H-index, especially between 2020 and 2022.

Figure 16. Author Local Impact my H Index

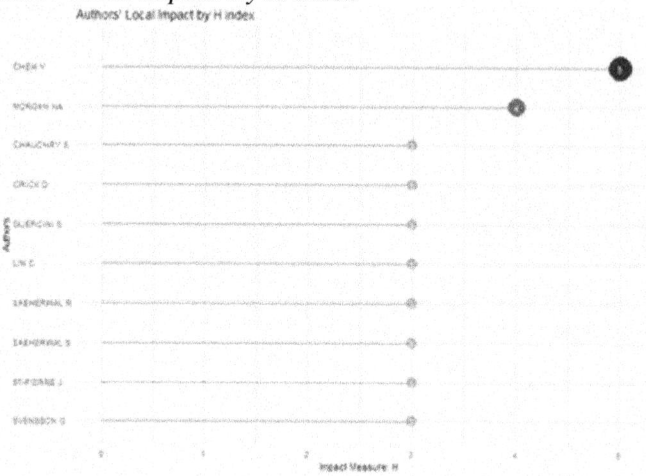

The impact of the paper was also increased by collaboration with organizations such as Copenhagen Business School and the Central University of Finance and Economics. Furthermore, the paper's global reach—especially in China and the United States—solidifies its academic and practical significance in AI research for business management.

Article Production Over time

The "Country Production over Time" graph shows how the output of scholarly articles changed in many important nations, including the USA, China, Germany, the UK, and Italy, between 1971 and 2024. Article production in the USA has been leading continuously since the early 2000s; the growth has been rapid and is expected to reach over 300 articles by 2024. China started producing more articles about 2010, and after 2020, its rise accelerated due to the nation's growing commitment to research. Growth has been more moderate and steadier in Germany, the UK, and Italy. Italy is marginally behind Germany and the UK, with Germany experiencing a discernible increase in output about 2015. In summary, the graph indicates that the United States of America has long been in the forefront of research, but China is closing the gap while European countries are growing at a slower but consistent rate.

Figure 17. Articles production in the countries.

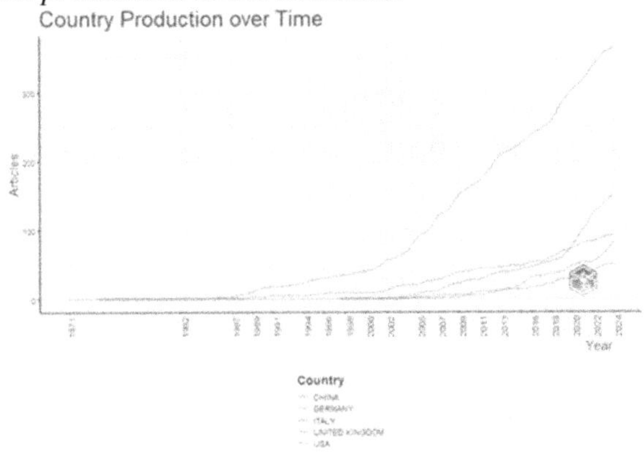

DISCUSSION

From 1971 to 2023, several research have looked at the development of AI and continuous learning in business management. Applying AI and business management successfully in a learning environment is challenging due to several barriers and constraints, as evidenced by the substantial amount of research on the issue. Providing a thorough examination and assessment of the corpus of literature that has been written on the topic throughout the years is the goal of this research project.

The goals are to fully understand the roles of business management and artificial intelligence (AI) by analysing the corpus of data that has been collected over time. The 343 publications that were especially chosen to emphasize the AI and business management culture in this investigation provided the basis for a sizable amount of the results.

Artificial Intelligence has a significant impact on management learning culture. Multiple study endeavors have focused on stakeholders' viewpoints about the deployment of artificial intelligence within a company management culture.

CONCLUSION

The increasing number of studies and publications shows how artificial intelligence (AI) has been used into company management over the past few decades. The examination of patterns between 1971 and 2023 indicates that artificial intelligence (AI) is becoming more and more relevant and influential in terms of decision-making, process automation, and overall operational efficiency in business. As seen by the significant rise in publications and citations over time, artificial intelligence (AI) has notably transformed important business management domains including marketing, operations, human resources, and strategic planning.

The results suggest that the adoption of AI in business management is widespread across industries and is not limited to scholarly discourse. The durability and persistent interest in the use of AI is highlighted by the research output's continuous increase in spite of obstacles like the COVID-19 epidemic. The conversation has been folded by prominent ties and notable participants from organizations like Copenhagen Business School and the Central University of Finance and Economics, guaranteeing that the application of AI to business management is thoroughly examined and recognised.

Anticipating the future, the growing cooperation between nations—most notably, the US and China—signals a worldwide movement toward using AI to support innovative and sustainable business practices. Research on the moral, societal, and financial ramifications of AI in corporate management is still desperately needed, nevertheless. By taking care of these issues, we can guarantee that AI will keep pushing forward and balancing the needs of human-centered management with those of technology.

Ultimately, artificial intelligence (AI) has solidified its position as a pillar in the development of corporate management, and its capacity to transform entire sectors of the economy only grows. Its potential to stimulate creativity, boost organizational effectiveness, and adjust to the dynamic global business environment will probably determine how AI is used in company management in the future.

Future Implication

Artificial intelligence (AI) in business management has a bright future ahead of it, as its uses are expected to spread into increasingly crucial and sophisticated fields. The growing importance of AI in data-driven decision-making is among the most important ramifications. AI will play a critical role in the analysis and synthesis of the massive volumes of data that organizations continue to produce in order to provide insights that can be put to use. In addition to increasing operational efficiency, this will help businesses better anticipate market trends, streamline their supply chains, and customize their interactions with customers. AI-powered analytics will replace conventional management techniques as a go-to tool for executives looking to make better, faster choices.

AI also has the potential to completely transform workforce management. As intelligent automation technologies proliferate, more efficient procedures will result, allowing businesses to reallocate staff members to higher-value jobs requiring imagination, compassion, and analytical thinking. Challenges will also arise from this change, such as the requirement for the workforce to retrain and upskill in order to collaborate with AI systems. Businesses will need to spend money on training programs to assist staff in adjusting to new jobs in the AI-driven economy as AI automates manual and repetitive activities. Business management in the future will put a greater emphasis on striking a balance between AI skills and human intellect to create a hybrid workforce that makes the most of both.

The ethical and legal environment that surrounds AI in corporate management is another potential future impact. Concerns about algorithmic bias, transparency, and data privacy will grow as AI systems become increasingly integrated into decision-making procedures. For AI to be employed in a responsible and morally sound manner in the corporate world, governments and regulatory agencies will need to create strong frameworks. To preserve confidence with stakeholders and clients, businesses must also implement best practices for AI governance. Navigating the tricky ethical landscape of artificial intelligence in corporate management will require constant cooperation between legislators, business executives, and engineers.

Finally, AI will continue to have a significant worldwide influence on company management, especially as emerging economies use AI to spur innovation and growth. The study of artificial intelligence (AI) and its commercial applications are already advanced in nations like China and India. Future worldwide business environments will be more linked due to growing cooperation between developed and emerging countries. AI's capacity to transcend national borders will open up new markets for companies, allowing them to develop more inclusive business models that serve a wide range of clientele.

To sum up, artificial intelligence will significantly change corporate management in the future. Although artificial intelligence has a lot of potential benefits, businesses will need to successfully integrate AI if they want to overcome issues with worker adaption, ethical issues, and international cooperation. Leading companies in the upcoming era of commercial innovation will be those who can successfully leverage AI's potential.

REFERENCES

Agarwal, P., Swami, S., & Malhotra, S. K. (2024). Artificial intelligence adoption in the post COVID-19 new-normal and role of smart technologies in transforming business: A review. *Journal of Science and Technology Policy Management*, *15*(3), 506–529. DOI: 10.1108/JSTPM-08-2021-0122

Åström, J., Reim, W., & Parida, V. (2022). Value creation and value capture for AI business model innovation: A three-phase process framework. *Review of Managerial Science*, *16*(7), 2111–2133. DOI: 10.1007/s11846-022-00521-z

Aziki, A., & Fadili, M. H. (2022). Highlighting artificial intelligence roles in business area Amid the COVID-19 crisis. *Procedia Computer Science*, *203*, 450–455. DOI: 10.1016/j.procs.2022.07.060 PMID: 35974967

Basri, W. (2020). Examining the impact of artificial intelligence (AI)-assisted social media marketing on the performance of small and medium enterprises: Toward effective business management in the Saudi Arabian context. *International Journal of Computational Intelligence Systems*, *13*(1), 142–152. DOI: 10.2991/ijcis.d.200127.002

Borges, A. F., Laurindo, F. J., Spínola, M. M., Gonçalves, R. F., & Mattos, C. A. (2021). The strategic use of artificial intelligence in the digital era: Systematic literature review and future research directions. *International Journal of Information Management*, *57*, 102225. DOI: 10.1016/j.ijinfomgt.2020.102225

Burström, T., Parida, V., Lahti, T., & Wincent, J. (2021). AI-enabled business-model innovation and transformation in industrial ecosystems: A framework, model and outline for further research. *Journal of Business Research*, *127*, 85–95. DOI: 10.1016/j.jbusres.2021.01.016

Chatterjee, S., Chaudhuri, R., & Vrontis, D. (2022). AI and digitalization in relationship management: Impact of adopting AI-embedded CRM system. *Journal of Business Research*, *150*, 437–450. DOI: 10.1016/j.jbusres.2022.06.033

Chen, J., Chen, Y., Ou, R., Wang, J., & Chen, Q. (2022). How to use artificial intelligence to improve entrepreneurial attitude in business simulation games: Implications from a quasi-experiment. *Frontiers in Psychology*, *13*, 856085. DOI: 10.3389/fpsyg.2022.856085 PMID: 36467165

Cubric, M. (2020). Drivers, barriers and social considerations for AI adoption in business and management: A tertiary study. *Technology in Society*, *62*, 101257. DOI: 10.1016/j.techsoc.2020.101257

Di Vaio, A., Palladino, R., Hassan, R., & Escobar, O. (2020). Artificial intelligence and business models in the sustainable development goals perspective: A systematic literature review. *Journal of Business Research, 121*, 283–314. DOI: 10.1016/j.jbusres.2020.08.019

Dwivedi, Y. K., Hughes, L., Ismagilova, E., Aarts, G., Coombs, C., Crick, T., Duan, Y., Dwivedi, R., Edwards, J., Eirug, A., Galanos, V., Ilavarasan, P. V., Janssen, M., Jones, P., Kar, A. K., Kizgin, H., Kronemann, B., Lal, B., Lucini, B., & Williams, M. D. (2021). Artificial Intelligence (AI): Multidisciplinary perspectives on emerging challenges, opportunities, and agenda for research, practice and policy. *International Journal of Information Management, 57*, 101994. DOI: 10.1016/j.ijinfomgt.2019.08.002

Enholm, I. M., Papagiannidis, E., Mikalef, P., & Krogstie, J. (2022). Artificial intelligence and business value: A literature review. *Information Systems Frontiers, 24*(5), 1709–1734. DOI: 10.1007/s10796-021-10186-w

Feuerriegel, S., Shrestha, Y. R., von Krogh, G., & Zhang, C. (2022). Bringing artificial intelligence to business management. *Nature Machine Intelligence, 4*(7), 611–613. DOI: 10.1038/s42256-022-00512-5

Gligor, D. M., Pillai, K. G., & Golgeci, I. (2021). Theorizing the dark side of business-to-business relationships in the era of AI, big data, and blockchain. *Journal of Business Research, 133*, 79–88. DOI: 10.1016/j.jbusres.2021.04.043

Haefner, N., Wincent, J., Parida, V., & Gassmann, O. (2021). Artificial intelligence and innovation management: A review, framework, and research agenda . *Technological Forecasting and Social Change, 162*, 120392. DOI: 10.1016/j.techfore.2020.120392

Han, R., Lam, H. K., Zhan, Y., Wang, Y., Dwivedi, Y. K., & Tan, K. H. (2021). Artificial intelligence in business-to-business marketing: A bibliometric analysis of current research status, development and future directions. *Industrial Management & Data Systems, 121*(12), 2467–2497. DOI: 10.1108/IMDS-05-2021-0300

Ho, S. P. S., & Chow, M. Y. C. (2024). The role of artificial intelligence in consumers' brand preference for retail banks in Hong Kong. *Journal of Financial Services Marketing, 29*(2), 292–305. DOI: 10.1057/s41264-022-00207-3

Huang, M. H., & Rust, R. T. (2021). Engaged to a robot? The role of AI in service. *Journal of Service Research, 24*(1), 30–41. DOI: 10.1177/1094670520902266

Jarrahi, M. H., Askay, D., Eshraghi, A., & Smith, P. (2023). Artificial intelligence and knowledge management: A partnership between human and AI. *Business Horizons, 66*(1), 87–99. DOI: 10.1016/j.bushor.2022.03.002

Kong, K. Y., & Yuen, K. F. (2024). Sustainability risk management: Exploring the role of artificial intelligence capabilities through an information-processing lens. *Risk Analysis*, risa.17448. DOI: 10.1111/risa.17448 PMID: 39179518

Kulkov, I. (2021). The role of artificial intelligence in business transformation: A case of pharmaceutical companies. *Technology in Society*, *66*, 101629. DOI: 10.1016/j.techsoc.2021.101629

La Torre, D., Appio, F. P., Masri, H., Lazzeri, F., & Schiavone, F. (2023). *Impact of artificial intelligence in business and society: Opportunities and Challenges*. Routledge. DOI: 10.4324/9781003304616

Lannon, F., Lyons, R., & O'Connor, C. (2024). Generation AI and family business: A perspective article. *Journal of Family Business Management*, *14*(3), 470–474. DOI: 10.1108/JFBM-07-2023-0116

Lee, J., Suh, T., Roy, D., & Baucus, M. (2019). Emerging technology and business model innovation: The case of artificial intelligence. *Journal of Open Innovation*, *5*(3), 44. DOI: 10.3390/joitmc5030044

. Lopes da Costa, R., Dias, Á., Pereira, L., António, N., & Capelo, A. (2019). The impact of artificial intelligence on commercial management. *The impact of artificial intelligence on commercial management*, (4), 441-452.

. Palanivelu, V. R., & Vasanthi, B. (2020). Role of artificial intelligence in business transformation. *International journal of advanced science and technology, 29*(4), 392-400.

Rahman, M. S., Bag, S., Gupta, S., & Sivarajah, U. (2023). Technology readiness of B2B firms and AI-based customer relationship management capability for enhancing social sustainability performance. *Journal of Business Research, 156*, 113525. DOI: 10.1016/j.jbusres.2022.113525

Rajagopal, N. K., Qureshi, N. I., Durga, S., Ramirez Asis, E. H., Huerta Soto, R. M., Gupta, S. K., & Deepak, S. (2022). Future of Business Culture: An Artificial Intelligence-Driven Digital Framework for Organization Decision-Making Process. *Complexity*, *2022*(1), 7796507. DOI: 10.1155/2022/7796507

Rana, N. P., Chatterjee, S., Dwivedi, Y. K., & Akter, S. (2022). Understanding dark side of artificial intelligence (AI) integrated business analytics: Assessing firm's operational inefficiency and competitiveness. *European Journal of Information Systems*, *31*(3), 364–387. DOI: 10.1080/0960085X.2021.1955628

Reim, W., Åström, J., & Eriksson, O. (2020). Implementation of artificial intelligence (AI): A roadmap for business model innovation. *AI, 1*(2), 11. DOI: 10.3390/ai1020011

Rožman, M., Oreški, D., & Tominc, P. (2022). Integrating artificial intelligence into a talent management model to increase the work engagement and performance of enterprises. *Frontiers in Psychology, 13*, 1014434. DOI: 10.3389/fpsyg.2022.1014434 PMID: 36506984

Saad, M. (2023). The influence of accounting information system adoption on business performance amid COVID-19. *Computers in Human Behavior Reports, 10*, 100286. DOI: 10.1016/j.chbr.2023.100286 PMID: 37122822

Svetlana, N., Anna, N., Svetlana, M., Tatiana, G., & Olga, M. (2022). Artificial intelligence as a driver of business process transformation. *Procedia Computer Science, 213*, 276–284. DOI: 10.1016/j.procs.2022.11.067

Tanveer, M., Khan, N., & Ahmad, A. R. (2021, April). AI support marketing: Understanding the customer journey towards the business development. In *2021 1st international conference on artificial intelligence and data analytics (CAIDA)* (pp. 144-150). IEEE.

Wamba-Taguimdje, S. L., Wamba, S. F., Kamdjoug, J. R. K., & Wanko, C. E. T. (2020). Influence of artificial intelligence (AI) on firm performance: The business value of AI-based transformation projects. *Business Process Management Journal, 26*(7), 1893–1924. DOI: 10.1108/BPMJ-10-2019-0411

Wang, X., Lin, X., & Shao, B. (2022). How does artificial intelligence create business agility? Evidence from chatbots. *International Journal of Information Management, 66*, 102535. DOI: 10.1016/j.ijinfomgt.2022.102535

Chapter 10
AI-Powered Business Process Automation:
Revolutionizing Firm Management

Muhammad Usman Tariq
https://orcid.org/0000-0002-7605-3040
Abu Dhabi University, UAE & University College Cork, Ireland

ABSTRACT

This chapter examines how automating business processes and changing management practices can be achieved through the use of artificial intelligence (AI). It draws attention to the increasing use of AI across a range of industries and emphasizes how it can improve productivity judgment and overall business performance. The chapter looks at the major managerial tasks that AI supports like employee engagement and performance management and offers case studies and real-world application insights. Businesses can use AI without sacrificing data security or fairness by taking ethical issues privacy concerns and the significance of responsible AI deployment into account. The potential for ongoing innovation and the difficulties businesses may encounter in putting these technologies into practice are highlighted in this exploration of future trends in AI-powered automation. Businesses looking to implement AI in their processes can use the best practices and practical lessons gleaned from industry case studies as a guide.

INTRODUCTION

This chapter presents a discussion on Artificial Intelligence (AI) that has become one of the most influential forces of change recognized to be transforming industries and redesigning the management of firms. BPA with the help of AI is

DOI: 10.4018/979-8-3693-7357-6.ch010

Copyright © 2025, IGI Global Scientific Publishing. Copying or distributing in print or electronic forms without written permission of IGI Global Scientific Publishing is prohibited.

the biggest innovation that firms have seen to tackle work mapping and workflow management. The capability of mimicking the everyday human decision-making datetime and performing tasks with improved efficiency, faster and accurate make AI the most dominant influencing factor to efficiency, productivity, and innovation. Major industries in the global market are adopting the use of Artificial Intelligence when it comes to solving problems that would take time to solve, and also be prone to mistakes. The identification of opportunities for cost efficiency in all of a company's operations, such as customer service and supply chain management, shows that artificial intelligence is precisely changing the way it works to help businesses stay relevant on the international stage in an ever-changing economic climate faster and faster, where a large number of innovations appear annually (Yakovenko & Shaptala, 2023).

Modern smart automation extends beyond Business Process Automation by embedding sophisticated features including machine learning, voice and text recognition and data controlling that enable the system to operate independently and improve performance over time. For instance, it is now possible for automated chatbots powered by the technology to directly and independently respond to customers in real-time something that was unheard of in the past. As well, with help of predictive analytics driven by AI, demand can be predicted and businesses, thus making strategic decisions are improved. The incorporation of Artificial Intelligence in business is a significant change that moves the center of work from the human capability aspect into the technical capability aspect which shifts the focus on reliance on machines for both low value and higher value work leading to operations being made efficient yet effective and accurate at lower costs (Lodhi, Gill, & Hussain, 2024).

It is the aim of this chapter to explain the broad idea on how artificial intelligence has impacted the management of firms. The broader topics of discussion will include the factors that have led to the increased use of AI in the organization's business processes, particular cases of AI application across organization's business functions, and the overall use of AI and its effects on the organization's performance, decisions, and employees. Moreover, the chapter will discuss the problems, and the ethical issues related to artificial intelligence in businesses, and consequences depending on the high usage of technology in companies.

The main goal is to provide the business leaders, managers, and stakeholders with the appropriate knowledge for the best practices in the AI applications particularly within the process automation while taking into consideration the emerging challenges that are part of the AI evolution process (Yakovenko & Shaptala, 2023).

This chapter will be devoted to analysis of one of the critical fields that are becoming increasingly vital in the modern firm management – Artificial Intelligence. Organizations in today's cutthroat business context have to search for ways to enhance their efficiency, cut expenses, and satisfy customers. It is using artificial intelligence that has become the key to attaining all these objectives. This means that AI saves firms time in allowing them to outsource mundane tasks and set their focus on essential business skills that include innovation and analysis. For example, AI solutions can facilitate such processes as invoice and inventory processing, calculation and payment of employees' wages, which not only speeds up work but also minimizes the risk of mistakes. Such a transition from traditional models where the management mostly relied on manual tasks to automated systems based on the AI solutions radically transformed the role of managers within firms, while they are now focused on monitoring and further enhancing the efficiency of AI operational systems.

In addition, there is evident effort to integrate artificial intelligence in decision-making structures of the firms. AI helps in analysing large data set in real time where the information that would have taken ages to analyse could be generated in a matter of minutes. This analytic approach enables the firms to develop more effective strategies and enhanced the management procedures in response to the changes in the market. For instance, in the marketing area, an AI solution can be used to identify regular customers' behaviour and prescribe particular methods to target them, which would contribute to making them more involved and purchase more products. In the financial services, the AI algorithms are applied in the identification of the fraudulent activities as well as the risk analysis to be more efficient than the traditional practices thus improving the protection and stability of the firm. AI's capacity to improve the business managers' decision-making tools is a significant development that is changing leadership by providing business leaders with AI solutions to make strategic and key organizational decision (Lodhi, Gill, & Hussain, 2024).

Besides increasing efficiency and effectiveness of decision-making, utilization of Artificial Intelligence in business process automation has far-reaching consequences in the management of workforce. If the lower-skilled tasks defined by the Human Skills Taxonomy are automated by AI systems, then employees can focus on higher-value areas such as creativity, decision making and interpersonal relations. This shift is altering the employment relationships and dynamics within the firms meaning that employees ought to possess new skills and competencies at the workplace. The new challenges for the managers are to select and implement the courses for the employees' reskilling and upskilling. Also, the rise of the automated system is making many to lose their jobs as the system undertakes tasks that were previously done by employees. This chapter will further discuss ways through which firms can optimally utilise both Automation and Human capital, to ensure that the Human capital remains relevant to the firm even as technology advances (Sehrawat, 2023).

There are also several issues and ethics that firms face when employing AI automation solutions in their operation system as stated below. One of the major issues is the risks associated with worsening of existing disparities in the workforce by AI technologies. As AI systems are introduced in industries, there is the possibility that some employee segments especially those engaged in low-skill occupations will be replaced by the advanced systems. This brings ethics into question, asking what duty certain firms have to guarantee the effectiveness of intelligent applications as they work towards equal distribution. Further, due to the employment of AI within the decision-making systems some questions regarding the transparency of the decision-making mechanisms have emerged. For instance, if an AI system in a firm makes a strategic business decision that brings adverse consequences, then it becomes uneasy to ascertain whether the blame goes to the AI itself, the developer or the firm that adopted the AI system. These are issues that are not easy to address especially bearing in mind that most firms have begun relying on AI to run their businesses (Lodhi, Gill, & Hussain, 2024).

Another important consideration that organisations face in the introduction of the automation systems powered by artificial intelligence is the problem of data privacy and security. Data is a core component of any AI system and the storage, sharing and protection of large volume of data brings into question on how the information is managed. Businesses need to ensure that they have adequate security measures that they have put in place to protect the companies' data to avoid falling foul of the legislation on data protection. Furthermore, AI operations in customer service, marketing and recruitment activities has raised issues to do with bias and fairness. For example, algorithms used in hiring or lending that are developed to employ sources such as gender, race among others may further the discrimination of individuals in the community.

Even so, the use of artificial intelligence to drive business process automation presents a great potential in the future. With time AI technology is likely to develop more advanced types of applications that will add more value to the management of the firm. For instance, the AI automation could enhance the relationship between business functions which means that the departments in an organization would be in a position to work more closely. This may culminate in generation of radical new business strategies where companies can act much more flexibly and employ dynamic adjustment strategies to meet the market needs in a way that was not possible before. Further, the use of AI tools and systems will alter industries, which will include healthcare, the financial sector as well as manufacturing industries since those sectors benefit from the use of technology in enhancing performance, improving the results and cutting costs among other factors. The corrective task for anytime, anywhere, for everybody and especially for firms will be to keep on experimenting and innovating how to integrate AI into value adding business models and usage processes in order not to leave space for the competitor to take over (Sehrawat, 2023).

Therefore, it may be stated that the given subject of AI proactively modifies the nature of business process automation and firm management beyond the existing possibilities of the recent years. Whether it is in glorification of traditional administrative functions, improving organizational decision and workforce processes, AI is enabling business optimal skills, throughput and creativity. Even though, there are some problems connected with the use of AI, one can state that the advantages of this tool surpass the shortcomings. The future belongs to AI-Derived automation and the companies which are already incorporating it in their business models and investing in the right talent, hardware and ethical guidelines. In this chapter, the focus is to present a broad view of how AI change the business processes as well as present the useful information to the managers and the other interested parties for the AI's potential usage.

BACKGROUND

Artificial organisms known as "augmented digital beings" communicate with people via cutting-edge technology, imitating their responses and actions. These entities—which include chatbots, virtual assistants, and digital avatars—are made to interact with people in ways that seem instinctive and natural. For example, virtual assistants like as Apple's Siri and Amazon's Alexa may handle routine activities like answering inquiries, scheduling reminders, and managing smart home devices, facilitating a smooth communication between people and technology (Alizadeh et al., 2024). Another illustration is the usage of digital avatars in mental health apps like Replika, which provide emotional support and imitate social interactions to lessen

Artificial intelligence or AI coupled with business process automation or BPA is now a core effective value in setting up and sustaining modern firms. AI is therefore the ability of machines to mimic human attributes hence solving problems, making decisions among others. Business process automation, on the other hand, is a business strategy that employs technology to complete specific repetitive functions with the least amount of intervention from the employees. AI, when it is blended with BPA, helps business organizations to automate not only simple but complex tasks that require learning, reasoning, and reflection. The integration of AI and BPA has its advantages such as first, it provides efficiency, secondly, operational costs, and thirdly, it provides improved decision making (Lodhi, Gill, & Hussain, 2024).

AI automation systems are very different from the traditional automation tools that are in use in the market today in that they utilize machine learning, natural language processing and other robot-like features. Machine learning, for instance, enables the AI systems to Adapt to new environments and act like human beings do because they learn to change with time. This capability makes the BPA systems with AI more flexible thus being able to address more problems. For instance, the use of AI to help computers handle and respond to clients' queries based on those used in their interaction with the services. One of the subfields of artificial intelligence is natural language processing that enables machines to understand and create human language making it easy for Business to look for such features as document scanners, sentiment analysis of customers' reviews, or the creation of automatic reports (Lodhi, Gill, & Hussain, 2024). AI has been in existence several decades with the advancement in business operations but its application in automating processes has widely adopted in recent decades due to increase in the number of computations, big data, and algorithms. The concerns and thoughts of early AI were to build machines capable of doing logical reasoning and solving complex problems which were actively researched in the 1950s. However, these early systems suffer from the technology in use at the time and their further applications in business were not popular. AI in business, however, did not start visibly and was continually launched from the loop in the late twentieth century with the application of enhanced computers and largeness data sets thereafter. Early applications of AI in business involved applications regarded as expert systems that aimed at emulating the processes of decision-making of specialists in different areas of human business including financial and medical fields (Sehrawat, 2023).

The inclusion of AI into business process automation started from the year 2000s when businesses tried to find ways on how to cut costs and time in the process of automating business activities. Robotic process automation (RPA) turned out to be the first attempt towards managing the dull processes on a large scale. RPA tools were developed with the intention to perform human activities such as inputting data, copying and pasting information, performing other clerical tasks among others. While RPA proved to deliver great results in term of speed and accuracy, the programing-based tool is only capable of performing predefined tasks with decision making capability which AI offers (Khan, 2023). When AI technologies started to improve, business followed the question on how the RPA could be enhanced with AI in order to make the systems more intelligent and adaptive capable for appointment not only on repetitive tasks but also on decision making processes (Yakovenko & Shaptala, 2023). Nowadays, AI applications are successfully used in processes where task implementation requires data analysis combined with decision-making, as well as interactions with people. Machine learning is one of the main classifications of the AI technologies used in BPA which involves the ability of a system to learn from the past data. For instance, the use of AI automation in supply chain may involve the use of analytical models to foretell the volume of sales of certain products, thus helping firms to order the right quantity of products to avoid storing products for long or even having excess products. Likewise with Automation of financial services, through Artificial Intelligence systems, it is possible to crunch financial data to produce intelligent patterns of fraudulent activities, making it easy for firms to protect themselves against financial crimes (Khan, 2023).

The two main fields of AI technology applicability are business process automation and natural language processing (NLP). NLP is a way of allowing machines to understand and even create natural human language so that Business can employ automation for example in analysis of documents and contracts, and interaction with consumers and even legal procedures. For instance, end-user communication through application of natural language processing in such tools as chatbots can address customers' inquiries in real-time without involving human personnel. These chatbots can be incorporated into a firm's facilities of the customer service department to afford a fully automated service 24/7 thus lightening the burden of the customer care officers while at the same time improving customer satisfaction. In the same way, legal contracts, and other legal documents can be scanned using NLP and Accused risks and firms can be protected to make sure they are following the laws set by the government. While being viewed as a subordinate type of automation, strongly cooperates with AI to improve business process automation. RPA tools are a means of handling tasks that can be defined as routine, prescribed, and re-iterative, usually including data entry, invoices' processing, and payroll management. PA becomes even more flexible and capable of increasing the number of processes required for work when integrated with other AI technologies, such as machine learning and NLP. For instance, in the health sector, RPA systems can schedule appointments and process patient details while AI systems use information derived from patients' records to help the doctors in diagnosing patient's ailments and admission. This combination of AI and RPA helps in obtaining even higher automation level which directly leads to the reduction of organizational costs and optimization of business processes (Mishra & Tripathi, 2021).

Other technology that is utilized in BPA includes computer vision which is a part of AI technology and is more utilized in industries such as manufacturing and logistics. Computer vision refers to the natural capability of the computer to understand visual data and information within the physical world and consequently automates visual recognition tasks. For instance, in manufacturing AI integrated systems with computer vision can be used to inspect products for defects which are faster and more efficient than employing human talents. Likewise in logistics, AI systems can keep track of stocks by identifying images of products and shelves and therefore eliminating the need for back checking. This capability not only works in enhancing the accuracy of such processes, but also offloads human workers to embrace other advanced and relevant tasks related to the overall organizational job (Khan, 2023). AI's capability to parse large datasets or massive flows of information within seconds or even minutes and come up with relevant decision-making insights is also changing decision-making processes. The use of business process automation systems through artificial intelligence is capable of processing massive data inputs from different areas and will generate an output containing recommendations for enhancement of these processes. For instance, in the retail business, AI-driven automation technologies can identify consumers' behavioral patterns to determine the right quantities of products to order or even end consumers' demand for products and even in segmentation, marketing promotions can be made. Such automation not only reduces cost but also helps the business be flexible, to adapt to changes in customer demand and market status (Mishra & Tripathi, 2021). Another benefit of utilizing artificial intelligence in business process automation is that the technology gets to acquire knowledge of the ongoing process and consistently enhance the processes' performance. AI unlike other automation tools need not be updated manually as the tool itself learns from the new data and new experiences. This capability ensures that automation systems under artificial intelligence transform into systems that are more capable of managing change than persistent systems. For instance, an AI supply chain management system can shift from specific historical events as a disaster, including bad weather conditions or a strike by suppliers and implement changes on the prediction and the main strategy modelled. This capability of learning and adaptation rationalises the functionalities of the advanced and enhanced AI powered automation systems to yield consistent performance and value even in dynamically altered and complex scenarios

Therefore, AI and business process automation are innovating new ways of operations of organizations by reducing time- consuming and inaccuracies results from previous manual work. These technologies include but not limited to machine learning, natural language processing, and computer vision that have had made some business processes become more efficient and cost effective to run besides facilitating better decision making processes. While AI is still a developing technology in automation, companies will have to be more responsive in order to fully realize the benefits of leveraging on AI. Thus, knowing the key ideas and the historical background of the AI application as well as the different types of technologies applied in process automation managers and leaders will be able to perform in this unpredictable field effectively and their companies will remain competitive in the digital environment.

AI-Driven Digital Transformation

It is obvious that artificial intelligence (AI) is among the more critical digital transformation enablers and drivers of change throughout the business as organizations navigate the new environment and address various challenges in today's digital environment. Essentially, digital transformation entails the adoption of technology into different areas of operations in an organization with a view of improving on services and transforming experiences.AI is among the most influential agents of this transformation since it offers organisations the capability to automate tasks and functions, process large volumes of information and make decisions in the process. In fact, there is hardly any firm today that has not leveraged – or is not thinking of leveraging – AI as a major enabler of their digital transformation initiatives, since it creates considerable efficiencies in terms of workflows and resource management and is therefore crucial for maintaining competitiveness in today's highly digitalised global environment (Mishra & Tripathi, 2021). Digital transformation of businesses has impacted a company in various ways with the help of AI. Automation of business procedures is one of the areas that AI has a significant impact on by cutting down the amount of work that needs to be done by the employees. For example, chatbots may handle customer relations, while big data analysis may be applied for generating insights as well as predictive supply chain management can be used to reduce interruptions. They also help businesses cut costs, speed up response time and improve customers' experience of the products and services provided. With the help of implementing AI solutions, organisations can increase the efficiency of the business processes at the same time enhancing the strategic management of the organisations' development processes and innovations (Kaushik, 2024).

Another area is that AI helps companies adapt to the needs of their consumers; in today's world, by personalization, which has become a driver of organizational transformation. With the help of advanced data analysis, AI systems thus have the capability of decoding and even predicting customers' tendencies and reactions. It becomes possible to carry out this level of customization with the help of machine learning algorithms that can talk more about the customers' information and their probable future actions. For instance, in e-commerce, AI in an application enables Amazon to recommend products to a customer based on the customers' browse history as well as their past purchases. In the banking industry, AI friendly systems can take in customer's financial data to recommend on the best investment opportunity or credit product to offer customers the products most suitable for their needs.

A prominent instance is Netflix's metamorphosis, wherein artificial intelligence has revolutionized the way it provides content to its viewership. Large volumes of data on user viewing preferences, habits, and even the time of day when users are most active are analysed by Netflix's AI algorithms. The aforementioned data is subsequently employed to generate tailored content suggestions, guaranteeing that users consistently encounter choices that align with their preferences. Netflix's success has been largely attributed to this personalized experience, which has helped it sustain high user engagement levels and dramatically increase its subscriber base (Kaushik, 2024). Additionally, Netflix uses AI to create content by evaluating viewership data to forecast which films and television series will succeed, enabling the business to make well-informed choices about content expenditures. The successful application of AI to digital transformation in the healthcare sector is another example. AI applications in healthcare, particularly in the areas of medical diagnostics and treatment recommendations, have been pioneered by companies such as IBM Watson. Artificial intelligence (AI) systems are capable of analyzing patient data, medical records, and even research literature to provide physicians diagnosis and treatment recommendations. This has changed the way medical professionals handle complicated cases, allowing for more rapid and accurate diagnosis as well as individualized treatment regimens.

AI, for example, has been used to diagnose diseases like cancer more rapidly and reliably than human radiologists by analyzing medical pictures. Along with bettering patient outcomes, this has also lessened the workload for healthcare professionals, freeing them up to concentrate more on patient care. Additionally, supply chain management is being drastically changed by AI for businesses worldwide. AI has been integrated into supply chain operations by businesses like Amazon and Walmart in an effort to increase productivity, save expenses, and improve customer happiness. For example, AI-driven systems are able to forecast product demand by examining market trends, past sales data, and other external factors. By doing this, businesses may maximize their stock levels and steer clear of overstocking or understocking, which can both have a detrimental effect on profitability. Furthermore, AI may be used to spot possible supply chain interruptions like supplier delays or problems with transportation, giving businesses the opportunity to take preventative action to lower risks. Supply chain management has changed from being a reactive process to one that is more proactive and predictive because to these capabilities (Kaushik, 2024).

General Electric's (GE) use of AI to enhance its industrial processes is one of the most noteworthy case studies of AI-driven digital transformation. As part of its digital transformation plan, GE used AI to produce "digital twins" of its industrial machinery, including gas turbines and jet engines. These digital twins are virtual copies of the actual machinery that track performance, anticipate maintenance requirements, and maximize efficiency using real-time data and AI algorithms. GE can save downtime and save money by doing maintenance before a breakdown happens by utilizing AI to forecast when a machine is likely to fail. This has not only changed the way GE runs its manufacturing division, but it has also made it possible for the business to provide new services to its clients, such predictive maintenance programs (Nair & Nathiya, 2024). Walmart, a massive retailer, is another impressive example of how AI has improved its digital transformation initiatives. AI has been incorporated into Walmart's operations in a number of areas, including customer service and inventory management. For example, Walmart employs automated systems driven by AI in its warehouses to manage inventory, improve product placement, and expedite the packaging and shipping procedures. By predicting demand and ensuring that popular items are constantly in stock, these AI systems may improve consumer happiness by analyzing real-time data. Furthermore, Walmart has integrated artificial intelligence (AI)-driven chatbots into its online customer support operations, enabling users to get prompt, precise answers to their questions without requiring human assistance. As a result, the company's operating expenses have decreased and the entire purchasing experience has been improved (Hamid, 2024). The financial services sector is another one where AI is clearly having an influence on digital transformation. Businesses there are using AI to boost client experiences, cut costs, and increase efficiency. For instance, JPMorgan Chase has automated the evaluation of legal papers using artificial intelligence (AI), replacing the need for hundreds of hours of human work in the past. The bank has lowered the time and expense of legal reviews dramatically by utilizing AI to scan and process documents. Additionally, by evaluating transaction data in real time and spotting suspect activity, AI-powered solutions are being employed in the financial sector to detect and prevent fraud. In addition to protecting consumers, this proactive strategy to fraud identification aids financial institutions in upholding their regulatory obligations and preserving their good names (Gu, 2024).

AI is accelerating digital change in the automotive sector by enabling the creation of driverless cars. Self-driving vehicles, which depend on machine learning algorithms, computer vision, and real-time data analysis to traverse roadways, avoid obstacles, and make driving judgments, are a product of the technological innovation of companies like Tesla. Because of the possible reduction in accidents, increase in fuel efficiency, and development of new business models focused on autonomous mobility, this might radically revolutionize the automobile industry. Robots with AI capabilities are automating welding and assembly, for example, in the car manufacturing process. This increases production efficiency and quality (Hamid, 2024). To sum up, artificial intelligence (AI) is a potent catalyst for digital transformation in a variety of sectors, allowing companies to automate procedures, boost productivity, and provide individualized consumer experiences. AI is revolutionizing the way businesses operate, compete, and innovate in a variety of industries, including healthcare, retail, banking, and manufacturing. Promising instances, including GE's digital twins, Walmart's AI-powered inventory control, and Netflix's tailored content suggestions, highlight how AI is revolutionizing corporate operations. AI's influence on the direction of digital transformation will only expand as more businesses use it; this will present fresh chances for development and creativity in the digital era.

AI in Human Resources and Recruitment

Human resources (HR) and recruiting are changing as a result of artificial intelligence (AI), which is increasing the accuracy and efficiency of formerly labor- and time-intensive procedures. AI technologies and methods are being utilized to automate HR processes, ranging from maintaining employee performance to screening resumes. These developments assist HR professionals make more objective decisions by reducing prejudice and human error, as well as by saving time (Gu, 2024). The hiring process is one of the main areas where AI is having a big influence. The first steps of the recruiting process may be automated by AI-driven systems, which use algorithms to scan and evaluate applications and find the best prospects based on predetermined standards. This saves time and eliminates the possibility of unconscious bias in manual resume evaluations, which are necessary for shortlisting possible candidates for a job. By evaluating candidate data and assigning candidates to positions that best fit their qualifications and expertise, AI may also aid in personalizing the hiring process. Employers may get more insight into candidates' talents by using AI-powered platforms like HireVue and Pymetrics, which utilize machine learning algorithms to evaluate candidates based on how well they do in gamified tests and video interviews.

AI is being utilized for HR tasks including performance monitoring, onboarding, and training in addition to recruiting. For example, AI-powered chatbots may help new hires with the onboarding process by assisting with routine queries, directing them through tasks, and giving them crucial information about the norms and procedures of the organization. This simplifies the onboarding process and frees up HR personnel time for more important tasks. Artificial intelligence (AI) systems in performance management are able to track worker performance in real time by evaluating key performance indicators (KPIs). This makes it possible for businesses to pinpoint high performers, pinpoint areas in need of development, and design individualized strategies for each employee's personal growth (Hamid, 2024). AI-driven hiring methods have several advantages. They help get rid of human biases that might influence recruiting decisions, shorten the time and expense involved in the hiring process, and increase the accuracy of applicant matching. Artificial Intelligence (AI) frees HR practitioners to concentrate on higher-level responsibilities like strategy planning and employee development by automating monotonous operations. Large-scale data analysis is another capability of AI technologies, which may yield insightful information that enhances retention and talent management tactics (Gu, 2024).

AI-driven hiring systems do, however, come with certain difficulties. The possibility of bias in AI algorithms is a significant worry, particularly if the data used to train these algorithms reflects prejudices that are already present in the workforce. For instance, an AI system may inadvertently reinforce prejudices in future employment decisions if it is educated on recruiting data from the past that Favors particular groups. Since AI systems need a lot of personal data to work well, there are also worries over data security and privacy. Employers need to make sure AI is used appropriately and that policies are in place to safeguard applicant and staff data (Lodhi, Gill, & Hussain, 2024). Unilever's use of AI technologies to expedite their employment process is a noteworthy case study of AI in recruitment. The business put in place an artificial intelligence (AI) driven hiring platform that analyzes applicants' video interviews and game-based tests using algorithms. With this strategy, Unilever was able to hire people 75% faster and with a more varied pool of applicants. In a similar vein, IBM has introduced artificial intelligence (AI) tools to oversee worker performance, employing data analytics to pinpoint top performers and provide tailored growth prospects.

AI is transforming HR and hiring by streamlining procedures, enhancing judgment, and offering insightful data. While there are many advantages to AI-driven systems, like less prejudice and better efficiency, there are drawbacks, including issues with algorithmic fairness and data privacy. As AI develops further, businesses need to find a way to utilize technology responsibly and ethically while still maximizing its potential.

AI FOR STRATEGIC DECISION-MAKING

Organizations are using artificial intelligence (AI) more and more to improve strategic planning and decision-making. Businesses may make more informed decisions based on real-time information and forecast insights thanks to artificial intelligence (AI), which processes massive volumes of data rapidly and effectively. Conventional methods of making decisions frequently rely on human intuition and experience, which might be constrained by biases and insufficient information. As an impartial, data-driven approach, artificial intelligence (AI) may assist executives in anticipating obstacles, seeing opportunities, and refining their strategy (Lodhi, Gill, & Hussain, 2024). Machine learning models for forecasting and predictive analytics are a major method AI improves strategic decision-making. In order to anticipate future events, machine learning algorithms can study previous data to find patterns and trends. AI, for instance, can estimate product demand, anticipate consumer behaviour, and evaluate risks, all of which may improve company planning. This is especially useful for businesses in the retail sector, where they can use AI to predict sales during high seasons and modify inventory levels based on customer habits. Artificial intelligence (AI) models in the financial sector enable financial organizations to make more informed lending and investing choices by forecasting stock market movements or evaluating credit risks

Artificial intelligence (AI) may offer real-time insights in addition to predictive analytics, facilitating speedier and more accurate decision-making.AI-powered technologies, for example, may track and evaluate competitive activity, market circumstances, and internal performance measures. This knowledge gives executives the ability to promptly modify their strategy. Artificial intelligence (AI) systems in the healthcare industry are capable of analyzing patient data to assist strategic choices on resource allocation, including where to invest in new medical technology or which therapies to prioritize. Analogously, AI in manufacturing may be applied to enhance supply chain management, forecast equipment breakdowns, and optimize production processes (Nair & Nathiya, 2024). Systems for strategic decision-making powered by AI have been effectively deployed in a number of sectors.For instance, Amazon leverages AI to streamline its logistics and supply chain processes. Amazon employs AI to assist the corporation make strategic decisions about where to place warehouses, how to deploy resources, and how to maximize delivery times. The system analyses data on consumer demand, inventory levels, and shipping routes. Because of this, Amazon has been able to increase productivity and save expenses without sacrificing customer pleasure (Lodhi, Gill, & Hussain, 2024).

Another illustration comes from the automobile sector, where businesses such as Tesla employ AI to make strategic decisions related to the development of autonomous vehicles. Artificial intelligence (AI) systems use data from sensors, cameras, and radar to make choices in real time regarding driving conditions, obstacle avoidance, and navigation. By using a data-driven approach, Tesla is able to make strategic decisions on the development and application of autonomous cars as well as continuously enhance its self-driving technology. In a similar vein, AI-driven decision-making is revolutionizing industries such as banking, where organizations employ AI to identify fraud, forecast market trends, and make investment choices (Nair & Nathiya, 2024). AI has developed into a potent instrument for strategic decision-making, enabling companies to evaluate information, predict results, and take well-informed decisions instantly. Organizations in a variety of sectors may improve their operations, lower risks, and maintain competitiveness in a market that is changing quickly by utilizing predictive analytics and machine learning models.AI technology will play an even more important role in influencing strategic decision-making as it develops, enabling firms to make judgments that are quicker, more accurate, and more effective (Hamid, 2024).

AI-Supported Management

Managerial tasks are assigned a much bigger importance to artificial intelligence the more they advance with technologies. Employees' duty includes decision making, sourcing for resources and setting goals and objectives which are activities that can be greatly supported by an AI system. As a result, AI systems can work with big data to generate useful information that can be used to inform strategic decisions by catching trends and predicting what might occur thus enhancing the stream of business. For instance, predictive analytics can assist the managers to estimate the market trends or the customers' behaviour to enable the businesses to make necessary preparations (Nair & Nathiya, 2024). Also, the process of timetabling and recording of activities, generating and maintaining reports can be effectively done by the AI while the manager can undertake other complicated tasks which requires human intervention. Thus, AI is a necessity as the business environment becomes a labyrinth, for managers eager to enhance their performance and optimise workflow (Aldoseri et al., 2024). AI tools are also influencing the area of performance management and employees' engagement as well. More often than not, the traditional approach to performance management entails carrying out regular appraisals which are not specific, accurate and can be driven by assumptions. AI tools, however, provide support through ongoing evaluation thus allowing performance tracking on a continuous basis. For instance, AI-based platforms can monitor the performance of the employees and give suggestions based on use, which may be helpful in goal setting and towards the achievement of organizational goals (Yakovenko & Shaptala, 2023). Further, the analysis of several activities such as employees' feedback, communication or social media posts reveals the overall satisfaction level of employees through sentiment analysis assuring that any concern will be addressed immediately (Lodhi et al., 2024). AI can also assist in creating and recommending unique training and development for every worker depending on their performance data, which could lead to increased productivity, inter alia employee satisfaction and attrition rates (Nduka, 2023).

Applying AI case studies to discuss different management tools and practices illustrate how the implementation of AI can revolutionise modern business. For example, a multinational firm was able to apply the technology in its supply channel efficiency. They are able to analyse demand patterns and optimize the inventory levels by applying machine learning algorithms, thus cutting down their costs on inventories while at the same time meeting customer expectations on delivery. Not only did this prove to be an effective method for increasing the efficiency of the process, but it also helped to cut costs dramatically; Shobhana 2024. For instance, a giant financial services firm used the concept of artificial intelligence in solving its recruitment problem. Working with the AI-based systems, the candidates' filtering and sorting occurred according to the skills and demands of the vacancies, which dramatically shrunk the recruitment time and increased the quality of the occupants (Eboigbe et al., 2023). Likewise, the firms that aided customer service through chatbots and automated help desks have been able to maintain constant and round-the-clock customer service which enhanced customer experience and saved operational expenses (Bhattacharyya et al., 2023). The above examples show how AI can be implemented to improve on management practices such that flows become optimized. Thus, the use of AI in management means a new form of interaction between the manager and other employees since it provides a set of tools and data to improve decision making, workers' productivity, and their motivation. AI helps managers to pay more attention to other important tasks that require their close attention while automating the various monotonous assignments that may take a lot of their time and other resources. This means that the importance of AI in management will keep increasing as more firms implement AI solutions in their operations, hence obtaining enhanced efficiency. Let's mention supply chain management, recruitment, and other essential spheres where AI can become a decisive factor for companies that want to strengthen their positions in the markets.

FUTURE TRENDS AND INNOVATIONS

As the application of Artificial Intelligence (AI) in business increase the following ethical issues emerge; Bias is another critical issue that can be caused by AI systems; the ability of the AI system to make bias decisions is a great concern. Machine learning relies on data feeds, and if the inputs are prejudiced in some way existing in the society, then AI becomes a betrayer in aspects such as employment, promotions or customer relations. For instance, if the AI system applied in the recruitment process was trained from gender or racially biased data then such a system will tend to Favor a particular gender or race leading to unethical hiring (Jabbouri & Issa, 2023). Thirdly, more and more decision-making processes are being 'outsourced' to the computers, which raises the issues of responsibility. When an AI system makes a wrong decision, it is often unclear who should be held responsible: proposed to benefit the business, the developers or the AI itself? Such conditions of vagueness result in organizational ethical ambiguity that organisational strategies have to resolve (Bhadra et al., 2023).

Lack of privacy is the other major concern that is likely to facing business entities with the increasing implementation of AI. Personal data is the most valuable resource for AI systems as they operate with customer data, employee records, or financial information, for example. The collection and use of this data pose some questions regarding data security and right to privacy. For instance, AI systems used in customer relationship management gather a lot of information about customers' behaviors as well as their preferences; this information if not secured adequately can be exploited (Allioui & Mourdi, 2023). Companies have to develop adequate safeguards for the protection of personal data in line with data encryption and anonymization methods to prevent the leakage of information to unauthorized persons (Cerruti & Valeri, 2022). Also, there are legal requirements that need to be met in regard to data protection acts such as the General Data Protection Regulation (GDPR) in Europe that requires that the data of the individuals should be given the highest form of consideration and that the data subjects must be informed as well (Nair & Nathiya, 2024). In order to mitigate these ethical and privacy issues we need well defined rules and regulation for the use of AI in businesses. First, AI system must be devised and implemented in a manner that is transparent. Decision making processes are easier explained to people in business organizations when the ai tools affect the employees or customer, therefore organizations should be able to explain how decisions are made when using such ai tools. For example, if a company incorporated the use of AI in pre-screening the potential employees, they ought to reveal the criteria used by AI and how it ranks them (Yakovenko & Shaptala, 2023). Second, it involves providing for checks and balances to confirm whether the AI systems are favourable or have formed biases towards certain entities. Last, AI should be developed with the aspect of privacy considering the use of technologies including differential privacy by enabling companies to glean useful data about people without disclosing their identities (Enholm et al., 2022).

Last but not the least; it is the responsibility of the business to ensure the ethical use of AI systems by incorporating the fundamental principles of ethics into the organizational DNA. This could include formation of ethics boards or committees to overs gears AI projects as well as program to train the employees on the ethics of AI (Hamid, 2024). Such guidelines will assist the organizations in the appropriate application of AI while at the same time avoiding any form of infringement of people's rights and privacy. In conclusion, therefore, this paper agrees with the view that, although AI can be of great and substantial benefit to business management, this technology is not entirely free from ethical and privacy concerns that ought to be well managed. Thus, it is possible to state that with the further reinforcement of transparency, data protection, and ethical management, businesses will be able to take advantage of AI without facing severe challenges from the part of social impact. This is the reason why there is a great outlook for the development of the Artificial Intelligence (AI) in business process automation. Another trend you can discuss is known as 'hyper-automation' which basically involves the total or close to total automation of business processes leveraging advanced Artificial Intelligence, Machine Learning and Robotic Process Automation. Hyper automation can be described as a process of automating several non-associated methods that use artificial intelligence in making decision, thereby decreasing the chances of making errors. Likewise, in organizations, the emerging trend of artificial intelligence means that companies are using chatbots for responding to customer service support enquires and follow-up and thus relieving human workers for higher valued added activities (George et al., 2023). Likewise, the process of supply chain has been made radical through the implementation of AI for managing supply-chain inventory as well as for accurate prediction of the demands (Shobhana, 2024). Thus, with the growing number of companies integrating such AI-based tools, the phenomenon of hyper automation should develop and render various industries more distinct.

As we look into the future, one can forecast that AI is going to revolutionize firm management in many ways. The use of AI thus brings up the ability to process large quantities of information in real time implying that managers would rely heavily on the use of AI in their decision-making processes. For instance, human resource data retrieved by AI can assist the manager to obtain patterns of performances, thus being in a position to develop, train, and promote employees appropriately (Lodhi et al., 2024). It can also allow managers to respond faster to the changes for example by analyzing customer behaviour and trends in the market. Embracing such fluidity will be equally important in ensuring that there is the ability to determine change and adapt to it in a manner that will keep an edge over competitors. However, as the AI systems evolve in the complex functionalities and capacities, they are likely to be adopted fundamental utility in the firm management where the companies will have added responsibility of designing long term visions and targeting the uncertainties of the business models by Karulkar et al., 2025.

However, together with these opportunities, the advancement of AI also opens new risks to the society. It also presents some limitations; lack of critical decision making since people tend to rely heavily on the systems. Although AI always out-performs human beings in doing data analysis, it is not capable of comprehending human emotions, intentions and various ethical considerations. Organizations should be careful in the process of AI implementation so that it does not remove human control or decisions completely especially when decisions may require ethical feelings (Bolotova, 2024). Fourth, the fact remains that businesses have to update the AI systems to meet the emerging advanced technological features. Larger firms have larger budgets and thus can afford to invest in infrastructure, training, and security of the data for the AI solutions, however, this is a significant challenge for the small firms (Bhadra et al., 2023). There are also the same threats that make AI in business management's future full of opportunities. There is one big benefit in using AI and that is the ability to transform innovation. By this method, a business firm can collect copious amounts of data which they can feed to an AI tool, and the tool will reveal trends that would be difficult to identify on one's own if the business firm is to develop a new product, a new service, or a new process. For instance, analytics formed by AI can assist the firms to detect the unsolved problem areas or customers' needs which have not been met adequately for firms to win over their competitors and innovate more than them (Nduka, 2023). Moreover, AI can also be useful in managing sales and targeting the customer and their needs more effectively and offer an improved and engaging interaction (Gu, 2024).

Finally, it can be stated that there are rather bright perspectives for AI in business processes automation and management in the future. Despite the costs of implementation and the risk of dependency on such a system there are significant benefits to be realised. Since the advancement and adoption of AI technologies is not finite, the organizations that are strategic in the management and adoption of AI courses will likely innovate, compete and sustain themselves in the cutthroat world that is characteristic of the fourth industrial revolution. Over a period further into the future of AI, this future will indeed revolutionize the field of business management in enabling entities unveil new methods towards the improvement of business processes, decision making as well as business growth.

CASE STUDIES AND REAL-WORLD APPLICATIONS

Many organisations in the global realm are incorporating use of AI to enhance business interoperations and gain competitive advantage. Another example of implementation of AI and machine learning is amazon where these technologies are used for logistics and supply chain. Having applied the AI algorithms in customer demand forecasting, inventory control, and delivery routes optimization, Amazon has improved its efficiency, cut costs, and increased customers' satisfaction (Yakovenko & Shaptala, 2023). This is shown by the case of the company using AI in its warehouses where robots pick, pack, and ship products together with human employees showing how AI optimises speed and precision of its operations. More real-world success story is also available from financial and banking sector where JP Morgan Chase is using Artificial Intelligence for preventing fraud and risk. The current revolutionary approach for credit card fraud detection in JP Morgan is the application of machine learning models since they can handle a large volume of transaction data in real time with improved accuracy as compared to the traditional method (Bhadra et al., 2023). Most importantly, this application of AI in the bank has enhanced the customers' protection and at the same time lowered the operating costs of the bank in the control of fraud. The experiences of JP Morgan show that the financial industry can benefit from the use of AI and improve security as well as risk management in the organization, and also analyse the data available in organizations for gaining insights.

Experience with such and other organizations shows that the use of AI in business processes needs to follow certain guidelines, which are described below. One important lesson that one can deduce is the fact that companies need to begin slowing by creating a small market before expanding their operations. For example, instead of implementing AI as a means of digitising complex processes at a go, the various programs can be introduced gradually starting with particular activities or divisions like Amazon's case of gradual incorporation of robotics in its storage facilities (George et al., 2023). This approach enables companies to determine the efficiency of the application of artificial intelligence in reducing and managing small-scale risks while at the same time engaging the employees in the program to increase acceptance before a broader adoption of the use of artificial intelligence is carried out. The second is the need to invest in training and upskilling of the workforce which is recognised throughout the business ecosystem. That is why, people will have to learn new skills that would allow them to work in conjunction with artificial intelligence; an approach used by Amazon to balance the use of AI with the need for employees.

The use of AI across the different industries has been a subject of debate, with some industries evidenced to have recorded high success rates. For instance, in healthcare, AI is applied in diagnosing patients as well as enhancing the delivery of the patients' need. Another example, IBM Watson, widely used artificial intelligence platform, has been used in the hospitals to in the medical data analysis and to help doctors to get better accurate disease diagnostic results (Karulkar et al., 2025). Through analysing a large amount of data concerning patient, Watson is able to find correlations and make suggestions which can be useful from the standpoint of practical health activities. This has led to increase in accuracy of diagnosis and increase in the survival of the patients. Likewise in the automotive sector the self-driving cars use AI from companies such as Tesla. Currently, self-driving cars from Tesla utilize artificial intelligence to interpret data from the machine and cameras in real-time, thereby enabling the vehicle to drive on the roads safely without human help (Shobhana, 2024). This can be viewed as a great step forward, not only in car development but also in case of AI integration into people's daily lives.

These case studies show the great impact that has been experienced by various industries due to the use of AI. In all cases, the organizations leveraged artificial intelligence functionalities for operational procedures, decision making and customer relations. The best practices of AI that can be observed in these examples include the capability of analysing data faster than the human personnel can ultimately enhance the result of the operations performed. Businesses that engage in systematic

AI planning, develop the capabilities of their employees, and are adaptable are more likely to fully unlock AI's potential and reap its benefits in the long term.

CONCLUSION

In this chapter we have been able to look at the areas which AI is used in in aiding business process automation, advantages and disadvantage. Decision making has been another area that organizations using AI to enhance their efficiency and effectiveness in running their organizations. We also explored how it has been adopted in performance management, engaging the employees, and even in managing risks in profession such as finance and healthcare. By use of samples like how Amazon adopted the use of AI to enhance its supply chain and JP Morgan on AI on fraud detection, the effectiveness of the technology is proved by revealing how organizations in various industries are using it to gain competitive advantage. Thus, these examples give the picture of how AI is valuable not only from an operational standpoint but also regarding the customers and business advantages. Another point that was made clear in this chapter is to begin with a small-scale application of AI and then expand it further. Such a modification enables organisations to use the technology primarily in certain areas and identify its efficiency and any changes that may be required before implementation in other departments. Further, we highlighted the issue of workforce reskilling as the roles of humans become obsolete with AI taking over repetitive operations while they have to switch to other roles thereby working hand in hand with AI. Many organizations have also realized the importance of apportioning resources towards supporting their people, facilitate them to move to new responsibilities that have potential in positions other than implementing AI while enjoying the gains that come with the application of automation.

The implementation of AI in corporate operations raises ethical and privacy problems, which were also covered in this chapter. Organizations must provide strong data protection protocols and uphold openness in the collection and use of data, as AI systems handle sensitive data more and more. Businesses must create precise policies for the moral use of AI, guaranteeing that their technology usage upholds privacy and is devoid of prejudice or discrimination. To ensure that AI's advantages are achieved without violating people's rights or trust, it will be essential to strike a balance between ethical concerns and the technology's transformational potential.

We investigated upcoming developments and trends in corporate automation and artificial intelligence. AI is developing quickly, and new technologies provide even more opportunities to improve corporate procedures. The potential for innovation is enormous, ranging from autonomous systems to more advanced AI-driven analytics. But these developments also bring with them new difficulties, such handling the intricacy of AI systems, protecting data, and adjusting to changing regulations. Organizations that maintain their adaptability, are dedicated to ongoing learning, and keep ahead of these changing difficulties will be the most likely to succeed. The case examples examined in this chapter provide insightful insights for companies considering AI implementation. Organizations may optimize the advantages of artificial intelligence by emphasizing gradual modifications, allocating resources for staff training, and upholding a strong emphasis on moral behaviour. Artificial Intelligence has demonstrated its capacity to revolutionize several industries, including manufacturing, banking, logistics, and healthcare. The corporate environment will continue to change as more organizations use AI-driven automation. Some advantages of this automation include improved customer satisfaction, quicker decision-making, and enhanced productivity.

To sum up, artificial intelligence (AI) has the ability to drastically change corporate processes, ranging from simple activities to intricate decision-making. Its capacity to swiftly and precisely analyse enormous volumes of data enables businesses to streamline processes, cut expenses, and raise service standards. Adopting AI has its obstacles, but with the correct strategy, these issues—like privacy concerns and the requirement for ethical deployment—can be overcome. Businesses that carefully and deliberately integrate AI will be better positioned to prosper in an increasingly digital environment as technology develops. AI will play a major role in business automation in the future, and companies who successfully leverage its potential will surely excel in both performance and innovation.

REFERENCES

Aldoseri, A., Al-Khalifa, K., & Hamouda, A. (2023). A roadmap for integrating automation with process optimization for AI-powered digital transformation.

Aldoseri, A., Al-Khalifa, K. N., & Hamouda, A. M. (2024). AI-powered innovation in digital transformation: Key pillars and industry impact. *Sustainability (Basel)*, *16*(5), 1790. DOI: 10.3390/su16051790

Allioui, H., & Mourdi, Y. (2023). Unleashing the potential of AI: Investigating cutting-edge technologies that are transforming businesses. [IJCEDS]. *International Journal of Computer Engineering and Data Science*, *3*(2), 1–12.

Bhadra, P., Chakraborty, S., & Saha, S. (2023). Cognitive IoT meets robotic process automation: The unique convergence revolutionizing digital transformation in the Industry 4.0 era. In *Confluence of artificial intelligence and robotic process automation* (pp. 355–388). Springer Nature Singapore. DOI: 10.1007/978-981-19-8296-5_15

Bhattacharyya, S., Banerjee, J. S., & De, D. (Eds.). (2023). *Confluence of artificial intelligence and robotic process automation* (Vol. 335). Springer Nature. DOI: 10.1007/978-981-19-8296-5

Bolotova, I. (2024). *Artificial intelligence technologies in business process management (based on "Advertising and production group NBS" case)* (Doctoral dissertation, Private Higher Educational Establishment-Institute "Ukrainian-American Concordia University").

Cerruti, C., & Valeri, A. (2022). *AI-powered platforms: Automated transactions in digital marketplaces* (Doctoral dissertation, Master of Science in Business Administration, Università degli Studi di Roma "Tor Vergata" Department of Management and Law).

Eboigbe, E. O., Farayola, O. A., Olatoye, F. O., Nnabugwu, O. C., & Daraojimba, C. (2023). Business intelligence transformation through AI and data analytics. *Engineering Science & Technology Journal*, *4*(5), 285–307. DOI: 10.51594/estj.v4i5.616

Elhajjar, S., Yacoub, L., & Yaacoub, H. (2023). Automation in business research: Systematic literature review. *Information Systems and e-Business Management*, *21*(3), 675–698. DOI: 10.1007/s10257-023-00645-z

Enholm, I. M., Papagiannidis, E., Mikalef, P., & Krogstie, J. (2022). Artificial intelligence and business value: A literature review. *Information Systems Frontiers*, *24*(5), 1709–1734. DOI: 10.1007/s10796-021-10186-w

Farayola, O. A., Abdul, A. A., Irabor, B. O., & Okeleke, E. C. (2023). Innovative business models driven by AI technologies: A review. *Computer Science & IT Research Journal*, *4*(2), 85–110. DOI: 10.51594/csitrj.v4i2.608

George, A. S., George, A. H., Baskar, T., & Sujatha, V. (2023). The rise of hyper-automation: A new frontier for business process automation. *Partners Universal International Research Journal*, *2*(4), 13–35.

Gu, S. (2024). Exploring the role of AI in business decision-making and process automation. *International Journal of High School Research*, *6*(3).

Hamid, M. (2024). AI-powered business intelligence: Revolutionizing data analysis and reporting. *Asian Bulletin of Business Analytics & Artificial Intelligence*, *1*(1).

Jabbouri, R., & Issa, H. (2023). The AI-powered business ecosystem and its associated business models. *Journal of Research in Administrative Sciences*, *12*(1), 9–27.

Karulkar, Y., Shah, A., & Naik, R. (2025). AI-powered business evolution: Transformative strategies for success of evolving industries. In *Creating AI synergy through business technology transformation* (pp. 39–72). IGI Global.

Kaushik, S. (2024). The rise of AI-powered competitive intelligence: Transforming market analysis. *Blockchain and AI in Business,* 112.

Khan, D. (2023). Unleashing business intelligence: Text analytics and AI-driven ERP transformations towards an intelligent enterprise. *Social Sciences Spectrum*, *2*(1), 103–110.

Lahlali, M., Berbiche, N., & El Alami, J. (2021). How enterprise must be prepared to be "AI first"? *International Journal of Advanced Computer Science and Applications*, *12*(5). Advance online publication. DOI: 10.14569/IJACSA.2021.0120542

Lodhi, S. K., Gill, A. Y., & Hussain, I. (2024). AI-powered innovations in contemporary manufacturing procedures: An extensive analysis. *International Journal of Multidisciplinary Sciences and Arts*, *3*(4), 15–25. DOI: 10.47709/ijmdsa.v3i4.4616

Mishra, S., & Tripathi, A. R. (2021). AI business model: An integrative business approach. *Journal of Innovation and Entrepreneurship*, *10*(1), 18. DOI: 10.1186/s13731-021-00157-5

Nair, S. S., & Nathiya, R. (2024, May). AI-powered business revolution: Elevating efficiency and boosting sales through cutting-edge process re-engineering with machine learning. In *2024 Second International Conference on Data Science and Information System (ICDSIS)* (pp. 1-7). IEEE. DOI: 10.1109/ICDSIS61070.2024.10594289

Nduka, W. (2023). The significance of artificial intelligence in business process management.

Qureshi, J. (2024). AI-powered cloud-based e-commerce: Driving digital business transformation initiatives.

Sehrawat, S. K. (2023). The role of artificial intelligence in ERP automation: State-of-the-art and future directions. *Transactions on Latest Trends in Artificial Intelligence, 4*(4).

Shobhana, N. (2024). AI-powered supply chains towards greater efficiency. In *Complex AI Dynamics and Interactions in Management* (pp. 229–249). IGI Global. DOI: 10.4018/979-8-3693-0712-0.ch011

Siddiqui, A. T., Jahangeer, G. S. B., & Basha, A. F. (2024). AI-empowered devices and strategies to reduce cost in business. In *Harnessing AI and digital twin technologies in businesses* (pp. 40–52). IGI Global. DOI: 10.4018/979-8-3693-3234-4.ch004

Yakovenko, Y., & Shaptala, R. (2023). *Intelligent process automation, robotic process automation, and artificial intelligence for business processes transformation.* Publishing House "Baltija Publishing". DOI: 10.30525/978-9934-26-378-1-20

ADDITIONAL READING

Tariq, M. U. (2025). Unlocking Competitive Edge: Harnessing the Power of Collaborative Innovation. In J. Martínez-Falcó, E. Sánchez-García, & B. Marco-Lajara (Eds.), *Open Innovation Strategies for Effective Competitive Advantage* (pp. 315-344). IGI Global Scientific Publishing. https://doi.org/10.4018/979-8-3693-9266-9.ch011

Tariq, M. U. (2025). Empowering Patients With AI-Ethical Digital Tools for Health Data Management and Decision. In A. Pesqueira & A. de Bem Machado (Eds.), *Navigating Privacy, Innovation, and Patient Empowerment Through Ethical Healthcare Technology* (pp. 197-216). IGI Global Scientific Publishing. https://doi.org/10.4018/979-8-3693-7630-0.ch008

Tariq, M. U. (2025). Leveraging Libraries and Information Centers for Startup Innovation and Growth. In V. Gupta & C. Gupta (Eds.), *Navigating Strategic Partnerships for Sustainable Startup Growth* (pp. 1-28). IGI Global Scientific Publishing. https://doi.org/10.4018/979-8-3693-4066-0.ch001

Tariq, M. U. (2025). Revolutionizing Retail: Enhancing Customer Experiences With the Metaverse. In M. Gonçalves Rodrigues, M. Carvalho, & J. Monteiro Pratas (Eds.), *Cases on Metaverse and Consumer Experiences* (pp. 175-202). IGI Global Scientific Publishing. https://doi.org/10.4018/979-8-3693-7245-6.ch007

Tariq, M. U. (2025). AI-Driven Research Methodologies: Revolutionizing Data-Driven Discoveries in Engineering and Physical Sciences. In J. Basha, T. Alade, M. Al Khazimi, R. Vasudevan, & J. Khan (Eds.), *Optimizing Research Techniques and Learning Strategies With Digital Technologies* (pp. 97-122). IGI Global Scientific Publishing. https://doi.org/10.4018/979-8-3693-7863-2.ch004

KEY TERMS AND DEFINITIONS

AI Ethics: The study and implementation of ethical standards in the development and deployment of AI systems.

Artificial Intelligence (AI): The simulation of human intelligence by machines, enabling them to perform tasks like decision-making, problem-solving, and learning.

Business Process Automation (BPA): The use of technology to automate repetitive tasks, streamline processes, and increase efficiency in business operations.

Machine Learning: A subset of AI focused on the development of algorithms that allow systems to learn from data and improve performance without explicit programming.

Predictive Analytics: A branch of data analytics that uses statistical models and machine learning to predict future events or trends based on historical data.

Chapter 11
Models of Elasticity of Key Indicators of Market Activity With a Neutral Approach to Dividend Policy:
Elasticity Models With a Neutral Dividend Policy

Sergey Krylov
https://orcid.org/0000-0001-6750-085X
Ural Federal University, Russia

ABSTRACT

The chapter is devoted to consideration of the conceptual basis for analyzing the sensitivity of key indicators of a public company's activity on the stock market (market activity) to the main determining factors with a neutral approach to the implementation of its dividend policy in the context of the possible use of artificial intelligence. The methodological basis of the study was the concept of a neutral approach to the dividend policy of a public company and the concept of sensitivity analysis. Analysis of the sensitivity of key indicators of market activity to the main determining factors in the conditions of a neutral approach to the implementation of the dividend policy of a public company involves the construction of appropriate elasticity models that make it possible to determine changes in these indicators depending on changes in their determining factors. The constructed elasticity models can be used in forecasting and analytical assessments of changes in key indicators of market activity under a neutral dividend policy.

DOI: 10.4018/979-8-3693-7357-6.ch011

Copyright © 2025, IGI Global Scientific Publishing. Copying or distributing in print or electronic forms without written permission of IGI Global Scientific Publishing is prohibited.

1. INTRODUCTION

In the conditions of a modern developed market economy, a rather important characteristic of the activity of a public company (public joint stock company) is its activity in the stock market (market activity), which should be understood as the choice of optimal strategies and tactics in using profit, accumulating it, increasing capital by issuing additional shares, as well as the impact on the market price of the share. Ensuring the level of market activity required by a public company, as a rule, involves the development of a set of management decisions that contribute, at least, to the non-deterioration of its position in the capital market in terms of the dynamics of market indicators (absolute - the market price of an ordinary share, earnings per ordinary share and dividend per ordinary share, as well as relative – financial coefficients of market activity).

The activity of a public company in the stock market can be considered as an essential component of its sustainable development, which implies the possibility of long-term continuation of its effective activities, which is determined by the availability and level of efficiency in the use of relevant resources and, as the author of this chapter believes, lies primarily in the sustainability of growth in production volumes. and sale of products (works, services), innovative and investment activity, as well as welfare of employees and shareholders of a public company.

Obviously, the problem of sustainable development of companies cannot be solved without the formation of appropriate information support related to the development of recommendations for compiling the so-called integrated report on the sustainable development of the company, among which the GRI standards (Global Reporting Initiative), focused on the principle of "triple outcome" (Triple bottom Line): company economics, company production ecology and company social policy (Global Reporting Initiative (GRI), 2013). At the same time, indicators that characterize their activity in the securities market can be included in the list of key indicators of economic performance of public companies.

In fairness, it should be noted that the indicators of market activity mentioned above are widely considered in numerous publications, for example, (Akhigbe & Madura, 1996; Ang, Cole & Lin, 2000; Bernstein, Wild & Subramanyam, 2001; Black, 1976; Block, Hirt & Danielsen, 2011; Brealey, Mayers & Allien, 2017; Brigham & Houston, 2015; Brooks, 1996; Fama & French, 1989; Goetzmann & Jorion, 1995; Hauser, 2013; Helfert, 2001; Higgins, Koski & Mitton, 2016; Lambrecht & Myers, 2012; Lee & Finnerty, 1990; McLaney, 1992; Penman, 2004; Petit, 1972; Rozeff, 1982; Shim & Siegel, 2008; Subramanyam, 2014; Van Horne, 1989; Van Horne & Wachowicz, 2009).

Having generalized and systematized the points of view of the above researchers, we will single out the key financial ratios that characterize the market activity of a public company, dividing them into two interrelated groups (Table 1).

Table 1. Key financial ratios characterizing the market activity of a public company

Name of indicator	Calculation formula	
	Numerator	**Denominator**
1. Indicators characterizing the investment attractiveness of common stock		
Common stock quote ratio	Market price of an ordinary share	Profit per ordinary share
Dividend yield on common stock	Dividend per ordinary share	Market price of an ordinary share
Market Price to Dividend Ratio per Common Share	Market price of an ordinary share	Dividend per ordinary share
2. Indicators characterizing the dividend policy		
Dividend yield ratio (Formula 1)	Dividend per ordinary share	Profit per ordinary share
Dividend yield ratio (Formula 2)	Dividends on ordinary shares	Net profit - Dividends on preferred shares
Dividend coverage ratio	Earnings per ordinary share	Dividend per ordinary share
The rate of distribution of net profit for dividends	Dividends on all types of shares	Net profit
Preferred share dividend coverage ratio	Net profit	Dividends on preferred shares
Ratio of dividends on ordinary and preferred shares	Dividends on ordinary shares	Dividends on preferred shares

Source: compiled by the author of the chapter

The indicators of the first group (quotation ratio of an ordinary share, dividend yield of an ordinary share, ratio of the market price of an ordinary share and dividend per ordinary share) characterize, first of all, the investment attractiveness of ordinary shares of a public company for potential investors.

The indicators of the second group (dividend yield ratio, dividend coverage ratio, the rate of distribution of net profit for dividends, the dividend coverage ratio for preferred shares, the ratio of dividends for ordinary and preferred shares) characterize exclusively the dividend policy of a public company.

Since the investment attractiveness of ordinary shares of a public company largely depends on its dividend policy, the indicators of the second group should be considered as basic, which determines their particular importance in the analysis of market activity. At the same time, many determining factors influence both groups of indicators.

It should be especially noted that the dividend policy, on the one hand, should contribute to the achievement of the main goal of financial management - maximizing the material well-being of shareholders, and, on the other hand, take into account the interests of all other stakeholders interested in the activities of a public company (including potential investors) to ensure its sustainable development in the long term. Fulfillment of this requirement is possible only within the framework of a neutral approach to the implementation of the dividend policy of a public company (Krylov, 2020, 2021, 2025).

At the same time, special attention should be paid to the fact that the dividend policy is usually developed only in relation to ordinary shares, since the dividend yield of preferred shares is in most cases (but not always) fixed.

All of the above makes it expedient to study the market activity of a public company by analyzing the sensitivity of its key indicators to the main factors that determine them, precisely in the context of a neutral approach to the implementation of dividend policy.

An important tool for solving this problem is artificial intelligence (AI), which is usually viewed in two aspects: firstly, as the ability of a computer to learn, make decisions and perform actions characteristic of human intelligence, and secondly, as a science at the intersection of mathematics, biology, psychology, cybernetics and some other fields of knowledge, which studies technologies that allow a person to write "intelligent" programs and teach computers to solve problems independently.

In financial management, artificial intelligence helps optimize investment and financial processes and obtain the final result with less effort, increasing the accuracy, speed and efficiency of transactions in financial markets. AI is a powerful financial market analysis tool that can predict future prices, trends and events by using big data, machine learning and deep learning to study various factors that influence market dynamics.

In addition, AI can also recognize complex patterns and signals in data that may be hidden to the human eye or traditional methods, not only improving existing investment and financial decisions and processes, but also opening up new opportunities for the financial industry by meeting needs and expectations customers in the era of digital transformation. AI enhances interaction and collaboration between different financial market participants, promoting social and environmental well-being.

2. MATERIALS AND METHODS

2.1. Previous Research

Previously in a number of publications (in particular, (Krylov, 2020, 2021, 2025)) formulated and substantiated a neutral approach to the dividend policy of a public company, based on the joint use of the dividend irrelevance theory, the dividend policy materiality theory and the concept of sustainable development companies.

It was shown that the "cornerstone" of the dividend policy, which determines its types (methods), is ultimately the ratio between dividend and earnings per ordinary share (dividends on ordinary shares and net income minus dividends on preferred shares), which makes the dividend ratio output (or its inversely proportional indicator - the dividend coverage ratio) is the most important indicator when analyzing the dividend policy of a public company.

The results of assessing its value largely depend on the chosen approach to the implementation of the dividend policy of a public company: passive or active (Van Horne, 1989; Van Horne & Wachowicz, 2009).

The passive approach to dividend policy implementation, or dividend irrelevance theory, to which F. Modiliani and M. Miller (Miller & Modiliani, 1961) made a crucial contribution, arguing that for a given choice of investment decisions, the dividend yield ratio is no more than a detail of the big picture. It does not affect the welfare of shareholders. Miller and Modigliani argue that the value of a public company is determined solely by the return on its assets or its investment policy, and that the way in which net income is distributed between dividends and reinvested earnings does not affect this valuation.

In other words, the payment of dividends acts as a "passive balance" after the investment projects of the public company have been financed. The value of the dividend yield ratio will change from period to period in accordance with fluctuations in the number of investment projects acceptable from the point of view of the management of a public company. If a public company has many favorable investment opportunities, then the dividend yield ratio is likely to be zero. In contrast, if a public company does not have profitable investment opportunities, the dividend yield ratio is likely to be 1. For any situation in between, the value of the dividend yield ratio will take values from 0 to 1 (Van Horne, 1989). At the same time, shareholders allegedly do not care what factor will increase their material well-being: dividends or an increase in the market value of ordinary shares as a result of the implementation of investment projects by a public company.

A formalized illustration of a passive approach to dividend policy is the model of James E. Walter (Walter, 1956), which is considered one of the first and has the advantages of relative simplicity and clarity:

$$P = \frac{D + \frac{r}{\rho} * (E - D)}{\rho} \quad (1)$$

where P is the predicted market price of an ordinary share,

D – dividend per ordinary share;
E – earnings per ordinary share;
r – return on investment of a public company;
ρ– market capitalization level (average market discount rate used to determine expected cash flows).

According to the active approach to the implementation of the dividend policy, or the theory of the materiality of the dividend policy, the main ideologists of which were M. Gordon (Gordon, 1963) and J. Lintner (Lintner, 1962), decisions on the payment of dividends play a significant, active role. The fact is that in the conditions of uncertainty, which is more or less typical for the activities of almost any public company in market conditions, shareholders do not care whether they receive their income in the form of dividends or in the form of an increase in the market value of ordinary shares. The payment of dividends gives shareholders a sense of certainty, since dividends are a type of current income, and the prospect of a return on capital can be pushed far into the future. Therefore, shareholders are not at all indifferent to what factor will increase their material well-being: dividends or an increase in the market value of ordinary shares as a result of the implementation of investment projects by a public company. In addition, if potential investors prefer early resolution of uncertainty, they will be willing, other things being equal, to pay a higher price for shares that entitle them to receive a larger current dividend (Van Horne, 1989).

A formalized argument in favor of an active approach to the implementation of dividend policy is M. Gordon's model of economic growth (Gordon, 1959):

$$P_0 = \frac{D_1}{k-g} = \frac{D_0 * (1+g)}{k-g} \quad (2)$$

where P_0 is the predicted current (theoretical) value of an ordinary share at the zero moment,

D_1 – expected dividend per ordinary share of the future period;
D_0 – dividend per ordinary share of the current period;
k – acceptable discount rate (the rate of return required by investors per ordinary share of the company);
g – dividend growth rate per ordinary share (assumed to be constant over time).

The above models (1) and (2) can be considered as formalized tools for forecasting and, accordingly, managing the dividend policy within the framework of passive and active approaches to its implementation.

At the same time, it should be borne in mind that the dividend policy of a public company, as noted earlier, should not only help maximize the material well-being of its shareholders, but also take into account the interests of all other stakeholders interested in the company's activities (suppliers, buyers, employees, the state, etc.) to ensure its long-term sustainability by contributing to the long-term value of the public company (Dunphy, Griffiths & Suzanne, 2007; Freeman, 2010; Friedman & Miles, 2006).

All this leads to the need to achieve a kind of "balance" between passive and active approaches within the framework of the so-called neutral approach to the implementation of dividend policy, which takes into account both the need to finance profitable investment projects and pay dividends to shareholders of a public company (not on a residual basis), thus leading to the maximization of the market value of its common stock.

Formalization of the idea of a neutral approach to the implementation of the dividend policy involves the construction of corresponding models of the dividend yield ratio and the dividend coverage ratio, as well as the expected price of an ordinary share.

To build models of the dividend yield ratio and the dividend coverage ratio, we equate the predicted market price of an ordinary share, calculated according to the model of D.E. Walter (formula (1)), to the predicted current (theoretical) value of an ordinary share at the zero moment, determined according to the M. Gordon economic growth model (formula (2)) based on the assumption that the current value of the flow of expected future dividends on an ordinary share corresponds to its market price (Van Horne, 1989), which is most relevant in a highly efficient securities market:

$$P = P_0 \qquad (3)$$

while introducing a single designation of the dividend per ordinary share as D ($D = D_0$).

As a result, we have the following equality:

$$\frac{D+\frac{r}{\rho}*(E-D)}{\rho} = \frac{D*(1+g)}{k-g} \qquad (4)$$

Through a series of transformations from formula (4), we obtain models of the dividend output ratio (DP) and the dividend coverage ratio (DC):

$$DP = \frac{D}{E} = \frac{\frac{r}{\rho}}{\frac{\rho*(1+g)}{k-g}+\frac{r}{\rho}-1} \quad (5)$$

$$DC=\frac{E}{D}=(\frac{\rho*(1+g)}{k-g} - 1)*\frac{\rho}{r} + 1 \quad (6)$$

Formulas (5) and (6) show that in the context of a neutral approach to the implementation of dividend policy, the following factors influence the dividend yield and dividend coverage ratios: the return on investment of a public company, the market capitalization level, the rate of return required by investors per ordinary share of the company, and the accepted constant in time rate of growth of dividend per ordinary share. The calculation of the influence of determining factors on the deviation of performance indicators in models (5) and (6) can be carried out using the appropriate methods of factor analysis.

The models of the dividend yield coefficient (formula (5)) and the dividend coverage ratio (formula (6)) can be used in predictive and analytical estimates of the values of these coefficients within the framework of a neutral approach to the implementation of the dividend policy directly, as well as some other indicators, characterizing market activity (for example, the dividend yield of an ordinary share and the quote coefficient of an ordinary share), calculated on their basis.

To build a model of the market price of an ordinary share, we first express the amount of dividend per ordinary share from the D.E. Walter (formula (1)) and the dividend per ordinary share of the current period from the M. Gordon economic growth model (formula (2)) respectively as follows:

$$D=\frac{\rho*P-\frac{r}{\rho}*E}{1-\frac{r}{\rho}} \quad (7)$$

$$D_0=\frac{P_0*(k-g)}{1+g} \quad (8)$$

Then we equate the amount of dividend per ordinary share from the D.E. Walter (formula (7)) to the dividend per ordinary share of the current period from the economic growth model of M. Gordon (formula (8)):

$$D = D_0 \quad (9)$$

while introducing a single designation of the expected, i.e. equilibrium in relation to the position of a particular investor and the situation on the stock market, the price of an ordinary share as P ($P = P_0$).

As a result, we have the equality:

$$\frac{\rho^*P - \frac{r}{\rho}^*E}{1-\frac{r}{\rho}} = \frac{P^*(k - g)}{1+g} \qquad (10)$$

from which we obtain a model of the expected price of an ordinary share:

$$P=\frac{\frac{r}{\rho}^*E}{\rho\text{-}(k\text{-}g)^*\frac{1-\frac{r}{\rho}}{1+g}} \qquad (11)$$

According to formula (11), under the conditions of a neutral approach to the implementation of the dividend policy, the expected price of an ordinary share is influenced by the following factors: the return on investment of the company, the market capitalization level, earnings per ordinary share, the rate of return required by investors per ordinary share of the company, and the rate assumed to be constant over time increase in dividend per ordinary share. The calculation of the influence of determining factors on the deviation of the effective indicator in model (11) can be carried out using the appropriate methods of factor analysis.

The model of the expected price of an ordinary share (formula (11)) can be used in predictive and analytical estimates of the values of this rather important indicator of the market activity of a public company within the framework of a neutral approach to the implementation of the dividend policy directly, as well as some other indicators characterizing the market activity of a public company. company (for example, the dividend yield of an ordinary share and the quote ratio of an ordinary share), calculated on its basis.

So, in the conditions of a neutral approach to the implementation of the dividend policy, based on the previously introduced symbols, a model of the dividend yield of an ordinary share (DY) can be formed:

$$DY=\frac{D^*(\rho\text{-}(k - g)^*\frac{1-\frac{r}{\rho}}{1+g})}{\frac{r}{\rho}^*E} \qquad (12)$$

In accordance with formula (12), under the conditions of a neutral approach to the implementation of dividend policy, the dividend yield of an ordinary share is determined by the influence of the following factors: dividend per ordinary share, market capitalization level, the rate of return required by investors on an ordinary share of the company, the assumed constant time rate of dividend growth per ordinary share and earnings per ordinary share. The calculation of the influence of determining factors on the deviation of the effective indicator in model (12) can be carried out using the appropriate methods of factor analysis.

The model of dividend yield of an ordinary share (formula (12)) can be used in predictive and analytical estimates of the values of this ratio within the framework of a neutral approach to the implementation of the dividend policy directly, as well as some other indicators characterizing the market activity of a public company, calculated on its basis (for example, the quotation ratio of an ordinary share).

The factor model of the quote coefficient of an ordinary share (13) is constructed as follows:

$$P/E = \frac{P}{E} = \frac{P}{D} * \frac{D}{E} = \frac{DP}{DY} = \frac{\frac{CD}{NP\text{-}PD}}{DY} = \frac{\frac{\frac{CD}{PD}}{\frac{NP}{PD}\text{-}1}}{DY} = \frac{DCD}{(CPD\text{-}1)*DY} \qquad (13)$$

where P/E – quote ratio of an ordinary share (Price / Earnings ratio);

DCD – ratio of dividends on ordinary and preference shares;
CPD – dividend coverage ratio for preferred shares;
DP – dividend yield ratio (Dividend payout);
DY – dividend yield of an ordinary share (Dividend Yield);
P – market price of an ordinary share;
E – earnings per ordinary share (Earnings per share);
D – dividend per ordinary share;
CD – total amount of dividends on ordinary shares;
PD – total amount of dividends on preferred shares;
NP – net profit.

In the context of a neutral approach to the implementation of the dividend policy, based on the above conventions, the model of the quotation ratio of an ordinary share (P / E) has the following form:

$$P/E = \frac{DCD * \frac{r}{\rho} * E}{(CPD\text{-}1) * D * (\rho\text{-}(k - g) * \frac{1\text{-}\frac{r}{\rho}}{1+g})} \qquad (14)$$

Based on formula (14), in the conditions of a neutral approach to the implementation of the dividend policy, the quote ratio of an ordinary share depends on the influence of such factors as earnings per ordinary share, the ratio of dividends on ordinary and preferred shares, the company's return on investment, market capitalization level, coverage ratio dividends on preferred shares, the rate of return required by investors per ordinary share of the company, the rate of growth of the dividend per ordinary share assumed to be constant over time, and the dividend per ordinary share. The calculation of the influence of determining factors on the deviation of the effective indicator in the model (14) can be carried out using the appropriate methods of factor analysis.

The model of the quote coefficient of an ordinary share (formula (14)) can be used in predictive and analytical assessments of the values of this rather important coefficient characterizing the market activity of a public company in the framework of a neutral approach to the implementation of its dividend policy, depending on its key indicators.

The forecast values of the above indicators of the market activity of a public company, obtained using models (5), (6), (11), (12) and (14), can be analyzed from the perspective of one or another stakeholder interested in the sustainable development of this company, based on the results of which they can be given a predictive assessment of the level of efficiency in managing its market activity (high, medium, low, extremely low).

It should also be noted that, as mentioned earlier, it is of particular interest to analyze the sensitivity of these indicators to changes in the main determining factors presented in their models, which leads to an increase in the effectiveness of the analysis and forecasting of the market activity of a public company in the framework of a neutral approach to its dividend policy, defining the methodological basis of this study.

2.2. Methodological Basis of the Research

The methodological basis of the study, the results of which are presented in this article, was a neutral approach to the dividend policy of a public company and the concept of sensitivity analysis.

Since the neutral approach to the dividend policy of a public company was described in sufficient detail in the previous subsection "Previous Research", let's turn to the concept of sensitivity analysis.

The concept of sensitivity analysis has by now been widely used and deeply considered in many literary sources, in particular, (Cacuci, 2003; Griewank, 2000; Helton, Johnson, Salaberry & Storlie, 2006; Leamer, 1985; Pannell, 1997; Saltelli, 2002; Saltelli, Chan & Scott, 2000).

Let's take a brief look at it.

As is well known, sensitivity analysis is designed to model the impact of various factors on the bottom line in the financial model of a business or project. It can be used for the following purposes:

- identification of the most significant parameters of the model, which will require special attention when collecting data and in the course of further business;
- assessment of expected results in conditions when important characteristics of the project or business are not known exactly;
- stress testing to determine the ability of a business to withstand fluctuations in parameters, in particular, the calculation of the maximum deviations of these parameters, at which there are problems with the profitability or financial stability of the company.

It should be noted that sensitivity analysis is a rather general term, and includes many possible tasks and modeling methods that combine four main elements:

1. There is a prepared business model. This model is quite complex, and there is no way to derive a direct mathematical dependence of the result on one or another parameter in the form of a simple formula. The model for researchers is a "black box" that can be experimented with to study the effect of parameters on the result.
2. Researchers are interested in one of the results of the model, which is expressed as a number. For example, the NPV of an investment project, or a business valuation, or the company's total capital requirement.
3. Researchers choose one or more model parameters, change them, and collect information about how the result changes. They have a great selection here. You can change the parameters evenly by trying all the values of some interval. You can choose their values randomly, taking into account the statistical distribution (this is how the Monte Carlo method works).
4. The final data on how the result is distributed with the studied parameter fluctuations is presented visually in the form of graphs or tables and used in business analysis.

Although in general statistical methods such as Monte Carlo are also sensitivity analysis, in financial models, sensitivity analysis usually means a narrower set of approaches. This is a visual display of the dependence of the final indicator on changes in one or more parameters in a given range.

In general, the sensitivity of a function is considered as the degree to which the function changes for a given absolute or relative change in the arguments. In economic and mathematical analysis, it is often necessary to determine how sensitive an economic indicator is to changes in the factors that determine it. In this case, two approaches are used – incremental and tempo. In the first case, the growth of the factor and the growth of the studied indicator are compared - the average rate of change of the function or the limiting rate of change of the function. In the second case, the growth rate of the factor and the growth rate of the studied indicator are compared, usually meaning percentage changes.

Sensitivity analysis of indicators is widely used in the practice of financial management. In the general case, it comes down to studying the dependence of some effective indicator on the variation in the values of the factors involved in its determination. In other words, this method allows you to get answers to questions like: what will happen to the resulting value if the value of some factor value changes? Hence its second name is "what if" analysis.

As a rule, such an analysis involves the following steps:

1. The relationship between the performance indicator and the factors determining it is set in the form of a mathematical equation or inequality.
2. The most probable values for the determining factors and possible ranges of their changes are determined.
3. By changing the values of the determining factors, their influence on the performance indicator is investigated.

The usual procedure for sensitivity analysis is to change one determinant while keeping the rest constant.

Sensitivity analysis is one of the simplest and most common methods of risk analysis. With its help, you can find out which factors (estimated parameters) can be attributed to the most risky.

As an indicator of the sensitivity of the object of risk regarding changes in certain factors, elasticity, or sensitivity of response, is used, which in economic theory in modern conditions is one of the fundamental values. Elasticity is a measure of the response of one variable (function) to a change in another (argument), is calculated as the limit of the ratio of the relative increment of the function to the relative increment of the argument when the increment of the argument tends to zero and is considered as an important statistical measurement tool widely used in marketing research, and economic analysis tool.

So the elasticity of the function $y=f(x)$ with respect to the argument x is determined by the following formula:

$$E_x(y) = \lim_{\Delta x \to 0}\left(\frac{\Delta y}{y}:\frac{\Delta x}{x}\right) = \frac{x}{y} * \frac{dy}{dx} \tag{15}$$

It can be seen from formula (15) that the elasticity $E_x(y)$ of the function $y=f(x)$ is directly proportional to the derivative of this function $\frac{dy}{dx}$ and expresses an approximate percentage increment of the function, which corresponds to 1% argument increments.

Sensitivity analysis is implemented in financial models using three common methods:

1) sensitivity graphs;
2) sensitivity tables;
3) tornado charts.

The sensitivity graph helps to demonstrate the dependence of a performance indicator on a change in one of its determinants. factors and shows how a change in one of the factors affects the performance indicator. As a rule, to build a sensitivity graph, several model calculations are carried out and a graph is built using the obtained points. Most often, the dependence will be linear, so 2-3 calculations are enough to build a graph, but in order not to miss a more complex dependence, it is better to use at least 5-7 points. Here you can see one trick used in a situation where the parameter being studied is not a single number, but a whole series of numbers. Instead of absolute values, a sensitivity plot usually uses a percentage of the baseline forecast.

Sensitivity tables track the change in the effective indicator when two factors fluctuate. For sensitivity analysis in Excel, a data table service is often used, which automates multiple recalculation of models with different initial parameters. Data tables have two parameters – in terms and columns, that is, they allow you to calculate the dependence on two characteristics at once. This has led to the popularity of the tabular approach to sensitivity analysis. In the case of tabular analysis, for better visualization, conditional formatting is usually used, separating good and bad values of the effective indicator.

Tornado charts focus only on the extreme values of the deviation of the studied factors, but on the other hand, on one such chart, you can combine the analysis of several factors at once. The Tornado diagrams show the change in the effective indicator with the same fluctuations of several factors of the model. Unlike graphs or sensitivity tables, the entire range of values is not studied here, but only two values are calculated for each factor: for positive and negative deviation. Since the most influential factors are usually located at the top of the graph, it takes on a look a bit like a tornado pattern, hence the name of these charts.

Having described in a rather concise form the methodological basis of the study, the main results of which are presented in this article, the author considers it appropriate to proceed to their consideration.

3. RESULTS

The results of the research by the author of this chapter are the models developed by him of elasticity of key indicators of the activity of a public company in the stock market according to the main factors determining them in the conditions of a neutral approach to the implementation of dividend policy: dividend yield ratio, dividend coverage ratio, expected price of an ordinary share, dividend yield of an ordinary share and quote ratio of an ordinary share - based on the models of the listed indicators (5), (6), (11), (12) and (14), using the formula (15) and previously introduced symbols.

Models of elasticity of the dividend yield coefficient of a public company with respect to the profitability of its investments ($E_r(DP)$), market capitalization level ($E_\rho(DP)$), the rate of return required by investors per ordinary share of a public company ($E_k(DP)$) and the rate of dividend growth per ordinary share assumed to be constant over time ($E_g(DP)$) are respectively represented by formulas (16), (17), (18) and (19):

$$E_r(DP) = \frac{r}{DP} * \frac{\partial DP}{\partial r} = \frac{\frac{\rho*(1+g)}{k-g} - 1}{\frac{\rho*(1+g)}{k-g} + \frac{r}{\rho} - 1} \tag{16}$$

$$E_\rho(DP) = \frac{\rho}{DP} * \frac{\partial DP}{\partial \rho} = \frac{1 - \frac{2*\rho*(1+g)}{k-g}}{\frac{\rho*(1+g)}{k-g} + \frac{r}{\rho} - 1} \tag{17}$$

$$E_k(DP) = \frac{k}{DP} * \frac{\partial DP}{\partial k} = \frac{\frac{k*\rho*(1+g)}{(k-g)^2}}{\frac{\rho*(1+g)}{k-g} + \frac{r}{\rho} - 1} \tag{18}$$

$$E_g(DP) = \frac{g}{DP} * \frac{\partial DP}{\partial g} = \frac{\frac{g*\rho*(k+1)}{(k-g)^2}}{1 - \frac{r}{\rho} - \frac{\rho*(1+g)}{k-g}} \tag{19}$$

Models of elasticities of the dividend coverage ratio of a public company with respect to the profitability of its investments ($E_r(DC)$), market capitalization level ($E_\rho(DC)$), the rate of return required by investors per ordinary share of a public company ($E_k(DC)$), and the dividend growth rate per ordinary share assumed to be constant over time ($E_g(DC)$) are respectively represented by formulas (20), (21), (22) and (23):

$$E_r(DC) = \frac{r}{DC} * \frac{\partial DC}{\partial r} = \frac{\rho - \frac{\rho^2*(1+g)}{k-g}}{\frac{\rho^2*(1+g)}{k-g} - \rho + r} \tag{20}$$

$$E_\rho(DC) = \frac{\rho}{DC} * \frac{\partial DC}{\partial \rho} = \frac{\frac{2*\rho^2*(1+g)}{k-g} - \rho}{\frac{\rho^2*(1+g)}{k-g} - \rho + r} \tag{21}$$

$$E_k(DC) = \frac{k}{DC} * \frac{\partial DC}{\partial k} = \frac{k*\rho^2*(1+g)}{\left(g-k\right)^2*\left(\frac{\rho^2*(1+g)}{k-g} - \rho + r\right)} \tag{22}$$

$$E_g(DC) = \frac{g}{DC} * \frac{\partial DC}{\partial g} = \frac{g*(k+1)}{\left(k-g\right)^2*\left(\left(\frac{\rho*(1+g)}{k-g} - 1\right)*\frac{\rho}{r} + 1\right)} \tag{23}$$

Formulas (16-23) show that the elasticity of the dividend yield and dividend coverage ratios of a public company with respect to the profitability of its investments to the market capitalization level, the rate of return required by investors per ordinary share of a public company, and the dividend growth rate per ordinary share assumed to be constant over time is influenced by the following factors: the return on investment of a public company, the market capitalization level, the rate of return required by investors per ordinary share of a public company, and the rate of dividend growth per ordinary share assumed to be constant over time. The calculation of the influence of determining factors on the deviation of performance indicators in formulas (16-23) can be carried out using the appropriate methods of factor analysis.

Elasticity models of the expected price of an ordinary share of a public company with respect to earnings per common share ($E_E(P)$), the return on investment of a public company ($E_r(P)$), market capitalization level ($E_\rho(P)$), the rate of return required by investors per common share of a public company ($E_k(P)$), and an assumed time-constant dividend growth rate per ordinary share ($E_g(P)$) are represented by formulas (24), (25), (26), (27) and (28), respectively:

$$E_E(P) = \frac{E}{P} * \frac{\partial P}{\partial E} = 1 \tag{24}$$

$$E_r(P) = \frac{r}{P} * \frac{\partial P}{\partial r} = \left(\rho - (k-g)*\frac{1-\frac{r}{\rho}}{1+g}\right)^2 + \frac{r*(g-k)}{1+g} + \frac{r*\left(g-k\right)^2*\left(1-\frac{r}{\rho}\right)}{\rho*(1+g)^2} \tag{25}$$

$$E_\rho(P) = \frac{\rho}{P} * \frac{\partial P}{\partial \rho} = \frac{\frac{r}{\rho}*\frac{k-g}{1+g} + \frac{(k-g)*\left(1-\frac{r}{\rho}\right)}{1+g} - \rho}{\rho - (k-g)*\frac{1-\frac{r}{\rho}}{1+g}} \tag{26}$$

$$E_k(P) = \frac{k}{P} * \frac{\partial P}{\partial k} = \frac{k*\left(1-\frac{r}{\rho}\right)}{\rho*(1+g) - (k-g)*\left(1-\frac{r}{\rho}\right)} \tag{27}$$

$$E_g(P) = \frac{g}{P} * \frac{\partial P}{\partial g} = \frac{g*\rho*(2*g-k)*\left(1-\frac{r}{\rho}\right)}{\left(\rho - (k-g)*\frac{1-\frac{r}{\rho}}{1+g}\right)*\left(1+g\right)^2} \tag{28}$$

According to formulas (25-28), the elasticity of the expected price of an ordinary share of a public company with respect to the return on investment, the market capitalization level, the rate of return required by investors per ordinary share of a public company, and the dividend growth rate assumed to be constant over time on its ordinary share is influenced by the following factors: the return on investment of a public company, the market capitalization level, the rate of return required by investors per ordinary share of a public company, and the rate of dividend growth per ordinary share assumed to be constant over time. The calculation of the influence of determining factors on the deviation of performance indicators in formulas (25-28) can be carried out using the appropriate methods of factor analysis.

Elasticity models for the dividend yield of a public company common stock to dividend and earnings per common share ($E_D(DY)$ *и* $E_E(DY)$ *соответственно*), public company return on investment ($E_r(DY)$), market capitalization level ($E_\rho(DY)$), investors' required rate of return per share of a public company common share ($E_k(DY)$), and assumed time-constant growth rate dividends per its ordinary share ($E_g(DY)$) are represented by formulas (29), (30), (31), (32), (33) and (34) respectively:

$$E_D(DY) = \frac{D}{DY} * \frac{\partial DY}{\partial D} = 1 \tag{29}$$

$$E_E(DY) = \frac{E}{DY} * \frac{\partial DY}{\partial E} = -1 \tag{30}$$

$$E_r(DY) = \frac{r}{DY} * \frac{\partial DY}{\partial r} = \frac{\frac{k-g}{1+g} - \rho}{\rho - (k-g) * \frac{1-\frac{r}{\rho}}{1+g}} \tag{31}$$

$$E_\rho(DY) = \frac{\rho}{DY} * \frac{\partial DY}{\partial \rho} = \frac{2*\rho - \frac{k-g}{1+g} * \left(1 + \frac{2*r}{\rho}\right)}{\rho - (k-g) * \frac{1-\frac{r}{\rho}}{1+g}} \tag{32}$$

$$E_k(DY) = \frac{k}{DY} * \frac{\partial DY}{\partial k} = \frac{k * \left(\frac{r}{\rho} - 1\right)}{\rho * (1+g) - (k-g) * \left(1 - \frac{r}{\rho}\right)} \tag{33}$$

$$E_g(DY) = \frac{g}{DY} * \frac{\partial DY}{\partial g} = \frac{g * (1+k) * \left(1 - \frac{r}{\rho}\right)}{\rho * (1+g)^2 - (k-g) * \left(1 - \frac{r}{\rho}\right) * (1+g)} \tag{34}$$

In accordance with formulas (31-34), the elasticity of the dividend yield of an ordinary share of a public company by the return on investment of a public company, the market level of capitalization, the rate of return required by investors on an ordinary share of a public company and the assumed constant time rate of dividend growth on its ordinary share are influenced by the following factors: the return on investment of a public company, the market capitalization level, the rate of return required by investors on a common share of a public company, and the assumed rate of dividend growth per common share that is constant over time. Calculation of the influence of determining factors on the deviation of performance indicators in formulas (31-34) can be carried out using appropriate methods of factor analysis.

Elasticity models for the quoted ratio of a public company's ordinary share in terms of dividend and earnings per ordinary share ($E_D(P/E)$ *и* $E_E(P/E)$ *соответственно*), the ratio of dividends on ordinary and preferred shares of a public company ($E_{DCD}(P/E)$), its dividend coverage ratio on preferred shares ($E_{CPD}(P/E)$), the return on investment of a public company ($E_r(P/E)$), market the level of capitalization ($E_\rho(P/E)$), the rate of return required by investors per ordinary share of a public company ($E_k(P/E)$) and the dividend growth rate assumed to be constant in time per its ordinary share ($E_g(P/E)$) are respectively represented by formulas (35), (36), (37), (38), (39), (40), (41) and (42):

$$E_D(P/E) = \frac{D}{(P/E)} * \frac{\partial\left(\frac{P}{E}\right)}{\partial D} = \frac{\rho}{(k-g)*\frac{1-\frac{r}{\rho}}{1+g} - \rho} \tag{35}$$

$$E_E(P/E) = \frac{E}{(P/E)} * \frac{\partial(P/E)}{\partial E} = 1 \tag{36}$$

$$E_{DCD}(P/E) = \frac{DCD}{(P/E)} * \frac{\partial(P/E)}{\partial DCD} = 1 \tag{37}$$

$$E_{CPD}(P/E) = \frac{CPD}{(P/E)} * \frac{\partial(P/E)}{\partial CPD} = \frac{CPD}{1-CPD} \tag{38}$$

$$E_r(P/E) = \frac{r}{(P/E)} * \frac{\partial(P/E)}{\partial r} = \frac{\rho - \frac{k-g}{1+g} * \left(1 - \frac{2*r}{\rho}\right)}{\rho - (k-g)*\frac{1-\frac{r}{\rho}}{1+g}} \tag{39}$$

$$E_\rho(P/E) = \frac{\rho}{(P/E)} * \frac{\partial(P/E)}{\partial \rho} = \frac{\frac{k-g}{1+g} - 2*\rho}{\rho - (k-g)*\frac{1-\frac{r}{\rho}}{1+g}} \tag{40}$$

$$E_k(P/E) = \frac{k}{(P/E)} * \frac{\partial(P/E)}{\partial k} = \frac{k*\left(1-\frac{r}{\rho}\right)}{(1+g)*\left(\rho - (k-g)*\frac{1-\frac{r}{\rho}}{1+g}\right)} \tag{41}$$

$$E_g(P/E) = \frac{g}{(P/E)} * \frac{\partial(P/E)}{\partial g} = \frac{g*(k+1)*\left(\frac{r}{\rho}-1\right)}{\left(1+g\right)^{2}*\left(\rho - (k-g)*\frac{1-\frac{r}{\rho}}{1+g}\right)} \tag{42}$$

Based on formulas (35) and (38-42), on the elasticity of the quoted ratio of an ordinary share of a public company on dividend per ordinary share, the dividend coverage ratio of a public company on preferred shares, the profitability of its investment, the market capitalization level, the rate of return required by investors on ordinary share of a public company and its assumed constant rate of dividend growth over time, its ordinary share is influenced by the following factors: dividend coverage ratio on preferred shares of a public company, return on investment of a public company, market capitalization level, the rate of return required by investors on ordinary share of a public company and the rate of dividend growth per ordinary share assumed to be constant over time. The calculation of the influence of determining factors on the deviation of effective indicators in formulas (35) and (38-42) can be carried out by the appropriate methods of factor analysis.

The sufficient complexity of the elasticity models developed by the author for key indicators of the activity of a public company in the stock market according to the main factors determining them in the context of a neutral approach to the implementation of dividend policy makes it difficult to determine the direction of the influence of these factors on the corresponding performance indicators without considering an example of the practical use of these models on a specific digital material.

Let us apply the elasticity models developed by the author of key indicators of the activity of a public company in the stock market in terms of the main factors determining them in the conditions of a neutral approach to the implementation of dividend policy (16-42) to the corresponding data of the public company Gamma (the real name has been changed), based on the assumption that it focuses on a neutral approach to dividend policy.

The values of some indicators of the public company "Gamma" at the end of the reporting year are presented in Table. 2.

Table 2. Values of some indicators of the public company "Gamma" at the end of the reporting year

Index	Meaning
Return on investment of a public company (r), %	23.9
Market capitalization level (ρ), %	15.3
Rate of return required by investors for an ordinary share of a public company (k), %	12
Dividend growth rate per ordinary share (assumed to be constant over time) (g), %	5
Earnings per ordinary share (E), rubles	157.48
Dividend per ordinary share (D), rubles	86.14
Dividend ratio for common and preferred shares (DCD)	23
Preferred Dividend Coverage Ratio (CPD)	60
Expected market price of an ordinary share (P), rubles	1294.73
Dividend yield ratio (DP), %	54.7
Dividend Cover Ratio (DC)	1.829

continued on following page

Table 2. Continued

Index	Meaning
Dividend yield per share (DY), %	5.4
Common share price ratio (P/E)	7.256

Source: compiled by the author of the chapter

Based on contained in the Table 2 data were calculated according to the models (16-42) of the elasticities of the key indicators of the activity of the public company "Gamma" in the stock market (expected market price of an ordinary share (P), dividend output ratio (DP), dividend coverage ratio (DC), dividend common stock return (DY), common stock quote ratio (P/E)) by their main determinants (return on investment of a public company (r), market capitalization level (ρ), rate of return required by investors per ordinary share of a public company (k), assumed to be a time-constant growth rate of dividend per ordinary share (g), dividend per ordinary share (D), earnings per ordinary share (E), dividend ratio for ordinary and preferred shares (DCD), dividend coverage ratio for preferred shares (CPD)) presented in Table 3.

Table 3. Values of elasticity of key indicators of the activity of the public company "Gamma" in the stock market by the main factors determining them

Index	Determining Factors							
	r	ρ	k	g	D	E	DCD	CPD
P	0.016	-0.453	-0.335	0.00041	-	1	-	-
DP	0.453	-1.257	1.337	-0.612	-	-	-	-
DC	-0.453	1.256	1.401	6.249	-	-	-	-
DY	-0.453	0.163	0.335	-0.148	1	-1	–	–
P/E	1.552	-1.258	-0.335	0.148	-0.805	1	1	-1.017

Source: compiled by the author of the chapter

Contained in the Table 3 values of elasticities of the key indicators of the activity of the public company "Gamma" in the stock market according to the main factors determining them approximately show by what percentage upward ("+") or decrease ("-") the value of one or another key indicator will change depending on 1% increments the value of one or another factor determining it.

For greater clarity, Table 4 shows the expected percentage changes in the values of key indicators of the activity of the public company "Gamma" in the stock market in the event of an increase / decrease in the value of each of the main factors determining them separately (with the values of all other factors unchanged) by 10%.

Table 4. Percentage changes in the values of key indicators of the activity of the public company "Gamma" in the stock market in the event of an increase / decrease in the value of each of the main factors determining them separately (with the values of all other factors unchanged) by 10%

Index	Determining Factors							
	r	ρ	k	g	D	E	DCD	CPD
P	+0.16 -0.16	-4.53 +4.53	-3.35 +3.35	+0.0041 -0.0041	-	+10 -10	-	-
DP	+4.53 -4.53	-12.57 +12.57	+13.37 -13.37	-6.12 +6.12	-	-	-	-
DC	-4.53 +4.53	+12.56 -12.56	+14.01 -14.01	+62.49 -62.49	-	-	-	-
DY	-4.53 +4.53	+1.63 -1.63	+3.35 -3.35	-1.48 +1.48	+10 -10	-10 +10	–	–
P/E	+15.52 -15.52	-12.58 +12.58	-3.35 +3.35	+1.48 -1.48	-8.05 +8.05	+10 -10	+10 -10	-10.17 +10.17

Source: compiled by the author of the chapter

Then the predicted values of the key indicators of the activity of the public company "Gamma" in the stock market in the event of an increase / decrease in the value of each of the main factors determining them separately (with the values of all other factors unchanged) by 10% can be summarized in Table 5.

Table 5. Forecast values of key indicators of the activity of the public company "Gamma" in the stock market in the event of an increase / decrease in the value of each of the main factors determining them separately (with the values of all other factors unchanged) by 10%

Index	Determining Factors							
	r	ρ	k	g	D	E	DCD	CPD
P, rubles	1296.80 1292.66	1236.08 1353.38	1251.36 1338.10	1294.78 1294.66	-	1424.20 1165.26	-	-
DP, %	57.2 52.2	47.8 61.6	62.0 47.4	51.3 58.0	-	-	-	-
DC	1.746 1.912	2.059 1.599	2.085 1.573	2.972 0.686	-	-	-	-
DY, %	5.155 5.645	5.489 5.312	5.581 5.219	5.320 5.480	5.940 4.860	4.86 5.94	–	–
P/E	8.383 6.130	6.343 8.169	7.013 7.499	7.363 7.149	6.672 15.306	7.982 6.530	7.982 6.530	6.518 7.994

Source: compiled by the author of the chapter

Concluding the consideration of the above example, it should be noted that in the context of a neutral approach to the implementation of the dividend policy of a public company, it allows not only to determine for a particular public company the degree of sensitivity of the values of key indicators of its activity in the stock market to changes in the values of the main factors determining them, but also the direction the impact of these factors on the key indicators of the dividend policy in the direction of increasing or decreasing their values. All this makes it possible to predict the values of key indicators of the activity of a particular public company in the stock market in the event of an increase / decrease in the value of each of the main factors determining them separately (with the values of all other factors unchanged) by a given percentage, if this public company adheres to a neutral approach to implementation dividend policy.

In addition, the models of elasticities of key indicators of the activity of a public company in the stock market built by the author of this chapter according to the main factors determining them (16-42) can be used as tools for managing the values of these elasticities by adjusting the values of the factors that determine them in a neutral approach to the implementation of the dividend policies of this public company.

4. DISCUSSION

The scientific results considered in this chapter, obtained by its author and related to the development of models of elasticity of key indicators of the activity of a public company in the stock market according to the main factors determining them (16-42) in the context of a neutral approach to the implementation of the dividend policy of this public company, can be characterized as fundamentally new, unparalleled developments on this issue.

The fundamental novelty of the author's developments is determined by the fact that a neutral approach to the dividend policy of a public company was formulated, and the underlying models (5), (6), (11), (12) and (14) were again developed by the author of this chapter (in particular, (Krylov, 2020, 2021, 2025)).

Since analogues for comparison with the scientific results obtained by the author were not found in the relevant scientific literature, it seems appropriate to focus on the merits of the above models of elasticity of key indicators of the activity of a public company in the stock market in terms of the main factors determining them in the context of a neutral approach to the implementation of its dividend policy. manifested in the fact that these models:

- focused on maintaining a balance of interests of all stakeholders of a public company, contributing to its sustainable development;

- are based on a repeatedly tested and proven methodology;
- characterized by objectivity and rationality;
- make it possible to calculate the influence of determining factors on the deviation of the effective indicators determined by them by the appropriate methods of factor analysis;
- are effective tools for analyzing and forecasting the values of key indicators of the market activity of a public company, which makes it possible to rationalize and improve the process of managing it.

At the same time, it should be noted that there are certain limitations inherent in the elasticity models developed by the author of key indicators of the activity of a public company in the stock market in terms of the main factors determining them in the context of a neutral approach to the implementation of its dividend policy.

First, in accordance with these models, the change in the value of each of the main factors that determine the key indicators of the activity of a public company in the stock market is taken into account separately (isolated), that is, with the values of all other factors unchanged.

Secondly, these models are focused on the constant growth rate of dividends per ordinary share of a public company.

Thirdly, they proceed from a sufficiently high efficiency of the securities market.

Overcoming these limitations will be the subject of further research.

5. CONCLUSIONS

Summing up the consideration of models of elasticity of key indicators of the activity of a public company in the stock market according to the main factors determining them in the conditions of a neutral approach to the implementation of its dividend policy, which are the results of the research and development of the author of this chapter, it is advisable to formulate the following conclusions:

- the key indicators of the activity of a public company in the stock market in the context of a neutral approach to the implementation of its dividend policy should include dividend yield ratio, dividend coverage ratio, expected price of a common share, dividend yield of a common share, and quote ratio of a common share;
- models of elasticity of key indicators of the activity of a public company in the stock market in terms of the main factors determining them in the conditions of a neutral approach to the implementation of its dividend policy

are built on the basis of models of these indicators developed earlier by the author;

- the construction of these models involved the use of the well-known and repeatedly tested mathematical apparatus of sensitivity analysis, associated with the calculation of the elasticities of performance indicators by the factors that determine them;
- the main factors that determine the key indicators of the activity of a public company in the stock market in the context of a neutral approach to the implementation of its dividend policy include the return on investment of a public company, the market level of capitalization, the rate of return required by investors per ordinary share of a public company, and the dividend growth rate assumed to be constant over time per ordinary share, dividend per ordinary share, earnings per ordinary share, ratio of dividends on ordinary and preferred shares, as well as the dividend coverage ratio on preferred shares;
- the constructed models make it possible to determine the elasticities of the key indicators of the activity of a public company in the stock market according to the main factors determining them in the context of a neutral approach to the implementation of its dividend policy and approximately show by how many percent the value of one or another key indicator will change upward or downward depending on an increment of 1% the value of one or another factor determining it;
- these models can be used as sufficiently effective tools for analysis and forecasting, and, consequently, for managing the market activity of a public company in the context of a neutral approach to the implementation of its dividend policy.

6. DIRECTIONS FOR FURTHER RESEARCH

The above conceptual foundations for analyzing the sensitivity of key indicators of the activity of a public company in the stock market (market activity) to the main determining factors in the context of a neutral approach to the implementation of its dividend policy largely determine only some of its general outlines as a new direction of scientific research and practice. They are a kind of theoretical basis for further development of modeling the elasticity of key indicators of the activity of a public company in the stock market in terms of the main factors determining them in the context of a neutral approach to the implementation of its dividend policy.

The following can be considered as the main directions for further development of modeling the elasticity of key indicators of the activity of a public company in the stock market (market activity) according to the main determining factors in the context of a neutral approach to the implementation of its dividend policy:

- development of such models with a changing growth rate of dividends per ordinary share of a public company;
- building models of elasticity of key indicators of the activity of a public company in the stock market according to several main factors that determine them, acting jointly, interconnectedly and simultaneously, in the conditions of a neutral approach to the implementation of dividend policy: dividend yield ratio, dividend coverage ratio, expected price of an ordinary share, dividend yield of an ordinary share and quote ratio of an ordinary share - based on the models of the listed indicators (5), (6), (11), (12) and (14);
- derivation of calculation formulas that make it possible to determine the impact on the elasticity deviation of key indicators of a public company's activity in the stock market for each factor that determines them, acting in isolation, and for several main factors that determine them, acting jointly and simultaneously, in the conditions of a neutral approach to the implementation of dividend policy: the dividend yield ratio, the dividend coverage ratio, the expected price of an ordinary share, the dividend yield of an ordinary share and the quote ratio of an ordinary share, based on the relevant models;
- computerization of the elasticity models formed by the author of key indicators of the activity of a public company in the stock market according to the main factors determining them in the conditions of a neutral approach to the implementation of dividend policy in order to more effectively use these models in practice in the process of managing the market activity of a public company.

REFERENCES

Akhigbe, A., & Madura, J. (1996). Dividend Policy and Corporate Performance. *Journal of Business Finance & Accounting*, *23*(9-10), 1267–1289. DOI: 10.1111/1468-5957.00079

Ang, J. S., Cole, R. A., & Lin, J. W. (2000). Agency Costs and Ownership Structure. *The Journal of Finance*, *55*(1), 81–106. DOI: 10.1111/0022-1082.00201

Bernstein, L. A., Wild, J., & Subramanyam, K. R. (2001). *Financial Statement Analysis*. McGraw-Hill Higher Education.

Black, F. (1976). The Dividend Puzzle. *Journal of Portfolio Management*, *2*(2), 5–8. DOI: 10.3905/jpm.1976.408558

Block, S. B., Hirt, G. A., & Danielsen, B. (2011). *Foundations of Financial Management*. McGraw-Hill Education.

Brealey, R. A., Mayers, S. C., & Allien, F. (2017). *Principles of Corporate Finance*. McGraw-Hill Education.

Brigham, E. F., & Houston, J. F. (2015). *Fundamentals of Financial Management: Concise*. Cengage Learning.

Brooks, R. M. (1996). Changes in Asymmetric Information at Earnings and Dividend Announcements. *Journal of Business Finance & Accounting*, *23*(3), 359–370. DOI: 10.1111/j.1468-5957.1996.tb01127.x

Cacuci, D. G. (2003). *Sensitivity and Uncertainty Analysis – Theory*. Chapman and Hall/CRC.

Dunphy, D. D., Griffiths, A., & Suzanne, B. (2007). *Organizational Change for Corporate Sustainability: A Guide for Leaders and Change Agents of the Future*. Rountledge.

Fama, E. F., & French, K. R. (1989). Business Conditions and Expected Returns on Stocks and Bonds. *Journal of Financial Economics*, *25*(1), 23–49. DOI: 10.1016/0304-405X(89)90095-0

Freeman, R. E. (2010). *Strategic Management: A Stakeholder Approach*. Cambridge University Press. DOI: 10.1017/CBO9781139192675

Friedman, R. E., & Miles, S. (2006). *Stakeholders: Theory and Practice*. Oxford University Press. DOI: 10.1093/oso/9780199269860.001.0001

Global Reporting Initiative (GRI). (2013). *G4 Sustainability Reporting Guidelines*. EYGM Limited.

Goetzmann, W. N., & Jorion, P. (1995). A Longer Look at Dividend Yields. *The Journal of Business*, *68*(4), 483–508. DOI: 10.1086/296674

Gordon, M. J. (1959). Dividends, Earnings and Stock Prices. *The Review of Economics and Statistics*, *41*(2), 99–105. DOI: 10.2307/1927792

Gordon, M. J. (1963). Optimal Investment and Financial Policy. *The Journal of Finance*, *18*(2), 264–272.

Griewank, A. (2000). *Evaluating Derivatives, Principles and Techniques of Algorithmic Differentiation*. SIAM.

Hauser, R. (2013). Did Dividend Policy Change During the Financial Crisis? *Managerial Finance*, *39*(6), 584–606. DOI: 10.1108/03074351311322861

Helfert, E. A. (2001). *Financial Analysis: Tools and Techniques. A Guide for Managers*. McGraw-Hill.

Helton, J. C., Johnson, J. D., Salaberry, C. J., & Storlie, C. B. (2006). Survey Of Sampling Based Methods for Uncertainty and Sensitivity Analysis. *Reliability Engineering & System Safety*, *91*(10-11), 1175–1209. DOI: 10.1016/j.ress.2005.11.017

Higgins, R. C., Koski, J., & Mitton, T. (2016). *Analysis for Financial Management*. McGraw-Hill Education.

Krylov, S. (2020). Dividend Policy Scores Models: Neutral Approach. *SBS Journal of Applied Business Research*, *8*, 23–33.

Krylov, S. (2021). Dividend Policy: Scores Modeling within Neutral Implementation Approach Conditions. *Academy of Accounting and Financial Studies Journal*, *25*(1), 1–10.

Krylov, S. (2025). Neutral Approach at Dividend Policy Modeling. In M. Khosrow-Pour, D.B.A. (Ed.), *Encyclopedia of Information Science and Technology, Sixth Edition*. Advance online publication. DOI: 10.4018/978-1-6684-7366-5.ch008

Lambrecht, B. M., & Myers, S. C. (2012). A Lintner Model of Payout and Managerial Rents. *The Journal of Finance*, *67*(5), 1761–1810. DOI: 10.1111/j.1540-6261.2012.01772.x

Leamer, E. E. (1985). Sensitivity Analyses Would Help. *The American Economic Review*, *75*(3), 308–313.

Lee, C. F., & Finnerty, J. E. (1990). *Corporate Finance: Theory, Method, and Applications*. Harcourt Brace & Company.

Lintner, J. (1962). Dividend, Earnings, Leverage, Stock Prices and the Supply of Capital to Corporations. *The Review of Economics and Statistics*, *44*(3), 243–269. DOI: 10.2307/1926397

McLaney, E. J. (1992). *Business Finance for Decision Makers*. Pitman Publishing.

Miller, M. H., & Modiliani, F. (1961). Dividend Policy, Growth and the Valuation of Share. *The Journal of Business*, *34*(4), 411–433. DOI: 10.1086/294442

Pannell, D. J. (1997). Sensitivity Analysis of Normative Economic Models: Theoretical Framework and Practical Strategies. *Agricultural Economics*, *16*(2), 139–152. DOI: 10.1111/j.1574-0862.1997.tb00449.x

Penman, S. (2004). *Financial Statement Analysis and Security Valuation*. McGraw-Hill / Irwin.

Petit, R. R. (1972). Dividend Announcement, Security Performance and Capital Market Efficiency. *The Journal of Finance*, *27*(5), 993–1007. DOI: 10.1111/j.1540-6261.1972.tb03018.x

Rozeff, M. S. (1982). Growth, Beta, and Agency Cost as Determinants of Dividend Payout Ratios. *Journal of Financial Research*, *5*(3), 461–488. DOI: 10.1111/j.1475-6803.1982.tb00299.x

Saltelli, A. (2002). Sensitivity Analysis for Importance Assessment. *Risk Analysis*, *22*(3), 1–12. DOI: 10.1111/0272-4332.00040 PMID: 12088235

Saltelli, A., Chan, K., & Scott, M. (2000). *Sensitivity Analysis*. John Wiley and Sons.

Shim, J. K., & Siegel, J. G. (2008). *Financial Management*. New York: Barron's Educational Series, Inc.

Subramanyam, K. R. (2014). *Financial Statement Analysis*. McGraw-Hill Education.

Van Horne, J. C. (1989). *Fundamentals of Financial Management*. Prentice-Hall.

Van Horne, J. C., & Wachowicz, J. M. (2009). *Fundamentals of Financial Management*. Pearson Education Limited.

Walter, J. E. (1956). Dividend Policies and Common Stock Prices. *The Journal of Finance*, *11*(1), 29–41. DOI: 10.1111/j.1540-6261.1956.tb00684.x

ADDITIONAL READING

Bernstein, L. A. (1993). *Financial Statement Analysis: Theory, Application and Interpretation*. Irwin.

Brigham, E. F. (1983). *Fundamentals of Financial Management*. Holt Saunders.

Brigham, E. F., & Gordon, M. J. (1970). Leverage, dividend policy and cost of capital [reply]. *The Journal of Finance, 25*(4), 904–908. DOI: 10.1111/j.1540-6261.1970.tb00563.x

Brooks, Ch. (2014). *Introductory Econometrics for Finance*. Cambridge University Press. DOI: 10.1017/CBO9781139540872

Helfert, E. A. (1994). *Techniques of Financial Analysis*. Irwin.

Higgins, R. C. (1972). The corporate dividend-saving decisions. *Journal of Financial and Quantitative Analysis*, *7*(2), 1527–1541. DOI: 10.2307/2329932

Knot, G. (1985). *Understanding Financial Management*. Pan Books.

Krylov, S. (2012). Methodological Approach to Company Cash Flows Target-Oriented Forecasting Based on Financial Position Analysis. *Economic Bulletin*, *32*(1), 830–836.

Krylov, S. (2015). Financial Analysis in Balanced Scorecard. *Journal of Global Economics. Management and Business Research*, *4*(1), 1–14.

Krylov, S. (2018). Target Financial Forecasting as an Instrument to Improve Company Financial Health. *Cogent Business & Management*, *5*(1), 1–42. DOI: 10.1080/23311975.2018.1540074

Subramanyam, K. R., & Venkatachalam, M. (2007). Earnings, cash flow and ex post intrinsic value of equity. *The Accounting Review*, *82*(2), 457–481. DOI: 10.2308/accr.2007.82.2.457

Van Horne, J. C. (1985). Of financial innovations and excesses. *The Journal of Finance*, *40*(3), 621–631. DOI: 10.1111/j.1540-6261.1985.tb04984.x

Watsham, T. J., & Parramore, K. (2004). *Quantitative Methods in Finance*. International Thomson Business Press.

KEY TERMS DEFINITIONS

A neutral approach to the implementation of a dividend policy: is an approach that takes into account both the need to finance profitable investment projects and pay dividends to shareholders of the company (not on a residual basis), thereby leading to the maximization of the market value of its ordinary shares.

Artificial Intelligence (AI): The ability of a computer to learn, make decisions and perform actions characteristic of human intelligence, as well as a science at the intersection of mathematics, biology, psychology, cybernetics and some other fields of knowledge, which studies technologies that allow a person to write "intelligent" programs and teach computers to solve problems on their own.

Dividend Policy: A set of decisions related to the payment of dividends to shareholders.

Elasticity: A measure of the sensitivity of one variable to a change in another, showing by how many percent the first value will change when the second changes by 1%.

Financial Model: A system of indicators that will help predict revenue, cash flow, business profit, and also calculate how changes within the company or in the market will affect the financial position in the future.

Financial Modeling: The task of constructing an abstract representation (model) of a financial situation in the real world.

Indicators of Market Activity: A group of indicators characterizing the position of the enterprise in the securities market.

Sensitivity Analysis: A tool used in financial modeling to analyze how different values of a set of independent variables affect a particular dependent variable under certain specific conditions.

Stakeholders: Are interested parties: people, groups or organizations who can influence or who can perceive themselves to be affected by a decision, operation or outcome of a project, program or portfolio.

The Market Activity of a Public Company: Is to choose the optimal strategy and tactics in using profits, accumulating them, increasing capital by issuing additional shares, and influencing the market price of the shares.

Chapter 12
What Can AI Maturity Models Achieve in Business Practice?

Silvio Andrae
https://orcid.org/0000-0002-8586-7812
Independent Researcher, Germany

ABSTRACT

Artificial intelligence (AI) is a key driver of digital transformation. However, companies need help with introducing and integrating AI into business processes. This paper examines how AI maturity models can help companies assess and strategically develop their AI maturity. The focus is on the dimensions of strategy, data, technology, people, and governance, which structure progress in five development phases from exploration to transformation. Specific challenges and success factors are analyzed based on empirical case studies of medium-sized companies. An additional focus is on the enlightening role of Large Language Models (LLMs) as a driving force behind AI development. The article shows the importance of AI maturity models as a valuable tool for companies to assess and strategically develop their use of AI.

1. INTRODUCTION

Artificial intelligence (AI) has evolved from an experimental technology into a pivotal driver of digital transformation in recent years. Companies across diverse industries are increasingly realizing the potential of AI to optimize their business processes, develop innovative products and services, and gain competitive advantages. This rapid development underscores the need for companies to assess their

DOI: 10.4018/979-8-3693-7357-6.ch012

Copyright © 2025, IGI Global Scientific Publishing. Copying or distributing in print or electronic forms without written permission of IGI Global Scientific Publishing is prohibited.

AI usage and devise a clear strategy for further development, promising a future of enhanced efficiency and innovation.

In business practice, there often needs to be an overview of the extent to which AI technology is already being used in other areas. Furthermore, it sometimes needs to be clarified to what extent the framework parameters for using the technology are even guaranteed. Finally, there are differences in the concept of AI readiness for implementation in business practice (Schuster et al., 2021). The challenges for companies range from the inability to accurately determine implementation costs and a lack of experience handling the corresponding data sets to problems aligning strategy (Sadiq et al., 2021). These factors make it clear that introducing AI involves much work for companies. The maturity and readiness of the company, often referred to as 'AI maturity ', are also crucial (Sadiq et al., 2021; Sonntag et al., 2024).

The decision to operate AI systems is contingent on the benefits they offer, which can sometimes be challenging to identify, even for companies (Perifanis & Kitsios, 2023). Assessing the company's stage of development can drive the adoption of new, intelligent technologies and the ability to harness AI. Moreover, understanding the company's status can inspire decision-makers and the organization to chart a path towards further development and advancement, underscoring their pivotal role in the AI strategy (Sonntag et al., 2024).

This paper addresses how companies can systematically determine and improve their AI maturity. To this end, the concept of the AI Maturity Model is presented (Al-Sai et al., 2023). Such a model serves as a framework for self-assessment and enables companies to determine their current status compared to an ideal state, which represents the highest level of AI implementation and strategy. Companies can take targeted measures to optimize their AI initiatives by identifying strengths and weaknesses. In addition to maturity models, there are other models, such as funnel dynamics for introducing AI technology (Ameye et al., 2024) or business model innovations (Jorzik et al., 2024). However, these need to be more relevant here.

This paper aims to elucidate the crucial role of AI maturity models for companies and provide a comprehensive overview of the various dimensions of AI maturity. Furthermore, empirical case studies shed light on the challenges and success factors in integrating AI into companies. A particular focus is placed on the role of general-purpose artificial intelligence models, such as large language models (LLMs), as a driving force behind AI development. Their significant influence on AI development in companies and their impact on AI architecture are highlighted, enlightening the reader about their importance.

The following is an overview of various AI maturity models, in which the central dimensions and phases of AI maturity are examined in more detail. Subsequently, the results of an empirical study analyzing the AI maturity level of medium-sized companies are presented. Based on this, the significance of LLMs for corporate practice is discussed, and finally, an outlook on future developments is given.

This structure makes it possible to answer the following research questions:

- What are the central dimensions of AI maturity, and how can they be operationalized?
- What challenges and success factors are associated with introducing AI in companies?
- What role do LLMs play in the development of AI applications?
- What recommendations can be given to companies for designing a successful AI strategy?

The chapter is structured as follows: Section 2 provides a theoretical overview of a model of an AI maturity level. Section 3 uses three medium-sized companies from different industries to test the model at different maturity stages. Data collection uses a mixed-methods approach that combines qualitative and quantitative methods. The results are then compared. Finally, in Section 5, the Large Language Models are introduced. They can significantly influence companies in the respective phases of further developing their AI maturity. The chapter ends with a summary (Section 5), which also addresses the limitations of a maturity model and the opportunities for future research.

2. AI MATURITY MODELS: AN OVERVIEW

The rapid development of artificial intelligence (AI) has presented companies with the challenge of adapting their business models and processes to new technological possibilities. To ensure the success of AI initiatives and enable systematic further development, a comprehensive understanding of one's own level of maturity in the field of AI, a complex and evolving field, is required. In this context, AI maturity models are becoming increasingly important.

2.1 Definition and Purpose

The starting point is AI deployment capability. According to Stecher et al. (2020), this refers to the use of specific AI applications within the company structure that enable AI systems to be implemented to support and improve company processes, thus making optimal use of the full potential of AI systems. In this chapter, AI systems are understood as a combined form of AI applications, algorithms, and information to solve complex challenges in collaboration (Monod et al., 2023). AI readiness is not only about AI for business processes but also about its use in products and services, such as large language models in customer service in the automotive industry. This paper focuses on AI readiness because AI deployment is essential for adopting AI in organizations (Mariani et al., 2023). Wagire et al. (2021) model includes seven dimensions and 38 maturity elements and has been validated for an automotive parts manufacturing company. The results show that the company is at the "Digital Novice" level of maturity, with a maturity level of 2.88 on a scale of 1 to 5, ending at 5. Lichtenthaler's (2020) model has five levels, ranging from no automation (level 1) to full automation (level 5).

In practice, when it comes to AI maturity, there is always a mix of AI technologies (e.g., NLP and computer vision) and business applications (e.g., prediction and risk analysis). Based on the European Artificial Intelligence Act (AIA) (Regulation (EU) 2024/1689), the focus should be on the various core characteristics of AI:

- **System**: AI is a system that can make decisions or perform tasks based on data and rules without being explicitly programmed.
- **Learning**: A central component of AI is learning from data and adapting to new situations.
- **Autonomy**: AI systems can act autonomously to a certain extent, i.e., make decisions without constant human intervention.

There is no explicit distinction between business applications and technologies. Rather, the focus is on a system's functionalities. A system is classified as an AI system if it has the above-mentioned characteristics, regardless of the area in which it is used. In this respect, statistical models or rule-based systems that function strictly according to predefined rules without adapting to new situations are not AI systems.

A maturity model serves as a framework for assessing a company's current state regarding its use of AI. The chosen AI definition should be considered here. Maturity models are "multi-stage models that describe typical patterns in developing organizational capabilities" (Comuzzi & Patel, 2016). The maturity model describes the corresponding levels for relevant areas for each maturity level. These stages should be logically connected and generalizable to determine the right level of maturity for a company or sector (Hausladen & Schosser, 2020; Fornasiero et al., 2024). Maturity models have established assessment tools for identifying strengths and weaknesses in AI and deriving recommendations for further development. Such a model enables companies to measure their progress, identify best practices, and develop a clear roadmap for the future (Chen et al., 2022). From a scientific perspective, the methodology of Design Science Research (DSR) is used to develop maturity models, according to Becker et al. (2009). DSR provides a framework for the scientific investigation of maturity models (Hevner et al., 2004).

AI maturity models are powerful tools that can help companies manage their AI initiatives in a targeted manner and fully exploit the opportunities presented by AI. By transparently assessing their maturity level, companies can identify potential risks and take early action to minimize them. Moreover, an AI maturity model fosters better communication within the company and facilitates collaboration between different departments, paving the way for a more efficient and innovative future in AI.

There are countless AI maturity models in science and practice. For example, Sonntag et al. (2024) identify eleven maturity models. On this basis, they create an industry-specific maturity model for the manufacturing industry that includes 29 indicators. Gökalp and Martinez (2021) examine 18 existing maturity models in digital transformation. They conclude that all suitability, completeness, clarity, and objectivity criteria are never fully met. They develop a holistic maturity model in digital transformation (DX-CMM) to address this research gap by applying a theoretically sound development approach. The purpose of DX-CMM is to support companies in a standardized way by providing an up-to-date assessment of their capabilities and maturity, deriving a gap analysis, and creating a comprehensive roadmap for improvements.

The cross-industry application of a unified AI maturity model offers the advantage of comparability across different sectors. It not only enables an accelerated transfer of knowledge but also fosters a sense of community, as companies can learn from each other and drive innovation faster. This collaborative approach to AI maturity models ensures that no company is left behind in the rapidly evolving AI landscape.

However, individual sectors' specific requirements and characteristics must be considered when developing a cross-industry model. One possible approach would be to develop a basic model that covers fundamental aspects of AI use and maturity, supplemented by industry-specific modules.

2.2 Dimensions of AI Maturity

Among the myriad of existing maturity models, the types of dimensions can be quite diverse. The five dimensions presented here, based on earlier studies, are particularly practical. This proposal is designed to underscore the organizational benefits of using a maturity model, without unnecessarily complicating it with additional characteristics.

A comprehensive AI maturity model, which measures the organization's readiness and capability to effectively use AI, considers various dimensions that influence the use of AI in companies (Element AI, 2020). The most important dimensions include:

- **Strategy** (S): A clear AI strategy, which is in perfect alignment with overarching business objectives, is the cornerstone of successful AI initiatives. It involves defining goals, identifying use cases, and setting priorities, providing a clear roadmap for AI implementation.

- **Data** (D): Data, the heart of every AI application, is best managed with robust data management systems. The quality, accessibility, and management of data are pivotal to the success of AI projects. A mature organization has clear data governance policies and the ability to use data effectively for AI applications.
- **Technology** (T): The selection of suitable AI tools and technologies and their integration into existing IT landscapes are further important. It also includes the data processing and storage infrastructure and the ability to efficiently develop, train, and deploy AI models.
- **People** (P): Employee skills, corporate culture, and effective change management are crucial to the success of AI initiatives. This includes developing AI skills, fostering a data-driven culture, and empowering employees to use AI tools effectively.
- **Governance** (G): A solid governance structure encompasses ethical aspects such as fairness and transparency in AI decision-making, compliance requirements like data privacy regulations, and risk management strategies to mitigate potential AI-related risks. It ensures that AI applications are developed and deployed responsibly and by legal and ethical standards.

These SDTPG dimensions are closely interwoven and influence each other. An effective AI maturity model considers these interdependencies and enables a holistic assessment of a company's AI maturity.

2.3 Stages of AI Maturity

The development of AI maturity can be described in different phases (Figure 1). Each of these dimensions, which include strategy, data, technology, people, and governance, is essential. Lack of progress in one of these dimensions hinders overall progress in AI, even if other dimensions are more advanced.

- **Exploring**: In this initial phase, companies experiment with AI technologies and gain initial experience. They explore potential use cases and build a basic understanding of AI technologies.
- **Experimenting**: Companies carry out pilot projects to demonstrate the feasibility and potential benefits of AI applications. They test various use cases and evaluate their value proposition.
- **Formalizing**: In this phase, AI applications are scaled and standardized. Processes and structures are established to systematically manage the use of

AI. This includes developing AI governance guidelines and integrating AI into existing business processes.

- **Optimizing**: The implemented AI applications are continuously improved and optimized. Organizations focus on increasing the efficiency and effectiveness of their AI solutions through continuous learning and adaptation.
- **Transforming**: In this advanced phase, AI becomes the organization's core competence, enabling new business models and products. AI is deeply integrated into the corporate strategy and drives innovation and value creation.

The framework presented here is a 5×5 model that illustrates the relationship between the organizational dimensions required to implement AI and the five maturity levels companies pass through to achieve these dimensions. The 5x5 model is a comprehensive tool that helps organizations understand the complexity of AI implementation and the various dimensions that need to be considered. It provides a structured approach to assess and improve AI maturity, guiding companies through the different phases of AI development (Element AI, 2020).

Figure 1. AI maturity model (5x5)

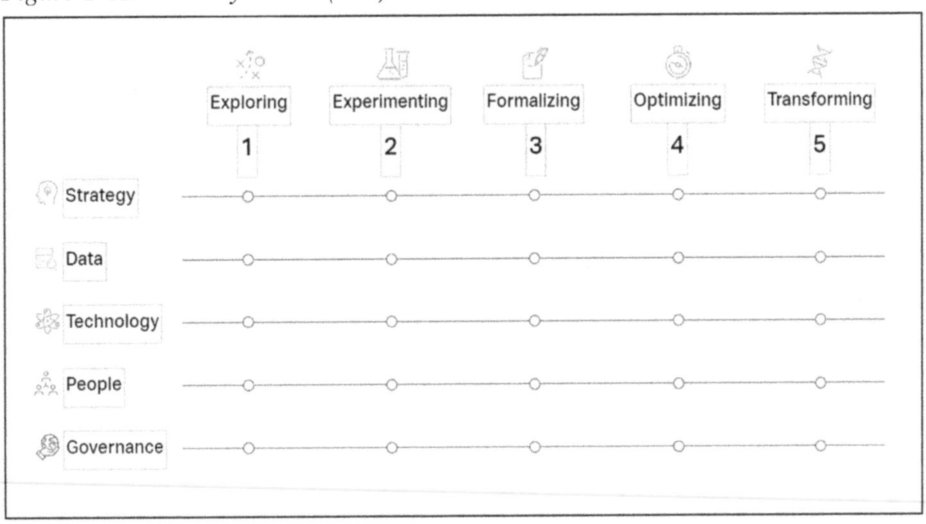

Source: own representation

It is important to emphasize that each company goes through these phases at an individual pace and possibly in a different order. Moving from one phase to the next requires continuously adapting corporate strategy, organizational structures, and technological infrastructure. Moreover, of course, the path is not linear. For example, companies are more likely to initially build AI on top of existing data-driven applications than to invest in entirely new applications. In addition to compatibility with existing systems, companies base their decisions on introducing AI on the relative advantage of technology over the technology already in place and the visibility of these improvements.

The five phases, which include exploring, experimenting, formalizing, optimizing, and transforming, are merely turning points in a company's journey to achieve AI impact. First, companies need to find out what AI can do and how it could benefit them. Experimenting companies find out what works and at what cost. Formalizing organizations put their first models into production with clear performance metrics and typically use this process to guide further investments. Optimizing organizations focus on building their capabilities to select, deploy, and manage AI solutions in production. Finally, transforming organizations use AI to push the technology's and their strategy's boundaries.

The best way to move forward, wherever you are today, is to take stock of your organization and determine your current status based on the status of each dimension. Then, you can determine which dimensions have the critical leverage you need to move forward. From there, it is easy to design projects and work plans that will move forward.

AI maturity models provide a valuable framework for organizations to assess and improve their progress in using AI. By considering various dimensions such as strategy, data, technology, people, and governance, organizations can identify their strengths and weaknesses. This reassures you of the model's value in optimizing your AI initiatives.

Applying an AI maturity model enables organizations to:

- objectively assess the current state of their AI capabilities,
- identify gaps and areas for improvement,
- establish a clear roadmap for further AI development,
- measure and compare progress over time,
- identify and implement best practices,
- improve communication and collaboration around AI initiatives.

It's crucial to understand that AI maturity models are not rigid prescriptions, but rather flexible guides. When applying these models, it's essential to consider each company's specific requirements and circumstances, empowering you to tailor the model to your organization's unique needs.

In the following section, we will delve into case studies that examine the challenges and success factors involved in introducing AI in individual companies. These practical examples will not only illustrate how companies progress through the various stages of AI maturity, but also inspire and motivate you to develop and scale your own AI capabilities successfully.

3. EMPIRICAL STUDY: CASE STUDIES OF MEDIUM-SIZED COMPANIES

An empirical study is being conducted to illustrate and deepen the theoretical foundations of the AI maturity model. The focus is on medium-sized companies from different industries in different phases of their AI maturity.

3.1 Methodology

Three medium-sized companies from different industries were selected for the study: an online fashion retailer, an automotive manufacturing company, and a financial services company. All three companies are headquartered in Germany. The selection was made according to the principle of maximum variation, which considers factors such as company size, market position, and AI adoption history. This approach was chosen to reflect the broadest possible range of AI maturity levels and capture different AI application scenarios. Each company represents a different phase of AI maturity.

Our data collection process is comprehensive, employing a mixed-methods approach that combines qualitative and quantitative methods:

Semi-structured interviews: We conducted in-depth interviews with a diverse range of participants, including executives, IT experts, and employees directly involved in AI projects. This approach ensured a comprehensive understanding of AI strategy, specific AI projects, the technologies used, organizational aspects, challenges, and success factors.

Online questionnaires: We employed a rigorous approach to quantitative data collection, distributing a standardized questionnaire to a larger group of employees. This questionnaire covered aspects such as the company's perception of AI, the level of knowledge of AI technologies, and the willingness to use AI tools.

Document analysis: Internal documents such as strategy papers, project reports, and technical documentation were analyzed to obtain a comprehensive picture of AI initiatives and their integration into corporate structures.

On-site observations: One-day observation sessions were conducted in each company to capture the practical application of AI tools in everyday work. The researchers acted as passive observers, not interfering with the normal course of operations, to ensure the data's validity. The data collection spanned three months, with multiple visits to each company. The collected data was then analyzed using qualitative content analysis and statistical methods.

The key dimensions of the study are:

- AI strategy and vision,
- Implemented AI projects and their impact,
- Technological infrastructure and AI tools used,
- Data management and quality,
- Skills and training in the field of AI,
- Organizational structure and change management,
- Ethical considerations and governance structures,
- Challenges and success factors in AI implementation.

This comprehensive study provided detailed insights into the practical application of AI in medium-sized companies and analyzed the various dimensions of AI maturity (Sonntag et al., 2024).

3.2 Case Studies

3.3.2 Case 1: Online Retailer in the "Exploring" Phase

The medium-sized online fashion retailer is in the exploratory phase of AI use, characterized by curiosity and uncertainty. The company has launched initial AI initiatives focusing on proof of concepts and experiments. These include implementing a rudimentary chatbot for frequently asked customer questions, using image analysis AI to create product descriptions semi-automatically, and developing a simple recommendation system based on customer purchase history.

These initiatives reflect typical entry points for AI in e-commerce, which aim to improve customer service, optimize processes, and personalize the shopping experience. The ultimate goal is to align these AI initiatives with the company's strategic goals, such as increasing customer satisfaction and operational efficiency. This phase is characterized by a high degree of openness towards AI technologies and uncertainty regarding long-term AI strategy and implementation. In general, in the initial phase, the maturity of AI typically focuses on improving operations to help companies achieve their existing strategic goals. In later stages, AI becomes increasingly important for the company's strategy.

Despite the challenges, the company is agile and adaptable. A lack of data quality and quantity, the complexity of selecting and integrating suitable AI tools, and the need for more clarity regarding the legal and ethical implications of using AI are all being addressed. The company is also working on measuring the return on investment (ROI) of AI initiatives.

Despite these hurdles, success factors are already emerging: Agile project management with short iteration cycles enables rapid adjustments. Close collaboration with external AI experts promotes knowledge transfer. An open error culture supports experimentation and learning from failures. However, one of the most crucial success factors is the strong support for AI initiatives from top management. Their backing not only provides the necessary resources but also sets the tone for the entire company's approach to AI.

Ambitious individuals or teams typically drive research. They focus on creating informed interest and buy-in. They make progress by evaluating business use cases, costs, and benefits. Technical teams can begin AI experiments, but mainly as a tool for learning and creating internal awareness and enthusiasm. The organization can reach an inflection point if it can distinguish good from inadequate AI opportunities. Then, teams can create a roadmap that shows what work is needed to define compelling AI solutions.

The company is committed to making essential investments in improving data infrastructure and quality. This commitment, along with the incremental building of internal AI capabilities and the systematic evaluation and scaling of successful AI pilots, will be critical to unlocking AI's full potential in the business.

Summarized for the SDTPG dimensions of an online fashion retailer:

S. There has yet to be a strategic direction on what the company wants to achieve with AI or how it can achieve it. Internal experts or enthusiasts typically study use cases or experiment with personal side projects.

D. The company needs specialized expertise to understand data. There is no standard infrastructure or procedures in place to facilitate access to data, and the company is barely able to define data requirements for AI.

T. The company typically does not have specialized AI or machine learning solutions, and executives are unsure of what is needed. Any initial experiments will be on PCs or in cloud-based environments.

P. The company has not defined the roles and responsibilities of AI. In the short term, business teams are using the literature to help them create valid use cases for AI. They also need help understanding technical AI techniques.

G. Board members, management teams, and employees are actively educating themselves on responsible AI to understand risks and opportunities. This focus on responsible AI, coupled with the collaborative work on a strategic roadmap, will help teams identify the most significant risks associated with priority use cases.

3.3.3 Case 2: Automotive Company in the "Formalizing" Phase

The second case describes a manufacturing company in the automotive industry that is proactively formalizing its AI implementation. After initial successful experiences with AI technologies, the company is now ready to scale up its AI initiatives. The first AI projects have been successfully transferred to production, usually as limited pilots. The goal is no longer to experiment to find out what works but to use the insights and results of the experiment to achieve measurable business impact.

Bringing AI solutions into production at this stage requires a significant effort, but the company is committed to ensuring that each solution has a clear business case with agreed key performance indicators. Furthermore, due to internal risk policies and industry regulations, AI projects will only go into operation if appropriate processes and relevant software tools are in place to ensure responsible and ethical use.

The company is setting up an AI center and building a data science team to consolidate and develop AI expertise within the company. The company's AI applications span various areas of production and quality management. One focus is on predictive maintenance, where AI models identify potential machine failures early on and address them proactively. In addition, the company uses machine learning algorithms to optimize its production processes, which increases efficiency and reduces costs. In quality control, advanced image processing technologies enable more precise and faster defect detection than conventional methods.

Despite the progress already made, the company is facing various challenges. Integrating AI solutions into existing IT landscapes and production processes is one key task. This often requires taking into account legacy systems and creating interfaces, which can be technically demanding. Data protection concerns exist, particularly when processing sensitive production or employee data. Another obstacle is the resistance sometimes encountered among employees who fear changes to their familiar workflows or even the loss of their jobs.

Several aspects have emerged as success factors for AI implementation. A clear AI strategy aligned with overarching corporate goals and defining specific milestones is important. The company is addressing all dimensions that it has yet to develop. For example, the data needed to operate an AI solution in production could require expensive, customized system integrations, which raises awareness of the need for a more integrated data strategy. Close collaboration between IT and business departments, particularly production, has proven crucial to successfully implementing AI projects. Regular training and professional development help employees understand and effectively use the new technologies. In addition, clearly defining key performance indicators (KPIs) has proven important for measuring the success of AI initiatives and continuously optimizing them.

The company is now focused on the next phase of its AI journey, which involves rolling out successful AI pilot projects across the organization and establishing a culture of continuous innovation. This culture of innovation is crucial for the successful introduction of more complex AI applications in critical business processes. To achieve this, the company is engaging employees at all levels in the transformation process and transparently communicating the benefits of AI. It is also seeking support from senior management to increase budgets, mandates, and plans for AI initiatives.

Summarized for the SDTPG dimensions of the automotive company:

S. Executive sponsorship helps organizational teams define the AI strategy for the organization. This sponsorship typically comes from an executive at the VP level or higher. When a clear strategy is in place, it is not unlikely that AI investments will still generate little profit. However, the company is able to make clear ROI projections for the future. This allows the company to release the budgets and mandates for its strategy to be implemented.

D. The company has a core set of usable data accessible for developing AI solutions. It is different from a data collection strategy within the company. Instead, it results from prioritized data acquisition based on a strategic roadmap for AI use cases. However, data activation is identified as a strategic priority, providing funding for building or expanding common infrastructure (e.g., Catena X) and acquiring new data (e.g., by labeling existing data or installing new sensors for data collection).

T. To fully enter production, technical controls are in place to enable each "human in the loop" and explainability capabilities defined through AI governance practices. The AI deployment architecture and development tools are standardized and implemented. An automated system manages access and resource allocation for computing power. As the AI development and deployment process becomes more standardized and scalable, departments are experimenting with more complex AI solution designs.

P. New AI tasks have emerged and are being defined at the company level. Performance metrics are being created but have not been used in formal performance management processes. There are centers of excellence to provide skills and resources for new roles, guidance for attracting external talent, and training for others in the organization.

G. The guiding principles for AI governance are implemented in daily practices that track specific performance metrics for security, reliability, trustworthiness, and accountability. Reporting is centralized, and key stakeholders have access to the data. Commitment to AI governance is formalized as a critical component of the overall AI strategy. Everyday practices that increase reliability and trustworthiness are part of the standard development cycle.

3.3.4 Case 3: Financial Service Provider in the "Transforming" Phase

The third case vividly portrays a financial services provider in the transformative phase of the AI maturity model, standing as a beacon of innovation and a pioneer in the use of AI in its industry. The company's cutting-edge work, powered by a highly developed AI infrastructure and an experienced AI team, has set a new standard in the industry. By leveraging AI to automate and enhance business processes and introduce new business models, products, or services, the company has shattered organizational silos, integrated data, and redefined value creation. AI now steers decisions across the organization, bolstered by interconnected systems that learn and evolve over time.

Organizations are entering the transformation phase when all organizational prerequisites for AI are in place, and most business decisions can be made with or through AI. Widespread AI expertise and successful communication of the AI vision and roadmap have enabled support for cross-team work and the breaking down of silos to develop next-generation AI solutions (Hortovanyi et al., 2023).

The financial services provider's AI initiatives are diverse and impactful. Advanced chatbots provide personalized financial advice, leveraging complex data analysis to make tailored recommendations. Automated systems are revolutionizing the loan decision process, enhancing efficiency and accuracy. In the realm of security, the company's use of machine learning algorithms for fraud detection is setting new standards, enabling real-time identification and analysis of suspicious transactions.

Despite its advanced position, the financial services provider faces continuous challenges. Compliance with constantly changing regulatory requirements requires close coordination between the AI development and compliance departments. Given the sensitive nature of financial data, ensuring data security remains a priority. In addition, the continuous development of AI models requires significant resources to keep pace with rapid technological progress.

Several aspects have emerged as resounding success factors for the company. The investment in a robust IT infrastructure has laid a solid foundation for advanced AI applications. The formation of a strong data science team with diverse skills has fostered continuous innovation and optimization of AI systems. The company's close collaboration with regulators has not only ensured compliance but also facilitated the development of innovative solutions. These success factors reassure us about the company's future in the rapidly evolving AI landscape.

The financial services provider's agile corporate culture is a key factor in its success. This culture promotes rapid adaptation to new technologies and market conditions. Strong innovative capabilities, supported by dedicated research and development teams, drive the development of new AI-based products and services. The company's close collaboration with external partners, including fintech startups and research institutions, expands its innovation potential and provides access to the latest technologies and insights.

Once transformative AI is fully developed, the technology will be ubiquitous in business operations and throughout the company's value chain, making it fundamental to developing and implementing new strategic opportunities. The company's structure, employee skills, and strategic direction are continuously adapted. The financial services provider faces the challenge of maintaining its pioneering role while setting ethical and regulatory standards in the rapidly developing AI landscape.

Summarized the SDTPG dimensions of the financial services company:

S. AI is seamlessly embedded in the financial services company's overall strategy. Budget plans and indicators for business and AI technology are integrated, enabling the company to quickly identify and respond to new AI-based operational improvements and business models. The company has the necessary experience to realize significant innovations for its products and services over more extended periods with the support of Fintechs (financial technology startups).

D. The company has a data platform that is important to the functioning of its core capabilities. As a result, the infrastructure and tools for data consolidation are highly automated and enable teams to easily capture new data sets. The data is well documented, and both internal and external data sets are highly visible.

T. The AI delivery architecture is standardized and efficient. As AI becomes more critical to the organization's overall strategy, new use cases are pushing the boundaries of what technology can do to develop cutting-edge AI solutions.

P. All teams and employees have a high level of AI knowledge and foster a work culture in which they collaborate with or complement AI systems. AI is integrated into all roles to some extent, even at the management level.

G. Strong corporate governance allows the organization to go beyond compliance. Its multifaceted approaches to risk avoidance and stakeholder trust are a competitive advantage for applying AI in a high-performance way. It introduces the company to novel challenges related to AI ethics or fairness, accountability, and transparency.

3.3 Comparative analysis

The case studies' analysis reveals similarities and differences in the individual phases of AI maturity in the companies examined (Table 1). One unifying element is the realization by all companies that AI is crucial to their future success. This is reflected in the high expectations placed on AI technologies.

Table 1. Similarities and differences

Similarities	Differences
- High expectations of AI	- Scope of AI initiatives
- Lack of qualified specialists	- Maturity of IT infrastructure
- Difficulties with data quality	- Organizational structure
- Need for a clear AI strategy	- Culture

Source: own representation

Despite this shared insight, there are apparent differences in the complexity of the implemented AI applications, the maturity of the IT infrastructure, and the organizational embedding of AI. The online fashion retailer is still in the exploration phase with initial experiments, while the automotive company is already using AI in various areas, and the financial services provider has integrated AI deeply into its business processes.

All the companies analyzed faced common challenges, such as the lack of qualified specialists and difficulties ensuring data quality. These aspects prove to be critical factors for the success of AI initiatives, regardless of the company's level of maturity. Understanding these challenges can foster a sense of empathy and shared experience among business leaders.

The differences between the companies are particularly evident in the scope of their AI initiatives, the maturity of their IT infrastructure, and their organizational structure. While the online retailer is still experimenting with basic implementations, the financial services provider already has a highly developed AI infrastructure and an experienced AI team. Table 2 illustrates how the three companies analyzed differ in their maturity in AI use and the striking differences that emerge across the five dimensions.

Table 2. Differences in AI maturity levels

Dimension	Exploring (Online Retailer)	Experimenting	Formalizing (Automotive Company)	Optimizing	Transforming (Financial Service Provider)
Strategy	No clearly defined AI strategy, focus on experiments		First AI strategy with clear goals and KPIs		Complete integration of AI into the overall strategy
Data	Limited data quality and missing infrastructure		Strategic data collection for prioritized use cases		Automated and consolidated data platform
Technology	First AI tools, mostly cloud-based		Standardized AI deployment architecture		Sophisticated architecture with a focus on advanced innovations
People	A dedicated role, learning through literature		Center of Excellence and defined roles for AI		Broad AI expertise in all teams, integration into every role
Governance	Beginning discussions of responsible AI		Principles of AI governance in daily practices		Advanced governance with a focus on AI ethics and fairness

Source: own representation

Despite these differences, converging development paths can be seen. Data quality and management are becoming increasingly important for all companies. Likewise, the need for close collaboration between IT and business departments is becoming increasingly apparent to implement AI projects successfully.

The empirical study clearly demonstrates that medium-sized companies are at different stages of AI maturity, each with its own set of challenges and success factors. A clear strategy, appropriate technologies, skilled employees, and an agile organizational culture are all crucial components for a successful AI transformation.

These findings underscore the necessity of a tailored approach when implementing AI in companies. While fundamental challenges such as data quality and a shortage of skilled workers are prevalent across all industries, specific solutions must be adapted to the respective level of maturity and the unique circumstances of each company.

4. ROLE OF OF AI MODELS WITH GENERAL PURPOSE

Artificial intelligence models with general purpose (e.g., Large Language Models (LLMs) such as ChatGPT) have experienced an enormous upswing in recent years. They offer companies new opportunities to optimize their business processes and develop innovative products and services. Their influence on companies at different stages of AI maturity is significant and varies depending on the level of development, creating an urgent need to adapt and evolve. In all cases, LLMs offer the potential to accelerate the transition to the next maturity phase. However, the challenges of integrating and responsibly deploying this technology must be considered.

4.1 Significance of Large Language Models

Large Language Models (LLMs) are complex neural networks trained on large text corpora. They can generate, translate, summarize, or respond to questions in a human-like manner. LLMs often interface with users and other specialized AI models, enabling natural interaction and simplifying complex tasks such as searching large data sets or extracting information (Liao & Vaughan, 2024).

For companies, LLMs offer numerous advantages. They can significantly improve the customer experience by providing personalized recommendations, answering customer queries, and creating customized content, which leads to increased customer satisfaction. In addition, they enable the automation of routine tasks such as writing reports, summarizing documents, or translating texts. It frees up employees and allows them to focus on value-adding activities. Another significant advantage lies in the ability of LLMs to help companies gain new insights from large amounts of data, thus promoting the development of innovative products and services.

Despite the impressive possibilities, companies using LLMs face several challenges. One key issue is the potential bias in the training data, which could lead to discriminatory or unjust results. It's crucial to stress the importance of continuous monitoring for bias, as it's a vital part of using LLMs responsibly and effectively. Other challenges include the complexity and opacity of how LLMs work, which limit their transparency and ability to explain themselves, and the significant cost factor due to the considerable computing power required.

Companies must carefully weigh these pros and cons and develop strategies to maximize the potential of LLMs while minimizing the associated risks. This includes the crucial step of continuous monitoring for bias, which is essential for maintaining ethical standards in AI technologies.

Despite the challenges, LLMs hold the potential to revolutionize business processes and create new value opportunities. This transformative power is why they are likely to become a central element of many companies' AI strategies.

4.2 Architecture and Application

Large Language Models (LLMs) are based on a complex architecture that enables them to generate and process human-like text. At the core of this architecture are transformer models, which represent a groundbreaking innovation in natural language processing. These models can capture relationships between words in a sentence and between sentences in a text, which allows them to develop an in-depth understanding of context and meaning.

The transformer architecture uses a mechanism called "self-attention," which allows the model to evaluate the relevance of different parts of the input text to each other. This results in highly efficient processing of long-term dependencies in texts. LLMs are trained on enormous text corpora that include billions of words from various sources, such as books, articles, web pages, and other text documents. This extensive training enables the models to capture broad knowledge and linguistic nuances, impressively deepening their understanding of language.

Today, the most advanced LLMs and multimodal models are accessed primarily in three ways: through chatbots, through application programming interfaces (APIs) that allow programmers to target models on a larger scale, or indirectly through software that builds on LLMs. Those best placed to use and benefit from these systems can easily interact with software as part of their existing workflows, i.e., those who do much of their work on computers. Those working in agriculture, skilled trades, personal services, and other occupations, primarily physical labor, have much less direct access to the scalable productivity benefits these systems can provide within their existing workflows.

LLMs' application areas are diverse and are revolutionizing numerous industries. In customer service, they are used to develop advanced chatbots and virtual assistants that understand and respond to complex customer queries. In content creation, LLMs assist in the creation of marketing texts, product descriptions, and blog articles, significantly accelerating the content creation process.

LLMs have also transformed the translation industry by enabling unprecedented-quality automatic translations. They can summarize long texts accurately and extract valuable information in research and journalism. In software development, LLMs are increasingly used for code generation, where they can generate code for different programming languages and even implement complex algorithms.

LLMs' versatility and power make them a powerful tool in digital transformation. Their ability to understand and generate natural language opens up new possibilities in human-machine interaction and automated information processing. With the continuous development of this technology, LLMs can have an even more profound impact on various aspects of our daily lives and the world of work in the future, exciting us about the potential they hold.

4.3 Impact on Analyzed Companies

Using large language models (LLMs) has far-reaching implications for companies and requires extensive adjustments in several areas. Companies need to make significant investments in the development and operation of LLMs, including hardware and software investments and employee training. The integration of LLMs leads to a redesign of existing processes, with a focus on automation and optimization. It requires an adjustment of workflows and a realignment of employee tasks. A high-performance IT infrastructure is essential to process the enormous amounts of data LLMs require. In addition, companies need to recruit or train employees with the necessary skills to deploy and develop LLMs effectively.

The possible applications of LLMs vary across industries and companies' AI maturity (Table 3):

Case 1: Imagine the possibilities for an online fashion retailer in the 'exploring' phase. LLMs could revolutionize customer service by developing intelligent chatbots, relieving the burden on customer support and shortening response times. These models could automatically generate product descriptions based on product features and customer ratings, speeding up the creation of product catalogs. By analyzing customer behavior, LLMs could create personalized product recommendations, significantly increasing the likelihood of purchases. The potential for improvement is vast and exciting.

Case 2: In the automotive industry, which is in the "formalizing" phase, LLMs could be used in conjunction with sensor data to improve the accuracy of predictive models for machine failures. By analyzing image data, LLMs could detect product defects early, thus ensuring quality. LLMs could eventually create and update technical documentation automatically.

Case 3: Now, let's consider the financial services provider in the 'Transforming' phase. LLMs could be a game-changer, enabling advanced credit risk assessments by analyzing large amounts of financial data. By analyzing transaction data, LLMs could identify suspicious activities and prevent fraud. They could even assist in developing new financial products by analyzing market research results and identifying trends. The potential for transformation is significant and inspiring.

Table 3. Differentiation of effects

Case study	Phase	LLMs
Online fashion retailer	Exploring	• Support for customer service • Product descriptions • Personalization
Automotive industry	Formalizing	• Improvements to predictive maintenance • Quality control • Documentation
Financial services provider	Transforming	• Risk assessment • Fraud detection • Product development

Source: own representation

Despite the wide range of opportunities for process improvement and developing new business models, the successful deployment of LLMs requires careful planning and execution. Companies need to be aware of potential issues such as bias, lack of transparency, and high costs. Therefore, a clear strategy for LLM deployment and ensuring the necessary resources and skills are essential. This emphasis on strategy and preparedness should reassure companies about the importance of planning in the successful implementation of LLMs.

The new generation of AI agents is characterized by their ability to perform complex tasks autonomously without a specific command and to continuously improve themselves. In a business context, AI agents could, for example,

- automate routine administrative tasks, such as processing standard requests or generating reports,
- provide customer service around the clock, with the ability to respond accurately to a wide range of concerns,
- perform data analysis and develop decision proposals for management,
- support product development by analyzing market trends and generating innovative ideas.

Integrating such AI agents is expected to lead to redesigning work processes and organizational structures. Companies will need to prepare for certain positions to be replaced by AI, while new roles will emerge that focus on the monitoring, development, and ethical use of AI systems (Krijger et al., 2023). For the successful integration of AI agents, companies must develop a clear strategy that aligns technological innovation with ethical considerations and the needs of their employees. Only in this way can the full potential of this technology be realized without neglecting the human aspects of the working world.

5. CONCLUSIONS AND OUTLOOK

This paper has underscored the empowering role of AI maturity models as a crucial tool for companies, providing business leaders, researchers, and policymakers with the means to evaluate and strategically develop their AI use. These models empower companies to identify strengths and weaknesses and take targeted optimization measures for their AI initiatives. New AI initiatives often start as a technological proof of concept, but the true nature of ROI gains (e.g., productivity, efficiency, quality) and scaling to the entire organization should be included. Companies are still developing their applications internally due to the limited availability of field-proven enterprise AI applications. Knowing where the pain points are and where to deploy AI investments for the most significant impact is a major challenge for organizations, but AI maturity models provide a sense of control and direction in this journey.

The maturity model presented here offers managers a practical and feasible tool for evaluating and improving AI implementation for these challenges, with industry-specific customization to consider. In practice, the key to AI maturity—from exploring AI to transforming with it—is to envision what that end state might look like for the organization. Then, it requires a clear path to that vision, starting from the current state. Most business leaders are unable to grasp the current or future state clearly. Therefore, the maturity model is a useful and effective management tool, providing a practical roadmap for AI implementation.

Large Language Models (LLMs) are increasingly important in this context. They open up many opportunities for companies to automate and optimize processes and develop new products and services. However, challenges such as bias, transparency, and costs must be addressed.

There are several practical implications for companies: developing a clear AI strategy that is aligned with individual business objectives is not just important, it's essential. Investing in data quality is crucial to the success of AI projects. Building skills through qualified employees is indispensable. Collaborating with external partners can accelerate AI initiatives. An agile organizational culture promotes adaptability to new AI technologies.

In the future, AI maturity models are expected to evolve to include new dimensions such as sustainability and ethical aspects. LLMs will become more widespread in various industries, their integration into existing IT landscapes will be simplified, and specialized LLMs will be developed for specific application areas. Regulation of AI will advance to address ethical and social implications.

The limitations of the case study analysis are the limited generalizability and possible distortions due to the limited sample. One of the biggest challenges is the generalizability of the results. Case studies are usually limited to individual companies or industries and cannot be easily transferred to other contexts. The representativeness of the selected cases is also a critical factor. A small sample size can lead to skewed results that do not reflect the full diversity of companies.

Further research is needed to deepen and generalize the insights from this work. The following aspects could be examined in more detail in future studies:

- Longitudinal studies could shed light on how companies' AI maturity develops over time and which factors influence the change.
- Quantitative studies with larger samples increase the generalizability of the results and uncover statistical relationships.

- Comparative studies between different industries and countries could help to identify cultural and institutional differences in AI adoption.
- The ethical implications of using AI should be considered more in future studies.
- The impacts of AI on the world of work and society should be investigated.

In conclusion, AI maturity models and LLMs offer companies great opportunities to increase competitiveness and develop new business models. A clear AI strategy, investments in employee training, and an agile organizational culture are required to take advantage of these. Further research is needed to understand better the complex relationships between technology, business, and society and to develop evidence-based recommendations for companies and policymakers.

REFERENCES

Al-Sai, Z. A., Husin, M. H., Syed-Mohamad, S. M., Abdullah, R., Zitar, R. A., & el Abualigah, L. (2023). Big Data maturity assessment models: A systematic literature review. *Big Data and Cognitive Computing*, *7*(1), 2. DOI: 10.3390/bdcc7010002

Ameye, N., Bughin, J., & van Zeebroeck, N. (2024). From experimentation to scaling: What shapes the funnel of AI adoption? *Economics of Innovation and New Technology*, 1–15. Advance online publication. DOI: 10.1080/10438599.2024.2413940

Becker, J., Knackstedt, R., & Pöppelbuß, J. (2009). Developing maturity models for IT management. *Business & Information Systems Engineering*, *1*(3), 213–222. DOI: 10.1007/s12599-009-0044-5

Chen, W., Liu, C., Xing, F., Peng, G., & Yang, X. (2022). Establishment of a maturity model to assess the development of industrial AI in smart manufacturing. *Journal of Enterprise Information Management*, *35*(3), 701–728. DOI: 10.1108/JEIM-10-2020-0397

Comuzzi, M., & Patel, A. (2016). How organisations leverage Big Data: A maturity model. *Industrial Management & Data Systems*, *116*(8), 1468–1492. DOI: 10.1108/IMDS-12-2015-0495

Element, A. I. (2020). The AI maturity framework: A strategic guide to operationalize and scale enterprise AI solutions. https://s3.amazonaws.com/external_clips/3430107/AI-Maturity-Framework_White-Paper_EN.pdf?1589551996

Fornasiero, R., Kiebler, L., Falsafi, M., & Sardesai, S. (2024). Proposing a maturity model for assessing Artificial Intelligence and Big data in the process industry. *International Journal of Production Research*. Advance online publication. DOI: 10.1080/00207543.2024.2372840

Gökalp, E., & Martinez, V. (2021). Digital transformation maturity assessment: Development of the digital transformation capability maturity model. *International Journal of Production Research*, *60*(20), 6282–6302. DOI: 10.1080/00207543.2021.1991020

Hausladen, I., & Schosser, M. (2020). Towards a maturity model for Big Data analytics in airline network planning. *Journal of Air Transport Management*, *82*, 101721. DOI: 10.1016/j.jairtraman.2019.101721

Hevner, A. R., March, S. T., Park, J., & Ram, S. (2004). Design science in information systems research. *Management Information Systems Quarterly*, *28*(1), 75–105. DOI: 10.2307/25148625

Hortovanyi, L., Morgan, R. E., Herceg, I. V., Djuricin, D., Hanak, R., & Dora Horvath, D.. (2023). Assessment of digital maturity: The role of resources and capabilities in digital transformation in B2B firms. *International Journal of Production Research, 61*(23), 8043–8061. DOI: 10.1080/00207543.2022.2164087

Hua, S. Y., Jin, S. C., & Jiang, S. Y. (2024). The limitations and ethical considerations of ChatGPT. *Data Intelligence, 6*(1), 201–239. DOI: 10.1162/dint_a_00243

Jorzik, P., Klein, S. P., Kanbach, D. K., & Kraus, S. (2024). AI-driven business model innovation: A systematic review and research agenda. *Journal of Business Research, 182*, 114764. DOI: 10.1016/j.jbusres.2024.114764

Krijger, J., Thuis, T., de Ruiter, M., Ligthart, E., & Broekman, I. (2023). The AI ethics maturity model: A holistic approach to advancing ethical data science in organizations. *AI and Ethics, 3*(2), 355–367. DOI: 10.1007/s43681-022-00228-7

Liao, V., & Vaughan, J. W. (2024). AI transparency in the age of LLMs: A human-centered research roadmap. *Harvard Data Science Review, 5*(Special Issue 5). Advance online publication. DOI: 10.1162/99608f92.8036d03b

Lichtenthaler, U. (2020). Five maturity levels of managing AI: From isolated ignorance to integrated intelligence. *Journal of Innovation Management, 8*(1), 39–50. DOI: 10.24840/2183-0606_008.001_0005

Mariani, M. M., Machado, I., & Nambisan, S. (2023). Types of innovation and artificial intelligence: A systematic quantitative literature review and research agenda. *Journal of Business Research, 155*(113364), 1–14. DOI: 10.1016/j.jbusres.2022.113364

Monod, E., Lissillour, R., Köster, A., & Jiayin, Q. (2023). Does AI control or support? Power shifts after AI system implementation in customer relationship management. *Journal of Decision Systems, 32*(3), 542–565. DOI: 10.1080/12460125.2022.2066051

Perifanis, N.-A., & Kitsios, F. (2023). Investigating the influence of artificial intelligence on business value in the digital era of strategy: A literature review. *Information (Basel), 14*(2), 85. DOI: 10.3390/info14020085

Sadiq, R. B., Safie, N., Abd Rahman, A. H., & Goudarzi, S. (2021). Artificial intelligence maturity model: A systematic literature review. *PeerJ. Computer Science, 7*, e661. DOI: 10.7717/peerj-cs.661 PMID: 34541308

Schuster, T., Waidelich, L., & Volz, R. (2021). Maturity models for the assessment of artificial intelligence in small and medium-sized enterprises. In Wrycza, S., & Maślankowski, J. (eds.), *Digital transformation*. PLAIS EuroSymposium 2021. *Lecture Notes in Business Information Processing, 429*, Springer, 22–36. https://doi.org/DOI: 10.1007/978-3-030-85893-3_2

Sonntag, M., Mehmann, S., Mehmann, J., & Teuteberg, F. (2024). Development and evaluation of a maturity model for AI deployment capability of manufacturing companies. *Information Systems Management*, *42*(1), 37–67. Advance online publication. DOI: 10.1080/10580530.2024.2319041

Stecher, P., Pohl, M., & Turowski, K. (2020). Enterprise architecture's effects on organizations' ability to adopt artificial intelligence-A resource-based perspective. Proceedings of the 2020 28th European Conference on Information Systems (ECIS), 1–16. https://aisel.aisnet.org/ecis2020_rp/173/

Wagire, A. A., Joshi, R., Rathore, A. P. S., & Jain, R. (2021). Development of maturity model for assessing the implementation of Industry 4.0: Learning from theory and practice. *Production Planning and Control*, *32*(8), 603–622. DOI: 10.1080/09537287.2020.1744763

Compilation of References

Abdelfattah, R. M. M. (2023). The Impact of Fintech on Financial Inclusion in Egypt (Doctoral dissertation, The German University in Cairo).

Abdulla, M., & Darwish, A. (2022). The Effect Of Artificial Intelligence In Smart Decision-Making In The UAE Government. *International Business Research.*

Abugri, B. A. (2008). Empirical relationship between macroeconomic volatility and stock returns: Evidence from Latin American markets. *International Review of Financial Analysis*, *17*(2), 396–410. DOI: 10.1016/j.irfa.2006.09.002

Acharya, V., Pedersen, L. H., Philippon, T., & Richardson, M. (2010). Measuring systemic risk, Working Paper, NYU Stern Schook of Business.

Acharya, V. (2009). A theory of systemic risk and design of prudential bank regulation. *Journal of Financial Stability*, *5*(3), 224–255. DOI: 10.1016/j.jfs.2009.02.001

Acharya, V., Engle, R., & Richardson, M. (2012). Capital shortfall: A new approach to ranking and regulating systemic risks. *The American Economic Review*, *102*(3), 59–64. DOI: 10.1257/aer.102.3.59

Adam, A. M., & Tweneboah, G. (2008). Macroeconomic factors and stock market movement: evidence from Ghana. Unpublished Working Paper. https://mpra.ub .unimuenchen. De/11256/.

Adamson, B., Dixon, M., & Toman, N. (2012). *The end of solution sales*. Harvard Business School.

Addy, W. A., Ajayi-Nifise, A. O., Bello, B. G., Tula, S. T., Odeyemi, O., & Falaiye, T. (2024). AI in credit scoring: A comprehensive review of models and predictive analytics. *Global Journal of Engineering and Technology Advances*, *18*(02), 118–129.

Adrian, T., & Boyarchenko, N. (2012). Intermediary leverage cycles and financial stability, Working Paper, Federal Reserve Bank of New York.

Adrian, T., & Brunnermeier, M. (2014). *CoVaR*. Federal Reserve Bank of New York Staff Reports.

Adu-Gyamfi, M., (2016), 'The bankruptcy of Lehman Brothers: Causes, effects and lessons learnt', Journal of Insurance and Financial Management, Vol. 1(4).

Agarwal, P., Swami, S., & Malhotra, S. K. (2024). Artificial intelligence adoption in the post COVID-19 new-normal and role of smart technologies in transforming business: A review. *Journal of Science and Technology Policy Management*, *15*(3), 506–529. DOI: 10.1108/JSTPM-08-2021-0122

Agyei, S. K., Owusu, P.Junior, Bossman, A., Asafo-Adjei, E., Asiamah, O., & Adam, A. M. (2022). Spillovers and contagion between BRIC and G7 markets: New evidence from time-frequency analysis. *PLoS One*, *17*(7), e0271088. DOI: 10.1371/journal.pone.0271088 PMID: 35895731

Ahmad, H., Yaqub, M., & Lee, S. H. (2023). Environmental-, social-, and governance-related factors for business investment and sustainability: A scientometric review of global trends. *Environment, Development and Sustainability*, *26*(2), 2965–2987. Advance online publication. DOI: 10.1007/s10668-023-02921-x PMID: 36714213

Aims History – Aims international. (n.d.). http://www.aimsinternational.org/aims

Akhigbe, A., & Madura, J. (1996). Dividend Policy and Corporate Performance. *Journal of Business Finance & Accounting*, *23*(9-10), 1267–1289. DOI: 10.1111/1468-5957.00079

Aldoseri, A., Al-Khalifa, K., & Hamouda, A. (2023). A roadmap for integrating automation with process optimization for AI-powered digital transformation.

Aldoseri, A., Al-Khalifa, K. N., & Hamouda, A. M. (2024). AI-powered innovation in digital transformation: Key pillars and industry impact. *Sustainability (Basel)*, *16*(5), 1790. DOI: 10.3390/su16051790

Allied Market Research. (2023). Allied Market Research. Retrieved May 20, 2024 from www.alliedmarketresearch.com

Allioui, H., & Mourdi, Y. (2023). Unleashing the potential of AI: Investigating cutting-edge technologies that are transforming businesses. [IJCEDS]. *International Journal of Computer Engineering and Data Science*, *3*(2), 1–12.

Al-Sai, Z. A., Husin, M. H., Syed-Mohamad, S. M., Abdullah, R., Zitar, R. A., & el Abualigah, L. (2023). Big Data maturity assessment models: A systematic literature review. *Big Data and Cognitive Computing*, *7*(1), 2. DOI: 10.3390/bdcc7010002

Al-Shami, H. A. A., & Ibrahim, Y. (2013). The effects of macro-economic indicators on stock returns: Evidence from Kuwait stock market. *American Journal of Economics*, *3*(5C), 57–66.

Alzubaidi, L., Bai, J., Al-Sabaawi, A., Santamaría, J., Albahri, A. S., Al-dabbagh, B. S. N., Fadhel, M. A., Manoufali, M., Zhang, J., Al-Timemy, A. H., Duan, Y., Abdullah, A., Farhan, L., Lu, Y., Gupta, A., Albu, F., Abbosh, A., & Gu, Y. (2023). A survey on deep learning tools dealing with data scarcity: Definitions, challenges, solutions, tips, and applications. *Journal of Big Data*, *10*(1), 46. DOI: 10.1186/s40537-023-00727-2

Ameye, N., Bughin, J., & van Zeebroeck, N. (2024). From experimentation to scaling: What shapes the funnel of AI adoption? *Economics of Innovation and New Technology*, 1–15. Advance online publication. DOI: 10.1080/10438599.2024.2413940

Ancillai, C., Terho, H., Cardinali, S., & Pascucci, F. (2019). Advancing social media driven sales research: Establishing conceptual domains for B2B and B2C scholarship. *Industrial Marketing Management*, *81*, 325–337.

Anderson, E. G., Lopez, J., & Parker, G. G. (2022). Leveraging value creation to drive the growth of B2B platforms. *Production and Operations Management*, *31*(12), 4501–4514. DOI: 10.1111/poms.13866

Anderson, H. D., Balli, F., & Godber, C. (2018). The effect of macroeconomic announcements at a sectoral level in the US and European Union. *Research in International Business and Finance*, *44*(C), 256–272. DOI: 10.1016/j.ribaf.2017.07.095

Andrie , A. M., Ihnatov, I., & Tiwari, A. (2014). Analyzing time–frequency relationship between interest rate, stock price and exchange rate through continuous wavelet. *Economic Modelling*, *41*(C), 227–238. DOI: 10.1016/j.econmod.2014.05.013

Ang, J. S., Cole, R. A., & Lin, J. W. (2000). Agency Costs and Ownership Structure. *The Journal of Finance*, *55*(1), 81–106. DOI: 10.1111/0022-1082.00201

Antonakakis, N., Chatziantoniou, I., & Filis, G. (2017). Oil shocks and stock markets: Dynamic connectedness under the prism of recent geopolitical and economic unrest. *International Review of Financial Analysis*, *50*(C), 1–26. DOI: 10.1016/j.irfa.2017.01.004

Arouri, M., Estay, C., Rault, C., & Roubaud, D. (2016). Economic policy uncertainty and stock markets: Long-run evidence from the US. *Finance Research Letters*, *18*(C), 136–141. DOI: 10.1016/j.frl.2016.04.011

Ashraf, B. N., & Shen, Y. (2019). Economic policy uncertainty and banks' loan pricing. *Journal of Financial Stability*, *44*(C), 100695. DOI: 10.1016/j.jfs.2019.100695

Asmy, M., Rohilina, W., Hassama, A., & Fouad, M. (2009). *Effects of Macroeconomic Variables on Stock Prices in Malaysia: An Approach of Error Correction Model, MPRA Paper 20970*. University Library of Munich.

Assis, L. F., Ferreira, K. R., Vinhas, L., Maurano, L., Almeida, C., Carvalho, A., & Camargo, C. (2019). TerraBrasilis: A spatial data analytics infrastructure for large-scale thematic mapping. *International Journal of Geo-Information*, *8*(11).

Åström, J., Reim, W., & Parida, V. (2022). Value creation and value capture for AI business model innovation: A three-phase process framework. *Review of Managerial Science*, *16*(7), 2111–2133. DOI: 10.1007/s11846-022-00521-z

Aziki, A., & Fadili, M. H. (2022). Highlighting artificial intelligence roles in business area Amid the COVID-19 crisis. *Procedia Computer Science*, *203*, 450–455. DOI: 10.1016/j.procs.2022.07.060 PMID: 35974967

Babina, T., Fedyk, A., He, A., & Hodson, J. (2023). Artificial intelligence, firm growth, and product innovation. *Journal of Financial Economics*, *151*, 103745. DOI: 10.1016/j.jfineco.2023.103745

Balcilar, M., Cakan, E., & Gupta, R. (2017). Does US news impact Asian emerging markets? Evidence from nonparametric causality-in-quantiles test. *The North American Journal of Economics and Finance*, *41*, 32–43.

Bartsch, Z. (2019). Economic policy uncertainty and dollar-pound exchange rate return volatility. *Journal of International Money and Finance*, *98*(C), 102067. DOI: 10.1016/j.jimonfin.2019.102067

Basri, W. (2020). Examining the impact of artificial intelligence (AI)-assisted social media marketing on the performance of small and medium enterprises: Toward effective business management in the Saudi Arabian context. *International Journal of Computational Intelligence Systems*, *13*(1), 142–152. DOI: 10.2991/ijcis.d.200127.002

Bathaee, Y. (2017). The artificial intelligence black box and the failure of intent and causation. *Harv. JL & Tech.*, *31*, 889.

Baxter, N. D. (1967). Leverage, Risk of Ruin and the Cost of Capital. *The Journal of Finance*, (September), 395–403.

BDO USA. (2023). TOP 10 business cyber security threats in 2023. Available at: https://surl.li/jaran

Becker, J., Knackstedt, R., & Pöppelbuß, J. (2009). Developing maturity models for IT management. *Business & Information Systems Engineering*, *1*(3), 213–222. DOI: 10.1007/s12599-009-0044-5

Bedowska-Sojka, B., Demir, E., & Zaremba, A. (2022). Hedging geopolitical risks with different asset classes: A focus on the Russian invasion of Ukraine. *Finance Research Letters*, *103192*, 103192. Advance online publication. DOI: 10.1016/j.frl.2022.103192

Bekiros, S., Gupta, R., & Majumdar, A. (2016). Incorporating economic policy uncertainty in US equity premium models: A nonlinear predictability analysis. *Finance Research Letters*, *18*(C), 291–296. DOI: 10.1016/j.frl.2016.01.012

Bendapudi, N., & Leone, R. P. (2002). Managing business-to-business customer relationships following key contact employee turnover in a vendor firm. *Journal of Marketing*, *66*(2), 83–101. DOI: 10.1509/jmkg.66.2.83.18476

Bentalha, B. (2023). Consumer Perception of Robotic Mobile Fulfillment Systems: A Netnographic Case Study of Amazon. In Innovation, Strategy, and Transformation Frameworks for the Modern Enterprise (pp. 243-264). IGI Global. DOI: 10.4018/979-8-3693-0458-7.ch010

Bentalha, B., & Alla, L. (2024). Revealing the Subtleties: The Art of Qualitative Studies in Science and Management. In Applying Qualitative Research Methods to Management Science (pp. 1-21). IGI Global.

Bentalha, B., & Boukare, M. (2024). AI-Driven Territorial Intelligence: An Integrated Approach to Enhancing Digital Sovereignty. In Generative AI and Implications for Ethics, Security, and Data Management (pp. 231-261). IGI Global.

Berdiyeva, O. (2021). Artificial Intelligence in Accounting and Finance. *Meta-Analysis.*, (August). Advance online publication. DOI: 10.37435/NBR21032502

Bernanke, B. S., Gertler, M., Policy, M., & Volatility, A. P. (February 2000). NBER Working Paper No. w7559, Available at *SSRN*: https://ssrn.com/abstract=217836

Bernstein, L. A., Wild, J., & Subramanyam, K. R. (2001). *Financial Statement Analysis*. McGraw-Hill Higher Education.

Bhadra, P., Chakraborty, S., & Saha, S. (2023). Cognitive IoT meets robotic process automation: The unique convergence revolutionizing digital transformation in the Industry 4.0 era. In *Confluence of artificial intelligence and robotic process automation* (pp. 355–388). Springer Nature Singapore. DOI: 10.1007/978-981-19-8296-5_15

Bhat, A. (2023). Employee morale: definition, affecting factors, and how to boost morale. QuestionPro. https://www.questionpro.com/blog/employee-morale/

Bhuiyan, E. M., & Chowdhury, M. (2020). Macroeconomic Variables and Stock Market Indices: Asymmetric Dynamics in the US and Canada. *The Quarterly Review of Economics and Finance*, *77*, 62–74. DOI: 10.1016/j.qref.2019.10.005

Bhuiyan, M. (2024). The Role of AI-Enhanced Personalization in Customer Experiences. *Journal of Computer Science and Technology Studies.*, *6*(1), 162–169. DOI: 10.32996/jcsts.2024.6.1.17

Bjørnland, H., & Leitemo, K. (2009). Identifying the interdependence between US monetary policy and the stock market. *Journal of Monetary Economics*, *56*(2), 275–282. DOI: 10.1016/j.jmoneco.2008.12.001

Blackburne, E. F.III, & Frank, M. W. (2007). Estimation of Nonstationary Heterogeneous Panels. *The Stata Journal*, *7*(2), 197–208. DOI: 10.1177/1536867X0700700204

Black, F. (1976). The Dividend Puzzle. *Journal of Portfolio Management*, *2*(2), 5–8. DOI: 10.3905/jpm.1976.408558

Block, S. B., Hirt, G. A., & Danielsen, B. (2011). *Foundations of Financial Management.* McGraw-Hill Education.

Blomberg, S. B., Hess, G. D., & Weerapana, A. (2004, June). Economic conditions and terrorism. *European Journal of Political Economy*, *20*(2), 463–478. DOI: 10.1016/j.ejpoleco.2004.02.002

Bloom, N. (2009). The impact of uncertainty shocks. econometrica, 77(3), 623-685.

Boiko, M., Bovsh, L., & Okhrimenko, A. (2022). Crisis resilience of the tourism business in martial law. *The International Scientific-Practical Journal. Commodities and Markets*, *42*(2), 31–47. DOI: 10.31617/2.2022(42)03

Bolotova, I. (2024). *Artificial intelligence technologies in business process management (based on "Advertising and production group NBS" case)* (Doctoral dissertation, Private Higher Educational Establishment-Institute "Ukrainian-American Concordia University").

Borges, A. F., Laurindo, F. J., Spínola, M. M., Gonçalves, R. F., & Mattos, C. A. (2021). The strategic use of artificial intelligence in the digital era: Systematic literature review and future research directions. *International Journal of Information Management*, *57*, 102225. DOI: 10.1016/j.ijinfomgt.2020.102225

Bossman, A., & Gubareva, M. (2023): Asymmetric impacts of geopolitical risk on stock markets: A comparative analysis of the E7 and G7 equities during the Russian-Ukrainian conflict. Heliyon, https://www.sciencedirect.com/science/article/pii/S2405844023008332

Bossman, A., Gubareva, M., & Teplova, T. (2023). Asymmetric effects of geopolitical risk on major currencies: Russia-Ukraine tensions. *Finance Research Letters*, *51*, 103440. DOI: 10.1016/j.frl.2022.103440

Bostandzic, D., & Weiss, G. N. F. (2018). Why do some banks contribute more to global systemic risk? *Journal of Financial Intermediation*, *35*, 17–40. DOI: 10.1016/j.jfi.2018.03.003

Boudri, R., Bentalha, B., & Benjelloun, O. (2024). Phygital Marketing and the Pain of Paying: An Amazon Go Netnographic Case Study. In AI and Data Engineering Solutions for Effective Marketing (pp. 348-363). IGI Global.

Bouhtati, N., Alla, L., & Bentalha, B. (2023). Marketing Big Data Analytics and Customer Relationship Management: A Fuzzy Approach. In Integrating Intelligence and Sustainability in Supply Chains (pp. 75-86). IGI Global. DOI: 10.4018/979-8-3693-0225-5.ch004

Bovsh, L., Hopkalo, L., & Rasulova, A. (2023). The concept of investment risk management by subjects of the hotel business in the conditions of martial law. In M. Sahaidak & T. Sobolieva (Eds.), Management: Challenges in global world (pp. 236-247). Kyiv National Economic University named after Vadym Hetman. Available at: http://doi.org/doi.org/10.35668/978-966-926-425-1

Bovsh, L., Rasulova, A., & Muravyova, I. (2022). The impact of the war on the tourism brand of Ukraine. Creative space of Ukraine and the world (pp. 223-227). Collective monograph. Kharkiv. Available at: https://www.newroute.org.ua/wp-content/uploads/2022/11/6.pdf

Bovsh, L., Bosovska, M., & Okhrimenko, A. (2021). Compliance-strategizing of economic security of the business in digitalization conditions. *Herald of KNUTE.*, *6*(6), 42–60. DOI: 10.31617/visnik.knute.2021(140)03

BrandEquity. E. (2021, July 23). Theatres to OTT: A shift in the wake of pandemic. ETBrandEquity.com. https://brandequity.economictimes.indiatimes.com/news/digital/theatres-to-ott-a-shift-in-the-wake-of-pandemic/84666148

Brealey, R. A., Mayers, S. C., & Allien, F. (2017). *Principles of Corporate Finance*. McGraw-Hill Education.

Breitung, J. (2000). The local power of some unit root tests for panel data. In Baltagi, B. H. (Ed.), *Nonstationary panels, panel cointegration and dynamic panels* (pp. 161–177). Elsevier. DOI: 10.1016/S0731-9053(00)15006-6

Brigham, E. F., & Houston, J. F. (2015). *Fundamentals of Financial Management: Concise*. Cengage Learning.

Brogaard, J., & Detzel, A. (2015). The Asset-Pricing Implications of Government Economic Policy Uncertainty. *Management Science*, *61*(1), 3–18. DOI: 10.1287/mnsc.2014.2044

Brooks, R. M. (1996). Changes in Asymmetric Information at Earnings and Dividend Announcements. *Journal of Business Finance & Accounting*, *23*(3), 359–370. DOI: 10.1111/j.1468-5957.1996.tb01127.x

Brownlees, C. T., & Robert, E. (2012). Volatility, correlation and tails for systemic risk measurement, Working Paper, NYU Stern School of Business.

Bruneckiene, J., Jucevicius, R., Zykiene, I., & Rapsikevicius, J. (2019). *Assessment of Investment Attractiveness in European Countries by Artificial Neural Networks : What Competences are Needed to Make a Decision on Collective Well-Being ?*

Brynjolfsson, E., & McAfee, A. (2014). *The second machine age: Work, progress, and prosperity in a time of brilliant technologies*. WW Norton & Company.

Buchinsky, M. (2001). Quantile Regression with Sample Selection: Estimating Women's Returns to Education in the U.S. *Empirical Economics*, *26*(1), 87–113. DOI: 10.1007/s001810000061

Buckley, R. P., Zetzsche, D. A., Arner, D. W., & Tang, B. (2021). Regulating Artificial Intelligence in Finance: Putting the Human in the Loop, 2021. 43 Sydney Law Journal 43 University of Hong Kong Faculty of Law Research Paper 2021/016

Bureau of Competition. (2021, October 27). Federal Trade Commission. https://www.ftc.gov/about-ftc/bureaus-offices/bureau-competition

Burrell, J. (2016). How the machine 'thinks': Understanding opacity in machine learning algorithms. *Big Data & Society*, *3*(1), 2053951715622512. DOI: 10.1177/2053951715622512

Burström, T., Parida, V., Lahti, T., & Wincent, J. (2021). AI-enabled business-model innovation and transformation in industrial ecosystems: A framework, model and outline for further research. *Journal of Business Research*, *127*, 85–95. DOI: 10.1016/j.jbusres.2021.01.016

Cacuci, D. G. (2003). *Sensitivity and Uncertainty Analysis – Theory.* Chapman and Hall/CRC.

Caggiano, G., Castelnuovo, E., & Figueres, J. (2017). Economic policy uncertainty and unemployment in the United States: A nonlinear approach. *Economics Letters, 151*, 31–34. DOI: 10.1016/j.econlet.2016.12.002

Caldara, D., & Iacoviello, M. (2022). Measuring geopolitical risk. *The American Economic Review, 112*(4), 1194–1225.

Camilleria, S. J., Sciclunaa, N., & Baib, Y. (2019). Do stock markets lead or lag macroeconomic variables? Evidence from select European countries. *The North American Journal of Economics and Finance, 48*, 170–186. DOI: 10.1016/j.najef.2019.01.019

Cerruti, C., & Valeri, A. (2022). *AI-powered platforms: Automated transactions in digital marketplaces* (Doctoral dissertation, Master of Science in Business Administration, Università degli Studi di Roma "Tor Vergata" Department of Management and Law).

Chandra, P. (2005). *Financial Management: Theory and Practice* (6th ed.). Tata McGraw-Hill Publishing Company Limited.

ChatGPT. [Generated information]. Available at: https://chat.openai.com/chat# (access date: 07/03/2023).

Chatterjee, S., Chaudhuri, R., & Vrontis, D. (2022). AI and digitalization in relationship management: Impact of adopting AI-embedded CRM system. *Journal of Business Research, 150*, 437–450. DOI: 10.1016/j.jbusres.2022.06.033

Cheng, C. H. J. (2017). Effects of foreign and domestic economic policy uncertainty shocks on South Korea. *Journal of Asian Economics, 51*(C), 1–11. DOI: 10.1016/j.asieco.2017.05.001

Chen, H., Chiang, R. H., & Storey, V. C. (2012). Business intelligence and analytics: From big data to big impact. *Management Information Systems Quarterly, 36*(4), 1165–1188. DOI: 10.2307/41703503

Chen, J., Chen, Y., Ou, R., Wang, J., & Chen, Q. (2022). How to use artificial intelligence to improve entrepreneurial attitude in business simulation games: Implications from a quasi-experiment. *Frontiers in Psychology, 13*, 856085. DOI: 10.3389/fpsyg.2022.856085 PMID: 36467165

Chen, N.-F., Roll, R., & Ross, S. A. (1986). Economic Forces and the Stock Market. *The Journal of Business, 59*(3), 383–403. DOI: 10.1086/296344

Chen, W., Liu, C., Xing, F., Peng, G., & Yang, X. (2022). Establishment of a maturity model to assess the development of industrial AI in smart manufacturing. *Journal of Enterprise Information Management*, *35*(3), 701–728. DOI: 10.1108/JEIM-10-2020-0397

Chernikova, E.G., & Tarasyeva, L.V. (2010). The main directions of ensuring economic security of the enterprise. Problems of ensuring economic security: materials of the international scientific and practical conference. Donetsk, DonNTU, 163-165.

Cheung, Y.-W., & Ng, L. (1998). International evidence on the stock market and aggregate economic activity. *Journal of Empirical Finance*, *5*(3), 281–296. DOI: 10.1016/S0927-5398(97)00025-X

Chiang, T. C. (2019). Financial risk, uncertainty and expected returns: Evidence from Chinese equity markets. *China Finance Review International*, *9*(4), 425–454. Advance online publication. DOI: 10.1108/CFRI-09-2018-0129

Chiang, T. C. (2022). Evidence of economic policy uncertainty and COVID-19 pandemic on global stock returns. *Journal of Risk and Financial Management*, *15*(1), 28.

Choudhry, T. (2010). World War II events and the Dow Jones industrial index. *Journal of Banking & Finance*, *34*(5), 1022–1031.

Choudhry, T., Papadimitriou, F. I., & Shabi, S. (2016). Stock market volatility and business cycle: Evidence from linear and nonlinear causality tests. *Journal of Banking & Finance*, *66*(66), 89–101. DOI: 10.1016/j.jbankfin.2016.02.005

CNBC. (2024). CNBC. Retrieved May 12, 2024 from www.cnbc.com

Cogley, T., & Sargent, T. J. (2001). Evolving post-world war II US inflation dynamics. *NBER Macroeconomics Annual*, *16*, 331–373.

Competition Commission of India, Government of India. (n.d.). https://www.cci.gov.in/about-us

Comuzzi, M., & Patel, A. (2016). How organisations leverage Big Data: A maturity model. *Industrial Management & Data Systems*, *116*(8), 1468–1492. DOI: 10.1108/IMDS-12-2015-0495

Contractor, F. J. (2021). The world economy will need even more globalization in the post-pandemic 2021 decade. *Journal of International Business Studies*, •••, 1–16. PMID: 33551513

Copeland, T. E., & Weston, I. F. (1992). *Financial Theory and Corporate Policy* (3rd ed.). Addison-Wesley Publishing Company.

Cubric, M. (2020). Drivers, barriers and social considerations for AI adoption in business and management: A tertiary study. *Technology in Society*, *62*, 101257. DOI: 10.1016/j.techsoc.2020.101257

Dakalbab, F., Talib, M. A., Nasir, Q., & Saroufil, T. (2024). Artificial intelligence techniques in financial trading: A systematic literature review. *Journal of King Saud University. Computer and Information Sciences*, *36*(3), 102015. DOI: 10.1016/j.jksuci.2024.102015

Davis, S. J. (2016). "An Index of Global Economic Policy Uncertainty." Macroeconomic Review, October. Also available as NBER Working Paper No. 22740

De Jonghe, O. (2010). Back to basics in banking? A micro-analysis of banking system stability. *Journal of Financial Intermediation*, *19*(3), 387–417. DOI: 10.1016/j.jfi.2009.04.001

De Jonghe, O., Diepstraten, M., & Schepens, G. (2015). Banks' size, scope and systemic risk: What role for conflicts of interest? *Journal of Banking & Finance*, *61*, S3–S13. DOI: 10.1016/j.jbankfin.2014.12.024

DeAngelo, H., & Masulis, R. (1980). Optimal capital Structure under Corporate and Personal taxation. *Journal of Financial Economics*, *8*(1), 3–30. DOI: 10.1016/0304-405X(80)90019-7

Denisov, O. E. (2019). Methods of ensuring the economic security of industries in the system of economic security of Ukraine. *State and Regions*, *6*(111), 29–34. DOI: 10.32840/1814-1161/2019-6-6

Department of Technical Cybernetics(CPC). (2015). Electronic synopsis of lectures on the discipline "Empirical methods of software engineering". National Technical University of Ukraine "Kyiv Polytechnic Institute. Available at: https://surl.li/iwxjf

Derbali, A. (2016). Global systemic risk ranking of Chinese financial institutions. *Journal of Chinese Governance*, *1*(2), 340–372. DOI: 10.1080/23812346.2016.1165403

Derbali, A. (2017a). Systemic risk in the Chinese Financial System: Measuring and Ranking. *Chinese Economy*, *50*(1), 34–58. DOI: 10.1080/10971475.2016.1211904

Derbali, A. (2017b). Systemic risk ranking of US financial institutions. *International Journal of Management and Network Economics*, *4*(1), 1–41. DOI: 10.1504/IJMNE.2017.087574

Derbali, A., & Hallara, S. (2016). Systemic risk of European financial institutions: Estimation and ranking by the Marginal Expected Shortfall. *Research in International Business and Finance*, *37*(15), 113–134. DOI: 10.1016/j.ribaf.2015.10.013

Derbali, A., Hallara, S., & Sy, A. (2016). Athen's game of chicken or the conditional dependence between the Greek banks. *International Journal of Economics and Accounting*, *7*(1), 1–26. DOI: 10.1504/IJEA.2016.076747

Derbali, A., & Sy, A. (2016). The volatility of exchange rate between the US dollar and African emerging currencies: Analysing by GAS-GARCH-Student-t model. *International Journal of Critical Accounting*, *8*(2), 132–143. DOI: 10.1504/IJCA.2016.077538

Dewan, A. A., & Hayworth, S. C. (1993). Macroeconometrics of stock price fluctuations. *Quarterly Journal of Business and Economics*, *32*(1), 50.

Di Vaio, A., Palladino, R., Hassan, R., & Escobar, O. (2020). Artificial intelligence and business models in the sustainable development goals perspective: A systematic literature review. *Journal of Business Research*, *121*, 283–314. DOI: 10.1016/j.jbusres.2020.08.019

Dixon, M., & Adamson, B. (2011). *The Challenger Sale: Taking Control of the Customer Conversation*. Penguin.

Dsns. Emergency events. https://dsns.gov.ua/news/ nadzvicaini-podiyi (access date: 07/10/2023).

Dunphy, D. D., Griffiths, A., & Suzanne, B. (2007). *Organizational Change for Corporate Sustainability: A Guide for Leaders and Change Agents of the Future*. Rountledge.

Duong, H. N., Nguyen, J. H., Nguyen, M., & Rhee, S. G. (2020). Navigating through economic policy uncertainty: The role of corporate cash holdings. *Journal of Corporate Finance*, *62*, 101607.

Dwivedi, Y. K., Hughes, L., Ismagilova, E., Aarts, G., Coombs, C., Crick, T., Duan, Y., Dwivedi, R., Edwards, J., Eirug, A., Galanos, V., Ilavarasan, P. V., Janssen, M., Jones, P., Kar, A. K., Kizgin, H., Kronemann, B., Lal, B., Lucini, B., & Williams, M. D. (2021). Artificial Intelligence (AI): Multidisciplinary perspectives on emerging challenges, opportunities, and agenda for research, practice and policy. *International Journal of Information Management*, *57*, 101994. DOI: 10.1016/j.ijinfomgt.2019.08.002

Dwivedi, Y. K., Ismagilova, E., Hughes, D. L., Carlson, J., Filieri, R., Jacobson, J., Jain, V., Karjaluoto, H., Kefi, H., Krishen, A. S., Kumar, V., Rahman, M. M., Raman, R., Rauschnabel, P. A., Rowley, J., Salo, J., Tran, G. A., & Wang, Y. (2021). Setting the future of digital and social media marketing research: Perspectives and research propositions. *International Journal of Information Management*, *59*, 102168. DOI: 10.1016/j.ijinfomgt.2020.102168

Dwivedi, Y. K., Kshetri, N., Hughes, L., Slade, E. L., Jeyaraj, A., Kar, A. K., & Wright, R. (2023). Opinion Paper: "So what if ChatGPT wrote it?" Multidisciplinary perspectives on opportunities, challenges and implications of generative conversational AI for research, practice and policy. *International Journal of Information Management*, *71*, 102642.

Eboigbe, E. O., Farayola, O. A., Olatoye, F. O., Nnabugwu, O. C., & Daraojimba, C. (2023). Business intelligence transformation through AI and data analytics. *Engineering Science & Technology Journal*, *4*(5), 285–307. DOI: 10.51594/estj.v4i5.616

Element, A. I. (2020). The AI maturity framework: A strategic guide to operationalize and scale enterprise AI solutions. https://s3.amazonaws.com/external_clips/3430107/AI-Maturity-Framework_White-Paper_EN.pdf?1589551996

Elhajjar, S., Yacoub, L., & Yaacoub, H. (2023). Automation in business research: Systematic literature review. *Information Systems and e-Business Management*, *21*(3), 675–698. DOI: 10.1007/s10257-023-00645-z

Engle, R., Moshirian, F., Sahgal, S., & Zhang, B. 2014. Banks non-interest income and global financial stability. Working Paper, New York University.

Enholm, I. M., Papagiannidis, E., Mikalef, P., & Krogstie, J. (2022). Artificial intelligence and business value: A literature review. *Information Systems Frontiers*, *24*(5), 1709–1734. DOI: 10.1007/s10796-021-10186-w

Enz, C. A. (2009). The physical safety and security features of U.S. hotels. *Cornell Hospitality Quarterly*, *50*(4), 553–560. DOI: 10.1177/1938965509345963

Eriksson, M., & Djoweini, C. (2020). Artificial Intelligence's Impact on Management. *The Innovation Journal*.

Fama, E. F. (1970). Efficient Capital Market: A Review Theory and Empirical Work. *The Journal of Finance*, *25*(May), 383–417. DOI: 10.2307/2325486

Fama, E. F. (1990). Stock returns, expected returns, and real activity. *The Journal of Finance*, *45*(4), 1089–1108.

Fama, E. F., & French, K. R. (1989). Business Conditions and Expected Returns on Stocks and Bonds. *Journal of Financial Economics, 25*(1), 23–49. DOI: 10.1016/0304-405X(89)90095-0

Farayola, O. A., Abdul, A. A., Irabor, B. O., & Okeleke, E. C. (2023). Innovative business models driven by AI technologies: A review. *Computer Science & IT Research Journal, 4*(2), 85–110. DOI: 10.51594/csitrj.v4i2.608

Fargo, W. (2022). Wells Fargo Newsroom. Retrieved May 12,2024 from www .newsroom.wf.com

Federico, B., Graeme, N., Giambattista, T., & Rob, W. (2019). Intelligent process automation: The engine at the core of the next-generation operating model | McKinsey. *The McKinsey Quarterly, 45*(October), •••. https://www.mckinsey.com/business-functions/mckinsey-digital/our-insights/intelligent-process-automation-the-engine-at-the-core-of-the-next-generation-operating-model

Feuerriegel, S., Shrestha, Y. R., von Krogh, G., & Zhang, C. (2022). Bringing artificial intelligence to business management. *Nature Machine Intelligence, 4*(7), 611–613. DOI: 10.1038/s42256-022-00512-5

Fischer, S., & Merton, R. C. (1984, January). Macroeconomics and finance: The role of the stock market. In *Carnegie-Rochester conference series on public policy* (Vol. 21, pp. 57–108). North-Holland.

Fornasiero, R., Kiebler, L., Falsafi, M., & Sardesai, S. (2024). Proposing a maturity model for assessing Artificial Intelligence and Big data in the process industry. *International Journal of Production Research*. Advance online publication. DOI: 10.1080/00207543.2024.2372840

Frank, M. R., Autor, D., Bessen, J. E., Brynjolfsson, E., Cebrian, M., Deming, D. J., Feldman, M., Groh, M., Lobo, J., Moro, E., Wang, D., Youn, H., & Rahwan, I. (2019). Toward understanding the impact of artificial intelligence on labor. *Proceedings of the National Academy of Sciences of the United States of America, 116*(14), 6531–6539. DOI: 10.1073/pnas.1900949116 PMID: 30910965

Freeman, R. E. (2010). *Strategic Management: A Stakeholder Approach*. Cambridge University Press. DOI: 10.1017/CBO9781139192675

Friedman, R. E., & Miles, S. (2006). *Stakeholders: Theory and Practice*. Oxford University Press. DOI: 10.1093/oso/9780199269860.001.0001

Frigo, M. L. (2018). Strategic Risk Management. In Augier, M., & Teece, D. J. (Eds.), *The Palgrave Encyclopedia of Strategic Management*. Palgrave Macmillan., DOI: 10.1057/978-1-137-00772-8_522

Gan, C., Lee, M., Yong, H. H. A., & Zhang, J. (2006). Macroeconomic variables and stock market interactions: New Zealand evidence. Investment management and financial innovations, (3, Iss. 4), 89-101.

George, A. S., George, A. H., Baskar, T., & Sujatha, V. (2023). The rise of hyper-automation: A new frontier for business process automation. *Partners Universal International Research Journal*, *2*(4), 13–35.

Ghazi, K. (2016). Safety and security measures in Egyptian hotels. *Journal of Association of Arab Universities for Tourism and Hospitality*, *13*(1), 165–190. DOI: 10.21608/jaauth.2016.49721

Gligor, D. M., Pillai, K. G., & Golgeci, I. (2021). Theorizing the dark side of business-to-business relationships in the era of AI, big data, and blockchain. *Journal of Business Research*, *133*, 79–88. DOI: 10.1016/j.jbusres.2021.04.043

Global Reporting Initiative (GRI). (2013). *G4 Sustainability Reporting Guidelines*. EYGM Limited.

Goetzmann, W. N., & Jorion, P. (1995). A Longer Look at Dividend Yields. *The Journal of Business*, *68*(4), 483–508. DOI: 10.1086/296674

Gökalp, E., & Martinez, V. (2021). Digital transformation maturity assessment: Development of the digital transformation capability maturity model. *International Journal of Production Research*, *60*(20), 6282–6302. DOI: 10.1080/00207543.2021.1991020

Gomber, P., Koch, J. A., & Siering, M. (2017). Digital Finance and FinTech: Current research and future research directions. *Journal of Business Economics*, *87*(5), 537–580. DOI: 10.1007/s11573-017-0852-x

Gomory, R., & Sylla, R. (2013). The American Corporation. Daedalus, 142(2), 102-118. Freeman, R. E. (2010). Strategic management: A stakeholder approach. Cambridge university press.

Goodell, J. W., McGee, R. J., & McGroarty, F. (2020). Election uncertainty, economic policy uncertainty and financial market uncertainty: A prediction market analysis. *Journal of Banking & Finance*, *110*(C), 105684. DOI: 10.1016/j.jbankfin.2019.105684

Gordon, M. J. (1959). Dividends, Earnings and Stock Prices. *The Review of Economics and Statistics*, *41*(2), 99–105. DOI: 10.2307/1927792

Gordon, M. J. (1962). The Savings, Investment, and Valuation of a Corporation. *The Review of Economics and Statistics*, *44*(1), 37–51. DOI: 10.2307/1926621

Gordon, M. J. (1963). Optimal Investment and Financial Policy. *The Journal of Finance, 18*(2), 264–272.

Graebner, M. E. (2021). Evolution of Qualitative Research Methods in Strategic Management. In Irene M. Duhaime, Michael A. Hitt, and Majorie A. Lyles (eds), *Strategic Management: State of the Field and Its Future* (pp. 99-114), online edn, Oxford Academic. https://doi.org/DOI: 10.1093/oso/9780190090883.003.0006

Greve, H. R. (2021). The Organizational View of Strategic Management. Strategic Management. In Irene M. Duhaime, Michael A. Hitt, and Majorie A. Lyles (eds), *Strategic Management: State of the Field and Its Future* (pp. 43-60), online edn, Oxford Academic. https://doi.org/DOI: 10.1093/oso/9780190090883.003.0003

Griewank, A. (2000). *Evaluating Derivatives, Principles and Techniques of Algorithmic Differentiation.* SIAM.

Gueznai, M. A., & Elboussadi, A. (2024). Exploratory Analysis of the Impact of Phygital on the Customer Experience. In AI and Data Engineering Solutions for Effective Marketing (pp. 364-387). IGI Global. DOI: 10.4018/979-8-3693-3172-9.ch018

Guliashki, V., & Stoyanova, K. (2023). Portfolio Risk Optimization Based on MVO Model. *Rcvt.Tu-Sofia.Bg, February.* http://rcvt.tu-sofia.bg/ICEST2018_14.pdf

Guo, Y., Ma, F., Li, H., & Lai, X. (2020). Oil price volatility predictability based on global economic conditions. *International Review of Financial Analysis.*

Gupta, P., Ding, B., Guan, C., & Ding, D. (2024). Generative AI: A systematic review using topic modelling techniques. *Data and Information Management, 8*(2), 100066. DOI: 10.1016/j.dim.2024.100066

Gu, S. (2024). Exploring the role of AI in business decision-making and process automation. *International Journal of High School Research, 6*(3).

Hacker, R. S., Karlsson, H. K., & Månsson, K. (2014). An investigation of the causal relations between exchange rates and interest rate differentials using wavelets. *International Review of Economics & Finance, 29*, 321–329. DOI: 10.1016/j.iref.2013.06.004

Haefner, N., Wincent, J., Parida, V., & Gassmann, O. (2021). Artificial intelligence and innovation management: A review, framework, and research agenda . *Technological Forecasting and Social Change, 162*, 120392. DOI: 10.1016/j.techfore.2020.120392

Hamid, M. (2024). AI-powered business intelligence: Revolutionizing data analysis and reporting. *Asian Bulletin of Business Analytics & Artificial Intelligence, 1*(1).

Handfield, R., Jenahingir, S., & Petersen, K. (2022). Artificial intelligence and machine learning for contract analytics: Opportunities and challenges. *Journal of Purchasing and Supply Management, 28*(4), 100772.

Han, R., Lam, H. K., Zhan, Y., Wang, Y., Dwivedi, Y. K., & Tan, K. H. (2021). Artificial intelligence in business-to-business marketing: A bibliometric analysis of current research status, development and future directions. *Industrial Management & Data Systems, 121*(12), 2467–2497. DOI: 10.1108/IMDS-05-2021-0300

Hauser, R. (2013). Did Dividend Policy Change During the Financial Crisis? *Managerial Finance, 39*(6), 584–606. DOI: 10.1108/03074351311322861

Hausladen, I., & Schosser, M. (2020). Towards a maturity model for Big Data analytics in airline network planning. *Journal of Air Transport Management, 82*, 101721. DOI: 10.1016/j.jairtraman.2019.101721

Helfat, C. E. (2021). The Economic View of Strategic Management. in Irene M. Duhaime, Michael A. Hitt, and Majorie A. Lyles (eds), *Strategic Management: State of the Field and Its Future* (pp. 61-80), online edn, Oxford Academic. https://doi.org/DOI: 10.1093/oso/9780190090883.003.0004

Helfert, E. A. (2001). *Financial Analysis: Tools and Techniques. A Guide for Managers*. McGraw-Hill.

Helton, J. C., Johnson, J. D., Salaberry, C. J., & Storlie, C. B. (2006). Survey Of Sampling Based Methods for Uncertainty and Sensitivity Analysis. *Reliability Engineering & System Safety, 91*(10-11), 1175–1209. DOI: 10.1016/j.ress.2005.11.017

Hevner, A. R., March, S. T., Park, J., & Ram, S. (2004). Design science in information systems research. *Management Information Systems Quarterly, 28*(1), 75–105. DOI: 10.2307/25148625

Higgins, R. C., Koski, J., & Mitton, T. (2016). *Analysis for Financial Management*. McGraw-Hill Education.

Hilal, W., Gadsden, S. A., & Yawney, J. (2022). Financial Fraud: A Review of Anomaly Detection Techniques and Recent Advances. *Expert Systems with Applications, 193*, 116429. DOI: 10.1016/j.eswa.2021.116429

Hmioui, A., Alla, L., Bentalha, B., & El Ghalfiki, J. (2019). La force de vente à l'épreuve de la performance commerciale: Le cas du profil Technico-Commercial. *Alternatives Managériales et Economiques, 1*(1), 72–91.

Hortovanyi, L., Morgan, R. E., Herceg, I. V., Djuricin, D., Hanak, R., & Dora Horvath, D.. (2023). Assessment of digital maturity: The role of resources and capabilities in digital transformation in B2B firms. *International Journal of Production Research, 61*(23), 8043–8061. DOI: 10.1080/00207543.2022.2164087

Ho, S. P. S., & Chow, M. Y. C. (2024). The role of artificial intelligence in consumers' brand preference for retail banks in Hong Kong. *Journal of Financial Services Marketing, 29*(2), 292–305. DOI: 10.1057/s41264-022-00207-3

Hosseini, S. M., Ahmad, Z., & Lai, Y. W. (2011). The Role of Macroeconomic Variables on Stock Market Index in China and India. In *MPRA Paper 112215*. University Library of Munich. DOI: 10.5539/ijef.v3n6p233

Hsia, C. C. (1981). Coherence of the Modern Theories of Finance. *Financial Review, 16*(Winter), 27–42. DOI: 10.1111/j.1540-6288.1981.tb01617.x

Hsing, Y., & Wen-jen, H. (2012). Impacts of macroeconomic variables on the stock market index in Poland: New evidence. *Journal of Business Economics and Management, 13*(2), 334–343. DOI: 10.3846/16111699.2011.620133

Huang, M. H., & Rust, R. T. (2021). Engaged to a robot? The role of AI in service. *Journal of Service Research, 24*(1), 30–41. DOI: 10.1177/1094670520902266

Huang, M.-H., & Rust, R. T. (2018). Artificial intelligence in service. *Journal of Service Research, 21*(2), 155–172. DOI: 10.1177/1094670517752459

Hua, S. Y., Jin, S. C., & Jiang, S. Y. (2024). The limitations and ethical considerations of ChatGPT. *Data Intelligence, 6*(1), 201–239. DOI: 10.1162/dint_a_00243

Humpe, A., & Macmillan, P. (2009). Can macroeconomic variables explain long-term stock market movements? A comparison of the US and Japan. *Applied Financial Economics, 19*(2), 111–119.

Hussain, A., Rafique, M., Khalil, A., & Nawaz, M. Macroeconomic Determinants of Stock Price Variations: An Economic Analysis of KSE-100 Index (January 12, 2016). Pakistan Journal of Humanities and Social Sciences, Jan-June 2013, Volume 1, No. 1, Pages 28-46, Available at SSRN: https://ssrn.com/abstract=2714202

Ikoku, A. E. (2010): « Is the stock market a leading indicator of economic activity in nigeria? CBN Journal of Applied Statistics [ISSN:] 2476-8472 Volume: 01 Issue: 1. The Central Bank of Nigeria. Abuja. 2010. pp 17-38

Im, K. S., Pesaran, M. H., & Shin, Y. (2003). Testing for unit roots in heterogeneous panels. *Journal of Econometrics, 115*(1), 53–74. DOI: 10.1016/S0304-4076(03)00092-7

Intelligence, M. (2024). Mordor Intelligence. Retrieved May 01,2024 from www .mordorintelligence.com

Jabbouri, R., & Issa, H. (2023). The AI-powered business ecosystem and its associated business models. *Journal of Research in Administrative Sciences*, *12*(1), 9–27.

Jareño, F., Ferrer, R., & Miroslavova, S. (2016): « US stock market sensitivity to interest and inflation rates: a quantile regression approach » Pages 2469-2481 | Published online: 05 Jan 2016. Applied Economics. Volume 48, 2016 - Issue 26

Jarrahi, M. H., Askay, D., Eshraghi, A., & Smith, P. (2023). Artificial intelligence and knowledge management: A partnership between human and AI. *Business Horizons*, *66*(1), 87–99. DOI: 10.1016/j.bushor.2022.03.002

Javaheri, B., habibi, F., & Amani, R. (2022). habibi, F. & Amani, R. Economic policy uncertainty and the US stock market trading: non-ARDL evidence. *Futur Bus J*, *8*(1), 36. DOI: 10.1186/s43093-022-00150-8

Jel, O., Pandey, M. K., Sergeeva, I., Пандей, М. К., & Сергеева, И. (2022). *Менеджмент Научная статья Artificial Intelligence Impact Evaluation : Transforming Paradigms in Financial Institutions Оценка воздействия искусственного интеллекта : трансформация парадигм в финансовых учреждениях.* *22*(1), 147–164. DOI: 10.25205/2542-0429-2022-22-1-147-164

Jensen, M., & Meckling, W. (1976). Theory of the Firm: Managerial Behavior, Agency Costs, and Ownership Structure. *Journal of Financial Economics*, *3*(October), 305–360. DOI: 10.1016/0304-405X(76)90026-X

Johnston, M. W., & Marshall, G. W. (2013). CRM and Sales Technologies. In Contemporary Selling (pp. 131-150). Routledge. DOI: 10.4324/9780203120965-11

Jore, S. H., Utland, I.-L. F., & Vatnamo, V. H. (2018). The contribution of foresight to improve long-term security planning. *Foresight*, *20*(1), 68–83. DOI: 10.1108/FS-08-2017-0045

Jorzik, P., Klein, S. P., Kanbach, D. K., & Kraus, S. (2024). AI-driven business model innovation: A systematic review and research agenda. *Journal of Business Research*, *182*, 114764. DOI: 10.1016/j.jbusres.2024.114764

JPMorgan Chase. (2022). JPMorgan Chase. Retrieved May 15, 2024 from www .jpmorganchase.com

Jun-Hyung, Ko., & Lee, C.-M. (2015). International economic policy uncertainty and stock prices: Wavelet approach. *Economics Letters*, *134*(C), 118–122.

Juniper Research. (2019,2021). Juniper Research. Retrieved May 15, 2024 from www.juniperresearch.com

Kadve, Dipak, Kumar, Binod, Suryawanshi, Vaishali, Gupta, Karan, & Koul, Ritesh & Shreyash, (2024). *Impact of Quantum Computing on Artificial Intelligence.21.* 71-78.

Kahle, K. M., & Stulz, R. (2013). Access to capital, investment, and the financial crisis. *Journal of Financial Economics, 110*(2), 280–299. DOI: 10.1016/j.jfineco.2013.02.014

Kandir, S.Y. (2008) Macroeconomic Variables, Firm Characteristics and Stock Returns: Evidence from Turkey. International Research Journal of Finance and Economics, Issue 16.

Kang, W., & Ratti, R. (2013). Oil shocks, policy uncertainty and stock market return. *Journal of International Financial Markets, Institutions and Money, 26*(C), 305–318. DOI: 10.1016/j.intfin.2013.07.001

Kao, C. (1999). Spurious regression and residual-based tests for cointegration in panel data. *Journal of Econometrics, 90*(1), 1–44. DOI: 10.1016/S0304-4076(98)00023-2

Karulkar, Y., Shah, A., & Naik, R. (2025). AI-powered business evolution: Transformative strategies for success of evolving industries. In *Creating AI synergy through business technology transformation* (pp. 39–72). IGI Global.

Kasztelnik, K. (2024). *The Study on the Impact of Business Artificial Intelligence Innovation on Fair Value Investments in the United States The Study on the Impact of Business Artificial Intelligence Innovation on Fair Value Investments in the US. January.*

Kaur, B., & Kour, M. (2024, September). Exploring the Growth and Future research directions on Robo advisors: A Bibliometric Study. In *2024 International Conference on Advances in Computing Research on Science Engineering and Technology (ACROSET)* (pp. 1-6).

Kaushik, S. (2024). The rise of AI-powered competitive intelligence: Transforming market analysis. *Blockchain and AI in Business,* 112.

Khan, D. (2023). Unleashing business intelligence: Text analytics and AI-driven ERP transformations towards an intelligent enterprise. *Social Sciences Spectrum, 2*(1), 103–110.

Khattak, B. H. A., Shafi, I., Khan, A. S., Flores, E. S., Lara, R. G., Samad, M. A., & Ashraf, I. (2023). A systematic survey of AI models in financial market forecasting for profitability analysis. *IEEE Access : Practical Innovations, Open Solutions*, *11*, 125359–125380.

Kim, H. (1978). A mean-Variance Theory of Optimal Capital Structure and Corporate Debt Capacity. *The Journal of Finance*, (March), 45–64.

Koenig, M. (2023a, March 13). CFO at Lehman Brothers worked at SVB - while risk manager worked at Deutsche Bank. Mail Online. https://www.dailymail.co.uk/news/article-11855245/CFO-Lehman-Brothers-worked-SVB-risk-manager-worked-Deutsche-Bank.html

Koenig, M. (2023b, March 13). CFO at Lehman Brothers worked at SVB - while risk manager worked at Deutsche Bank. Mail Online. https://www.dailymail.co.uk/news/article-11855245/CFO-Lehman-Brothers-worked-SVB-risk-manager-worked-Deutsche-Bank.html

Koku, P. S. (2022). Artificial intelligence (AI) and the future of sales management: A research agenda. *Journal of Personal Selling & Sales Management*, *42*(3), 177–190.

Kolluri, B., & Wahab, M. (2008). Stock returns and expected inflation: Evidence from an asymmetric test specification [May.]. *Review of Quantitative Finance and Accounting*, *30*(4), 371–395. DOI: 10.1007/s11156-007-0060-9

Kompanets, K., Antonyuk, I., & Medvedeva, A. (2022). Marketing techniques in the organization of the restaurant business of Ukraine during the war. *Science and Technology Today*, *5*(5). Advance online publication. DOI: 10.52058/2786-6025-2022-5(5)-78-86

Kong, K. Y., & Yuen, K. F. (2024). Sustainability risk management: Exploring the role of artificial intelligence capabilities through an information-processing lens. *Risk Analysis*, risa.17448. DOI: 10.1111/risa.17448 PMID: 39179518

Korstanje, M. E. (2020). Tourism Security: A Critical Insight, Korstanje, M.E. and Seraphin, H. (Ed.) *Tourism, Terrorism and Security: Tourism Security-Safety and Post Conflict Destinations* (pp. 1-20), Emerald Publishing Limited, Leeds. https://doi.org/DOI: 10.1108/978-1-83867-905-720201002

Korzeniewski, J. (2018). Efficient Stock Portfolio Construction by Means of Clustering. *Acta Universitatis Lodziensis.Folia Oecologica*, *1*(333), 85–92. DOI: 10.18778/0208-6018.333.06

Kotler, P., & Keller, L. K. (2016). *Marketing Management* (15th ed.). Pearson Education.

Kour, M. (2024a, September). Revolutionizing Finance: Unleashing Machine Learning's Potential for a New Financial Era. In *2024 International Conference on Advances in Computing Research on Science Engineering and Technology (ACROSET)* (pp. 1-5). IEEE.

Kour, M. (2024b), Dynamics of Big Data Analytics in the Banking Sector. *2024 IEEE International Conference on Interdisciplinary Approaches in Technology and Management for Social Innovation (IATMSI)*, (Vol. 2, pp. 1-6). IEEE. DOI: 10.1109/IATMSI60426.2024.10502648

Krijger, J., Thuis, T., de Ruiter, M., Ligthart, E., & Broekman, I. (2023). The AI ethics maturity model: A holistic approach to advancing ethical data science in organizations. *AI and Ethics*, *3*(2), 355–367. DOI: 10.1007/s43681-022-00228-7

Krylov, S. (2025). Neutral Approach at Dividend Policy Modeling. In M. Khosrow-Pour, D.B.A. (Ed.), *Encyclopedia of Information Science and Technology, Sixth Edition*. Advance online publication. DOI: 10.4018/978-1-6684-7366-5.ch008

Krylov, S. (2020). Dividend Policy Scores Models: Neutral Approach. *SBS Journal of Applied Business Research*, *8*, 23–33.

Krylov, S. (2021). Dividend Policy: Scores Modeling within Neutral Implementation Approach Conditions. *Academy of Accounting and Financial Studies Journal*, *25*(1), 1–10.

Kulkov, I. (2021). The role of artificial intelligence in business transformation: A case of pharmaceutical companies. *Technology in Society*, *66*, 101629. DOI: 10.1016/j.techsoc.2021.101629

Kumar, B., Kumar, B., Nagesh, Y., Singh, S., & Rani, J. (2022). The continuous investment in artificial intelligence and its impact on ensuring customer satisfaction. Korea review of international studies, 15(03).

Kusi, B., Agbloyor, E., Gyeke-Dako, A., & Asongu, S. (2022). Financial sector transparency, financial crises and market power: A cross-country evidence. *International Journal of Finance & Economics*, *27*(4), 4431–4450.

Kuzmenko, O., Makliuk, O., & Chernyshova, O. (2022). Business Cybersecurity in a Time of War. *Economy and Society*, *44*. Advance online publication. DOI: 10.32782/2524-0072/2022-44-21

Kyiv School of Economics (KSE). (March 2023). Report on damages to infrastructure caused by Russia's war against Ukraine: One year after the start of the full-scale invasion. Available at: https://kse.ua/wp-content/uploads/2023/03/ENG_FINAL_Damages-Report_.pdf

La Torre, D., Appio, F. P., Masri, H., Lazzeri, F., & Schiavone, F. (2023). *Impact of artificial intelligence in business and society: Opportunities and Challenges.* Routledge. DOI: 10.4324/9781003304616

Lahlali, M., Berbiche, N., & El Alami, J. (2021). How enterprise must be prepared to be "AI first"? *International Journal of Advanced Computer Science and Applications, 12*(5). Advance online publication. DOI: 10.14569/IJACSA.2021.0120542

Lambrecht, B. M., & Myers, S. C. (2012). A Lintner Model of Payout and Managerial Rents. *The Journal of Finance, 67*(5), 1761–1810. DOI: 10.1111/j.1540-6261.2012.01772.x

Lannon, F., Lyons, R., & O'Connor, C. (2024). Generation AI and family business: A perspective article. *Journal of Family Business Management, 14*(3), 470–474. DOI: 10.1108/JFBM-07-2023-0116

Laopodis, N. (2011). Equity prices and macroeconomic fundamentals: International evidence. *Journal of International Financial Markets, Institutions and Money, 21*(2), 247–276. DOI: 10.1016/j.intfin.2010.10.006

LawGeex. (2021). LawGeex. Retrieved May 19, 2024 from www.lawgeex.com

Leamer, E. E. (1985). Sensitivity Analyses Would Help. *The American Economic Review, 75*(3), 308–313.

Lee, J., Schoenherr, D., & Starmans, J. (2023): « The Economics of Legal Uncertainty ». European Corporate Governance Institute - Law Working Paper No. 669/2022

Lee, C. F., & Finnerty, J. E. (1990). *Corporate Finance: Theory, Method, and Applications.* Harcourt Brace & Company.

Leeflang, P. S., Verhoef, P. C., Dahlström, P., & Freundt, T. (2014). Challenges and solutions for marketing in a digital era. *European Management Journal, 32*(1), 1–12. DOI: 10.1016/j.emj.2013.12.001

Lee, I., & Shin, Y. J. (2020). Fintech: Ecosystem, business models, investment decisions, and challenges. *Business Horizons, 63*(3), 357–370.

Lee, J. (2020). Access to Finance for Artificial Intelligence Regulation in the Financial Services Industry. *European Business Organization Law Review, 21*(4), 731–757. DOI: 10.1007/s40804-020-00200-0

Lee, J., Suh, T., Roy, D., & Baucus, M. (2019). Emerging technology and business model innovation: The case of artificial intelligence. *Journal of Open Innovation, 5*(3), 44. DOI: 10.3390/joitmc5030044

Lenddo, E. F. L. (2023). LenddoEFL. Retrieved May 16, 2024 from www.lenddoefl.com

Lepri, B., Oliver, N., Letouzé, E., Pentland, A., & Vinck, P. (2018). Fair, transparent, and accountable algorithmic decision-making processes: The premise, the proposed solutions, and the open challenges. *Philosophy & Technology*, *31*(4), 611–627.

Levin, A., Lin, C., & Chu, C. (2002). Unit root tests in panel data: Asymptotic and finite sample properties. *Journal of Econometrics*, *108*(1), 1–24. DOI: 10.1016/S0304-4076(01)00098-7

Liang, C., Ma, F., Li, Z., & Li, Y. (2020). Which types of commodity price information are more useful for predicting US stock market volatility? *Economic Modelling*, *93*, 642–650. DOI: 10.1016/j.econmod.2020.03.022

Liang, C., Tang, L., Li, Y., & Wei, Y. (2020). Which sentiment index is more informative to forecast stock market volatility? Evidence from China. *International Review of Financial Analysis*, *71*, 101552. DOI: 10.1016/j.irfa.2020.101552

Liao, V., & Vaughan, J. W. (2024). AI transparency in the age of LLMs: A human-centered research roadmap. *Harvard Data Science Review*, *5*(Special Issue 5). Advance online publication. DOI: 10.1162/99608f92.8036d03b

Lichtenthaler, U. (2020). Five maturity levels of managing AI: From isolated ignorance to integrated intelligence. *Journal of Innovation Management*, *8*(1), 39–50. DOI: 10.24840/2183-0606_008.001_0005

Lilien, G. L. (2016). The B2B Knowledge Gap. *International Journal of Research in Marketing*, *33*(3), 459–466. DOI: 10.1016/j.ijresmar.2016.01.003

Lintner, J. (1962). Dividend, Earnings, Leverage, Stock Prices and the Supply of Capital to Corporations. *The Review of Economics and Statistics*, *44*(3), 243–269. DOI: 10.2307/1926397

Liu, L., & Zhang, T. (2015). Economic policy uncertainty and stock market volatility. *Finance Research Letters*, *15*(C), 99–105. DOI: 10.1016/j.frl.2015.08.009

Li, X., Li, Z., Su, C. W., Umar, M., & Shao, X. (2022). Exploring the asymmetric impact of economic policy uncertainty on China's carbon emissions trading market price: Do different types of uncertainty matter? *Technological Forecasting and Social Change*, *178*(May), 121601. DOI: 10.1016/j.techfore.2022.121601

Lodhi, S. K., Gill, A. Y., & Hussain, I. (2024). AI-powered innovations in contemporary manufacturing procedures: An extensive analysis. *International Journal of Multidisciplinary Sciences and Arts*, *3*(4), 15–25. DOI: 10.47709/ijmdsa.v3i4.4616

M. Hashem Pesaran, Yongcheol Shin and Ron P. Smith (1999): « Pooled Mean Group Estimation of Dynamic Heterogeneous Panels » Journal of the American Statistical Association. Vol. 94, No. 446 (Jun., 1999), pp. 621-634 (14 pages). Published By: Taylor & Francis, Ltd.

Maddala, G. S., & Wu, S. (1999). A comparative study of unit root tests with panel data and a new simple test. *Oxford Bulletin of Economics and Statistics, 61*(S1), 631–652. DOI: 10.1111/1468-0084.0610s1631

Ma, F., Guo, Y., Chevallier, J., & Huang, D. (2022). Macroeconomic attention, economic policy uncertainty, and stock volatility predictability. *International Review of Financial Analysis, 84*(November), 102339. DOI: 10.1016/j.irfa.2022.102339

Ma, F., Lu, F., & Tao, Y. (2022). Geopolitical risk and excess stock returns predictability: New evidence from a century of data. *Finance Research Letters, 50*, 103211. DOI: 10.1016/j.frl.2022.103211

Ma, F., Lu, X., Liu, J., & Huang, D. (2022). Macroeconomic attention and stock market return predictability. *Journal of International Financial Markets, Institutions and Money, 79*, 101603. DOI: 10.1016/j.intfin.2022.101603

Ma, F., Wahab, M. I. M., & Zhang, Y. (2019). Forecasting the US stock volatility: An aligned jump index from G7 stock markets. *Pacific-Basin Finance Journal, 54*, 132–146. DOI: 10.1016/j.pacfin.2019.02.006

Magness, V. (2008). Who are the stakeholders now? An empirical examination of the Mitchell, Agle, and Wood theory of stakeholder salience. *Journal of Business Ethics, 83*(2), 177–192. https://economictimes.indiatimes.com/news/economy/policy/govt-amends-rules-governing-corporate-social-responsibility/articleshow/94381725.cms?from=mdr. DOI: 10.1007/s10551-007-9610-2

Mansour, N., & Ben Salem, S. (Eds.). (2022). *COVID-19's Impact on the Cryptocurrency Market and the Digital Economy*. IGI Global., DOI: 10.4018/978-1-7998-9117-8

Manyika, J., Chui, M., Miremadi, M., Bughin, J., George, K., Willmott, P., & Dewhurst, M. (2017). A future that works: AI, automation, employment, and productivity. McKinsey Global Institute Research. *Tech. Rep, 60*, 1–135.

Ma, R., Zhou, C., Cai, H., & Deng, C. (2019). The forecasting power of EPU for crude oil return volatility. *Energy Reports, 5*, 866–873. DOI: 10.1016/j.egyr.2019.07.002

Mariani, M. M., Machado, I., & Nambisan, S. (2023). Types of innovation and artificial intelligence: A systematic quantitative literature review and research agenda. *Journal of Business Research, 155*(113364), 1–14. DOI: 10.1016/j.jbusres.2022.113364

Markovska, A. V., & Zholobnyuk, D. O. (2023). *Restaurant business during the war*. Black Sea Scientific Studies., DOI: 10.36059/978-966-397-300-5-18

Mathew, A., & Arul, A. (2021). *Deep Learning Techniques : An Overview Deep Learning Techniques : An Overview. August 2020*. DOI: 10.1007/978-981-15-3383-9

Mathew, N. (2023). *Artificial Intelligence an enabler in Robo-Advisory services to enhance Investment returns – Empirical. 10*, 4008–4016.

Maysami, R. C., Howe, L. C., & Hamzah, M. A. (2004). *Relationship between Macroeconomic Variables and Stock Market Indices: Cointegration Evidence from Stock Exchange of Singapore's All-S Sector Indices*. Jurnal Pengurusan.

Maysami, R. C., & Koh, T. S. (2000). A vector error correction model of the Singapore stock market. *International Review of Economics & Finance*, *9*(1), 79–96. DOI: 10.1016/S1059-0560(99)00042-8

Mazaraki, A. A., & Bosovska, M. V. (2013). Theoretical and methodological foundations of the formation of the integration strategy of enterprises. *Business Info*, *7*, 299–308.

McLaney, E. J. (1992). *Business Finance for Decision Makers*. Pitman Publishing.

Mei, D., Ma, F., Liao, Y., & Wang, L. (2020). Geopolitical risk uncertainty and oil future volatility: Evidence from MIDAS models. *Energy Economics*, *86*, 104624.

Mhlanga, D. (2024). Big Data and Financial Technology (Fintech) Towards Financial Inclusion. SSRN Electronic Journal. 10.2139. DOI: 10.2139/ssrn.4697365

Mikalef, P., Boura, M., Lekakos, G., & Krogstie, J. (2019). Big data analytics and firm performance: Findings from a mixed-method approach. *Journal of Business Research*, *98*, 261–276. DOI: 10.1016/j.jbusres.2019.01.044

Milana, C., & Ashta, A. (2021). Artificial intelligence techniques in finance and financial markets: A survey of the literature. *Strategic Change*, *30*(3), 189–209. DOI: 10.1002/jsc.2403

Miller, M. H. (1977). Debt and Taxes. *The Journal of Finance*, (May), 261–275.

Miller, M. H., & Modiliani, F. (1961). Dividend Policy, Growth and the Valuation of Share. *The Journal of Business*, *34*(4), 411–433. DOI: 10.1086/294442

Mishra, S., & Tripathi, A. R. (2021). AI business model: An integrative business approach. *Journal of Innovation and Entrepreneurship*, *10*(1), 18. DOI: 10.1186/s13731-021-00157-5

Modigliani, F., & Miller, M. H. (1958). The Cost of Capital, Corporation Finance, and the Theory of Investment. *The American Economic Review*, (June), 261–297.

Modigliani, F., & Miller, M. H. (1963). Corporate Income taxes and the Cost of Capital. *The American Economic Review*, (June), 433–443.

Mok, H. M. (1993). Causality of interest rate, exchange rate and stock prices at stock market open and close in Hong Kong. *Asia Pacific Journal of Management*, *10*(2), 123–143. DOI: 10.1007/BF01734274

Monod, E., Lissillour, R., Köster, A., & Jiayin, Q. (2023). Does AI control or support? Power shifts after AI system implementation in customer relationship management. *Journal of Decision Systems*, *32*(3), 542–565. DOI: 10.1080/12460125.2022.2066051

Moore, K., & Zhou, C. 2014. The determinants of systemic importance. Discussion Paper, London School of Economics and Political Science.

Morgan, B. (2019, September 16). 10 Examples Of Customer Experience Turnarounds. Forbes. https://www.forbes.com/sites/blakemorgan/2019/09/16/10-examples-of-customer-experience-turnarounds/?sh=1f7c3deb4415

Moskalenko, V. V., Moskalenko, V. V., & Godlevskyi, M. D. (2018). Modeli ta metody stratehichnoho upravlinnia rozvytkom pidpryiemstva [Models and methods of strategic management of enterprise development]. Ministry of Education and Science of Ukraine, National Technical University "Kharkiv Polytechnic Institute". Tochka, Kharkiv.

Mukherjee, T. K., & Naka, A. (1995). Dynamic Relations between Macroeconomic Variables and the Japanese Stock Market: An Application of a Vector Error Correction Model ». *Journal of Financial Research*, *18*(2), 223–237. DOI: 10.1111/j.1475-6803.1995.tb00563.x

Naik, P. K., & Padhi, P. (2012). Interaction of macroeconomic factors and stock market index: Empirical evidence from Indian data. Available at *SSRN* 2150208.

Nair, S. S., & Nathiya, R. (2024, May). AI-powered business revolution: Elevating efficiency and boosting sales through cutting-edge process re-engineering with machine learning. In *2024 Second International Conference on Data Science and Information System (ICDSIS)* (pp. 1-7). IEEE. DOI: 10.1109/ICDSIS61070.2024.10594289

Narayan, P. K., Narayan, S., & Singh, H. (2014). The Determinants of Stock Prices: New Evidence from the Indian Banking Sector. *Emerging Markets Finance & Trade*, *50*(2), 5–15. DOI: 10.2753/REE1540-496X500201

Nasseh, A., & Strauss, J. (2000). Stock prices and domestic and international macroeconomic activity: A cointegration approach. *The Quarterly Review of Economics and Finance*, *40*(2), 229–245. DOI: 10.1016/S1062-9769(99)00054-X

Nduka, W. (2023). The significance of artificial intelligence in business process management.

Newsroom, P. (2024). Paypal Newsroom. Retrieved May 05,2024 from www.newsroom.paypal-corp.com

Nguyen, B., Schinckus, C., & Thanh, S. D. (2021). Economic Policy Uncertainty and Entrepreneurship: A Bad for a Good? *The Journal of Entrepreneurship*, *30*(1), 81–133. DOI: 10.1177/0971355720974819

Nova, M. (2020). Globalization-its influences & impacts on specific regions of Africa. In *SHS Web of Conferences* (Vol. 74, p. 06020). EDP Sciences., https://www.indiatimes.com/worth/news/svb-employee-joseph-gentile-worked-at-lehman-brothers-and-arthur-anderson-595887.html DOI: 10.1051/shsconf/20207406020

Nuti, G., Mirghaemi, M., Treleaven, P., & Yingsaeree, C. (2020). Algorithmic trading with machine learning and sentiment analysis: A survey. *The Journal of Financial Data Science*, *6*(4), 148–170.

Osamor, I. P., & Adeniran, O. S. (2023). *Effects of Artificial Intelligence on Financial Reporting : Evidence from KPMG and PwC Effects of Artificial Intelligence on Financial Reporting : Evidence from KPMG and PwC. April.*

Ozili, P. K. (2020). Impact of Digital Finance on Financial Inclusion and Stability. *Borsa Istanbul Review*, *20*(4), 329–340. DOI: 10.1016/j.bir.2017.12.003

Pannell, D. J. (1997). Sensitivity Analysis of Normative Economic Models: Theoretical Framework and Practical Strategies. *Agricultural Economics*, *16*(2), 139–152. DOI: 10.1111/j.1574-0862.1997.tb00449.x

Pattnaik, D., Ray, S., & Raman, R. (2024). Applications of artificial intelligence and machine learning in the financial services industry: A bibliometric review. *Heliyon*, *10*(1), e23492. DOI: 10.1016/j.heliyon.2023.e23492 PMID: 38187262

Pedroni, P. (2004). Panel Cointegration: Asymptotic and Finite Sample Properties of Pooled Time Series Tests with an Application to the Ppp Hypothesis. *Econometric Theory*, *20*(3), 597–625. DOI: 10.1017/S0266466604203073

Peiró, A. (2016). Stock prices and macroeconomic factors: Some European evidence. *International Review of Economics & Finance*, *41*(C), 287–294. DOI: 10.1016/j.iref.2015.08.004

Penman, S. (2004). *Financial Statement Analysis and Security Valuation*. McGraw-Hill / Irwin.

Perifanis, N.-A., & Kitsios, F. (2023). Investigating the influence of artificial intelligence on business value in the digital era of strategy: A literature review. *Information (Basel), 14*(2), 85. DOI: 10.3390/info14020085

Pesaran, M. H., & Smith, R. (1995, July). Estimating long-run relationships from dynamic heterogeneous panels. *Journal of Econometrics, 68*(1), 79–113. DOI: 10.1016/0304-4076(94)01644-F

Petit, R. R. (1972). Dividend Announcement, Security Performance and Capital Market Efficiency. *The Journal of Finance, 27*(5), 993–1007. DOI: 10.1111/j.1540-6261.1972.tb03018.x

Phan, D. H. B., Sharma, S. S., & Tran, V. T. (2018). Can economic policy uncertainty predict stock returns? Global evidence. *Journal of International Financial Markets, Institutions and Money, 55*(C), 134–150. DOI: 10.1016/j.intfin.2018.04.004

Piletska, S. T., Korytko, T. Yu., & Tkachenko, E. V. (2021). A model of integrated assessment of the enterprise economic security. *Economic Herald of Donbass, 65*(3), 56–66. DOI: 10.12958/1817-3772-2021-3(65)-56-65

Pillai, K. A. (2023). AI-DRIVEN DYNAMIC PRICING STRATEGIES FOR SUBSCRIPTION FEATURES: LEVERAGING ARTIFICIAL INTELLIGENCE FOR REAL-TIME PRICING OPTIMIZATION. *Cem Dilmegani (2023). Dynamic Pricing Algorithms in.*

Plíhal, T. (2016). Granger Causality between Stock Market and Macroeconomic Indicators: Evidence from Germany. *Acta Universitatis Agriculturae et Silviculturae Mendelianae Brunensis, 64*(6), 2101–2108. DOI: 10.11118/actaun201664062101

Pranckutė, R. (2021). Web of Science (WoS) and Scopus: The Titans of Bibliographic Information in Today's Academic World. *Publications / MDPI, 9*(1), 12. DOI: 10.3390/publications9010012

Prasad, A. (2023). Google predicts an increase in Russian cyberattacks on Ukraine and NATO members in 2023. Forbes.ua. Available at: https://surl.li/jaqxk

Qureshi, J. (2024). AI-powered cloud-based e-commerce: Driving digital business transformation initiatives.

Rada.gov.ua. (2003). Law of Ukraine "On Combating Terrorism", Article 1. https://zakon.rada.gov.ua/laws/show/638-15#Text

Radaelli, P. (2021). Enterprise Risk Management in Practice: A European Perspective, Maffei, M. (Ed.) *Enterprise Risk Management in Europe* (pp. 261-278). Emerald Publishing Limited, Leeds. https://doi.org/DOI: 10.1108/978-1-83867-245-420211015

Rahman, M. S., Bag, S., Gupta, S., & Sivarajah, U. (2023). Technology readiness of B2B firms and AI-based customer relationship management capability for enhancing social sustainability performance. *Journal of Business Research, 156*, 113525. DOI: 10.1016/j.jbusres.2022.113525

Rajagopal, N. K., Qureshi, N. I., Durga, S., Ramirez Asis, E. H., Huerta Soto, R. M., Gupta, S. K., & Deepak, S. (2022). Future of Business Culture: An Artificial Intelligence-Driven Digital Framework for Organization Decision-Making Process. *Complexity*, *2022*(1), 7796507. DOI: 10.1155/2022/7796507

Rana, N. P., Chatterjee, S., Dwivedi, Y. K., & Akter, S. (2022). Understanding dark side of artificial intelligence (AI) integrated business analytics: Assessing firm's operational inefficiency and competitiveness. *European Journal of Information Systems*, *31*(3), 364–387. DOI: 10.1080/0960085X.2021.1955628

Rane, N., Paramesha, M., Choudhary, S., & Rane, J. (2024). Artificial Intelligence in Sales and Marketing: Enhancing Customer Satisfaction, Experience and Loyalty. SSRN Electronic Journal. DOI: 10.2139/ssrn.4831903

Ratanapakorn, O., & Sharma, S. (2007). Dynamic Analysis between the U.S. Stock Returns and the Macroeconomic Variables. *Applied Financial Economics*, *17*(5), 369–377. DOI: 10.1080/09603100600638944

Reilly, F. K., & Brown, K. C. (2000). *Investment Analysis and Portfolio Management* (6th ed.). The Dryden Press.

Reim, W., Åström, J., & Eriksson, O. (2020). Implementation of artificial intelligence (AI): A roadmap for business model innovation. *AI*, *1*(2), 11. DOI: 10.3390/ai1020011

Ribeiro Ramos, O., Mironenko, E., Britchenko, I., Zhuk, O., & Patlachuk, V. (2022). Economic security as an element of corporate management. *Financial and Credit Activity: Problems of Theory and Practice*, *1*(42), 304–312. DOI: 10.55643/fcaptp.1.42.2022.3698

Rigobon, R., & Sack, B. (2005). The effects of war risk on US financial markets. *Journal of Banking & Finance*, *29*(7), 1769–1789. DOI: 10.1016/j.jbankfin.2004.06.040

Ring, D. (February 2019). Definition OKRs (Objectives and Key Results). Techtarget. Available at: https://www.techtarget.com/searchhrsoftware/definition/OKRs-Objectives-and-Key-Results (10/9/2023)

Riyako, E. (2023). Law Firm Metrics and KPIs: Management through Digital. Ligazakon.net. https://surl.li/jbiam

Rozeff, M. S. (1982). Growth, Beta, and Agency Cost as Determinants of Dividend Payout Ratios. *Journal of Financial Research*, *5*(3), 461–488. DOI: 10.1111/j.1475-6803.1982.tb00299.x

Rožman, M., Oreški, D., & Tominc, P. (2022). Integrating artificial intelligence into a talent management model to increase the work engagement and performance of enterprises. *Frontiers in Psychology*, *13*, 1014434. DOI: 10.3389/fpsyg.2022.1014434 PMID: 36506984

Rubinstein, M. E. (1973). A Mean-Variance Synthesis of Corporate Financial Theory. *The Journal of Finance*, (March), 167–181.

Rui, Z., & Yan, Z. (2019). A Survey on Biometric Authentication: Toward Secure and Privacy-Preserving Identification. *IEEE Access : Practical Innovations, Open Solutions*, *7*, 5994–6009. DOI: 10.1109/ACCESS.2018.2889996

Saad, M. (2023). The influence of accounting information system adoption on business performance amid COVID-19. *Computers in Human Behavior Reports*, *10*, 100286. DOI: 10.1016/j.chbr.2023.100286 PMID: 37122822

Sadiq, R. B., Safie, N., Abd Rahman, A. H., & Goudarzi, S. (2021). Artificial intelligence maturity model: A systematic literature review. *PeerJ. Computer Science*, *7*, e661. DOI: 10.7717/peerj-cs.661 PMID: 34541308

Salisu, A. A., Gupta, R., Karmakar, S., & Das, S. (2022). Forecasting output growth of advanced economies over eight centuries: The role of gold market volatility as a proxy of global uncertainty. *Resources Policy*, *75*, 102527.

Saltelli, A. (2002). Sensitivity Analysis for Importance Assessment. *Risk Analysis*, *22*(3), 1–12. DOI: 10.1111/0272-4332.00040 PMID: 12088235

Saltelli, A., Chan, K., & Scott, M. (2000). *Sensitivity Analysis*. John Wiley and Sons.

Samuelson, P. A. (1965). Proof that Properly Anticipated Prices Fluctuate Randomly. *Industrial Management Review*, (Spring), 41–49.

Saunders, A., Schmid, M., & Walter, I. (2020). Strategic scope and bank performance. *Journal of Financial Stability*, *46*, 100715. DOI: 10.1016/j.jfs.2019.100715

Schueffel, P. (2021). Taming the Beast: A Scientific Definition of Fintech. *Journal of Innovation Management, 9*(4), 32–54. DOI: 10.24840/2183-0606_004.004_0004

Schuster, T., Waidelich, L., & Volz, R. (2021). Maturity models for the assessment of artificial intelligence in small and medium-sized enterprises. In Wrycza, S., & Maślankowski, J. (eds.), *Digital transformation.* PLAIS EuroSymposium 2021. *Lecture Notes in Business Information Processing, 429*, Springer, 22–36. https://doi.org/DOI: 10.1007/978-3-030-85893-3_2

Schwert, G. W. (1990). Stock Returns and Real Activity: A Century of Evidence. *The Journal of Finance, 45*(4), 1237–1257. Advance online publication. DOI: 10.1111/j.1540-6261.1990.tb02434.x

Sehrawat, S. K. (2023). The role of artificial intelligence in ERP automation: State-of-the-art and future directions. *Transactions on Latest Trends in Artificial Intelligence, 4*(4).

Sesame, C. (2018). Credit Sesame. Retrieved May 23, 2024 from www.creditsesame .com

Shah, S. (2014). Corporate social responsibility: A way of life at the Tata Group. *Journal of Human Values, 20*(1), 59–74. DOI: 10.1177/0971685813515591

Shamim, R., & Bentalha, B. (2023). Blockchain-Enabled Machine Learning Framework for Demand Forecasting in Supply Chain Management. In Integrating Intelligence and Sustainability in Supply Chains (pp. 28-48). IGI Global. DOI: 10.4018/979-8-3693-0225-5.ch002

Shamsan Saleh, A. M. (2024). Blockchain for secure and decentralized artificial intelligence in cybersecurity: A comprehensive review. Blockchain: Research and Applications, 100193.

Sharif, A., Aloui, C., & Yarovaya, L. (2020). COVID-19 pandemic, oil prices, stock market, geopolitical risk and policy uncertainty nexus in the US economy: Fresh evidence from the wavelet-based approach. *International Review of Financial Analysis, 70*, 101496.

Sharitov, O. (2023). Rockets instead of visitors. The war damaged more than 1,000 restaurants, cafes and hotels. How does business restore them and how can the state help. ForbesUkraine. https://surl.li/ixncp

Shaver, J. M. (2021). Evolution of Quantitative Research Methods in Strategic Management. Strategic Management, 83-98. https://doi.org/DOI: 10.1093/oso/9780190090883.003.0005

Shim, J. K., & Siegel, J. G. (2008). *Financial Management.* New York: Barron's Educational Series, Inc.

Shin, Y., Yu, B., & Greenwood-Nimmo, M. (2014). Modelling asymmetric cointegration and dynamic multipliers in an ARDL framework. In: Horrace, W.C. DOI: 10.1007/978-1-4899-8008-3_9

Shneiderman, B. (2020). Human-centered artificial intelligence: Reliable, safe & trustworthy. *International Journal of Human-Computer Interaction, 36*(6), 495–504. DOI: 10.1080/10447318.2020.1741118

Shobhana, N. (2024). AI-powered supply chains towards greater efficiency. In *Complex AI Dynamics and Interactions in Management* (pp. 229–249). IGI Global. DOI: 10.4018/979-8-3693-0712-0.ch011

Shoetan, P., & Familoni, B. (2024). TRANSFORMING FINTECH FRAUD DETECTION WITH ADVANCED ARTIFICIAL INTELLIGENCE ALGORITHMS. *Finance & Accounting Research Journal., 6*(4), 602–625. DOI: 10.51594/farj.v6i4.1036

Siddiqui, A. T., Jahangeer, G. S. B., & Basha, A. F. (2024). AI-empowered devices and strategies to reduce cost in business. In *Harnessing AI and digital twin technologies in businesses* (pp. 40–52). IGI Global. DOI: 10.4018/979-8-3693-3234-4.ch004

Sims, C. A., Stock, J. H., & Watson, M. W. (1990, January). JAMWS H. STOCK, AND MARK W. WATSON (1990): « INFERENCE IN LINEAR TIME SERIES MODELS WITH SOME UNIT ROOTS. *Econometrica, 58*(1), 113–144. DOI: 10.2307/2938337

Soliman, M., Gulvady, S., Elbaz, A. M., Mosbah, M., & Wahba, M. S. (2023). Robot-delivered tourism and hospitality services: How to evaluate the impact of health and safety considerations on visitors' satisfaction and loyalty? *Tourism and Hospitality Research.* Advance online publication. DOI: 10.1177/14673584231153367

Sonnenfeld, J. A., Tian, S., Sokolowski, F., Wyrebkowski, M., & Kasprowicz, M. Business retreats and sanctions are crippling the Russian economy, SSRN Electron. J. 1–118 (2022). DOI: 10.2139/ssrn.4167193

Sonntag, M., Mehmann, S., Mehmann, J., & Teuteberg, F. (2024). Development and evaluation of a maturity model for AI deployment capability of manufacturing companies. *Information Systems Management, 42*(1), 37–67. Advance online publication. DOI: 10.1080/10580530.2024.2319041

Spencer, A., & Tarlow, P. (2021). *Tourism Security to Tourism Surety and Well-being, Tourism Safety and Security for the Caribbean (Tourism Security-Safety and Post Conflict Destinations)*. Emerald Publishing Limited., DOI: 10.1108/978-1-80071-318-520211004

Stecher, P., Pohl, M., & Turowski, K. (2020). Enterprise architecture's effects on organizations' ability to adopt artificial intelligence-A resource-based perspective. Proceedings of the 2020 28th European Conference on Information Systems (ECIS), 1–16. https://aisel.aisnet.org/ecis2020_rp/173/

Stiglitz, J. E. (1969). A Re-examination of the Modigliani-Miller Theorem. *The American Economic Review*, (December), 784–793.

Stolzer, A. J., Sumwalt, R. L., & Goglia, J. J. (2023). *Safety Management Systems in Aviation* (3rd ed.). CRC Press. DOI: 10.1201/9781003286127

Suhaibu, I., Harvey, S. K., & Amidu, M. (2017). The impact of monetary policy on stock market performance: Evidence from twelve (12) African countries. *Research in International Business and Finance*, *42*, 1372–1382.

Svetlana, N., Anna, N., Svetlana, M., Tatiana, G., & Olga, M. (2022). Artificial intelligence as a driver of business process transformation. *Procedia Computer Science*, *213*, 276–284. DOI: 10.1016/j.procs.2022.11.067

Syam, N., & Sharma, A. (2018). Waiting for a sales renaissance in the fourth industrial revolution: Machine learning and artificial intelligence in sales research and practice. *Industrial Marketing Management*, *69*, 135–146. DOI: 10.1016/j.indmarman.2017.12.019

Taherdoost, H., & Madanchian, M. (2023). Artificial Intelligence and Sentiment Analysis: A Review in Competitive Research. *Computers*, *12*(2), 37. DOI: 10.3390/computers12020037

Tanveer, M., Khan, N., & Ahmad, A. R. (2021, April). AI support marketing: Understanding the customer journey towards the business development. In *2021 1st international conference on artificial intelligence and data analytics (CAIDA)* (pp. 144-150). IEEE.

Ta, V. D., Liu, C. M., & Addis, D. (2018). Prediction and portfolio optimization in quantitative trading using machine learning techniques. In *Proceedings of the 9th International Symposium on Information and Communication Technology* (pp. 98-105). DOI: 10.1145/3287921.3287963

Thanh, S. D., Canh, N. P., & Maiti, M. (2020). Asymmetric effects of unanticipated monetary shocks on stock prices: Emerging market evidence. *Economic Analysis and Policy*, *65*, 40–55. DOI: 10.1016/j.eap.2019.11.005

Thomas, J. Sargent (1999) « The Conquest of American Inflation » Published by: Princeton University Press https://www.jstor.org/stable/j.ctv39x7tk

Töytäri, P., & Rajala, R. (2015). Value-based selling: An organizational capability perspective. *Industrial Marketing Management*, *45*, 101–112. DOI: 10.1016/j.indmarman.2015.02.009

Tradingeconomics.com. (2023). Global Terrorism Index. https://tradingeconomics.com/ukraine/terrorism-index

Tretyak, V., Lyakina, M., & Volkova, E. (2021). The ways of business digitalization in global corporations. *SHS Web of Conferences, 92*, 05027. DOI: 10.1051/shsconf/20219205027

Trim, P., & Lee, Y.-I. (2022). *Strategic Cyber Security Management* (1st ed.). Routledge., DOI: 10.4324/9781003244295

Tuna, A. A., & Türkmendağ, Z. (2022). Cyber Business Management, Özsungur, F. (Ed.) *Conflict Management in Digital Business* (pp. 281-301), Emerald Publishing Limited, Leeds. https://doi.org/DOI: 10.1108/978-1-80262-773-220221026

Ukrainian truth. (2023). Everything you need to know about the Kakhovskaya HPP disaster. Available at: https://www.pravda.com.ua/articles/2023/06/6/7405590/

Ullah, G. M. W., Islam, A., Alam, M. S., & Khan, M. K. (2017). Effect of macroeconomic variables on stock market performance of SAARC countries. *Asian Economic and Financial Review*, *7*(8), 770.

Umar, Z., Bossman, A., Choi, S., & Teplova, T. (2022). Does geopolitical risk matter for global asset returns? Evidence from quantile-on-quantile regression. *Finance Research Letters*, *48*, 102991. DOI: 10.1016/j.frl.2022.102991

Valcarcel, V. J. (2012). The dynamic adjustments of stock prices to inflation disturbances. *Journal of Economics and Business*, *64*(2), 117–144. DOI: 10.1016/j.jeconbus.2011.11.002

Van Horne, J. C. (1989). *Fundamentals of Financial Management*. Prentice-Hall.

Verbeke, W., Dietz, B., & Verwaal, E. (2011). Drivers of sales performance: A contemporary meta-analysis. Have salespeople become knowledge brokers? *Journal of the Academy of Marketing Science*, *39*(3), 407–428. DOI: 10.1007/s11747-010-0211-8

Verezomska, I., Bovsh, L., Prykhodko, K., & Baklan, H. (2022). Cyber protection of hotel brands. *Restaurant and hotel consulting.Innovation*, *5*(2), 190–209. DOI: 10.31866/2616-7468.5.2.2022.270089

Verhoef, P. C., Broekhuizen, T., Bart, Y., Bhattacharya, A., Qi Dong, J., Fabian, N., & Haenlein, M. (2020). Digital transformation: A multidisciplinary reflection and research agenda. *Journal of Business Research*, *122*, 889–901. DOI: 10.1016/j.jbusres.2019.09.022

Vo, H., Trinh, Q.-D., Le, M., & Nguyen, N. (2021). Does economic policy uncertainty affect investment sensitivity to peer stock prices? *Economic Analysis and Policy*, *72*, 685–699. Advance online publication. DOI: 10.1016/j.eap.2021.10.012

Wagire, A. A., Joshi, R., Rathore, A. P. S., & Jain, R. (2021). Development of maturity model for assessing the implementation of Industry 4.0: Learning from theory and practice. *Production Planning and Control*, *32*(8), 603–622. DOI: 10.1080/09537287.2020.1744763

Walter, J. E. (1956). Dividend Policies and Common Stock Prices. *The Journal of Finance*, *11*(1), 29–41. DOI: 10.1111/j.1540-6261.1956.tb00684.x

Wamba-Taguimdje, S. L., Wamba, S. F., Kamdjoug, J. R. K., & Wanko, C. E. T. (2020). Influence of artificial intelligence (AI) on firm performance: The business value of AI-based transformation projects. *Business Process Management Journal*, *26*(7), 1893–1924. DOI: 10.1108/BPMJ-10-2019-0411

Wang, X., Lin, X., & Shao, B. (2022). How does artificial intelligence create business agility? Evidence from chatbots. *International Journal of Information Management*, *66*, 102535. DOI: 10.1016/j.ijinfomgt.2022.102535

Wang, Y., Pan, Z., Liu, L., & Wu, C. (2019). Oil price increases and the predictability of equity premium. *Journal of Banking & Finance*, *102*, 43–58. DOI: 10.1016/j.jbankfin.2019.03.009

Watts, R., & Zimmerman, J. (1979). The Demand for and Supply of Accounting Theories: The market for Excuses. *The Accounting Review*, (April), 273–305.

Weiss, G. N. F., Bostandzic, D., & Neumann, S. (2014). What factors drive systemic risk during international financial crises? *Journal of Banking & Finance*, *41*, 78–96. DOI: 10.1016/j.jbankfin.2014.01.001

Wiersema, F. (2013). The B2B Agenda: The current state of B2B marketing and a look ahead. *Industrial Marketing Management*, *42*(4), 470–488. DOI: 10.1016/j.indmarman.2013.02.015

World Economic Forum. (2020). World Economic Forum (2020). Retrieved May 15,2024 from www.weforum.org

Xu, Y., Shi, Y., & Wang, C. (2022). AI-empowered sales optimization: A survey from the perspective of knowledge-driven sales analytics. arXiv preprint arXiv:2208.08985.

Yaiprasert, C., & Hidayanto, A. N. (2024). AI-powered ensemble machine learning to optimize cost strategies in logistics business. *International Journal of Information Management Data Insights*, *4*(1), 100209. DOI: 10.1016/j.jjimei.2023.100209

Yakovenko, Y., & Shaptala, R. (2023). *Intelligent process automation, robotic process automation, and artificial intelligence for business processes transformation*. Publishing House "Baltija Publishing". DOI: 10.30525/978-9934-26-378-1-20

Yousaf, I., Patel, R., & Yarovaya, L. (2022). The reaction of G20+ stock markets to the Russia–Ukraine conflict "black-swan" event: Evidence from event study approach. *Journal of Behavioral and Experimental Finance*, *35*, 100723.

Zekan, Y., Sekt, F., & Co, E. A. L. P. (2022).. . *The Role of Artificial Intelligence in Investment Decisions and Applications in The Turkish Finance Industry.*, *21*(4), 2208–2222.

Zhang, H., Chen, J., & Shao, L. (2021). Dynamic spillovers between energy and stock markets and their implications in the context of COVID-19. *International Review of Financial Analysis*, *77*, 101828.

Zhivko, Z. B., Cherevko, O. V., Zachosova, N. V., Zhivko, M. O., Bavorovska, O. B., & Zanora, V. O. (2019). Organization and management of the economic security system of the enterprise: educational and methodological manual. Eds. Z.B. Zhivko Cherkasy: Yu.A. Chabanenko publisher, 120. https://surl.li/hmcbr

Zirar, A., Ali, S. I., & Islam, N. (2023). Worker and workplace Artificial Intelligence (AI) coexistence: Emerging themes and research agenda. *Technovation*, *124*, 102747. DOI: 10.1016/j.technovation.2023.102747

Zou, P. X., & Sunindijo, R. Y. (2015). *Strategic safety management in construction and engineering*. John Wiley & Sons., DOI: 10.1002/9781118839362

About the Contributors

Abdelkader Mohamed Sghaier Derbali is an Associate Professor in Finance at the Department of Finance and Accounting, Higher Institute of Informatics and Management of Kairouan, Kairouan University, Kairouan, Tunisia and at the Department of Administrative and Financial Sciences and Techniques, Community College, Taibah University, Saudi Arabia. He is one of the Editorial Board Members in the Journal of Energy Markets, International Business Review, Cogent Economic & Finance, International Review of Applied Economics, African Journal of Accounting, Auditing and Finance, and African Journal of Economic and Sustainable Development. His research interests include Risk Management, Systemic risk, International finance, Capital markets and institutions, Banking and market microstructure and Islamic Finance. He has published articles, among others, in Research in International Business and Management, Finance Research Letters, International Journal of Critical Accounting, Journal of Asset Management, International Journal of Productivity and Quality Management, Cogent Business & Management, Cogent Economic & Finance, Journal of Chinese Governance, Pacific Accounting Review, International Journal of Financial Engineering, Virtual Economics, International Journal of Economics and Business Research, International Journal of Mathematics in Operational Research, The Chinese Economy, Journal of Energy Markets, and International Journal of Trade and Global Markets, International Journal of Social Economics, Journal of Business and Socio-economic Development, International Journal of the Economics of Business, China Economic Journal, Journal of Economics, Finance and Administrative Science.

***

Princy.A.S is working as Assistant Professor in the Department of Management studies, Sathyabama Institute of Science and Technology, Chennai, Tamilnadu. She has completed MBA from Bharathiar University and qualified UGC-NET in management. She has presented numerous papers at national and international conferences. Her research contributions are in Scopus indexed and UGC recommended journals. She has h 8 years of Industrial experience and 8years of teaching experience.

Badr Bentalha teaches Supply Chain and Operations Management at National School Of Business and Management – Fez, Sidi Mohamed Ben Abdellah University – Morocco. Dr. Bentalha investigates the structural dynamics and control of complex networks, applying his findings to supply chain management, Industry 4.0, risk analysis, and digital supply chains. His work emphasizes the intersection of supply chain management, operations research, industrial engineering, and digital technology. As a professor, he teaches undergraduate, graduate, and, doctoral courses in operations management, supply chain management, logistics, management information systems, and strategic management. Through guest lectures, webinars, and scholarly presentations, he engages students and fosters an active learning environment.Professor Bentalha specializes in supply chain and operations management, operations research, and service management. He is passionate about integrating knowledge across disciplines to solve real-world problems. He has delivered numerous invited plenary talks, keynotes, and panel discussions at conferences and global webinars.

Abdelfattah Bouri is a Professor of Finance at the Faculty of Economic Sciences and Management of Sfax, Tunisia. Affiliation: Department Head of Accounting and Finance and Director of Governance, Finance, and Accounting Laboratory, University of Sfax, Tunisia. E-mail: bouriabdelf@gmail.com

Chris Sherin D is affiliated with St. Joseph's College of Engineering. Her primary area of interest is finance and her work has been prominently featured in several esteemed journals, reflecting her significant contributions to the field. She has earned recognition and respect within the academic community.

Nizar Elouni is a Professor of Finance at the Faculty of Political & Economic Sciences, Tunisia. Affiliation: Dean of European University of Tunis and membre of Governance, Finance, and Accounting Laboratory, University of Sfax, Tunisia.

Dewanshi Ghosh A dynamic and results-oriented professional with a comprehensive background in business economics, I am poised to graduate from Amity University with a focus on economics, finance, statistics, and data analysis. With an outstanding academic track record and five years of rich leadership experience, I bring to the table a robust skill set and a passion for economics that propels me to excel in MS Word. In addition to my academic endeavors, I possess advanced proficiency in German and am fluent in two languages. I also have specialized knowledge in marketing, HR management, and statistical analysis. I am a naturally creative person who excels at utilizing new technologies and has a sharp eye for streamlining operational procedures. My work ethic is shaped by my belief in cooperation and respect for others, which creates atmospheres where teamwork is valued above individual achievement.

D. Joel Jebadurai, currently working as an Associate Professor in Department of MBA, St.Joseph's College of Engineering, OMR, Chennai, India. He has published more than 5o research articles in a reputed and indexed journal.

Kahkashan Khan is presently working as an Assistant Professor in MBA Department in Siddharth University, Kapilvastu, Siddharth Nagar, Uttar Pradesh, India. Earlier to this, Dr. Khan was working as an Assistant Professor in Humanities and Management Science Department, MMMUT, Gorakhpur, UP, India. She has an enriching work experience of more than 5 years with strong academic background. She has completed her Graduation (B.Com.), Post-Graduation (MBA), and PhD in Management from DDU Gorakhpur University, UP, India. She is Gold Medalist in MBA and has also qualified UGC NET/JRF in Management subject. She has authored more than 32 research papers, 11 book chapters and 7 conference papers which is published in different reputed journals of ABDC, SAGE, Scopus, UGC CARE etc., and has also presented research papers in different National & International seminars/Conferences.

Manjit Kour is working as Professor at University Business School at Chandigarh University. She holds a PhD in Business Management from IK Gujral Punjab Technical University, India. She has a good research record with several research papers published in reputed journals. She has presented numerous papers at international/national conferences and seminars. She has two books to her credit as well. She is an editorial board member and reviewer of many reputed journals including Scopus and ABDC-indexed journals. She has acted as a resource person in many seminars and workshops. She has also received International Researcher Award 2021 from the International Institute of Organized Research (I2OR). Her areas of interest include sustainability, green practices, Fintech, online marketing trends and business ethics.

Sergey Krylov He was born on 19th January, 1967, Sverdlovsk, USSR. He received doctor of science (economics) degree. He is a professor at Academic Department of Accounting, Analysis and Audit, Ural Federal University, Yekaterinburg, Russian Federation. He has 30 years of teaching experience and research experience. His areas of research interest include Financial Analysis,

Financial Forecasting, Dividend Policy, and Balanced Scorecard. He has published 205 research articles in the national and international journals. He knows Russian, English, and Spanish languages.

Bhupendra Kumar is a highly accomplished academic and researcher, currently serving as Professor of Accounting & Finance at Amity Business School, Amity University, Gwalior, India. With over 22 years of experience in academia, research, and administration, he is recognized for his global exposure and professional holds a Ph.D. (2009), an M.Phil. (Economics) with a Gold Medal, and an MBA, showcasing his outstanding academic credentials. He has published 85 high-quality research works, including seven international books, and has evaluated more than 20 foreign PhD theses. His expertise spans accounting, finance, data analysis, advisory, and consultancy services, along with curriculum development, expert talks, and international seminars. He is actively involved in strategic collaborations with global organizations such as THE, QS, Erasmus Europe, Africa Uninet, UNESCO, and the African Union, focusing on research partnerships and institutional recognition.

Kamal Kumar Prasad is working as Asst. Professor in CSE Department.My research is going on AI, Machine learning.

L. Rajeshkumar is an Assistant Professor in the Department of MBA. He has graduated BBA from Aditanar College of Arts and Sciences, MBA, and M.Phil from Manonmaniam Sundarnar University in Tirunelveli. In December 2012, he qualified for the UGC-NET examination. Then 2018, he received his Ph.D with a marketing specialization especially in FMCG. He started his career at Manonmaniam Sundaranar University College, Govindaperi, in September, 2012. After that, he moved to DMI. St. Eugune University, Zambia, for one year in the 2014–15 academic year. In 2015, he began his Ph.D. studies at Manonmaniam Sundarnar University in Tirunelveli. In July 2018, he submitted his thesis and started his journey at the Aarupadai Veedu Institute of Technology, Chennai, in February 2018. Then, in February 2020, he shifted his work to TNJFU - Fisheries Business School, Tamilnadu Dr.J. Jayalalithaa Fisheries University, OMR Campus, Chennai. After that, in October 2022, he joined as an assistant professor in the department of MBA at St.Joseph's College of Engineering, Chennai. Overall, he has 11 years of experience, including 3 years of research and 8 years of teaching. He has specialized in Marketing and

Surenthran David is an Assistant Professor at St. Joseph's College of Engineering in Chennai, India. His academic contributions include publications in both Scopus and UGC CARE indexed journals, reflecting his active engagement in research and scholarly activities. In addition to his academic endeavors, he has also shared his expertise as a resource person in the field of Finance, contributing to the development and dissemination of knowledge in this crucial area.

Ashwani Panesar is an Associate Professor in Mittal School of Business, Lovely Professional University, Punjab (India); Dr. Ashwani Panesar has a rich teaching experience of over 13 years, taking up various business management subjects at university level. Having worked closely with the sales aspect of the pharmaceutical industry (8 years), he had pursued his Doctorate in pharmaceutical marketing strategies from Jaipur National University, Rajasthan (India).

Sabyasachi Pramanik is a professional IEEE member. He obtained a PhD in Computer Science and Engineering from Sri Satya Sai University of Technology and Medical Sciences, Bhopal, India. Presently, he is an Associate Professor, Department of Computer Science and Engineering, Haldia Institute of Technology, India. He has many publications in various reputed international conferences, journals, and book chapters (Indexed by SCIE, Scopus, ESCI, etc). He is doing research in the fields of Artificial Intelligence, Data Privacy, Cybersecurity, Network Security, and Machine Learning. He also serves on the editorial boards of several international journals. He is a reviewer of journal articles from IEEE, Springer, Elsevier, Inderscience, IET and IGI Global. He has reviewed many conference papers, has been a keynote speaker, session chair, and technical program committee member at many international conferences. He has authored a book on Wireless Sensor Network. He has edited 8 books from IGI Global, CRC Press, Springer and Wiley Publications.

Jaideep Sharma is working as Associate Professor in Galgotias University, India.

Muhammad Usman Tariq has more than 16+ year's experience in industry and academia. He has authored more than 200+ research articles, 110+ case studies, 95+ book chapters and several books other than 4 patents. He is founder and CEO of The Case HQ, a unique repository for courses, narrative and video case studies. He has been working as a consultant and trainer for industries representing six sigma, quality, health and safety, environmental systems, project management, and information security standards. His work has encompassed sectors in aviation, manufacturing, food, hospitality, education, finance, research, software and transportation. He has diverse and significant experience working with accreditation agencies of ABET, ACBSP, AACSB, WASC, CAA, EFQM and NCEAC. Additionally, Dr. Tariq has operational experience in incubators, research labs, government research projects, private sector startups, program creation and management at various industrial and academic levels. He is Certified Higher Education Teacher from Harvard University,

USA, Certified Online Educator from HMBSU, Certified Six Sigma Master Black Belt and has been awarded PFHEA, SMIEEE, and CMBE.

Index

A

B

C

D

E

F

G

I

www.ingramcontent.com/pod-product-compliance
Lightning Source LLC
LaVergne TN
LVHW081338300926
849161LV00008B/2012